Chemistry for Biologists
The Text Book
Volume II Sections G–H

A Pearson Custom Publication

Chemistry for Biologists
The Text Book
Volume II Sections G–H

Compiled from:

The Organic Chemistry of Biological Pathways
by John McMurry and Tadhg Begley

Principles of Biochemistry
Third Edition
by H. Robert Horton, Laurence A. Moran, Raymond S. Ochs
J. David Rawn and K. Gray Scrimgeour

PEARSON
Custom
Publishing

Pearson Education Limited
Edinburgh Gate
Harlow
Essex CM20 2JE
And associated companies throughout the world

Visit us on the World Wide Web at:
www.pearsoned.co.uk

First published 2006
This Custom Book Edition © 2006 Published by Pearson Education Limited

Taken from:

The Organic Chemistry of Biological Pathways
by John McMurry and Tadhg Begley
ISBN 0 974 70771 6

Principles of Biochemistry Third Edition
by H. Robert Horton, Laurence A. Moran, Raymond S. Ochs,
J. David Rawn and K. Gray Scrimgeour
ISBN 0 13 026672 8

ISBN-10   1 84479 715 5
ISBN-13   978 1 84658 715 8

Printed and bound in Great Britain by Antony Rowe

Contents

Part 3

1 Common Mechanisms in Biological Chemistry

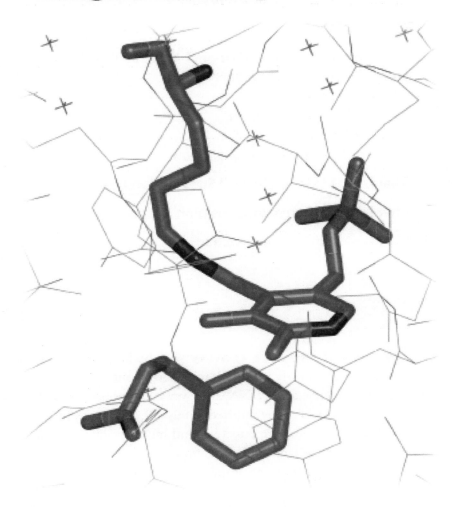

This scheme shows the active site of the enzyme that catalyzes the transamination reaction in the biosynthesis of phenylalanine from chorismate. A mechanistic understanding of biosynthetic pathways is a powerful tool for elucidating the chemical logic of living systems.

1.1 Functional Groups in Biological Chemistry

1.2 Acids and Bases; Electrophiles and Nucleophiles
Brønsted–Lowry Acids and Bases
Lewis Acids and Bases
Electrophiles and Nucleophiles

1

The final decades of the 20th century saw the beginning of a scientific revolution. Based on our newly acquired ability to manipulate, sequence, and synthesize deoxyribonucleic acid (DNA), the way is now open to isolate, study, and eventually modify each of the approximately 30,000 genes in our bodies. Medicines will become safer, more effective, and more specific; terrible genetic diseases such as sickle-cell anemia and cystic fibrosis will be cured; life spans will increase and the quality of life will improve as heart disease and cancer are brought under control.

None of these changes could occur without a detailed knowledge of chemistry, for it is our understanding of life processes at the molecular level that has made this revolution possible and that will sustain it. Biochemical processes are not mysterious. It's true that the many proteins, enzymes, nucleic acids, polysaccharides, and other substances in living organisms are enormously complex, but despite their complexity, they are still molecules. They are subject to the same chemical laws as all other molecules, and their reactions follow the same rules of reactivity and take place by the same mechanisms as those of far simpler molecules.

The focus of this book is on examining biochemical processes from a chemical perspective. We'll begin with a brief review of organic chemistry, looking first at the common functional groups found in biological molecules and then at some fundamental mechanisms by which organic molecules react. Following this general review of organic reactivity, we'll look at the structures and chemical characteristics of the main classes of biomolecules: carbohydrates, lipids, proteins, enzymes, and nucleic acids. Finally, we'll come to the heart of the matter: the organic chemistry of biological transformations. We'll dissect the details of important biochemical pathways to see both *how* and *why* these pathways occur. The result will be both a deeper understanding of biochemistry and a deeper appreciation for the remarkable subtleties by which living organisms function.

1.1 Functional Groups in Biological Chemistry

Chemists have learned through experience that organic compounds can be classified into families according to their structural features and that members of a given family have similar chemical reactivity. The structural features that make such classifications possible are called *functional groups*. A **functional group** is a group of atoms within a molecule that has a characteristic chemical behavior. Chemically, a functional group behaves in pretty much the same way in every molecule where it occurs. An ester (RCO_2R), for instance, usually undergoes a hydrolysis reaction with water to yield a carboxylic acid (RCO_2H) and an alcohol (ROH); a thiol (RSH) usually undergoes an oxidation reaction to yield a disulfide ($RSSR$); and so on. Table 1.1 lists some common functional groups found in biological molecules.

Table 1.1 Common Functional Groups in Biological Molecules

Structure*	Name	Structure*	Name
	Alkene (double bond)		Imine (Schiff base)
	Arene (aromatic ring)		Carbonyl group
	Alcohol		Aldehyde
	Ether		Ketone
	Amine		Carboxylic acid
	Thiol		Ester
	Sulfide		Thioester
	Disulfide		Amide
	Monophosphate		Acyl phosphate
	Diphosphate		

* The bonds whose connections aren't specified are assumed to be attached to carbon or hydrogen atoms in the rest of the molecule.

Alcohols, ethers, amines, thiols, sulfides, disulfides, and phosphates all have a carbon atom singly bonded to an electronegative atom. Alcohols, ethers, and phosphates have a carbon atom bonded to oxygen; amines have a carbon atom bonded to nitrogen; and thiols, sulfides, and disulfides have a carbon atom bonded to sulfur. In all cases, the bonds are polar, with the carbon atom being electron-poor and thus bearing a partial positive charge ($\delta+$), while the electronegative atom is electron-rich and thus bears a partial negative charge ($\delta-$). These polarity patterns are shown in Figure 1.1.

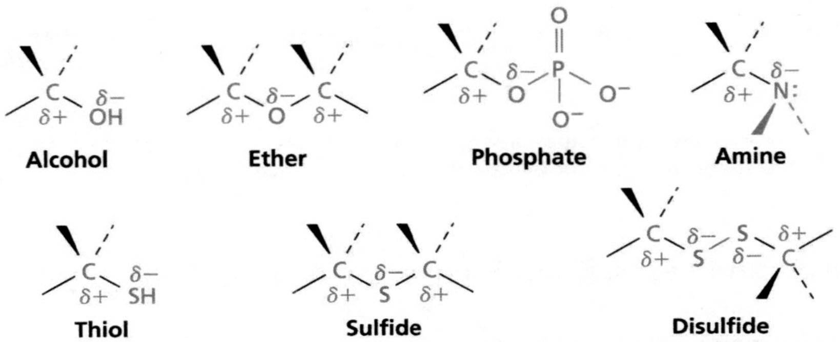

FIGURE 1.1 Polarity patterns of some common functional groups. The electronegative atom bears a partial negative charge ($\delta-$), and the carbon atom bears a partial positive charge ($\delta+$).

Note particularly in Table 1.1 the different families of compounds that contain the **carbonyl group, C=O**. Carbonyl groups are present in the vast majority of biological molecules. These compounds behave similarly in many respects but differ depending on the identity of the atoms bonded to the carbonyl-group carbon. Aldehydes have at least one hydrogen bonded to the C=O; ketones have two carbons bonded to the C=O; carboxylic acids have an —OH group bonded to the C=O; esters have an ether-like oxygen (−OR) bonded to the C=O; thioesters have a sulfide-like sulfur (−SR) bonded to the C=O; amides have an amine-like nitrogen (−NH$_2$, −NHR, or −NR$_2$) bonded to the C=O; and acyl phosphates have a phosphate group (−OPO$_3^{2-}$) bonded to the C=O. You might note that an acyl phosphate is structurally (and chemically) similar to a carboxylic acid anhydride.

As shown in Figure 1.2, carbonyl compounds are polar, with the electron-poor C=O carbon atom bearing a partial positive charge and the electron-rich oxygen atom bearing a partial negative charge.

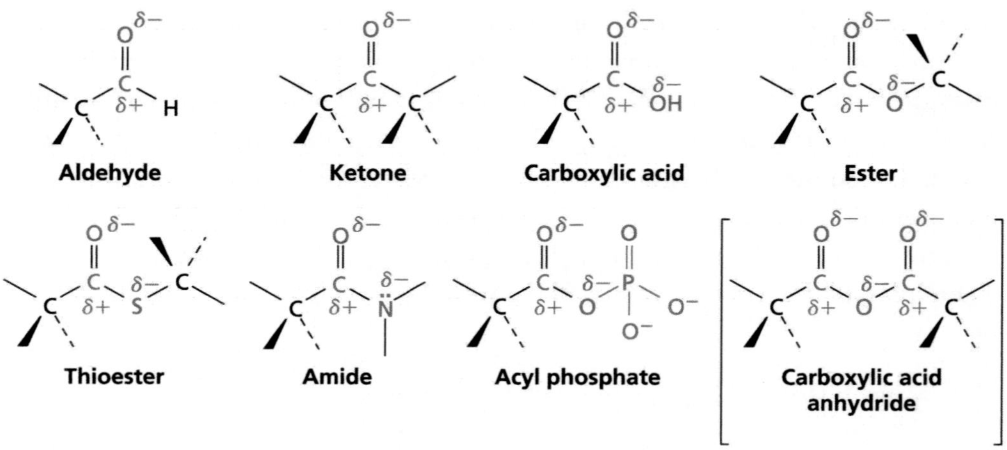

FIGURE 1.2 Polarity patterns in some carbonyl-containing functional groups. The carbonyl carbon atom is electron-poor ($\delta+$) and the oxygen atom is electron-rich ($\delta-$).

1.2 Acids and Bases; Electrophiles and Nucleophiles

Brønsted–Lowry Acids and Bases

Acids and bases are enormously important in biochemistry. The vast majority of biological transformations are catalyzed by acids or bases, and a thorough knowledge of acid–base chemistry is crucial for understanding how reactions occur.

According to the Brønsted–Lowry definition, an **acid** is a substance that donates a proton (hydrogen ion, H^+), and a **base** is a substance that accepts a proton. A carboxylic acid such as acetic acid, for example, can donate its —OH proton to a base such as methylamine in a reversible, **proton-transfer reaction**. The product that results by loss of H^+ from an acid is the **conjugate base** of the acid, and the product that results from addition of H^+ to a base is the **conjugate acid** of the base.

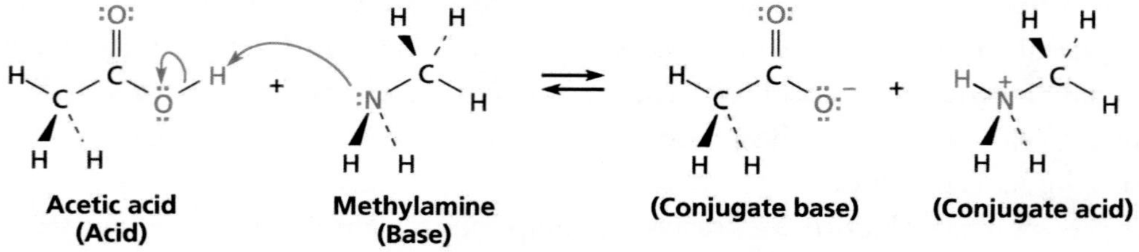

Acetic acid (Acid)   Methylamine (Base)   (Conjugate base)   (Conjugate acid)

Note the standard convention used to show how this proton-transfer reaction occurs: A curved arrow (red) indicates that a pair of electrons moves *from* the atom at the tail of the arrow (the nitrogen in methylamine) *to* the atom at the head of the arrow (the acidic hydrogen in acetic acid). That is, the electrons used to form the new N—H bond flow from the base to the acid. As the N—H bond forms, the O—H bond breaks and its electrons remain with oxygen, as shown by a second curved arrow. *A curved arrow always represents the movement of electrons, not atoms.*

Acids differ in their ability to donate protons. Recall from general chemistry that the strength of an acid HA in water solution is expressed by its pK_a, the negative common logarithm of its **acidity constant,** K_a. A stronger acid has a smaller pK_a (or larger K_a); a weaker acid has a larger pK_a (or smaller K_a).

For the reaction: $HA + H_2O \rightleftharpoons A^- + H_3O^+$

$$K_a = \frac{[H_3O^+][A^-]}{[HA]} \text{ and } pK_a = -\log K_a$$

Stronger acid—smaller pK_a
Weaker acid—larger pK_a

Table 1.2 lists the pK_a's of some typical acids encountered in biochemistry. Note that the pK_a of water is 15.74, the value that results when K_w, the ion-product constant for water, is divided by the molar concentration of pure water, 55.5 M:

$$HA + H_2O \rightleftharpoons A^- + H_3O^+ \qquad \text{where } HA = H_2O, A^- = OH^-$$

$$K_a = \frac{[H_3O^+][A^-]}{[HA]} = \frac{[H_3O^+][OH^-]}{[H_2O]} = \frac{K_w}{55.5}$$

$$= \frac{1.00 \times 10^{-14}}{55.5} = 1.80 \times 10^{-16}$$

$$pK_a = -\log 1.80 \times 10^{-16} = 15.74$$

Note also in Table 1.2 that carbonyl compounds are weakly acidic, a point we'll discuss in more detail in Section 1.7.

Table 1.2 Relative Strengths of Some Acids

Functional group	Example	pK_a	
Carboxylic acid	CH_3COH (with $\overset{O}{\overset{\|}{}}$)	4.76	Stronger acid
Imidazolium ion	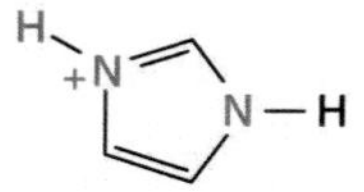 (imidazolium structure)	6.95	
Ammonia	NH_4^+	9.26	
Thiol	CH_3SH	10.3	
Alkylammonium ion	$CH_3NH_3^+$	10.66	
β-Keto ester	$CH_3CCH_2COCH_3$ (with two C=O)	10.6	
Water	H_2O	15.74	
Alcohol	CH_3CH_2OH	16.00	
Ketone	CH_3CCH_3 (with C=O)	19.3	
Thioester	CH_3CSCH_3 (with C=O)	21	
Ester	CH_3COCH_3 (with C=O)	25	Weaker acid

Just as acids differ in their ability to donate a proton, bases differ in their ability to accept a proton. The strength of a base B in water solution is normally expressed using the *acidity* of its conjugate acid, BH^+.

For the reaction: $BH^+ + H_2O \rightleftharpoons B + H_3O^+$

$$K_a = \frac{[B][H_3O^+]}{[BH^+]}$$

so

$$K_a \times K_b = \left(\frac{[B][H_3O^+]}{[BH^+]}\right)\left(\frac{[BH^+][OH^-]}{[B]}\right)$$

$$= [H_3O^+][OH^-] = K_w = 1.00 \times 10^{-14}$$

Thus $K_a = \dfrac{K_w}{K_b}$ and $K_b = \dfrac{K_w}{K_a}$

so $pK_a + pK_b = 14$ and $pK_b = 14 - pK_a$

Stronger base—larger pK_a for BH^+
Weaker base—smaller pK_a for BH^+

These equations say that we can determine the basicity of a base B by knowing the K_a of its conjugate acid BH^+. A stronger base holds H^+ more tightly, so it has a weaker conjugate acid (larger pK_a); a weaker base holds H^+ less tightly, so it has a stronger conjugate acid (smaller pK_a). Table 1.3 lists some typical bases found in biochemistry. Note that water can act as either a weak acid or a weak base, depending on whether it donates a proton to give OH^- or accepts a proton to give H_3O^+. Similarly with imidazole, alcohols, and carbonyl compounds, which can either donate or accept protons depending on the circumstances.

Table 1.3 Relative Strengths of Some Bases

Functional group	Example		pK_a of BH^+	
Hydroxide ion	$:\!\overset{..}{O}H^-$	H_2O	15.74	Stronger base
Guanidino	$\overset{\displaystyle :NH}{\underset{\displaystyle H_2NCNHCH_2CH_3}{\|\|}}$	$\overset{\displaystyle {}^+NH_2}{\underset{\displaystyle H_2NCNHCH_2CH_3}{\|\|}}$	12.5	
Amine	$CH_3\overset{..}{N}H_2$	$CH_3\overset{+}{N}H_3$	10.66	
Ammonia	$:NH_3$	$^+NH_4$	9.26	
Imidazole	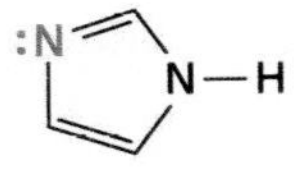	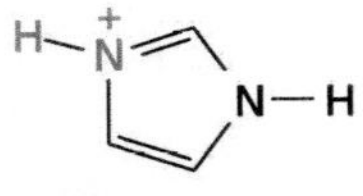	6.95	
Water	$H_2\overset{..}{O}:$	H_3O^+	−1.74	
Alcohol	$CH_3\overset{..}{O}H$	$CH_3\overset{+}{O}H_2$	−2.05	
Ketone	$\overset{\displaystyle :O:}{\underset{\displaystyle CH_3CCH_3}{\|\|}}$	$\overset{\displaystyle {}^+OH}{\underset{\displaystyle CH_3CCH_3}{\|\|}}$	−7.5	Weaker base

Lewis Acids and Bases

The Brønsted–Lowry definition of acids and bases covers only compounds that donate or accept H^+. Of more general use, however, is the Lewis definition. A **Lewis acid** is a substance that accepts an electron pair from a base, and a **Lewis base** is a substance that donates an electron pair to an acid. For all practical purposes, Lewis and Brønsted–Lowry bases are the same: Both have lone pairs of electrons that they donate to acids. Lewis and Brønsted–Lowry acids, however, are *not* necessarily the same.

The fact that a Lewis acid must be able to accept an electron pair means that it must have a vacant, low-energy orbital. Thus, the Lewis definition of acidity is much broader than the Brønsted–Lowry definition and includes many species in addition to H^+. For example, various metal cations and transition-metal compounds, such as Mg^{2+}, Zn^{2+}, and Fe^{3+} are Lewis acids.

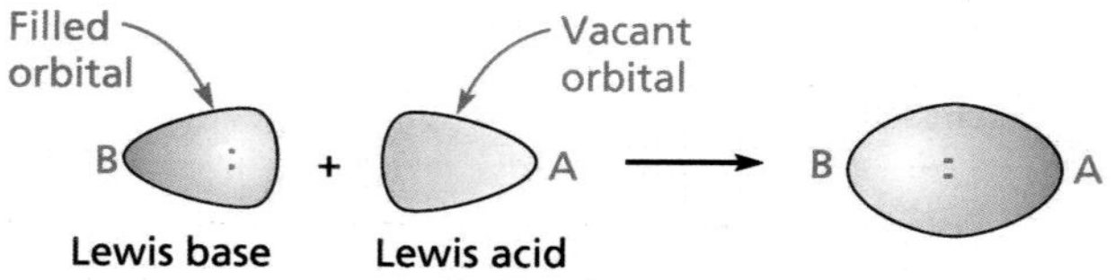

Lewis acids are involved in a great many biological reactions, often as cofactors in enzyme-catalyzed processes. Metal cations such as Mg^{2+} and Zn^{2+} are particularly common, but complex compounds such as iron–sulfur clusters are also found. We'll see an example in Section 4.4 where citrate undergoes acid-catalyzed dehydration to yield *cis*-aconitate, a reaction in the citric acid cycle.

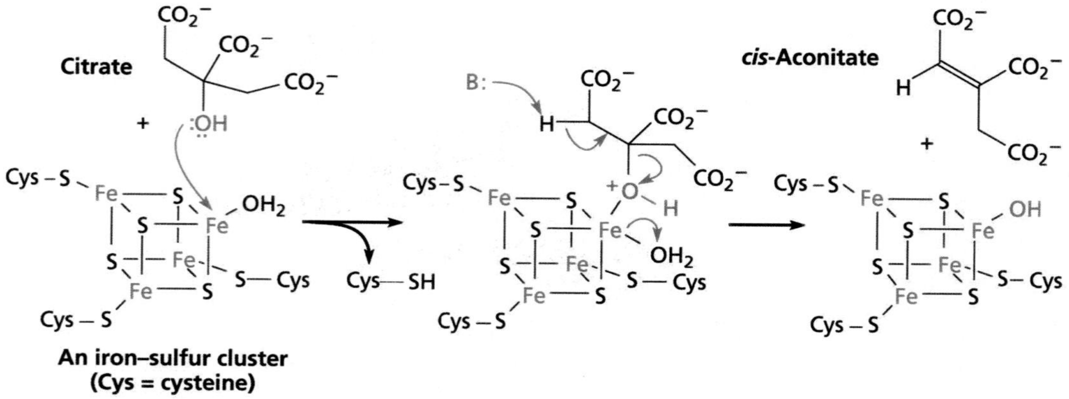

Electrophiles and Nucleophiles

Closely related to acids and bases are *electrophiles* and *nucleophiles*. An **electrophile** is a substance that is "electron-loving." It has a positively polarized, electron-poor atom and can form a bond by accepting a pair of electrons from an electron-rich atom. A **nucleophile**, by contrast, is "nucleus-loving." It has a negatively polarized, electron-rich atom and can form a bond by donating a pair of electrons to an electron-poor atom. Thus, electrophiles are essentially the same as Lewis acids and nucleophiles are the same as Lewis bases. In practice, however, the words "acid" and "base" are generally used when electrons are donated to H^+ or a metal ion, and the words "electrophile" and "nucleophile" are used when electrons are donated to a carbon atom.

Electrophiles are either positively charged or neutral and have a positively polarized, electron-poor atom that can accept an electron pair from a nucleophile/base. Acids (H^+ donors), trialkylsulfonium compounds (R_3S^+), and carbonyl compounds are examples (Figure 1.3).

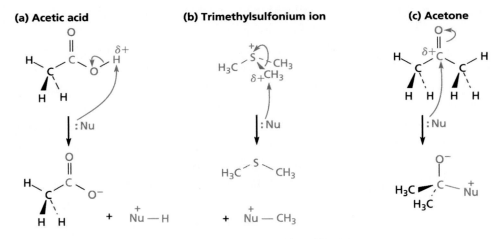

FIGURE 1.3 Some electrophiles and their reactions with nucleophiles (:Nu).

Nucleophiles are either negatively charged or neutral and have a lone pair of electrons they can donate to an electrophile/acid. Amines, water, hydroxide ion, alkoxide ions (RO^-), and thiolate ions (RS^-) are examples.

1.3 Mechanisms: Electrophilic Addition Reactions

Chemical reactions carried out in living organisms follow the same rules of reactivity as reactions carried out in the laboratory. The "solvent" is often different, the temperature is often different, and the catalyst is certainly different, but the reactions occur by the same fundamental mechanisms. That's not to say that *all* bioorganic reactions have obvious laboratory counterparts—some of the most chemically interesting biotransformations cannot be duplicated in the laboratory without an enzyme because too many side reactions would occur. Nevertheless, the chemical mechanisms of biotransformations can be understood and accounted for by organic chemistry. In this and the remaining sections of Chapter 1, we'll look at some fundamental organic reaction mechanisms, beginning with the electrophilic addition reactions of $C=C$ bonds.

An **electrophilic addition reaction** is initiated by addition of an electrophile to an unsaturated (electron-rich) partner, usually an alkene, and leads to formation of a saturated product. In the laboratory, for example, water undergoes an acid-catalyzed electrophilic addition to 2-methylpropene to yield 2-methyl-2-propanol. The reaction takes place in three steps and proceeds through a positively charged, carbocation intermediate (Figure 1.4). In the first step, electrons from the nucleophilic $C=C$ bond attack an electrophilic hydrogen atom of H_3O^+, forming a $C-H$ bond. The intermediate carbocation then reacts with water as nucleophile, giving first a protonated alcohol and then the neutral alcohol after a proton-transfer step that regenerates H_3O^+. Note that the initial protonation takes place on the less highly substituted carbon of the double bond, leading to the more highly substituted, more stable, carbocation.

Biological examples of electrophilic addition reactions occur frequently in the biosynthetic routes leading to steroids and other terpenoids, although they are less common elsewhere. The electrophile in such reactions is a positively charged or positively polarized carbon atom, which often adds to a $C=C$ bond within the same molecule. As an example, α-terpineol, a substance found in pine oil and used in perfumery, is derived biosynthetically from linalyl diphosphate by an internal electrophilic addition reaction. Following formation of an allylic carbocation by dissociation of the diphosphate (here abbreviated PPO),

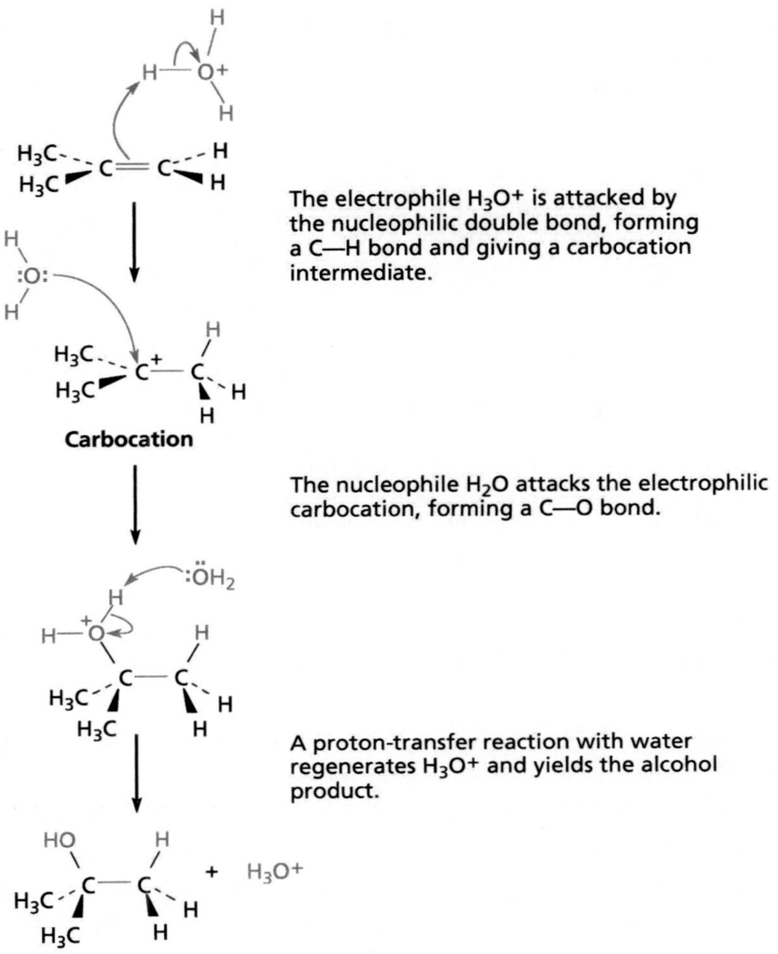

The electrophile H_3O^+ is attacked by the nucleophilic double bond, forming a C—H bond and giving a carbocation intermediate.

Carbocation

The nucleophile H_2O attacks the electrophilic carbocation, forming a C—O bond.

A proton-transfer reaction with water regenerates H_3O^+ and yields the alcohol product.

FIGURE 1.4 The mechanism of the acid-catalyzed electrophilic addition of water to 2-methylpropene. The reaction involves a carbocation intermediate.

electrophilic addition to the nucleophilic C≡C bond at the other end of the molecule occurs, giving a second carbocation that then reacts with nucleophilic water. A proton transfer from the protonated alcohol to water yields α-terpineol (Figure 1.5). We'll see more such examples when we look at steroid biosynthesis in Section 3.5.

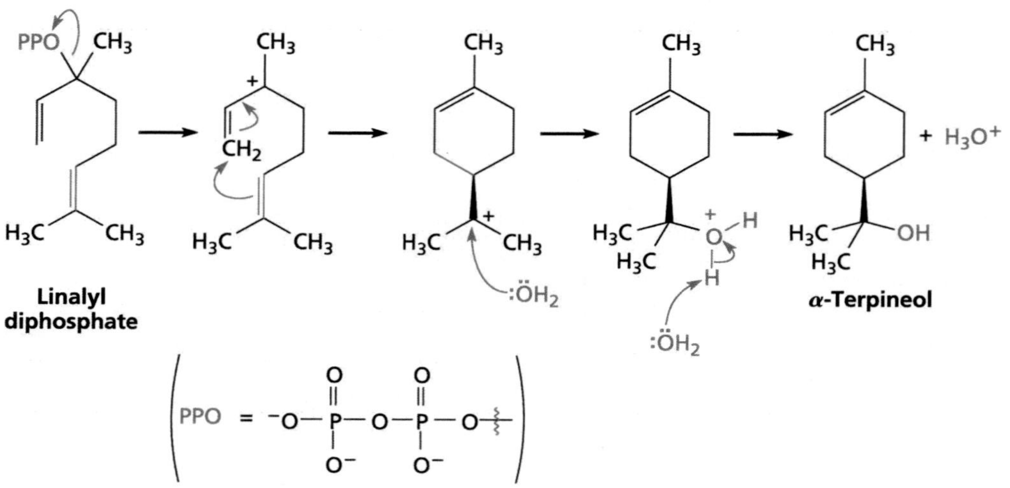

FIGURE 1.5 The biosynthesis of α-terpineol from linalyl diphosphate occurs by an electrophilic addition reaction.

1.4 Mechanisms: Nucleophilic Substitution Reactions

A **nucleophilic substitution reaction** is the substitution of one nucleophile (the *leaving group*) by another on a saturated, sp^3-hybridized carbon atom: Br^- by OH^-, for example. Nucleophilic substitution reactions in the laboratory generally proceed by either an S_N1 **mechanism** or an S_N2 **mechanism** depending on the reactants, the solvent, the pH, and other variables. S_N1 reactions usually take place with tertiary or allylic substrates and occur in two steps through a carbocation intermediate. S_N2 reactions usually take place with primary substrates and take place in a single step without an intermediate.

The mechanism of a typical S_N1 reaction is shown in Figure 1.6. As indicated, the substrate undergoes a spontaneous dissociation to generate a carbocation intermediate, which reacts with the substituting nucleophile to give product.

The mechanism of a typical S_N2 process is shown in Figure 1.7 for the reaction of hydroxide ion with (S)-2-bromobutane. The reaction takes place in a single step when the incoming nucleophile uses a lone pair of electrons to attack the

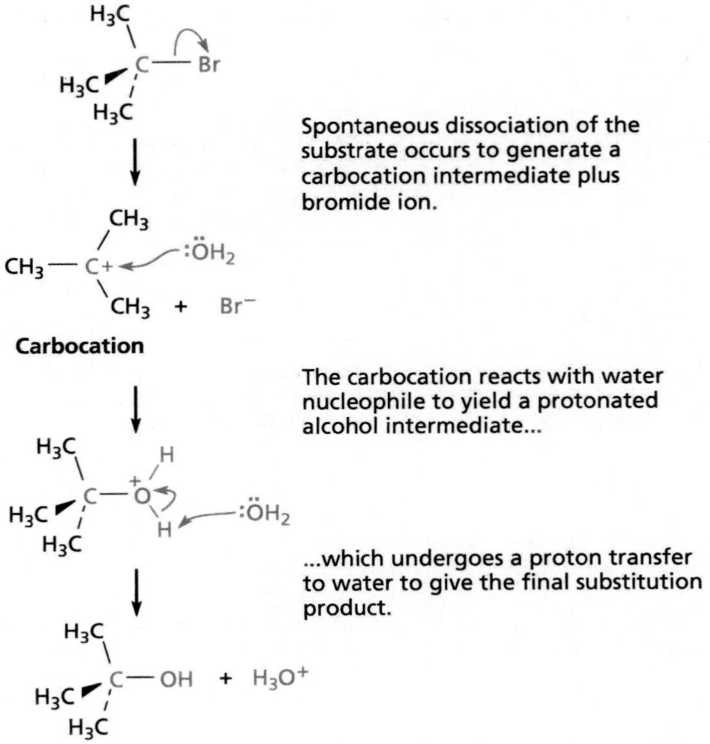

Spontaneous dissociation of the substrate occurs to generate a carbocation intermediate plus bromide ion.

Carbocation

The carbocation reacts with water nucleophile to yield a protonated alcohol intermediate...

...which undergoes a proton transfer to water to give the final substitution product.

FIGURE 1.6 Mechanism of the S_N1 reaction of 2-bromo-2-methylpropane with water to yield 2-methyl-2-propanol. The reaction occurs by a spontaneous dissociation to give a carbocation intermediate, which reacts with water.

electrophilic carbon atom of the alkyl halide from a direction 180° opposite the C—Br bond. As the OH⁻ comes in and a new O—C bond begins to form, the old C—Br bond begins to break and the Br⁻ leaves. Because the incoming and outgoing nucleophiles are on opposite sides of the molecule, the stereochemistry at the reacting center inverts during an S_N2 reaction. (*S*)-2-Bromobutane yields (*R*)-2-butanol, for example. (There is no guarantee that inversion will change the assignment of a stereocenter from *R* to *S* or vice versa, because the relative priorities of the four groups attached to the stereocenter may also change.)

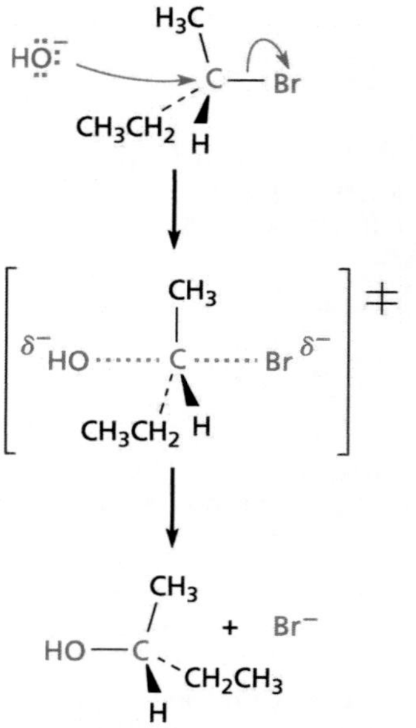

OH⁻ nucleophile uses a lone pair of electrons to attack the electrophilic alkyl halide carbon from a direction 180° oppoite the C—Br bond. The transition state has partially formed C—O and C—Br bonds.

The stereochemistry at carbon inverts as the C—H bond forms fully and the Br⁻ ion leaves.

FIGURE 1.7 Mechanism of the S_N2 reaction of (S)-2-bromobutane with hydroxide ion to yield (R)-2-butanol. The reaction occurs in a single step with inversion of stereochemistry at the reacting carbon atom.

Biochemical examples of both S_N1 and S_N2 reactions occur in numerous pathways. An S_N1 reaction, for instance, takes place during the biological conversion of geranyl diphosphate to geraniol, a fragrant alcohol found in roses and used in perfumery. Initial dissociation of the diphosphate gives a stable allylic carbocation, which reacts with water nucleophile and transfers a proton to yield geraniol.

An S_N1 reaction

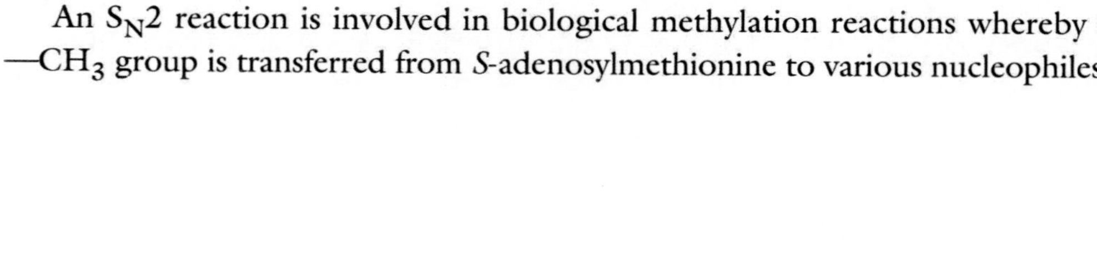

Geranyl diphosphate

Geraniol

An S_N2 reaction is involved in biological methylation reactions whereby a —CH_3 group is transferred from S-adenosylmethionine to various nucleophiles.

In the biosynthetic transformation of norepinephrine to epinephrine (adrenaline), for instance, the nucleophilic amine nitrogen atom of norepinephrine attacks the electrophilic methyl carbon atom of S-adenosylmethionine in an S_N2 reaction, displacing S-adenosylhomocysteine as the leaving group (Figure 1.8).

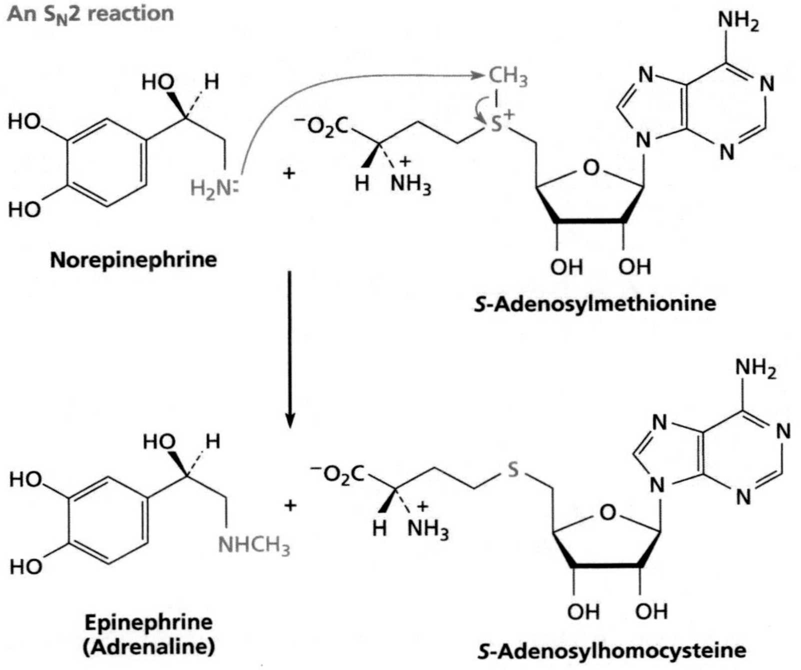

FIGURE 1.8 The biosynthesis of epinephrine from norepinephrine occurs by an S_N2 reaction with S-adenosylmethionine.

1.5 Mechanisms: Nucleophilic Carbonyl Addition Reactions

Carbonyl groups are present in the vast majority of biological molecules, and carbonyl reactions are thus encountered in almost all biochemical pathways. In discussing carbonyl-group chemistry, it's useful to make a distinction between two general classes of compounds. In one class are aldehydes and ketones, which have their carbonyl carbon bonded to atoms (C and H) that can't stabilize a negative charge and therefore don't typically act as leaving groups in substitution reactions. In the second class are carboxylic acids and their derivatives, which have their carbonyl carbon bonded to an electronegative atom (O, N, or S) that *can* stabilize a negative charge and thus *can* act as a leaving group in a substitution reaction.

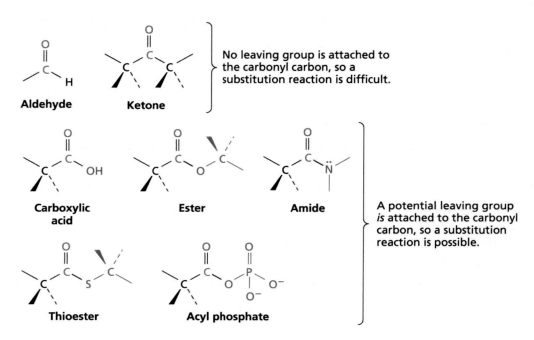

The C=O bond in every carbonyl compound, regardless of structure, is polarized with the oxygen negative and the carbon positive. As a result, the carbonyl oxygen is *nucleophilic* and reacts with acids/electrophiles, while the carbon is *electrophilic* and reacts with bases/nucleophiles. These simple reactivity patterns show up in almost all biological pathways.

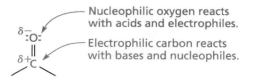

Nucleophilic Addition Reactions

A **nucleophilic addition reaction** is the addition of a nucleophile (:Nu) to the electrophilic carbon of an aldehyde or ketone. As an electron pair from the nucleophile forms a bond to the carbon, an electron pair from the C=O bond moves toward oxygen, giving an alkoxide ion, RO^-. The carbonyl carbon rehybridizes from sp^2 to sp^3 during the process, so the alkoxide product has tetrahedral geometry.

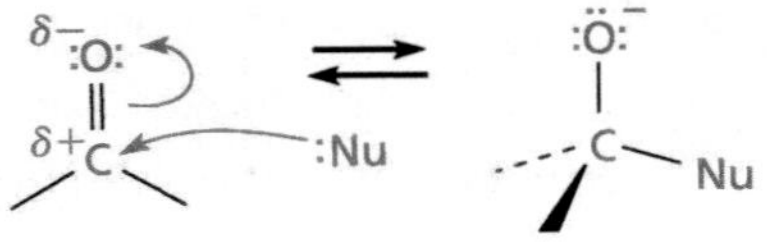

Once formed, the tetrahedral alkoxide ion can do any of several things, as shown in Figure 1.9. When a nucleophile such as hydride ion ($H:^-$) or a carbanion ($R_3C:^-$) adds, the alkoxide ion undergoes protonation to yield a stable alcohol.

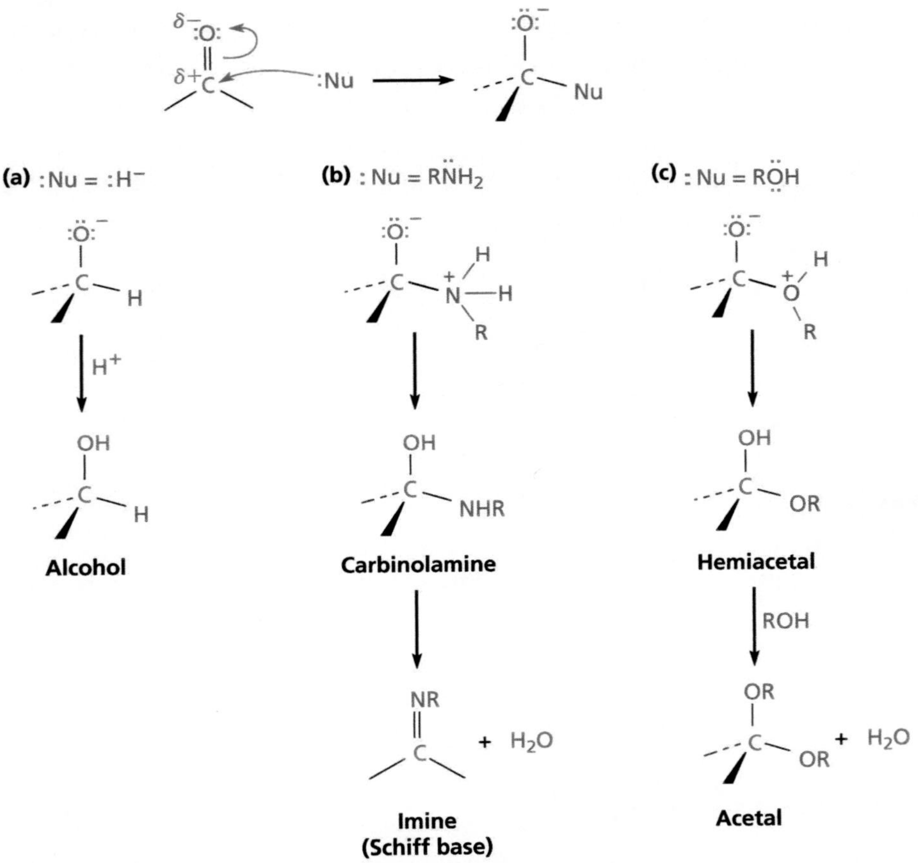

(a) :Nu = :H⁻

(b) :Nu = RṄH₂

(c) :Nu = RȮH

Alcohol

Carbinolamine

Hemiacetal

Imine
(Schiff base)

Acetal

FIGURE 1.9 Some typical nucleophilic addition reactions of aldehydes and ketones. (a) With a hydride ion as nucleophile, protonation of the alkoxide intermediate leads to an alcohol. (b) With an amine as nucleophile, proton transfer and loss of water leads to an imine. (c) With an alcohol as nucleophile, proton transfer leads to a hemiacetal, and further reaction with a second equivalent of alcohol leads to an acetal.

When a primary amine nucleophile (RNH_2) adds, the alkoxide ion undergoes a proton transfer to yield a **carbinolamine**, which loses water to form an **imine** ($R_2C=NR'$), often called a **Schiff base** in biochemistry. When an alcohol nucleophile (ROH) adds, the alkoxide undergoes proton transfer to yield a **hemiacetal**, which can react with a second equivalent of alcohol and lose water to give an **acetal** [$R_2C(OR')_2$]. In all the reactions that follow, note the role of acid and base catalysts.

Alcohol Formation

In the laboratory, the conversion of an aldehyde or ketone to an alcohol is generally carried out using $NaBH_4$ as the nucleophilic hydride-ion donor. In biological pathways, however, NADH (reduced nicotinamide adenine dinucleotide) or the closely related NADPH (reduced nicotinamide adenine dinucleotide phosphate) is the most frequently used hydride-ion donor. An example that occurs in the pathway by which organisms synthesize fatty acids is the conversion of acetoacetyl ACP (acyl carrier protein) to 3-hydroxybutyryl ACP. We'll look at the details of the process in Section 3.4.

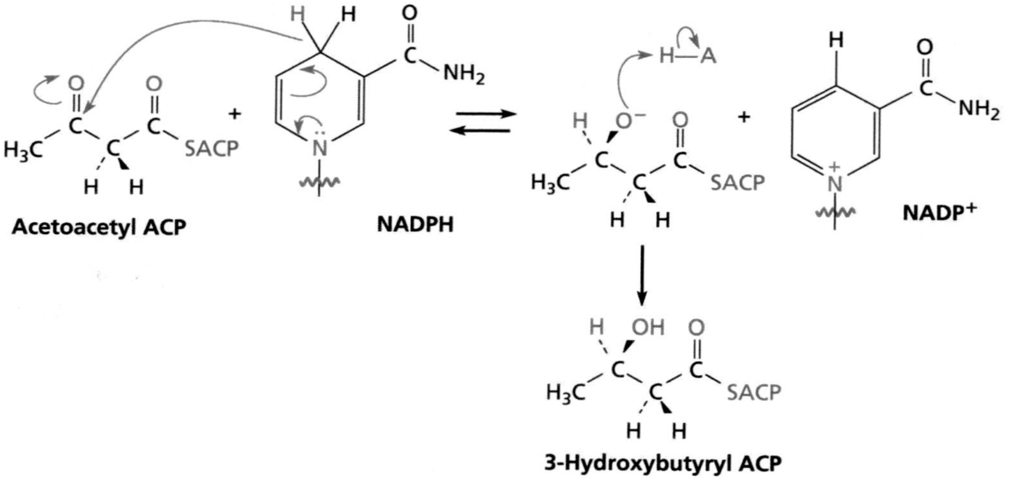

Acetoacetyl ACP   **NADPH**   **NADP+**

3-Hydroxybutyryl ACP

Imine (Schiff Base) Formation

Imines are formed in a reversible, acid-catalyzed process that begins with nucleophilic addition of a primary amine to the carbonyl group of an aldehyde or ketone. The initial dipolar addition product undergoes a rapid proton transfer that removes an H^+ from N and places another H^+ on O to give a carbinolamine, which is protonated on the oxygen atom by an acid catalyst. The effect of this protonation is to convert —OH into a much better leaving group (—OH$_2^+$) so that it can be expelled by the electrons on nitrogen. Deprotonation of the resultant iminium ion then gives the imine product. The mechanism is shown in Figure 1.10.

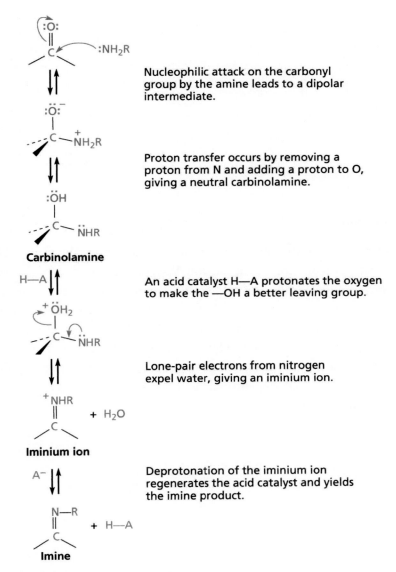

Nucleophilic attack on the carbonyl group by the amine leads to a dipolar intermediate.

Proton transfer occurs by removing a proton from N and adding a proton to O, giving a neutral carbinolamine.

An acid catalyst H—A protonates the oxygen to make the —OH a better leaving group.

Lone-pair electrons from nitrogen expel water, giving an iminium ion.

Deprotonation of the iminium ion regenerates the acid catalyst and yields the imine product.

FIGURE 1.10 Mechanism of acid-catalyzed imine (Schiff base) formation by reaction of an aldehyde or ketone with a primary amine, RNH$_2$.

The conversion of a ketone to an imine is a step in numerous biological pathways, including the route by which many amino acids are synthesized in the body. For instance, the ketone pyruvate and the amine pyridoxamine phosphate, a derivative of vitamin B_6, form an imine that is converted to the amino acid alanine. We'll look at the details in Section 5.1.

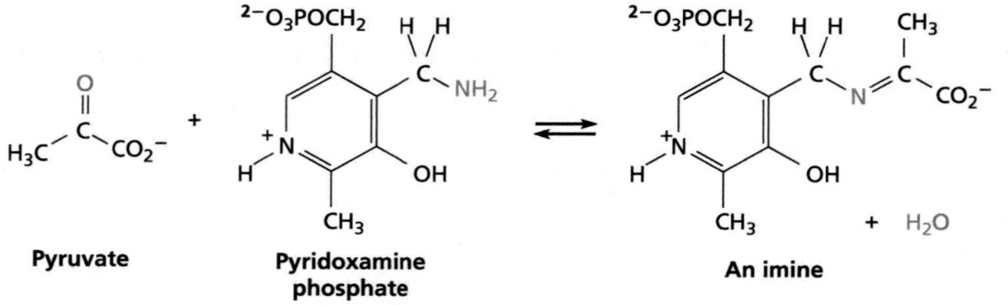

Acetal Formation

Acetals, like imines, are formed in a reversible, acid-catalyzed process. The reaction begins with protonation of the carbonyl oxygen to increase its reactivity, followed by nucleophilic addition of an alcohol. Deprotonation then gives a neutral hemiacetal, and reprotonation on the hydroxyl oxygen converts the —OH into a better leaving group so that it can be expelled by electrons on the neighboring —OR to produce an oxonium ion. This oxonium ion behaves much like the protonated carbonyl group in the first step, undergoing a second nucleophilic addition with alcohol. A final deprotonation then gives the acetal product. The mechanism is shown in Figure 1.11.

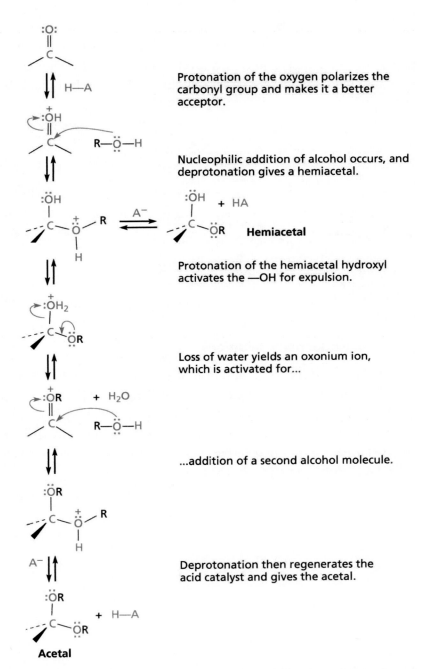

Protonation of the oxygen polarizes the carbonyl group and makes it a better acceptor.

Nucleophilic addition of alcohol occurs, and deprotonation gives a hemiacetal.

Hemiacetal

Protonation of the hemiacetal hydroxyl activates the —OH for expulsion.

Loss of water yields an oxonium ion, which is activated for...

...addition of a second alcohol molecule.

Deprotonation then regenerates the acid catalyst and gives the acetal.

Acetal

FIGURE 1.11 Mechanism of acid-catalyzed hemiacetal and acetal formation by reaction of an aldehyde or ketone with an alcohol.

The formation of hemiacetals and acetals is a central part of carbohydrate chemistry. Glucose, for instance, is in a readily reversible equilibrium between open (aldehyde + alcohol) and closed (cyclic hemiacetal) forms. Many glucose molecules can then join together by acetal links to form starch and cellulose (Section 4.1).

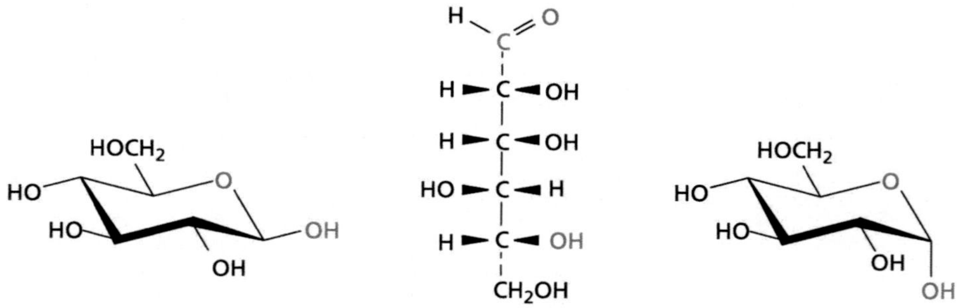

β-Glucose (hemiacetal)   **Glucose (open)**   **α-Glucose (hemiacetal)**

Conjugate (1,4) Nucleophilic Additions

Closely related to the direct (1,2) addition of a nucleophile to the C=O bond of an aldehyde or ketone is the **conjugate (1,4) addition**, or **Michael reaction**, of a nucleophile to the C=C bond of an α,β-unsaturated aldehyde or ketone (or thioester). The initial product, a resonance-stabilized **enolate ion**, typically undergoes protonation on the α carbon (the carbon *next to* the C=O) to give a saturated aldehyde or ketone (or thioester) product.

A direct (1,2) addition

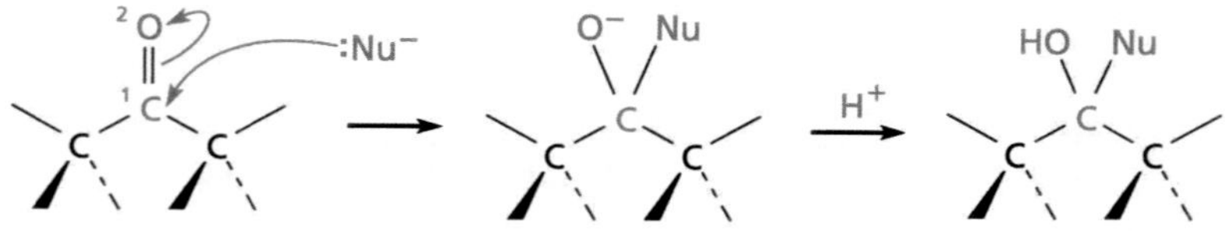

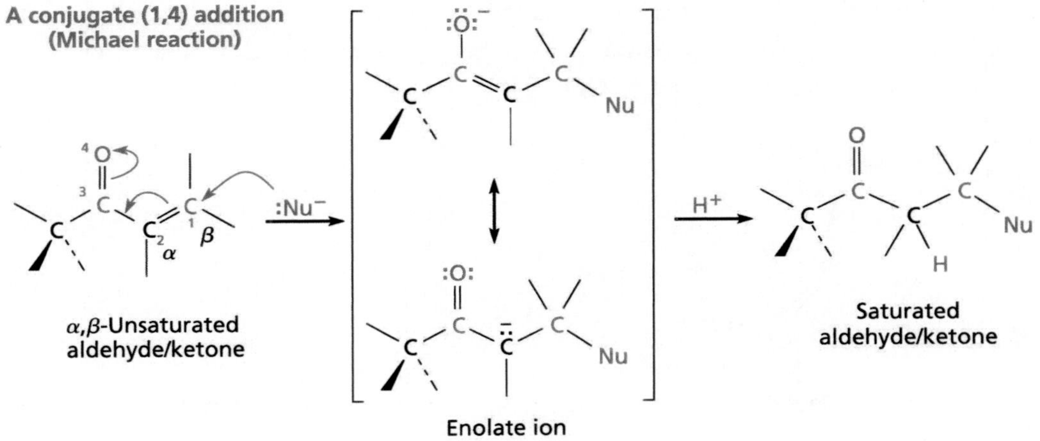

A conjugate (1,4) addition (Michael reaction)

Enolate ion

α,β-Unsaturated
aldehyde/ketone

Saturated
aldehyde/ketone

Note that this conjugate addition reaction gives an overall result similar to that of the electrophilic alkene addition discussed in Section 1.3, but the mechanisms of the two processes are entirely different. Isolated alkenes react with *electrophiles* and form carbocation intermediates; *α,β*-unsaturated carbonyl compounds react with *nucleophiles* and form enolate-ion intermediates. Conjugate addition occurs because the electronegative oxygen atom of the *α,β*-unsaturated carbonyl compound withdraws electrons from the *β* carbon, thereby making it more electron-poor and more electrophilic than a typical alkene C=C bond.

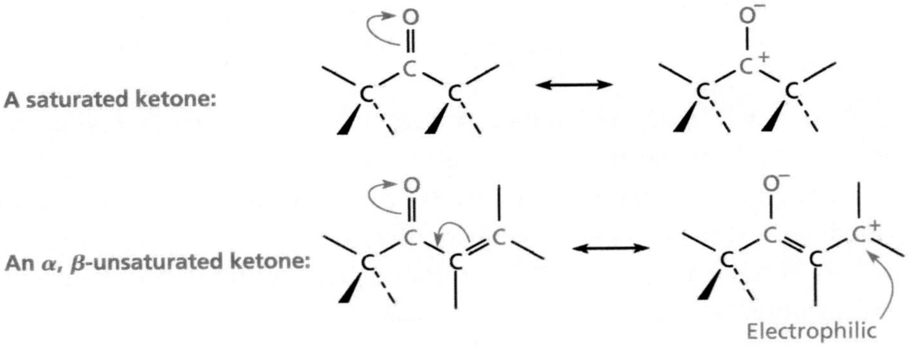

A saturated ketone:

An *α, β*-unsaturated ketone:

Electrophilic

Among the many biological examples of conjugate additions is the conversion of fumarate to malate by reaction with water, a step in the citric acid cycle by which acetate is metabolized to CO_2.

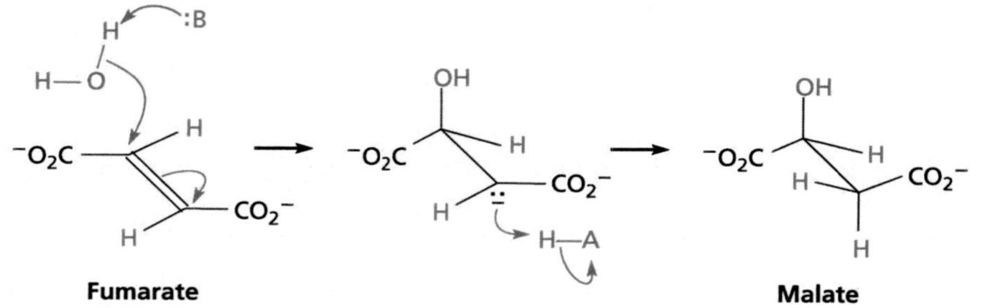

Fumarate   **Malate**

1.6 Mechanisms: Nucleophilic Acyl Substitution Reactions

Carboxylic acids and their derivatives are characterized by the presence of an electronegative atom (O, N, S) bonded to the carbonyl carbon. As a result, these compounds can undergo **nucleophilic acyl substitution reactions**—the substitution of the leaving group bonded to the carbonyl carbon (:Y) by an attacking nucleophile ($:Nu^-$).

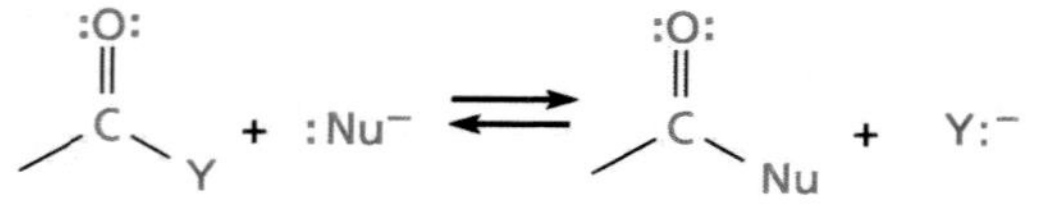

A nucleophilic acyl substitution reaction

As shown in Figure 1.12 for the reaction of OH^- with methyl acetate, a nucleophilic acyl substitution reaction is initiated by addition of the nucleophile to the carbonyl carbon in the usual way. But the tetrahedrally hybridized alkoxide intermediate is not isolated; instead, it reacts further by expelling the leaving group and forming a new carbonyl compound. The overall result of nucleophilic acyl substitution is the replacement of the leaving group by the attacking nucleophile, just as occurs in the nucleophilic *alkyl* substitutions discussed in Section 1.4. Only the *mechanisms* of the two substitutions are different.

Both the addition step and the elimination step can affect the overall rate of a nucleophilic acyl substitution reaction, but the first step is generally rate-limiting. Thus, the greater the stability of the carbonyl compound, the less reactive it is. We therefore find that, of the carbonyl-containing functional groups commonly

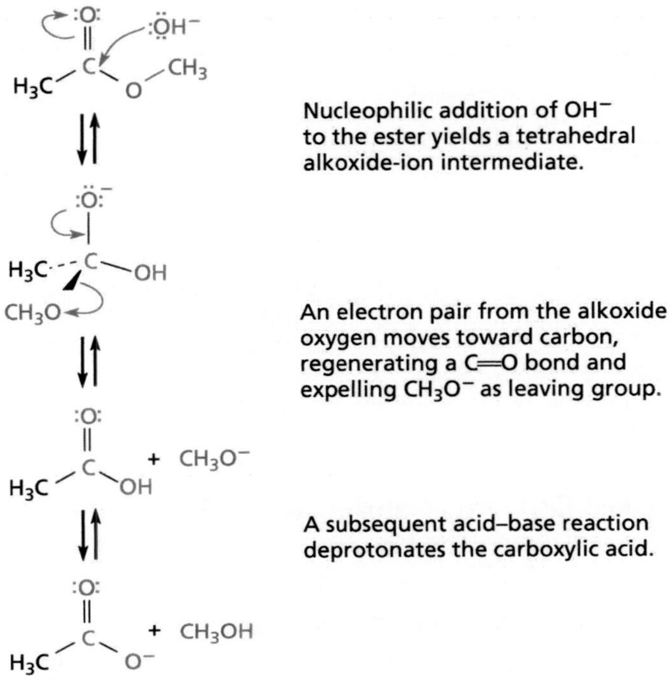

Nucleophilic addition of OH⁻ to the ester yields a tetrahedral alkoxide-ion intermediate.

An electron pair from the alkoxide oxygen moves toward carbon, regenerating a C=O bond and expelling CH₃O⁻ as leaving group.

A subsequent acid–base reaction deprotonates the carboxylic acid.

FIGURE 1.12 Mechanism of the nucleophilic acyl substitution reaction of OH⁻ with methyl acetate to give acetate. The reaction occurs by a nucleophilic addition to the carbonyl group, followed by expulsion of the leaving group in a second step.

found in living organisms, amides are the least reactive because of resonance stabilization; esters are somewhat more reactive; and thioesters and acyl phosphates are the most reactive toward substitution. (Acyl phosphates are generally further activated for substitution by complexation with a Lewis acidic metal cation such as Mg^{2+}.)

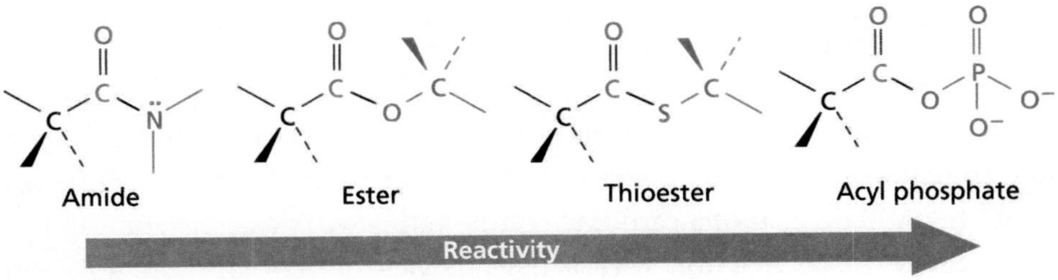

Amide   Ester   Thioester   Acyl phosphate

Reactivity

Nucleophilic acyl substitution reactions occur frequently in biochemistry. For example, the carboxypeptidase-catalyzed hydrolysis of the C-terminal amide bond in proteins is one such process.

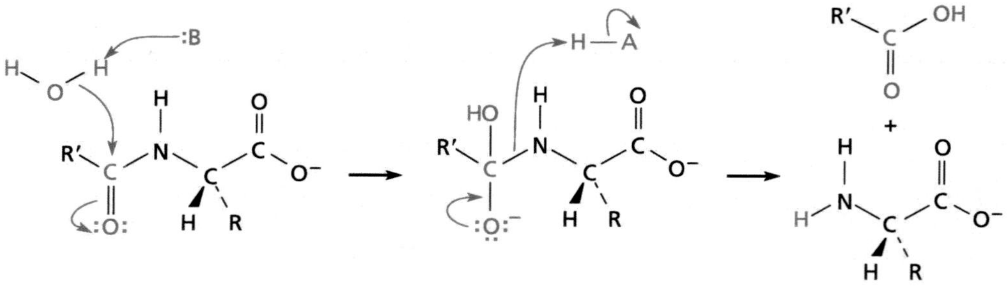

1.7 Mechanisms: Carbonyl Condensation Reactions

The third major reaction of carbonyl compounds, **carbonyl condensation**, occurs when two carbonyl compounds join to give a single product. When an aldehyde is treated with base, for example, two molecules combine to yield a β-hydroxy aldehyde product. Similarly, when an ester is treated with base, two molecules combine to yield a β-keto ester product.

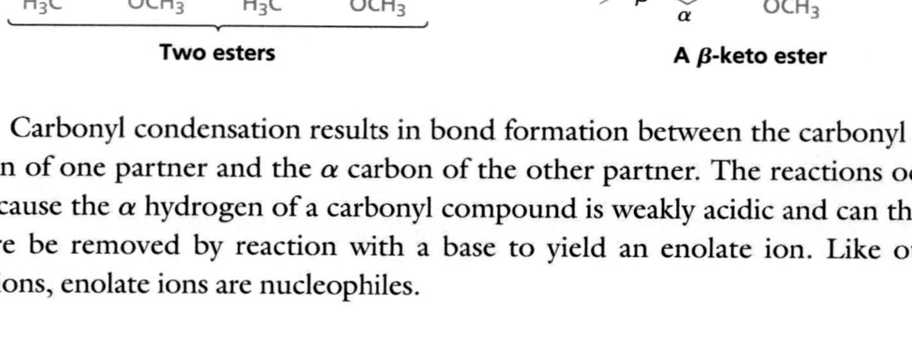

Two aldehydes   A β-hydroxy aldehyde

Two esters   A β-keto ester

Carbonyl condensation results in bond formation between the carbonyl carbon of one partner and the α carbon of the other partner. The reactions occur because the α hydrogen of a carbonyl compound is weakly acidic and can therefore be removed by reaction with a base to yield an enolate ion. Like other anions, enolate ions are nucleophiles.

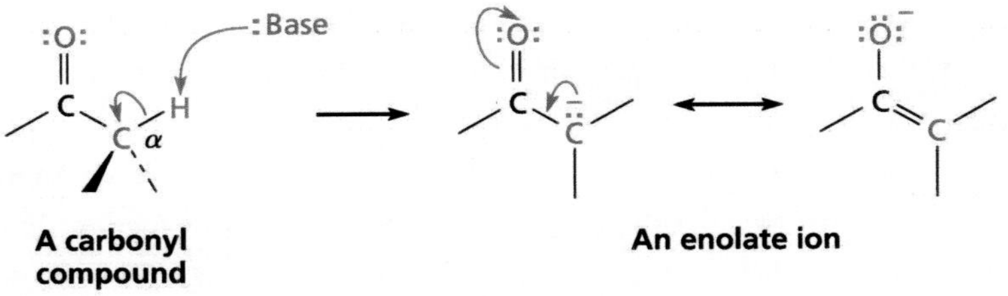

A carbonyl compound   **An enolate ion**

The acidity of carbonyl compounds is due to resonance stabilization of the enolate ion, which allows the negative charge to be shared by the α carbon and the electronegative carbonyl oxygen. As shown in Table 1.4, aldehydes and ketones are the most acidic monocarbonyl compounds, with thioesters, esters,

Table 1.4 Acidity Constants of Some Carbonyl Compounds

Carbonyl compound	Example	pK_a	
Carboxylic acid	CH_3COH (O)	4.7	Stronger acid
1,3-Diketone	$CH_3CCH_2CCH_3$ (O O)	9.0	
β-Keto ester	$CH_3CCH_2COCH_3$ (O O)	10.6	
1,3-Diester	$CH_3OCCH_2COCH_3$ (O O)	12.9	
Aldehyde	CH_3CH (O)	17	
Ketone	CH_3CCH_3 (O)	19.3	
Thioester	CH_3CSCH_3 (O)	21	
Ester	CH_3COCH_3 (O)	25	
Amide	$CH_3CN(CH_3)_2$ (O)	30	Weaker acid

Chemistry for Biologists

31

and amides less so. Most acidic of all, however, are 1,3-*dicarbonyl* compounds (β-dicarbonyl compounds), which have an α position flanked by *two* adjacent carbonyl groups.

The condensation of an aldehyde or ketone is called the **aldol reaction** and takes place by the mechanism shown in Figure 1.13. One molecule reacts with base to give a nucleophilic enolate ion, which then adds to the second molecule in a nucleophilic addition reaction. Protonation of the initially formed alkoxide ion yields the neutral β-hydroxy aldehyde or ketone product. Note that the condensation is reversible: A β-hydroxy aldehyde or ketone can fragment on treatment with base to yield two molecules of aldehyde or ketone.

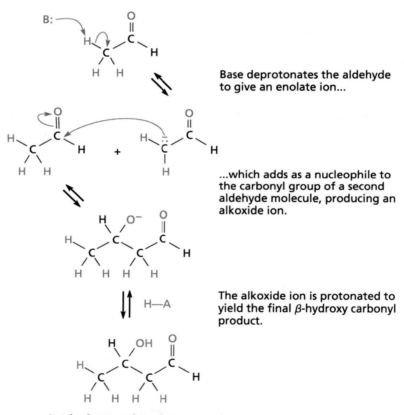

Base deprotonates the aldehyde to give an enolate ion...

...which adds as a nucleophile to the carbonyl group of a second aldehyde molecule, producing an alkoxide ion.

The alkoxide ion is protonated to yield the final β-hydroxy carbonyl product.

A β-hydroxy carbonyl compound

FIGURE 1.13 Mechanism of the aldol reaction, a reversible, base-catalyzed condensation reaction between two molecules of aldehyde or ketone to yield a β-hydroxy carbonyl compound. The key step is nucleophilic addition of an enolate ion to a C=O bond.

The condensation of an ester is called the **Claisen condensation reaction** and takes place by the mechanism shown in Figure 1.14. One molecule reacts with base to give a nucleophilic enolate ion, which adds to the second molecule in a nucleophilic acyl substitution reaction. The initially formed alkoxide ion

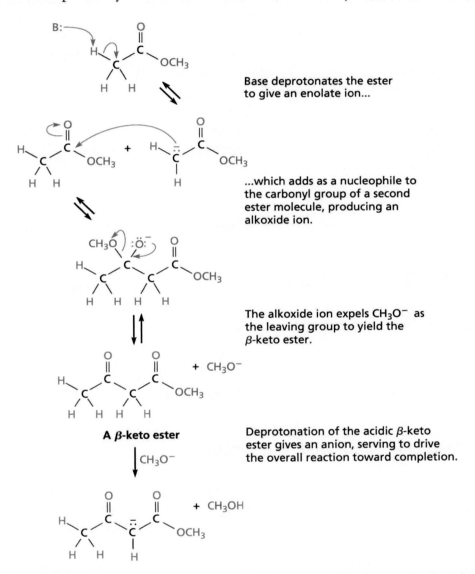

Base deprotonates the ester to give an enolate ion...

...which adds as a nucleophile to the carbonyl group of a second ester molecule, producing an alkoxide ion.

The alkoxide ion expels CH_3O^- as the leaving group to yield the β-keto ester.

A β-keto ester

Deprotonation of the acidic β-keto ester gives an anion, serving to drive the overall reaction toward completion.

FIGURE 1.14 Mechanism of the Claisen condensation reaction, a reversible, base-catalyzed condensation reaction between two molecules of ester to yield a β-keto ester. The key step is nucleophilic acyl substitution by an enolate ion, with expulsion of an alkoxide leaving group.

expels CH_3O^- as the leaving group to regenerate a $C\!\!=\!\!O$ bond and form the β-keto ester product. As with the aldol reaction, the Claisen condensation is reversible: A β-keto ester can fragment on treatment with base to yield two molecules of ester.

Carbonyl condensation reactions are involved in nearly all biochemical pathways and serve as the primary biological method for forming and breaking carbon–carbon bonds. For instance, one step in the biosynthesis of glucose from pyruvate is the aldol reaction of glyceraldehyde 3-phosphate with dihydroxyacetone phosphate. As another example, the biological pathway for terpenoid and steroid biosynthesis begins with a Claisen condensation of the thioester acetyl CoA (coenzyme A) to give acetoacetyl CoA. We'll look at the details of glucose biosynthesis in Section 4.5 and the details of steroid biosynthesis in Section 3.6.

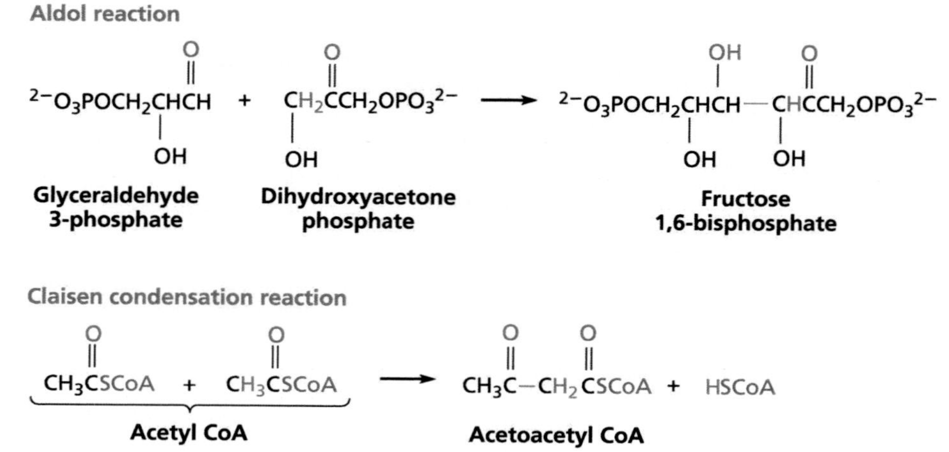

Aldol reaction

$$2^-O_3POCH_2\overset{\underset{OH}{|}}{C}HC\overset{O}{\overset{||}{H}} \;+\; CH_2\overset{O}{\overset{||}{C}}CH_2OPO_3{}^{2-} \longrightarrow\; 2^-O_3POCH_2\overset{\underset{OH}{|}}{C}HC\overset{OH}{\overset{|}{H}}\!\!-\!\!\overset{\underset{OH}{|}}{C}HC\overset{O}{\overset{||}{C}}H_2OPO_3{}^{2-}$$

Glyceraldehyde 3-phosphate   **Dihydroxyacetone phosphate**   **Fructose 1,6-bisphosphate**

Claisen condensation reaction

$$CH_3\overset{O}{\overset{||}{C}}SCoA \;+\; CH_3\overset{O}{\overset{||}{C}}SCoA \;\longrightarrow\; CH_3\overset{O}{\overset{||}{C}}\!\!-\!\!CH_2\overset{O}{\overset{||}{C}}SCoA \;+\; HSCoA$$

Acetyl CoA   **Acetoacetyl CoA**

1.8 Mechanisms: Elimination Reactions

The elimination of HX to yield an alkene appears to be the simple reverse of an electrophilic addition of HX. In fact, though, **elimination reactions** are a good deal more complex than additions and can occur by any of several mechanisms. In the laboratory, the three most common processes are the E1, E2, and E1cB reactions, which differ in the timing of C—H and C—X bond-breaking. In the E1 reaction, the C—X bond breaks first to give a carbocation intermediate, which then undergoes base abstraction of H^+ to yield the alkene (the exact reverse of the electrophilic addition reaction described in Section 1.3). In the E2 reaction, base-induced C—H bond cleavage is simultaneous with C—X bond cleavage, giving the alkene in a single step. In the E1cB reaction (cB for "conjugate base"), base abstraction of the proton occurs first, giving a carbanion intermediate that undergoes loss of X^- in a subsequent step to give the alkene.

E1 Reaction: C–X bond breaks first to give a carbocation intermediate, followed by base removal of a proton to yield the alkene.

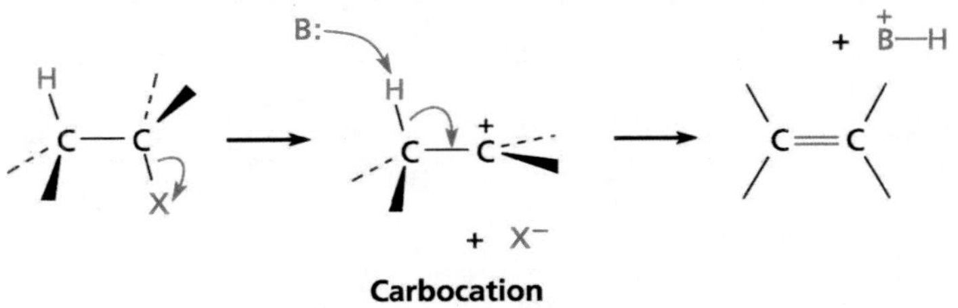

Carbocation

E2 Reaction: C–H and C–X bonds break simultaneously, giving the alkene in a single step without intermediates.

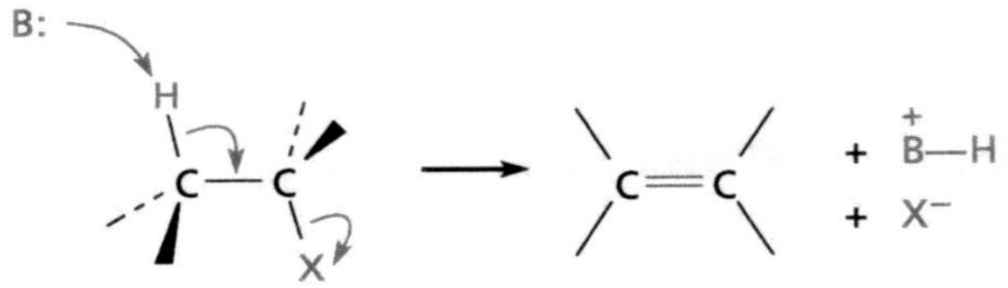

E1cB Reaction: C–H bond breaks first, giving a carbanion intermediate that loses X^- to form the alkene.

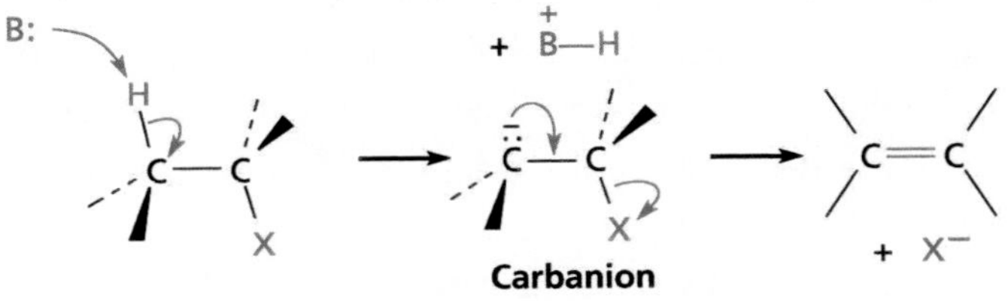

Carbanion

Examples of all three mechanisms occur in different biological pathways, but the E1cB mechanism is particularly common. The substrate is usually an alcohol (X = OH) or protonated alcohol (X = OH_2^+), and the H atom that is removed is usually made acidic, particularly in E1cB reactions, by being adjacent to a carbonyl group. Thus, β-hydroxy carbonyl compounds (aldol reaction products) are frequently converted to α,β-unsaturated carbonyl compounds by elimination reactions. An example is the dehydration of a β-hydroxy thioester to the corresponding unsaturated thioester, a reaction that occurs in fatty-acid biosynthesis (Section 3.4). The base in this reaction is a histidine residue in the enzyme, and the elimination is assisted by complexation of the —OH group to the protonated histidine as a Lewis acid. Note that the reaction occurs with *syn* stereochemistry, meaning that the —H and —OH groups in this example are eliminated from the same side of the molecule.

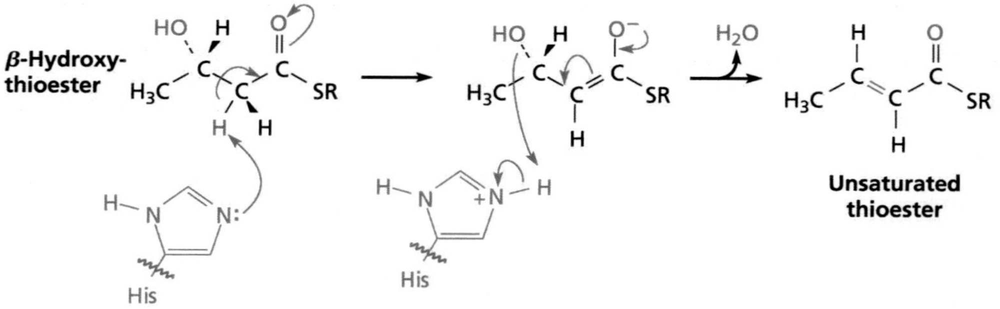

1.9 Oxidations and Reductions

Oxidation–reduction, or **redox**, chemistry is a large and complicated, but extremely important, topic. Rather than attempt a complete catalog of the subject at this point, however, let's focus on the mechanisms of two of the more commonly occurring biological redox processes: the oxidation of an alcohol and the reduction of a carbonyl compound. We'll look at the mechanisms of other kinds of biological oxidations in later chapters as the need arises when we discuss specific pathways.

In the laboratory, alcohol oxidations generally occur through a mechanism that involves attachment to oxygen of a leaving group X, usually a metal in a high oxidation state such as Cr(VI) or Mn(VII). An E2-like elimination reaction then forms the C=O bond and expels the metal in a lower oxidation state. Note that the C—H hydrogen is removed by base as H^+ during the elimination step.

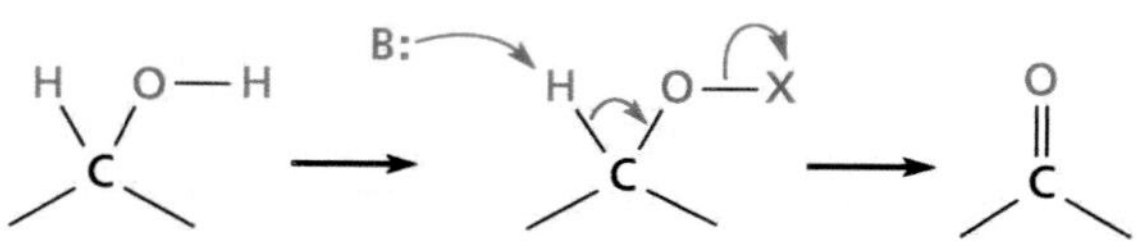

Although a similar mechanism does occasionally occur in biological pathways, many biological oxidations of an alcohol occur by a reversible hydride-transfer mechanism involving one of the coenzymes NAD$^+$ (oxidized nicotinamide adenine dinucleotide) or NADP$^+$ (oxidized nicotinamide adenine dinucleotide phosphate). As shown in Figure 1.15, the reaction occurs in a single step without intermediates when a base B: abstracts the acidic O—H proton, the electrons from the O—H bond move to form a C=O bond, and the hydrogen attached to carbon is transferred to NAD$^+$. Note that the C—H hydrogen is transferred as H$^-$, in contrast to the typical laboratory oxidation where it is removed as H$^+$. Note also that the hydride ion adds to the C=C—C=N$^+$ part of NAD$^+$ in a conjugate nucleophilic addition reaction, much as water might add to the C=C—C=O part of an α,β-unsaturated ketone (Section 1.5).

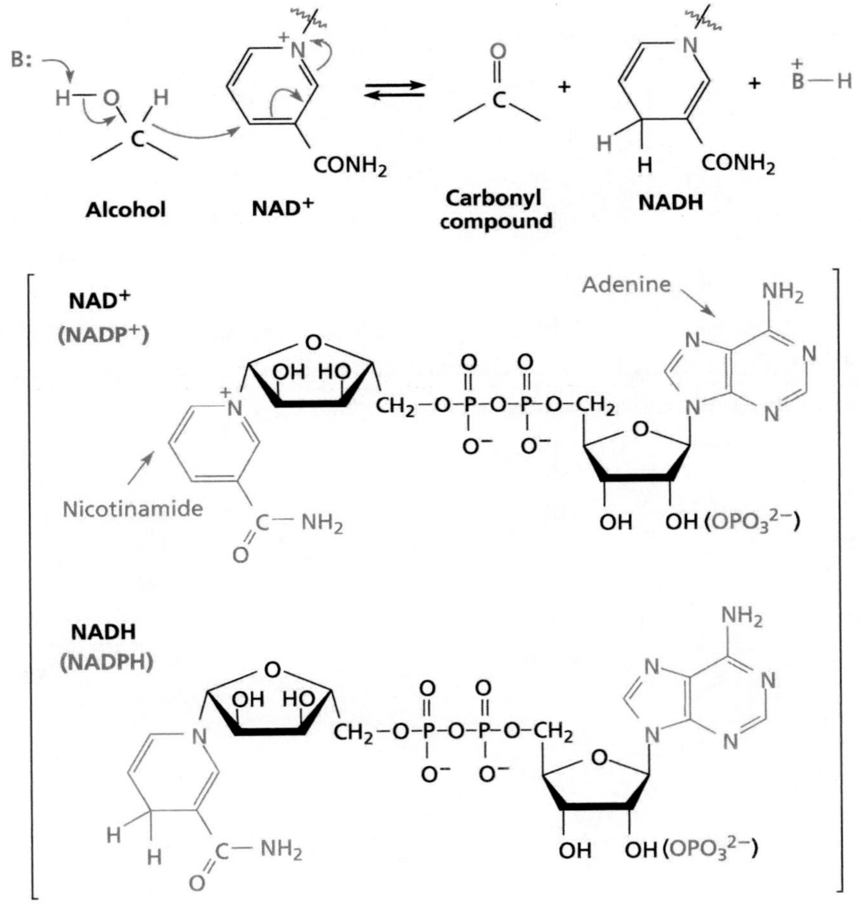

FIGURE 1.15 Mechanism of alcohol oxidation by NAD$^+$.

Expulsion of hydride ion is not often seen in laboratory chemistry because, as noted at the beginning of Section 1.5, H⁻ is a poor leaving group. One analogous process that does occur in laboratory chemistry, however, is the Cannizzaro reaction, which involves the disproportionation of an aromatic aldehyde on treatment with base. Benzaldehyde, for example, is converted to a mixture of benzyl alcohol and benzoic acid by reaction with NaOH. Hydroxide ion first adds to the aldehyde carbonyl group to give an alkoxide intermediate, which transfers a hydride ion to a second molecule of aldehyde. The first aldehyde is thereby oxidized, and the second aldehyde is reduced.

Cannizzaro reaction

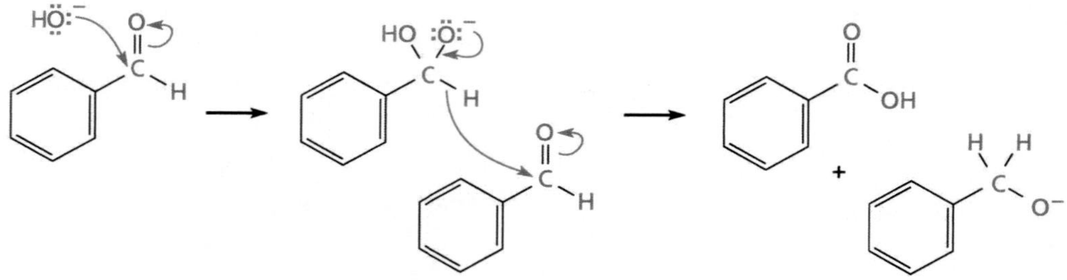

Biological reductions are the reverse of oxidations. As noted in Section 1.5, NADH transfers a hydride ion to the carbonyl group in a nucleophilic addition reaction, and the alkoxide intermediate is protonated.

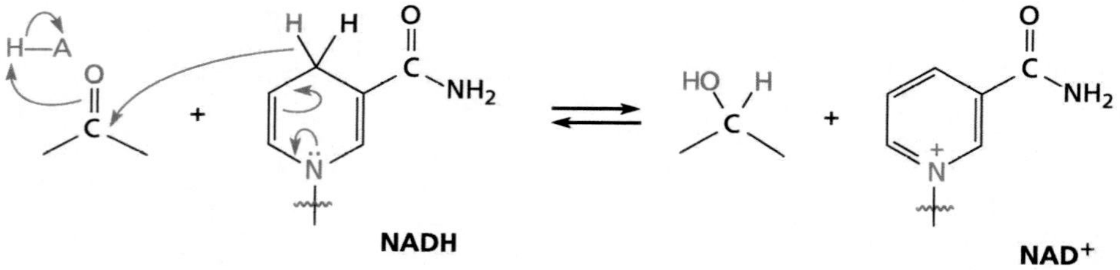

Problems

1.1 Which of the following substances can behave as either an acid or a base, depending on the circumstances?

(a) CH_3SH (b) Ca^{2+} (c) NH_3 (d) CH_3SCH_3

(e) NH_4^+ (f) $H_2C{=}CH_2$ (g) $CH_3CO_2^-$ (h) $^+H_3NCH_2CO_2^-$

1.2 Which $C{=}C$ bond do you think is more nucleophilic, that in 1-butene or that in 3-buten-2-one? Explain.

$$CH_3CH_2CH{=}CH_2 \qquad \overset{\displaystyle O}{\underset{\displaystyle}{CH_3\overset{\|}{C}CH{=}CH_2}}$$

1-Butene   **3-Buten-2-one**

1.3 Rank the following compounds in order of increasing acidity:

(a) Acetone, $pK_a = 19.3$ (b) Phenol, $pK_a = 9.9$

(c) Methanethiol, $pK_a = 10.3$ (d) Formic acid, $K_a = 1.99 \times 10^{-4}$

(e) Ethyl acetoacetate, $K_a = 2.51 \times 10^{-11}$

1.4 Rank the following compounds in order of increasing basicity:

(a) Aniline, $pK_{a(BH^+)} = 4.63$ (b) Pyrrole, $pK_{a(BH^+)} = 0.4$

(c) Dimethylamine, $pK_{a(BH^+)} = 10.5$

(d) Ammonia, $K_{a(BH^+)} = 5.5 \times 10^{-10}$

1.5 Protonation of acetic acid by H_2SO_4 might occur on either of two oxygen atoms. Draw resonance structures of both possible products, and explain why protonation occurs preferentially on the double-bond oxygen.

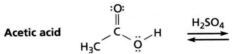

Acetic acid

1.6 Protonation of a guanidino compound occurs on the double-bond nitrogen rather than on either of the single-bond nitrogens. Draw resonance structures of the three possible protonation products, and explain the observed result.

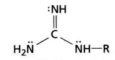

A guanidino compound

1.7   Predict the product(s) of the following biological reactions by interpreting the flow of electrons as indicated by the curved arrows:

(a)

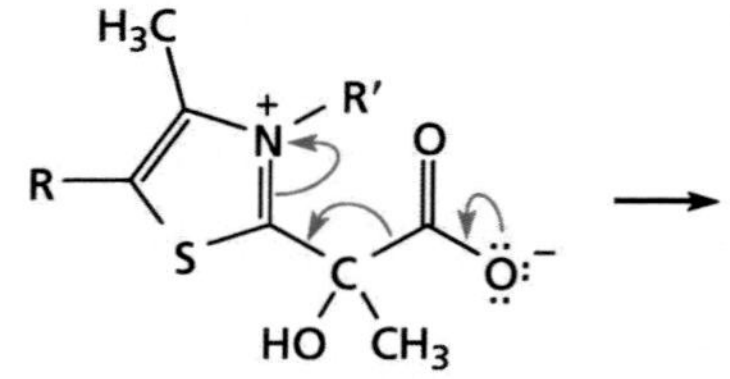

(b)

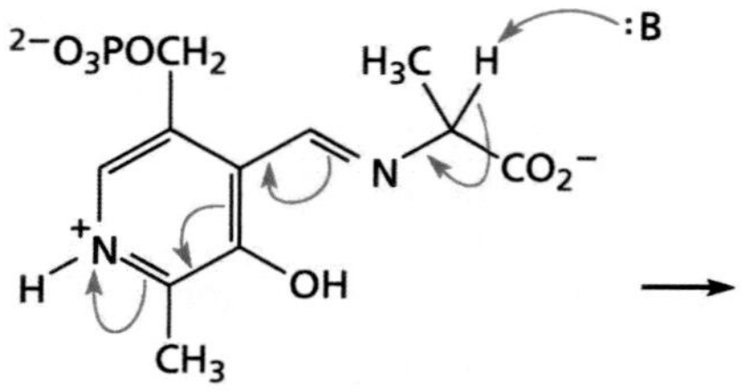

(c)

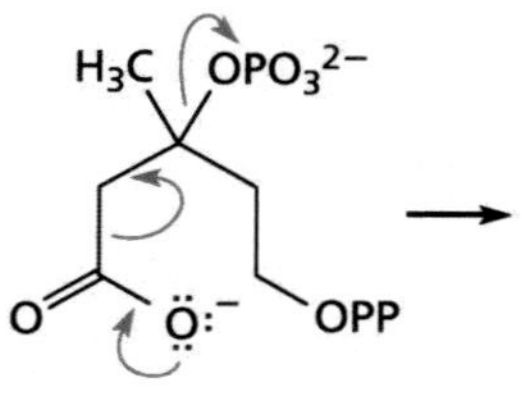

1.8   Complete the following biological mechanisms by adding curved arrows to indicate electron flow:

(a)

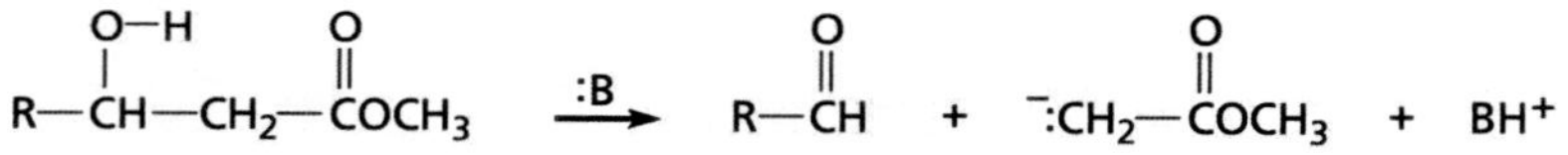

(b)

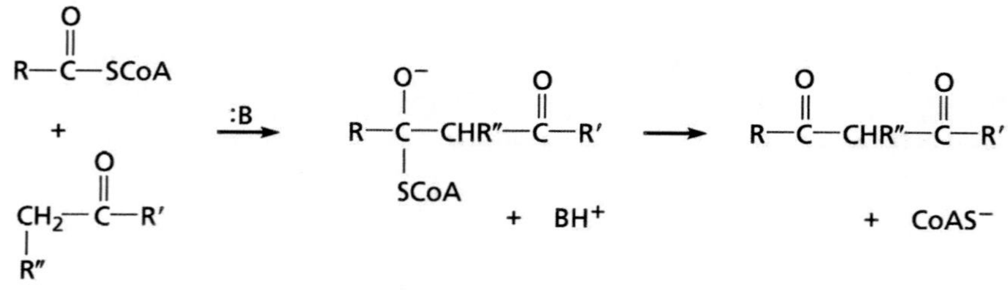

(c)

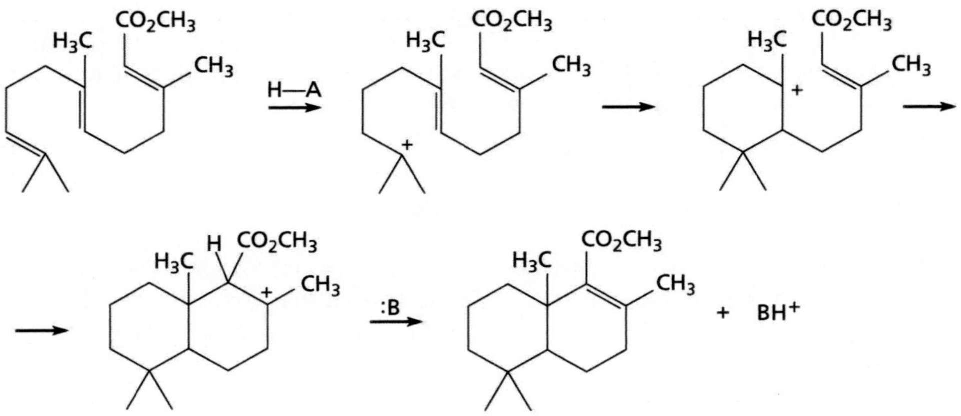

1.9 Propose a mechanism for the following step in the β-oxidation pathway for degradation of fatty acids. HSCoA is the abbreviation for coenzyme A, a thiol.

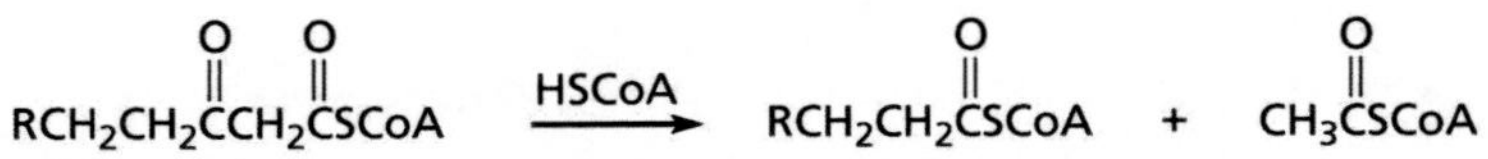

1.10 The conversion of fructose 1,6-bisphosphate to glyceraldehyde 3-phosphate plus dihydroxyacetone phosphate is a step in the glycolysis pathway for degrading carbohydrates. Propose a mechanism.

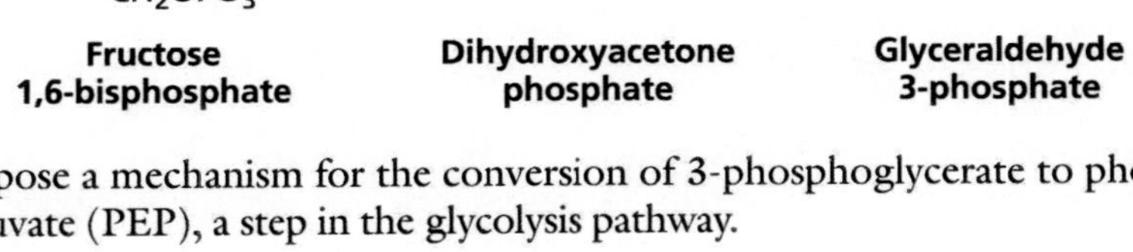

Fructose 1,6-bisphosphate   **Dihydroxyacetone phosphate**   **Glyceraldehyde 3-phosphate**

1.11 Propose a mechanism for the conversion of 3-phosphoglycerate to phosphoenolpyruvate (PEP), a step in the glycolysis pathway.

2-Phosphoglycerate   **Phosphoenolpyruvate**

1.12 The biological conversion of an aldehyde to a thioester occurs in two steps: (1) nucleophilic addition of a thiol to give a hemithioacetal, and (2) oxidation of the hemithioacetal by NAD^+. Show the structure of the intermediate hemithioacetal, and propose mechanisms for both steps.

$$\underset{RCH_2CH}{\overset{O}{\|}} \xrightarrow{R'SH} \text{Hemithioacetal} \xrightarrow{NAD^+} \underset{RCH_2CSR'}{\overset{O}{\|}}$$

1.13 The loss of CO_2 (decarboxylation) from a β-keto acid happens frequently in biological chemistry and takes place by a mechanism that is closely related to a retro-aldol reaction. Propose a mechanism for the following reaction that occurs in the citric acid cycle.

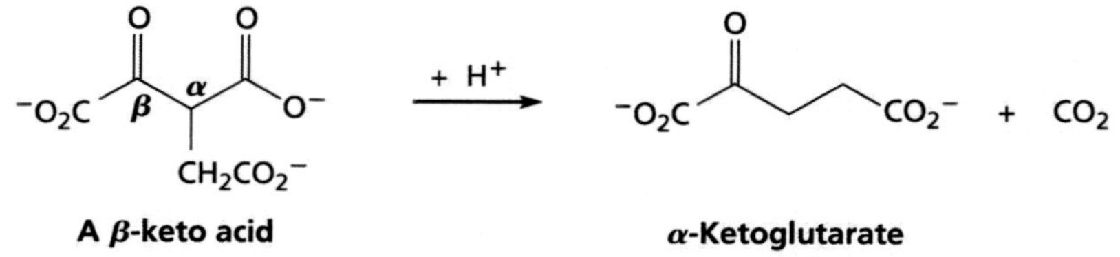

A β-keto acid   **α-Ketoglutarate**

1.14 One of the biological pathways by which an amine is converted to a ketone involves two steps: (1) oxidation of the amine by NAD^+ to give an imine, and (2) hydrolysis of the imine to give a ketone plus ammonia. Glutamate, for instance, is converted by this process into α-ketoglutarate. Show the structure of the imine intermediate, and propose mechanisms for both steps.

Glutamate   **α-Ketoglutarate**

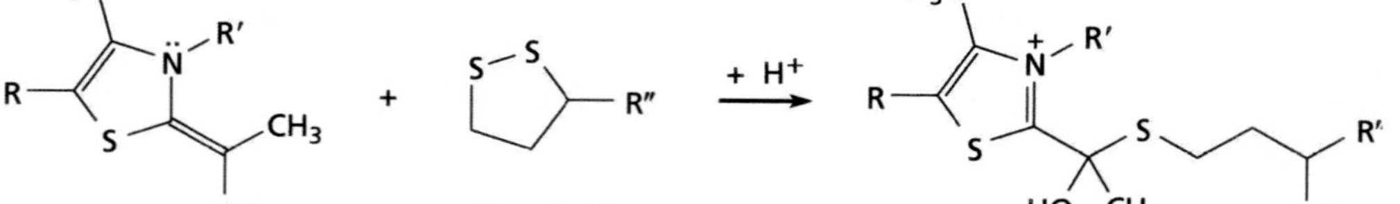

1.15 The following reaction is part of the sequence by which pyruvate is converted to acetyl CoA. Propose a mechanism, and tell what kind of reaction is occurring.

Lipoamide

1.16 The amino acid methionine is formed by a methylation reaction of homocysteine with *N*-methyltetrahydrofolate. The stereochemistry of the reaction has been probed by carrying out the transformation using a donor with a "chiral methyl group" in which deuterium (D) and tritium (T) isotopes of hydrogen are present. Does the methylation reaction occur with inversion or retention of configuration? What mechanistic inferences can you draw?

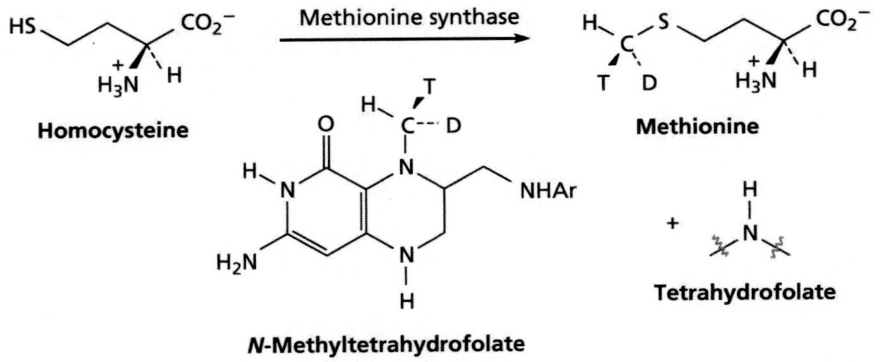

Homocysteine

Methionine synthase

Methionine

N-Methyltetrahydrofolate

Tetrahydrofolate

Part 4

Amino Acids and the Primary Structures of Proteins

The study of proteins has occupied biochemists for well over a century. Understanding the compositions, three-dimensional shapes, and chemical activities of proteins may be the key to meeting some of the most pressing scientific challenges. The process of photosynthesis, for example, is one of the most important biochemical pathways because of its role in capturing the sun's energy. A detailed examination of the structures of the many proteins that carry out photosynthesis is leading to an understanding of this fundamental process. Another active area of investigation is the study of proteins from thermophilic bacteria. These bacteria thrive at high temperatures, in some cases greater than 100°C, but they perform the same sorts of biochemical reactions that are common in all cells. What's different about the proteins of thermophilic bacteria that allows them to be active at temperatures that would destroy most other proteins?

Many medically related problems require an understanding of proteins and how they work. A case in point is human immunodeficiency virus 1 (HIV-1)—the virus associated with AIDS (acquired immune deficiency syndrome). Like most retroviruses, this virus mutates at a high frequency, leading to new strains that are resistant to the standard treatments. We now know that the enzyme responsible for the high mutation rate is reverse transcriptase, and its structure and function have been studied in detail. We also know the structures of the viral coat proteins whose genes are mutated in the new strains. Scientists are elucidating how these mutations allow the virus to overcome the best defenses that medical science can create. Hopefully, this information will lead to better treatments of AIDS and other diseases caused by retroviruses.

There are many different kinds of proteins. The following list, although not exhaustive, covers most of the important biological functions of proteins.

1. Many proteins function as enzymes, the biochemical catalysts. Enzymes catalyze nearly all reactions that occur in living organisms.

Top: L-Arginine, one of the 20 common amino acids.

51

2. Some proteins bind other molecules for storage and transport. For example, myoglobin binds oxygen in skeletal and cardiac muscle cells, and hemoglobin binds and transports O_2 and CO_2 in red blood cells.

3. Some proteins, such as tubulin, actin, and collagen, provide support and shape to cells and hence to tissues and organisms.

4. Assemblies of proteins can do mechanical work, such as the movement of flagella, the separation of chromosomes at mitosis, and the contraction of muscles.

5. Many proteins play a role in decoding information in the cell. Some are involved in translation, whereas others play a role in regulating gene expression by binding to nucleic acids.

6. Some proteins are hormones, which regulate biochemical activities in target cells or tissues; other proteins serve as receptors for hormones.

7. Some proteins have highly specialized functions. For example, antibodies defend vertebrates against bacterial and viral infections, and toxins, produced by bacteria, can kill larger organisms.

We begin our study of proteins—also called polypeptides—by exploring the structures and chemical properties of their constituent amino acids. We will also discuss the purification, analysis, and sequencing of polypeptides.

3.1 General Structure of Amino Acids

All organisms use the same 20 amino acids as building blocks for the assembly of protein molecules. These 20 amino acids are called the *common*, or *standard*, amino acids. Despite the limited number of amino acids, an enormous variety of different polypeptides can be produced by connecting the 20 common amino acids in various combinations.

Amino acids are called amino acids because they are amino derivatives of carboxylic acids. In the 20 common amino acids the amino group and the carboxyl group are bonded to the same carbon atom: the α-carbon atom. Thus, all of the standard amino acids found in proteins are α-amino acids. Two other substituents are

$$
\overset{R}{\underset{\alpha}{\overset{|}{H_3\overset{\oplus}{N}-CH}}}-COOH \qquad \overset{R}{\underset{2}{\overset{|}{H_3\overset{\oplus}{N}-CH}}}-\underset{1}{COOH}
$$

bound to the α-carbon—a hydrogen atom and a side chain (R) that is distinctive for each amino acid. In the chemical names of amino acids, carbon atoms are identified by numbers, beginning with the carbon atom of the carboxyl group. [The correct chemical name, or systematic name, follows rules established by the International Union of Pure and Applied Chemistry (IUPAC) and the International Union of Biochemistry and Molecular Biology (IUBMB).] If the R group is —CH_3, then the systematic name for that amino acid would be 2-aminopropanoic acid. (Propanoic acid is CH_3—CH_2—COOH.) The trivial name for CH_3—$CH(NH_2)$—COOH is alanine. An alternate nomenclature uses Greek letters to identify the α-carbon atom and the carbon atoms of the side chain.

Inside a cell, under normal physiological conditions, the amino group is protonated (—$NH_3^{\oplus}$) and the carboxyl group is ionized (—$COO^{\ominus}$). Thus, at the physiological pH of 7.4, amino acids are **zwitterions**, or dipolar ions, even though their net charge may be zero. We will see in Section 3.4 that some side chains can also ionize. Biochemists always represent the structures of amino acids in the form that is biologically relevant, which is why you will see the zwitterions in the following figures.

Figure 3.1a shows the general structure of an amino acid in perspective. Figure 3.1b shows a ball-and-stick model of a representative amino acid, serine, whose side

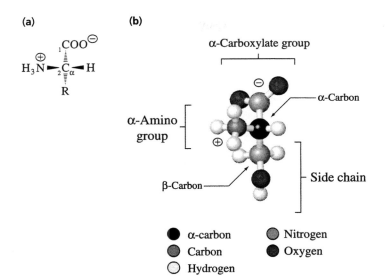

(a)   **(b)**

α-Carboxylate group

α-Carbon

α-Amino group

β-Carbon

Side chain

● α-carbon   ◉ Nitrogen
◉ Carbon   ● Oxygen
○ Hydrogen

chain is —CH$_2$OH. The carbon atoms of a side chain are sequentially labeled β, γ, δ, and ε, which refer to carbons 3, 4, 5, and 6, respectively. The systematic name for serine is 2-amino-3-hydroxypropanoic acid.

In 19 of the 20 amino acids used for the biosynthesis of proteins, the α-carbon atom is **chiral**, or asymmetric, since it has four different groups bonded to it. The exception is glycine, whose R group is simply a hydrogen atom (the molecule is not chiral because the α-carbon atom is bonded to two identical hydrogen atoms). The 19 chiral amino acids can therefore exist as stereoisomers. **Stereoisomers** are compounds that have the same molecular formula but differ in the arrangement, or configuration, of their atoms in space. The two stereoisomers are distinct molecules that can't be easily converted from one form to the other since a change in configuration requires the breaking of one or more bonds. Amino acid stereoisomers are nonsuperimposable mirror images. Such stereoisomers are called **enantiomers**. Two of the 19 chiral amino acids (isoleucine and threonine) have two chiral carbon atoms each, and therefore both can form four possible stereoisomers.

By convention, the mirror-image pairs of amino acids are designated D (for dextro, from the Latin *dexter*, right) and L (for levo, from the Latin *laevus*, left). The configuration of the amino acid in Figure 3.1a is L; that of its mirror image is D. To assign the stereochemical designation, one draws the amino acid vertically with its α-carboxylate group at the top and its side chain at the bottom, both pointing away from the viewer. In this orientation, the α-amino group of the L isomer is on the left of the α-carbon, and that of the D isomer is on the right, as shown in Figure 3.2.

The 19 chiral amino acids used in the assembly of proteins are all of the L configuration, although a few D-amino acids occur in nature. By convention, amino acids are assumed to be in the L configuration unless specifically designated D. Often it is convenient to draw the structures of L-amino acids in a form that is stereochemically uncommitted, especially when a correct stereochemical representation is not critical to a given discussion. For example, alanine—the amino acid with a methyl side chain—can be drawn simply as

$$\overset{\oplus}{H_3N} - \overset{\overset{\displaystyle CH_3}{\displaystyle |}}{CH} - COO^{\ominus} \qquad \textbf{(3.1)}$$

The fact that all living organisms use the same standard amino acids in protein synthesis is evidence that all species on Earth are descended from a common ancestor. Like modern organisms, the last common ancestor (LCA) must have used L-amino

Figure 3.2 ▶
Mirror-image pairs of amino acids.
(a) Ball-and-stick models of L-serine and
D-serine. Note that the two molecules are
not identical; they cannot be superimposed.
(b) L-Serine and D-serine.

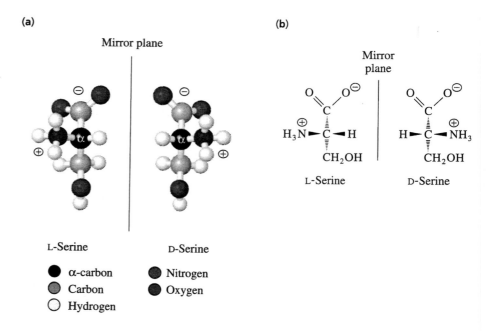

(a)

Mirror plane

L-Serine   D-Serine

● α-carbon   ● Nitrogen
● Carbon   ● Oxygen
○ Hydrogen

(b)

Mirror
plane

L-Serine   D-Serine

BOX 3.1   An Alternative Nomenclature

The *RS* system of configurational nomenclature is also some-times used to describe the chiral centers of amino acids. The *RS* system is based on the assignment of a priority sequence to the four groups bound to a chiral carbon atom. Once as-signed, the group priorities are used to establish the configu-ration of the molecule. Priorities are numbered 1 through 4 and are assigned to groups according to the following rules:

1. For atoms directly attached to the chiral carbon, the one with the lowest atomic mass is assigned the lowest pri-ority (number 4).

2. If there are two identical atoms bound to the chiral car-bon, the priority is decided by the atomic masses of the next atoms bound. For example, a —CH_3 group has a lower priority than a —CH_2Br group because bromine has a greater atomic mass than hydrogen.

3. If an atom is bound by a double or triple bond, the atom is counted once for each formal bond. Thus, —CHO,

with a double-bonded oxygen, has a higher priority than —CH_2OH. The order of priority for the most common groups, from lowest to highest, is —H, —CH_3, —C_6H_5, —CH_2OH, —CHO, —COOH, —COOR, —NH_2, —NHR, —OH, —OR, and —SH.

With these rules in mind, imagine the molecule as the steer-ing wheel of a car, with the group of lowest priority (numbered 4) pointing away from you (like the steering column) and the other three groups arrayed around the rim of the steering wheel. Trace the rim of the wheel, moving from the group of highest pri-ority to the group of lowest priority (1, 2, 3). If the movement is clockwise, the configuration is *R* (from the Latin *rectus*, right-handed). If the movement is counterclockwise, the configura-tion is *S* (from the Latin, *sinister*, left-handed). The figure demonstrates the assignment of *S* configuration to L-serine by the *RS* system. L-Cysteine has the opposite configuration, *R*. Because not all amino acids found in proteins have the same *RS* designation, the DL system is used more often in biochemistry.

▶ Assignment of configuration by the *RS* sys-tem. **(a)** Each group attached to a chiral carbon is assigned a priority based on atomic mass, 4 being the lowest priority. **(b)** By orienting the molecule with the priority 4 group pointing away (behind the chiral carbon) and tracing the path from the highest priority group to the lowest, the absolute configuration can be established. If the sequence 1, 2, 3 is clockwise, the configuration is *R*. If the sequence 1, 2, 3 is counterclockwise, the configuration is *S*. L-Serine has the *S* configuration.

(a)

②
$COO^{\ominus}$
① $H_3N^{\oplus}$ — C ◀ H ④
CH_2OH
③

L-Serine

(b)

S configuration

acids and not D-amino acids. Mixtures of L- and D-amino acids are formed under conditions that mimic those present when life first arose on Earth 4 billion years ago, and both enantiomers are found in meteorites and in the vicinity of stars. It is not known how or why primitive life forms selected L-amino acids from the presumed mixture of the enantiomers present when life first arose. Modern living organisms do not select L-amino acids from a mixture since only L-amino acids are synthesized in sufficient quantities. Thus, the predominance of L-amino acids in modern species is due to the evolution of metabolic pathways that produce L-amino acids and not D-amino acids (Chapter 17).

3.2 Structures of the 20 Common Amino Acids

The structures of the 20 amino acids commonly found in proteins are shown in the following figures as Fischer projections. In Fischer projections, horizontal bonds at a chiral center extend toward the viewer, and vertical bonds extend away (as in Figures 3.1 and 3.2). Examination of the structures reveals considerable variation in the side chains of the 20 amino acids. Some side chains are nonpolar and thus hydrophobic, whereas others are polar or ionized at neutral pH and are therefore hydrophilic. The properties of the side chains greatly influence the overall three-dimensional shape, or conformation, of a protein. For example, most of the hydrophobic side chains of a water-soluble protein fold into the interior, giving the protein a compact, globular shape.

Both the three-letter and one-letter abbreviations for each amino acid are shown in the figures. The three-letter abbreviation is self-evident, but the simple one-letter abbreviation is less obvious. Several amino acids begin with the same letter so other letters of the alphabet have to be used in order to provide a unique label; for example, threonine = T, tyrosine = Y, and tryptophan = W. These labels have to be memorized.

It is important to learn the structures of the standard amino acids because we refer to them frequently in the chapters on protein structure, enzymes, and protein synthesis. In the following sections, we have grouped the standard amino acids by their general properties and the chemical structures of their side chains. The side chains fall into the following chemical classes: aliphatic, aromatic, sulfur-containing, alcohols, bases, acids, and amides. Of the 20 amino acids, 5 are further classified as highly hydrophobic (blue), and 7 are classified as highly hydrophilic (red). Understanding the classification of the R groups will simplify memorizing the structures and names.

A. Aliphatic R Groups

Glycine (Gly, G) is the smallest amino acid since its R group is simply a hydrogen atom. As a result, the α-carbon of glycine is not chiral. The two hydrogen atoms of the α-carbon of glycine impart little hydrophobic character to the molecule. We will see that glycine plays a unique role in the structure of many proteins because its side chain is small enough to fit into niches that can accommodate no other amino acid.

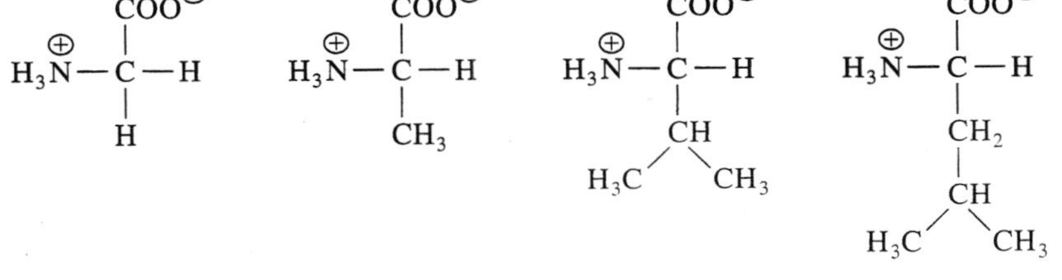

Glycine [G]   Alanine [A]   Valine [V]   Leucine [L]
(Gly)   (Ala)   (Val)   (Leu)

Figure 3.3 ▶
Stereoisomers of isoleucine

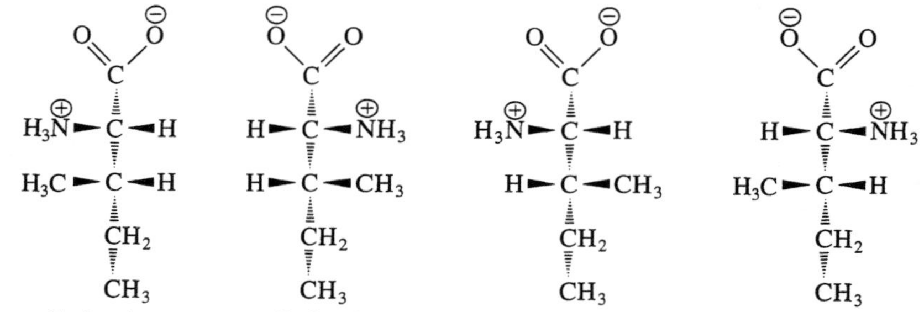

L-Isoleucine   D-Isoleucine   L-Alloisoleucine   D-Alloisoleucine

Four amino acids, alanine (Ala, A), valine (Val, V), leucine (Leu, L), and the structural isomer of leucine, isoleucine (Ile, I), have saturated aliphatic side chains. The side chain of alanine is a methyl group, whereas valine has a three-carbon branched side chain and leucine and isoleucine each contain a four-carbon branched side chain. Both the α- and β-carbon atoms of isoleucine are asymmetric. Because isoleucine has two chiral centers, it has four possible stereoisomers. The stereoisomer used in proteins is called L-isoleucine, and the amino acid that differs at the β-carbon is called L-alloisoleucine (Figure 3.3). The other two stereoisomers are D-isoleucine and D-alloisoleucine.

Although the side chains of alanine, valine, leucine, and isoleucine have no reactive functional groups, these amino acids play an important role in establishing and maintaining the three-dimensional structures of proteins because of their tendency to cluster away from water. Valine, leucine, and isoleucine are known as branched-chain amino acids because their side chains of carbon atoms contain branches. All three amino acids are highly hydrophobic.

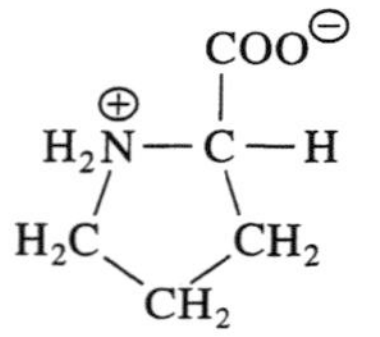

Proline (Pro, P) differs from the other 19 amino acids because its three-carbon side chain is bonded to the nitrogen of its α-amino group as well as to the α-carbon, creating a cyclic molecule. As a result, proline contains a secondary rather than a primary amino group. The heterocyclic pyrrolidine ring of proline restricts the geometry of polypeptides, sometimes introducing abrupt changes in the direction of the peptide chain.

Proline [P]
(Pro)

B. Aromatic R Groups

Phenylalanine (Phe, F), tyrosine (Tyr, Y), and tryptophan (Trp, W) have side chains with aromatic groups. Phenylalanine has a benzyl side chain. The benzene ring makes phenylalanine residues highly hydrophobic. Tyrosine is structurally similar to phenylalanine; the *para* hydrogen of phenylalanine is replaced in tyrosine by a hydroxyl group (—OH), making tyrosine a phenol. The hydroxyl group of tyrosine is ionizable but retains its hydrogen under normal physiological conditions. The side chain of tryptophan contains a bicyclic indole group. Tyrosine and tryptophan are not as hydrophobic as phenylalanine because their side chains include polar groups.

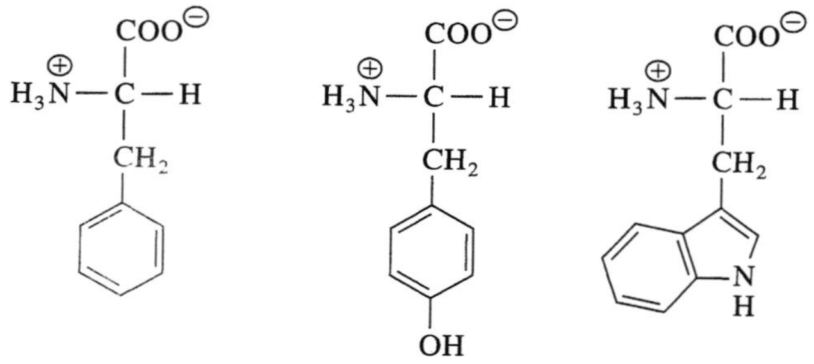

Phenylalanine [F]   Tyrosine [Y]   Tryptophan [W]
(Phe)   (Tyr)   (Trp)

Chemistry for Biologists

All three aromatic amino acids absorb ultraviolet (UV) light. At neutral pH, both tryptophan and tyrosine absorb light at a wavelength of 280 nm, whereas phenylalanine is almost transparent at 280 nm and absorbs light weakly at 260 nm. Since most proteins contain tryptophan and tyrosine they will absorb light at 280 nm. Absorbance at 280 nm is routinely used to estimate the concentration of proteins in solutions.

C. Sulfur-Containing R Groups

Methionine (Met, M) and cysteine (Cys, C) are the two sulfur-containing amino acids. Methionine contains a nonpolar methyl thioether group in its side chain, and this makes it one of the more hydrophobic amino acids. Methionine plays a special role in protein synthesis since it is almost always the first amino acid in a polypeptide chain. The structure of cysteine resembles that of alanine with a hydrogen atom replaced by a sulfhydryl group (—SH).

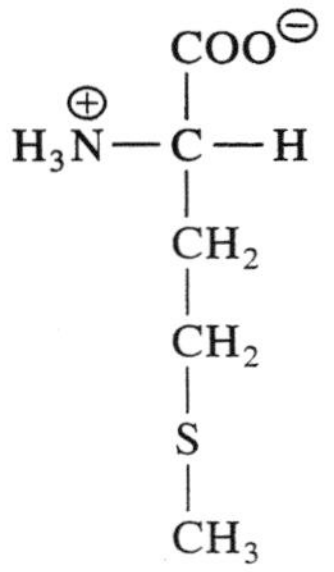

Although the side chain of cysteine is somewhat hydrophobic, it is also highly reactive. Because the sulfur atom is polarizable, the sulfhydryl group of cysteine can form weak hydrogen bonds with oxygen and nitrogen. Moreover, the sulfhydryl group of cysteine is a weak acid, which allows it to lose its proton to become a negatively charged thiolate ion.

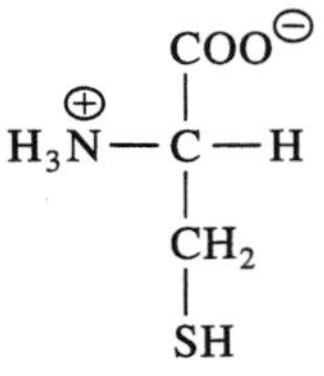

A compound called cystine can be isolated when some proteins are hydrolyzed. Cystine is formed from two oxidized cysteine molecules that are linked by a disulfide bond (Figure 3.4). Oxidation of the sulfhydryl groups of cysteine molecules proceeds most readily at slightly alkaline pH values, at which the sulfhydryl groups are ionized. The two cysteine side chains must be adjacent in three-dimensional space in order to form a disulfide bond, but they don't have to be close together in the amino acid sequence of the polypeptide chain. They may even be found in different polypeptide chains. Disulfide bonds, or disulfide bridges, may stabilize the three-dimensional structures of some proteins by covalently cross-linking cysteine residues in peptide chains. (Most proteins do not contain disulfide bridges because conditions inside the cell do not favor oxidation. However, many secreted, or extracellular, proteins contain disulfide bridges.)

D. Side Chains with Alcohol Groups

Serine (Ser, S) and threonine (Thr, T) have uncharged polar side chains containing β-hydroxyl groups; these alcohol groups give hydrophilic character to the aliphatic side chains. Unlike the more acidic phenolic side chain of tyrosine, the hydroxyl groups of serine and threonine have the weak ionization properties of primary and secondary alcohols. The hydroxymethyl group of serine (—CH₂OH) does not appreciably ionize in aqueous solutions; nevertheless, this alcohol can react within the

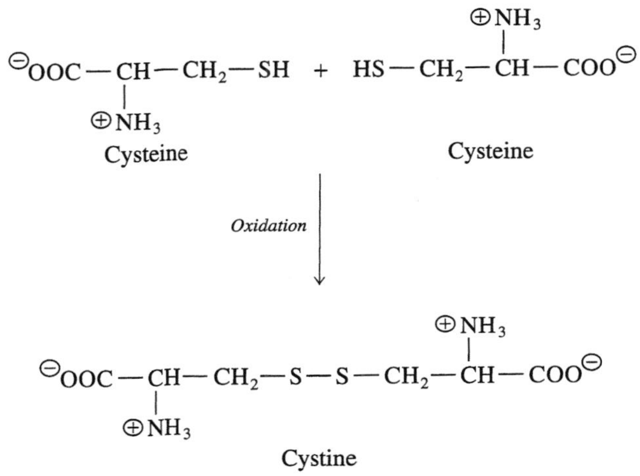

Methionine [M]
(Met)

Cysteine [C]
(Cys)

◄ Figure 3.4
Formation of cystine. When oxidation links the sulfhydryl groups of two cysteine molecules, the resulting compound is a disulfide called cystine.

Cysteine   Cysteine

Oxidation

Cystine

Serine [S]
(Ser)

Threonine [T]
(Thr)

active sites of a number of enzymes as though it were ionized. Threonine, like isoleucine, has two chiral centers, the α- and β-carbon atoms. L-Threonine is the only one of the four stereoisomers that commonly occurs in proteins. (The other stereoisomers are called D-threonine, L-allothreonine, and D-allothreonine.)

E. Basic R Groups

Histidine (His, H), lysine (Lys, K), and arginine (Arg, R) have hydrophilic side chains that are nitrogenous bases and are positively charged at pH 7. The side chain of histidine contains an imidazole ring substituent. The imidazole group can ionize, and the protonated form of this ring is called an imidazolium ion (Section 3.4). Lysine is a diamino acid, having both α- and ε-amino groups. The ε-amino group exists as an alkylammonium ion ($-CH_2-NH_3^{\oplus}$) at neutral pH and confers a positive charge on proteins. Arginine is the most basic of the 20 amino acids because its side-chain guanidinium ion is protonated under all conditions normally found within a cell. Arginine side chains also contribute positive charges in proteins.

Histidine [H]
(His)

Lysine [K]
(Lys)

Arginine [R]
(Arg)

F. Acidic R Groups and Their Amide Derivatives

Aspartate (Asp, D) and glutamate (Glu, E) are dicarboxylic amino acids and are negatively charged at pH 7. In addition to α-carboxyl groups, aspartate possesses a β-carboxyl group and glutamate possesses a γ-carboxyl group. Aspartate and glutamate confer negative charges on proteins because their side chains are ionized at pH 7. Aspartate and glutamate are sometimes called aspartic acid and glutamic acid, but under most physiological conditions they are found as the conjugate bases and, like other carboxylates, have the suffix -ate. Glutamate is probably familiar as its monosodium salt, monosodium glutamate (MSG), which is used in food as a flavor enhancer.

Asparagine (Asn, N) and glutamine (Gln, Q) are the amides of aspartic acid and glutamic acid, respectively. Although the side chains of asparagine and glutamine are uncharged, these amino acids are highly polar and are often found on the surfaces of proteins, where they can interact with water molecules. The polar amide groups of asparagine and glutamine can also form hydrogen bonds with atoms in the side chains of other polar amino acids.

Aspartate [D]
(Asp)

Glutamate [E]
(Glu)

Asparagine [N]
(Asn)

Glutamine [Q]
(Gln)

G. The Hydrophobicity of Amino Acid Side Chains

The various side chains of amino acids range from highly hydrophobic, through weakly polar, to highly hydrophilic. The relative hydrophobicity or hydrophilicity of each amino acid is called its **hydropathy**. There are several ways of measuring hydropathy, but most of them rely on calculating the tendency of an amino acid to prefer a hydrophobic environment over a hydrophilic environment. A commonly used hydropathy scale is shown in Table 3.1. Amino acids with highly positive hydropathy values are considered hydrophobic, whereas those with the largest negative values are hydrophilic. It is difficult to ascertain the hydropathy values of some amino acid residues that lie near the center of the scale. For example, there is disagreement over the hydrophilicity of the indole group of tryptophan, and in some scales tryptophan has a much lower hydropathy value.

Hydropathy is an important determinant of protein-chain folding because hydrophobic side chains tend to be clustered in the interior of a protein and hydrophilic residues are usually found on the surface. However, it is not yet possible to predict accurately whether a given residue will be found in the nonaqueous interior of a protein or on the solvent-exposed surface. Hydropathy measurements of free amino acids, such as those shown in Table 3.1, are used to predict which segments of membrane-spanning proteins are likely to be embedded in a hydrophobic lipid bilayer (Chapter 9).

3.3 Other Amino Acids and Amino Acid Derivatives

More than 200 different amino acids are found in living organisms. Most species contain a variety of L-amino acids that are either precursors of the common amino acids or intermediates in other biochemical pathways. Examples are homocysteine, homoserine, ornithine, and citrulline (see Chapter 17). S-Adenosylmethionine (SAM) is a common methyl donor in many biochemical pathways (Section 7.2). In addition to these L-amino acid intermediates, many species of bacteria and fungi synthesize D-amino acids that are used in cell walls and in complex peptide antibiotics such as actinomycin D.

Several common amino acids are chemically modified to produce biologically important amines. These are synthesized by enzyme-catalyzed reactions that include decarboxylation. In the mammalian brain, for example, glutamate is converted to the neurotransmitter γ-aminobutyrate (GABA) (Figure 3.5a). Mammals can also synthesize histamine (Figure 3.5b) from histidine. Histamine controls the constriction of certain blood vessels and also the secretion of hydrochloric acid by the stomach. In the adrenal medulla, tyrosine is metabolized to epinephrine, also known as adrenaline (Figure 3.5c). Epinephrine and its precursor, norepinephrine (a compound

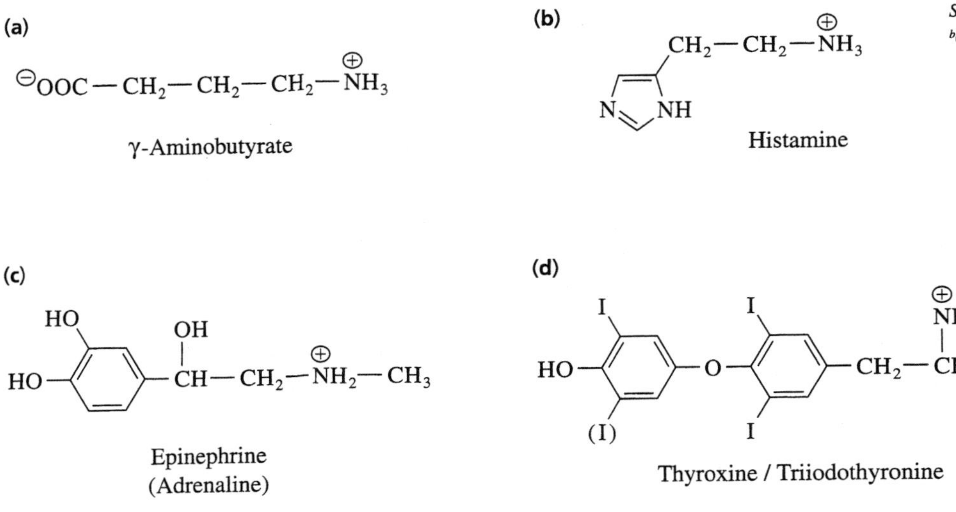

TABLE 3.1 Hydropathy scale for amino acid residues

Amino acid	Free-energy change for transfer^a (kj mol^{-1})
Highly hydrophobic	
Isoleucine	3.1
Phenylalanine	2.5
Valine	2.3
Leucine	2.2
Methionine	1.1
Less hydrophobic	
Tryptophan	1.5^b
Alanine	1.0
Glycine	0.67
Cysteine	0.17
Tyrosine	0.08
Proline	−0.29
Threonine	−0.75
Serine	−1.1
Highly hydrophilic	
Histidine	−1.7
Glutamate	−2.6
Asparagine	−2.7
Glutamine	−2.9
Aspartate	−3.0
Lysine	−4.6
Arginine	−7.5

^{a}The free-energy change is for transfer of an amino acid residue from the interior of a lipid bilayer to water.

[Adapted from Eisenberg, D., Weiss, R. M., Terwilliger, T. C., Wilcox, W. (1982). Hydrophobic moments in protein structure. *Faraday Symp. Chem. Soc.* 17:109–120.]

^{b}On other scales, tryptophan has a lower hydropathy value.

(a)

γ-Aminobutyrate

(b)

Histamine

(c)

Epinephrine
(Adrenaline)

(d)

Thyroxine / Triiodothyronine

Figure 3.5 ▲
Compounds derived from common amino acids. **(a)** γ-Aminobutyrate, a derivative of glutamate. **(b)** Histamine, a derivative of histidine. **(c)** Epinephrine, a derivative of tyrosine. **(d)** Thyroxine and triiodothyronine, derivatives of tyrosine. Thyroxine contains one more atom of iodine (in parentheses) than does triiodothyronine.

whose amino group lacks a methyl substituent), are hormones that help regulate metabolism in mammals. Tyrosine is also the precursor of the thyroid hormones thyroxine and triiodothyronine (Figure 3.5d). Biosynthesis of the thyroid hormones requires iodide. Small amounts of sodium iodide are commonly added to table salt to prevent goiter, a condition of hypothyroidism caused by a lack of iodide in the diet.

Some amino acids are chemically modified after they have been incorporated into polypeptides. For example, some proline residues in the protein collagen are oxidized to form hydroxyproline residues (Section 4.11). Another common modification is the addition of complex carbohydrate chains, a process known as glycosylation (Chapters 8 and 22). Many proteins are phosphorylated by the addition of phosphoryl groups to the side chains of serine, threonine, or tyrosine. The oxidation of pairs of cysteine residues to form cystine also occurs after a polypeptide has been synthesized. In bacteria, the first amino acid in a protein is usually methionine, which is modified by the addition of a formyl group to form *N*-formylmethionine (Chapter 22).

A surprising discovery was that a 21st amino acid, selenocysteine (which contains selenium in place of the sulfur of cysteine), is incorporated into a few proteins in a wide variety of species. Selenocysteine is formed from serine during protein synthesis. Although only 20 different types of amino acids are used in the biosynthesis of most proteins, a number of proteins have more than 20 different types of amino acid residues as a result of chemical modifications.

$$
\begin{array}{c}
COO^{\ominus} \\
| \\
\overset{\oplus}{H_3N} - C - H \\
| \\
CH_2 \\
| \\
SeH
\end{array}
$$

Selenocysteine

3.4 Ionization of Amino Acids

The physical properties of amino acids are influenced by the ionic states of the α-carboxyl and α-amino groups and of any ionizable groups in the side chains. Each ionizable group is associated with a specific pK_a value that corresponds to the pH at which the concentrations of the protonated and unprotonated forms are equal (Section 2.9). When the pH of the solution is below the pK_a, the protonated form predominates and the amino acid is then a true acid that is capable of donating a proton. When the pH of the solution is above the pK_a of the ionizable group, the unprotonated form of that group predominates and the amino acid exists as the conjugate base, which is a proton acceptor. Every amino acid has at least two pK_a values corresponding to the ionization of the α-carboxyl and α-amino groups. In addition, seven of the common amino acids have ionizable side chains with additional, measurable pK_a values. These values differ among the amino acids. Thus, at a given pH amino acids frequently have different net charges.

The ionic states of amino acid side chains influence the three-dimensional structures of proteins. In addition, because a number of ionizable amino acid residues are involved in catalysis by enzymes, an understanding of the ionic properties of amino acids helps one understand enzyme mechanisms (Chapter 6).

The pK_a values of amino acids are determined from titration curves such as those we saw in the previous chapter. The titration of alanine is shown in Figure 3.6. Alanine has two ionizable groups—the α-carboxyl and the protonated α-amino group. As more base is added to the solution of acid, the titration curve exhibits two pK_a values, at pH 2.4 and pH 9.9. Each pK_a value is associated with a buffering zone where the pH of the solution changes relatively little when more base is added.

As the pH at which the concentration of the acid form (proton donor) exactly equals the concentration of its conjugate base (proton acceptor), the pK_a of an ionizable group corresponds to a midpoint of the titration curve. In the example shown in Figure 3.6, the concentrations of the positively charged form of alanine and of the zwitterion are equal at pH 2.4.

$$
\overset{\oplus}{NH_3} - \underset{\underset{CH_3}{|}}{CH} - COOH \rightleftharpoons \overset{\oplus}{NH_3} - \underset{\underset{CH_3}{|}}{CH} - COO^{\ominus} + H^{\oplus} \qquad \textbf{(3.2)}
$$

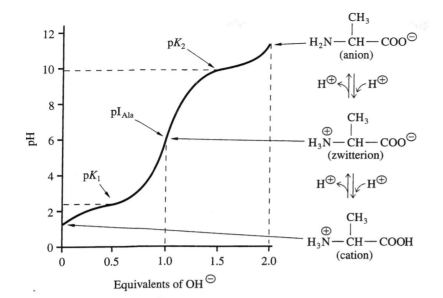

◀ **Figure 3.6**
Titration curve for alanine. The first pK_a value is 2.4; the second is 9.9. pI_{Ala} represents the isoelectric point of alanine.

At pH 9.9 the concentration of the zwitterion equals the concentration of the negatively charged form.

$$\overset{\oplus}{N}H_3-\underset{\underset{CH_3}{|}}{CH}-COO^{\ominus} \rightleftharpoons NH_2-\underset{\underset{CH_3}{|}}{CH}-COO^{\ominus} + H^{\oplus} \qquad \textbf{(3.3)}$$

Note that in the acid-base pair shown in the first equilibrium (3.2), the zwitterion is the conjugate base of the acid form of alanine. In the second acid-base pair (3.3), the zwitterion is the proton donor, or conjugate acid, of the more basic form that predominates at higher pH.

One can deduce that the net charge on alanine molecules at pH 2.4 averages $+0.5$ and that the net charge at pH 9.9 averages -0.5. Midway between pH 2.4 and pH 9.9, at pH 6.15, the average net charge on alanine molecules in solution is zero. For this reason, pH 6.15 is referred to as the isoelectric point (pI), or isoelectric pH, of alanine. If alanine were placed in an electric field at a pH below its pI, it would carry a net positive charge (in other words, its cationic form would predominate), and it would therefore migrate toward the cathode (defined by biochemists as the negative electrode). At a pH higher than its pI, alanine would carry a net negative charge and would migrate toward the anode (the positive electrode). At its isoelectric point (pH = 6.15), alanine would not migrate in either direction.

Histidine contains an ionizable side chain. The titration curve for histidine contains an additional inflection point that corresponds to the pK_a of its side chain (Figure 3.7a). As is the case with alanine, the first pK_a (1.8) represents the ionization of the α-COOH, and the most basic pK_a value (9.3) represents the ionization of the α-amino group. The middle pK_a (6.0) corresponds to the deprotonation of the imidazolium ion of the side chain of histidine (Figure 3.7b). At pH 7.0, the ratio of imidazole (conjugate base) to imidazolium ion (conjugate acid) is 10:1. Thus, the protonated and neutral forms of the side chain of histidine are both present in significant concentrations near physiological pH. A given histidine side chain in a protein may be either protonated or unprotonated, depending on its immediate environment within the protein. This property makes the side chain of histidine ideal for the transfer of protons within the catalytic sites of enzymes.

The isoelectric point of an amino acid that contains only two ionizable groups (the α-amino and the α-carboxyl groups) is the arithmetic mean of its two pK_a values (i.e., pI = $(pK_1 + pK_2)/2$). However, for an amino acid that contains three ionizable groups, such as histidine, one must assess the net charge of each ionic species.

Chemistry for Biologists

Figure 3.7 ▶
Ionization of histidine. **(a)** Titration curve for histidine. The three pK_a values are 1.8, 6.0, and 9.3. pI_{His} represents the isoelectric point of histidine. **(b)** Deprotonation of the imidazolium ring of the side chain of histidine.

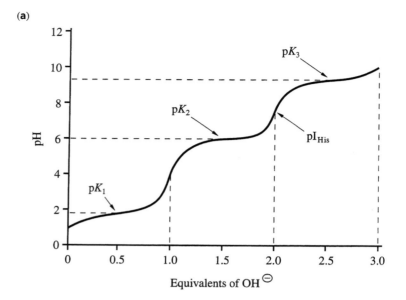

(a)

(b)

Imidazolium ion
(protonated form)
of histidine side chain

Imidazole
(deprotonated form)
of histidine side chain

The isoelectric point for histidine lies between the pK_a values on either side of the species with no net charge: midway between 6.0 and 9.3, or 7.65.

As shown in Table 3.2, the pK_a values of the α-carboxyl groups of free amino acids range from 1.8 to 2.5. These values are lower than those of typical carboxylic acids, such as acetic acid ($pK_a = 4.8$) because the neighboring $-NH_3^{\oplus}$ group withdraws electrons from the carboxylic acid group and this favors the loss of a proton from the α-carboxyl group. The side chains, or R groups, also influence the pK_a value, which is why different amino acids have different pK_a values. (We have just seen that the values for histidine and alanine are not the same.)

The α-COOH group of an amino acid is a weak acid. We can use the Henderson-Hasselbalch equation (Section 2.9) to calculate the fraction of the group that is ionized at any given pH.

$$pH = pK_a + \log \frac{[\text{proton acceptor}]}{[\text{proton donor}]} \qquad (3.4)$$

For a typical amino acid whose α-COOH group has a pK_a of 2.0, the ratio of proton acceptor (carboxylate anion) to proton donor (carboxylic acid) at pH 7.0 can be calculated using the Henderson-Hasselbalch equation.

$$7.0 = 2.0 + \log \frac{[\text{RCOO}^{\ominus}]}{[\text{RCOOH}]} \qquad (3.5)$$

Chemistry for Biologists

TABLE 3.2 pK_a values of acidic and basic constituents of free amino acids at 25°C

Amino acid	pKa value		
	α-Carboxyl group	α-Amino group	Side chain
Glycine	2.4	9.8	
Alanine	2.4	9.9	
Valine	2.3	9.7	
Leucine	2.3	9.7	
Isoleucine	2.3	9.8	
Methionine	2.1	9.3	
Proline	2.0	10.6	
Phenylalanine	2.2	9.3	
Tryptophan	2.5	9.4	
Serine	2.2	9.2	
Threonine	2.1	9.1	
Cysteine	1.9	10.7	8.4
Tyrosine	2.2	9.2	10.5
Asparagine	2.1	8.7	
Glutamine	2.2	9.1	
Aspartic acid	2.0	9.9	3.9
Glutamic acid	2.1	9.5	4.1
Lysine	2.2	9.1	10.5
Arginine	1.8	9.0	12.5
Histidine	1.8	9.3	6.0

[Adapted from Dawson, R. M. C., Elliott, D. C., Elliott, W. H., and Jones, K. M. (1986). *Data for Biochemical Research*, 3rd ed. (Oxford: Clarendon Press).]

In this case, the ratio of carboxylate anion to carboxylic acid is 100 000:1. This means that under the conditions normally found inside a cell, the carboxylate anion is the predominant species.

The α-amino group of a free amino acid can exist as a free amine, —NH$_2$ (proton acceptor), or as a protonated amine, —NH$_3^\oplus$ (proton donor). The pK_a values range from 8.7 to 10.7 as shown in Table 3.2. For an amino acid whose α-amino group has a pK_a value of 10.0, the ratio of proton acceptor to proton donor is 1:1000 at pH 7.0. In other words, under physiological conditions the α-amino group is mostly protonated and positively charged. These calculations verify our earlier statement that free amino acids exist predominantly as zwitterions at neutral pH. They also show that it is inappropriate to draw the structure of an amino acid with both —COOH and —NH$_2$ groups since there is no pH at which the carboxyl group is protonated and the amino group is unprotonated. Note that the secondary amino group of proline (pK_a = 10.6) is also protonated at neutral pH, so that proline—despite the bonding of the side chain to the α-amino group—is also zwitterionic at pH 7.

The seven standard amino acids with readily ionizable groups in their side chains are aspartate, glutamate, histidine, cysteine, tyrosine, lysine, and arginine. Ionization of these groups obeys the same principles as ionization of the α-carboxyl and α-amino groups, and the Henderson-Hasselbalch equation can be applied to each ionization. The ionization of the γ-carboxyl group of glutamate (pK_a = 4.1) is shown in Figure 3.8a. Note that the γ-carboxyl group is further removed from the influence of the α-ammonium ion and behaves as a weak acid with a pK_a of 4.1. This makes it similar in strength to acetic acid (pK_a = 4.8), whereas the α-carboxyl group is a

Chemistry for Biologists

Figure 3.8 ▶
Ionization of amino acid side chains. **(a)** Ionization of the protonated γ-carboxyl group of glutamate. The negative charge of the carboxylate anion is delocalized. **(b)** Deprotonation of the guanidinium group of the side chain of arginine. The positive charge is delocalized.

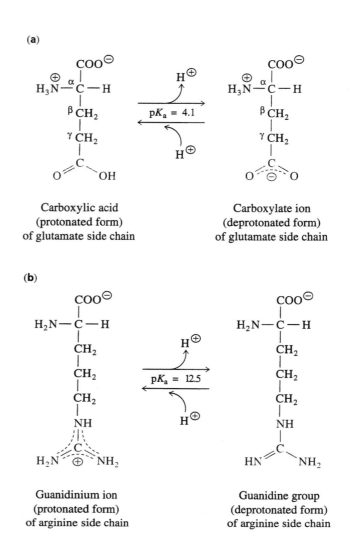

(a)

Carboxylic acid
(protonated form)
of glutamate side chain

$pK_a = 4.1$

Carboxylate ion
(deprotonated form)
of glutamate side chain

(b)

Guanidinium ion
(protonated form)
of arginine side chain

$pK_a = 12.5$

Guanidine group
(deprotonated form)
of arginine side chain

stronger acid ($pK_a = 2.1$). Figure 3.8b shows the deprotonation of the guanidinium group of the side chain of arginine in a strongly basic solution. Charge delocalization stabilizes the guanidinium ion, contributing to its high pK_a value of 12.5.

The pK_a values of ionizable side chains in proteins can differ from those of the free amino acids. Two factors cause this perturbation of ionization constants. First, α-amino and α-carboxyl groups lose their charges once they are linked by peptide bonds in proteins; consequently, they exert weaker inductive effects on their neighboring side chains. Second, the position of an ionizable side chain within the three-dimensional structure of a protein can affect its pK_a. For example, the enzyme ribonuclease A has four histidine residues, but the side chain of each residue has a slightly different pK_a as a result of differences in their immediate surroundings, or microenvironments.

3.5 Peptide Bonds Link Amino Acids in Proteins

The linear sequence of amino acids in a polypeptide chain is called the **primary structure** of a protein. Higher levels of structure are referred to as secondary, tertiary, and quaternary. The structure of proteins is covered more thoroughly in the next chapter, but it's important to understand peptide bonds and primary structure before discussing some of the remaining topics in this chapter.

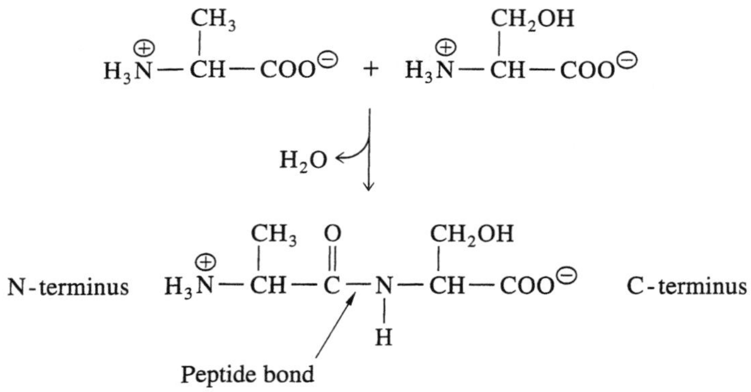

Peptide bond between two amino acids. The structure of the peptide linkage can be viewed as the product of a condensation reaction which the α-carboxyl group of one amino acid condenses with the α-amino group of another amino acid. The result is a dipeptide in which the amino acids are linked by a peptide bond. Here, alanine is condensed with serine to form alanylserine.

$$CH_3 \qquad\qquad\qquad CH_2OH$$
$$\overset{\oplus}{H_3N} - CH - COO^{\ominus} \;+\; \overset{\oplus}{H_3N} - CH - COO^{\ominus}$$

$$H_2O \leftharpoondown \Big\downarrow$$

$$CH_3 \quad O \qquad\quad CH_2OH$$

N-terminus $\quad \overset{\oplus}{H_3N} - CH - \overset{O}{\overset{\|}{C}} - N - CH - COO^{\ominus} \quad$ C-terminus

$$| \atop H$$

Peptide bond

The linkage formed between amino acids is a secondary amide bond called a **peptide bond** (Figure 3.9). This linkage can be thought of as resulting from a simple condensation of the α-carboxyl group of one amino acid with the α-amino group of another. Note that a water molecule is lost from the condensing amino acids in the reaction. (Recall from Section 2.6 that such simple condensation reactions are extremely unfavorable in aqueous solutions due to the huge excess of water molecules. The actual pathway of protein synthesis involves reactive intermediates that overcome this limitation.) Unlike the carboxyl and amino groups of free amino acids in solution, the groups involved in peptide bonds carry no ionic charges.

Linked amino acid moieties in a polypeptide chain are called amino acid residues. The names of residues are formed by replacing the ending *-ine* or *-ate* with *-yl*. For example, a glycine residue in a polypeptide is called glycyl, and a glutamate residue is called glutamyl. In the cases of asparagine, glutamine, and cysteine, *-yl* replaces the final *-e* to form asparaginyl, glutaminyl, and cysteinyl, respectively. The *-yl* ending indicates that the residue is an acyl unit (a structure that lacks the hydroxyl of the carboxyl group). The dipeptide in Figure 3.9 is called alanylserine because alanine is converted to an acyl unit but the amino acid serine retains its carboxyl group.

The free amino group and free carboxyl group at the opposite ends of a peptide chain are called the N-terminus (amino terminus) and the C-terminus (carboxyl terminus), respectively. At neutral pH, each terminus carries an ionic charge. By convention, amino acid residues in a peptide chain are numbered from the N-terminus to the C-terminus and are usually written from left to right.

Both the standard three-letter abbreviations for the amino acids (e.g., Gly–Arg–Phe–Ala–Lys) and the one-letter abbreviations (e.g., GRFAK) are used to describe the sequence of amino acid residues in peptides and polypeptides. It's important to know both abbreviation systems. The terms dipeptide, tripeptide, oligopeptide, and polypeptide refer to chains of two, three, several (up to about 20), and many (usually more than 20) amino acid residues, respectively. A dipeptide contains one peptide bond, a tripeptide contains two peptide bonds, and so on. As a general rule, each peptide chain, whatever its length, possesses one free α-amino group and one free α-carboxyl group. (Exceptions include covalently modified terminal residues and circular peptide chains.) Note that the formation of a peptide bond eliminates the ionizable α-carboxyl and α-amino groups found in free amino acids.

Most of the ionic charges associated with a protein molecule are contributed by the side chains of the constituent amino acids. This means that the solubility and ionic properties of a protein are largely determined by its amino acid composition. Furthermore, the side chains of the residues interact with each other, and these interactions contribute to the three-dimensional shape and stability of a protein molecule (Chapter 4).

Some peptides are important biological compounds, and the chemistry of peptides is an active area of research. Several hormones are peptides; for example, endorphins are the naturally occurring molecules that modulate pain in vertebrates. Some very simple peptides are useful as food additives; for example, the sweetening agent

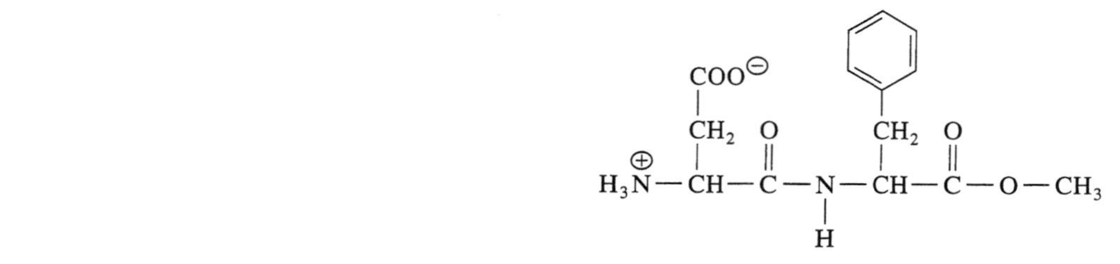

◀ **Figure 3.10**
Aspartame (aspartylphenylalanine methyl ester).

aspartame is the methyl ester of aspartylphenylalanine (Figure 3.10). Aspartame is about 200 times sweeter than table sugar and is widely used in diet drinks. There are also many peptide toxins, such as those found in snake venom and poisonous mushrooms.

3.6 Protein Purification Techniques

In order to study a particular protein in the laboratory, one must usually separate it from all other cell components, including other similar proteins. Few analytical techniques can be directly applied to crude mixtures of cellular proteins because they contain hundreds (or thousands) of different proteins. The purification steps are different for each protein. They are worked out by trying a number of different techniques until a procedure is developed that reproducibly yields highly purified protein that is still biologically active. Purification steps usually exploit minor differences in the solubilities, net charges, sizes, and binding specificities of proteins. In this section, we consider some of the common methods of protein purification. Most purification techniques are performed at 0° to 4°C to minimize temperature-dependent processes such as protein degradation and denaturation (unfolding).

The first step in protein purification is to prepare a solution of proteins. The source of a protein is often whole cells in which the target protein accounts for less than 0.1% of the total dry weight. Isolation of an intracellular protein requires that cells be suspended in a buffer solution and homogenized, or disrupted into cell fragments. Under these conditions, most proteins dissolve. (Major exceptions include membrane proteins, which require special purification procedures.) Let us assume that the desired protein is one of many proteins in this buffer solution.

The next step in protein purification is often a relatively crude separation, or **fractionation**, procedure that makes use of the different solubilities of proteins in solutions of salts. Ammonium sulfate is frequently used in such fractionations. Enough ammonium sulfate is mixed with the solution of proteins to precipitate the less soluble impurities, which are removed by centrifugation. The target protein and other, more soluble proteins remain in the fluid, called the supernatant fraction. Next, more ammonium sulfate is added to the supernatant fraction until the desired protein is precipitated. The mixture is centrifuged, the fluid removed, and the precipitate dissolved in a minimal volume of buffer solution. Typically, fractionation using ammonium sulfate gives a two- to threefold purification (i.e., one-half to two-thirds of the unwanted proteins have been removed from the resulting enriched protein fraction). At this point, the solvent (which contains residual ammonium sulfate) is exchanged by dialysis for a buffer solution suitable for chromatography. In dialysis, a protein solution is placed in a cylinder of cellophane tubing sealed at one end. The tubing is then sealed at the other end and suspended in a large volume of buffer. The cellophane membrane is semipermeable: high-molecular-weight proteins are too large to pass through the pores of the membrane so proteins remain inside the tubing while low-molecular-weight solutes (including, in this case, ammonium and sulfate ions) diffuse out and are replaced by solutes in the buffer.

Column chromatography can then be used to fractionate the mixture of proteins that remains after ammonium sulfate precipitation and dialysis. A cylindrical column is filled with an insoluble material such as substituted cellulose fibers or synthetic beads. The protein mixture is applied to the column and washed through the matrix of insoluble material by the addition of solvent. As solvent flows through the column, the **eluate** (the liquid emerging from the bottom of the column) is collected in many fractions, a few of which are represented in Figure 3.11a. The rate at which proteins travel through the matrix depends on interactions between matrix and protein. For a given column, different proteins are eluted at different rates. The concentration of protein in each fraction can be determined by measuring the absorbance of the eluate at a wavelength of 280 nm (Figure 3.11b). (Recall from Section 3.2B that at neutral pH, tyrosine and tryptophan absorb UV light at 280 nm.) To locate the target protein, the fractions containing protein must then be assayed, or tested, for biological activity or some other characteristic property. Column chromatography may be performed under high pressure using small, tightly packed columns, with solvent flow controlled by a computer. This technique is called **HPLC**, for high-pressure liquid chromatography.

Chromatographic techniques are classified according to the type of matrix. In **ion-exchange chromatography**, the matrix carries positive charges (anion-exchange resins) or negative charges (cation-exchange resins). Anion-exchange matrices bind negatively charged proteins, retaining them in the matrix for subsequent elution. Conversely, cation-exchange materials bind positively charged proteins. The bound proteins can be serially eluted by gradually increasing the salt concentration in the solvent. As the salt concentration is increased, it eventually reaches a concentration where the salt ions outcompete proteins in binding to the matrix. At this concentration, the protein is released and is collected in the eluate. Individual bound proteins are eluted at different salt concentrations, and this fractionation makes ion-exchange chromatography a powerful tool in protein purification.

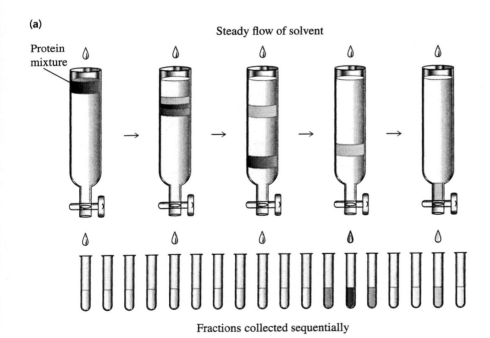

(a)

Steady flow of solvent

Protein mixture

Fractions collected sequentially

(b)

A_{280}

Fraction number

◀ **Figure 3.11**
Column chromatography. **(a)** A mixture of proteins is added to a column containing a solid matrix. Solvent then flows into the column from a reservoir. Washed by solvent, different proteins (represented by red and blue bands) travel through the column at different rates, depending on their interactions with the matrix. Eluate is collected in a series of fractions, a few of which are shown. **(b)** The protein concentration of each fraction is determined by measuring the absorbance at 280 nm. The peaks correspond to the elution of the protein bands shown in (a). The fractions are then tested for the presence of the target protein.

Chemistry for Biologists

Gel-filtration chromatography separates proteins on the basis of molecular size. The gel is a matrix of porous beads. Proteins that are smaller than the average pore size penetrate much of the internal volume of the beads and are therefore retarded by the matrix as the buffer solution flows through the column. The smaller the protein, the later it elutes from the column. Fewer of the pores are accessible to larger protein molecules. Consequently, the largest proteins flow past the beads and elute first.

Affinity chromatography is the most selective type of column chromatography. It relies on specific binding interactions between the target protein and some other molecule that is covalently bound to the matrix of the column. The molecule bound to the matrix may be a substance or a ligand that binds to a protein in vivo; an antibody that recognizes the target protein; or another protein that is known to interact with the target protein inside the cell. As a mixture of proteins passes through the column, only the target protein specifically binds to the matrix. The column is then washed with buffer several times to rid it of nonspecifically bound proteins. Finally, the target protein can be eluted by washing the column with a solvent containing a high concentration of salt that disrupts the interaction between the protein and column matrix. In some cases, bound protein can be selectively released from the affinity column by adding excess ligand to the elution buffer. The target protein preferentially binds to the ligand in solution instead of the lower concentration of ligand that is attached to the insoluble matrix of the column. This method is most effective when the ligand is a small molecule. Affinity chromatography alone can sometimes purify a protein 1000- to 10 000-fold.

Electrophoresis separates proteins based on their migration in an electric field. In **polyacrylamide gel electrophoresis (PAGE)**, protein samples are placed on a highly cross-linked gel matrix of polyacrylamide and an electric field is applied. The matrix is buffered to a mildly alkaline pH so that most proteins are anionic and migrate toward the anode. Typically, several samples are run at once, together with a reference sample. The gel matrix retards the migration of large molecules as they move in the electric field. Hence, proteins are fractionated on the basis of both charge and mass.

A modification of the standard electrophoresis technique uses the negatively charged detergent sodium dodecyl sulfate (SDS) to overwhelm the native charge on

Figure 3.12 ▶
SDS–PAGE. **(a)** An electrophoresis apparatus includes an SDS–polyacrylamide gel between two glass plates and buffer in the upper and lower reservoirs. Samples are loaded into the wells of the gel, and voltage is applied. Since proteins complexed with SDS are negatively charged, they migrate toward the anode. **(b)** The banding pattern of the proteins after electrophoresis can be visualized by staining. Since the smallest proteins migrate fastest, the proteins of lowest molecular weight are at the bottom of the gel.

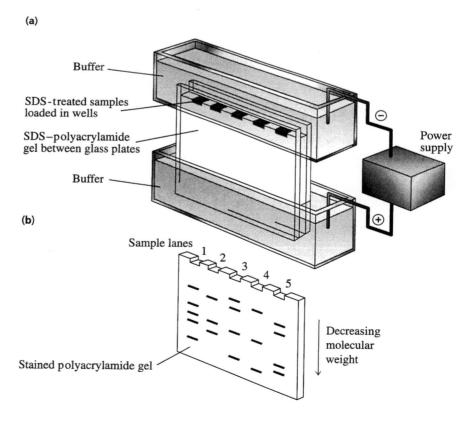

(a)

Buffer

SDS-treated samples loaded in wells

SDS–polyacrylamide gel between glass plates

Buffer

Power supply

(b)

Sample lanes

Stained polyacrylamide gel

Decreasing molecular weight

Chemistry for Biologists

proteins so that they are separated on the basis of mass only. SDS–polyacrylamide gel electrophoresis (SDS–PAGE) is used to assess the purity and to estimate the molecular weight of a protein. In SDS–PAGE, the detergent is added to the poly-acryamide gel as well as to the protein samples. A reducing agent is also added to the samples to reduce any disulfide bonds. The dodecyl sulfate anion, which has a long hydrophobic tail ($CH_3(CH_2)_{11}OSO_3^{\ominus}$; Figure 2.8), binds to hydrophobic side chains of amino acid residues in the polypeptide chain. SDS binds at a ratio of ap-proximately one molecule for every two residues of a typical protein. Since larger proteins bind proportionally more SDS, the charge-to-mass ratios of all treated proteins are approximately the same. All the SDS-protein complexes are highly negatively charged and move toward the anode, as diagramed in Figure 3.12a. However, their rate of migration through the gel is inversely proportional to the logarithm of their mass—larger proteins encounter more resistance and therefore migrate more slowly than smaller proteins. This sieving effect differs from gel-filtration chromatography because in gel filtration larger molecules are excluded from the pores of the gel and hence travel faster. In SDS–PAGE, all molecules pen-etrate the pores of the gel, so the largest proteins travel most slowly. The protein bands that result from this differential migration, as pictured in Figure 3.12b, can be visualized by staining. Molecular weights of unknown proteins can be estimat-ed by comparing their migration to the migration of reference proteins elec-trophoresed on the same gel.

SDS–PAGE is primarily an analytical tool, although it can be adapted for purify-ing proteins. Denatured proteins can be recovered from SDS–PAGE by cutting out the bands of a gel. The protein is then electroeluted by applying an electric current to allow the protein to migrate into a buffer solution. After concentration and the removal of salts, such protein preparations can be used for structural analysis or antibody production.

3.7 Amino Acid Composition of Proteins

Once a protein has been isolated, its amino acid composition can be determined. First, the peptide bonds of the protein are cleaved by acid hydrolysis, typically using 6 M HCl (Figure 3.13). Next, the hydrolyzed mixture, or hydrolysate, is subjected to a chromatographic procedure in which each of the amino acids is sep-arated and quantitated, a process called **amino acid analysis**. One method of amino acid analysis involves treatment of the protein hydrolysate with phenylisothio-cyanate (PITC) at pH 9.0 to generate phenylthiocarbamoyl (PTC)–amino acid de-rivatives (Figure 3.14). The PTC–amino acid mixture is then subjected to HPLC in a column of fine silica beads to which short hydrocarbon chains have been at-tached. The amino acids are separated by the hydrophobic properties of their side

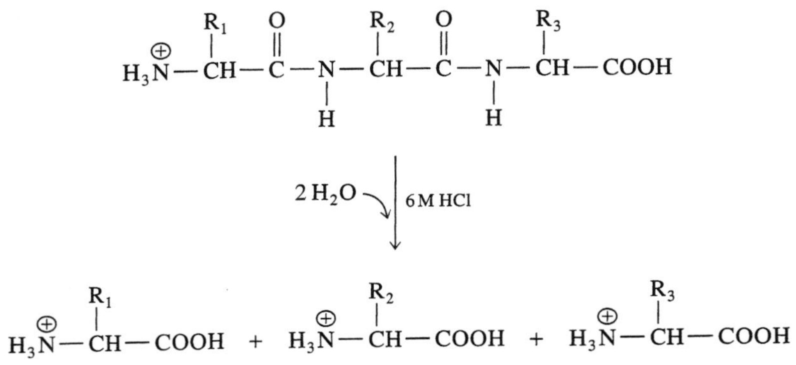

Figure 3.13 ▲
Acid-catalyzed hydrolysis of a peptide. Incubation with 6 M HCl at 110°C for 16 to 72 hours releases the constituent amino acids of a peptide.

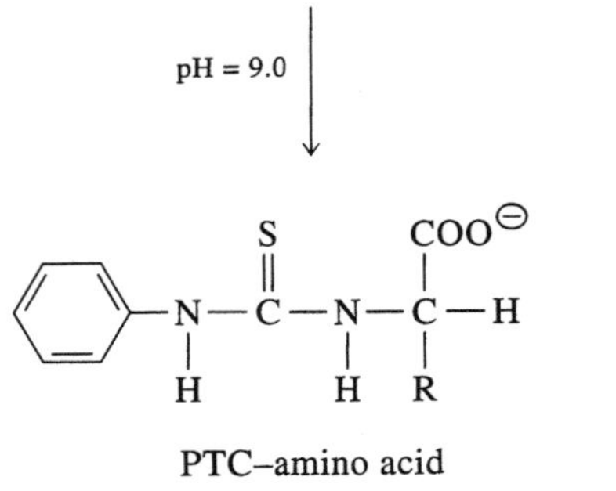

Figure 3.14 ▲
Amino acid treated with phenylisothio-cyanate (PITC). The α-amino group of an amino acid reacts with phenylisothiocyanate to give a phenylthiocarbamoyl–amino acid (PTC–amino acid).

chains. As each PTC–amino acid derivative is eluted, it is detected and its concentration is determined by measuring the absorbance of the eluate at 254 nm (the peak absorbance of the PTC moiety). A plot of the absorbance of the eluate as a function of time is given in Figure 3.15. Each peak corresponds to a specific PTC–amino acid representing a residue that was present in the original protein. Since different PTC–amino acid derivatives are eluted at different rates, the timing of the peaks identifies the amino acids. The amount of each amino acid in the hydrolysate is proportional to the area under its peak. With this method, amino acid analysis can be performed on samples as small as 1 picomole (10^{-12} mol) of a protein that contains approximately 200 residues.

Despite its usefulness, acid hydrolysis cannot yield a complete amino acid analysis. Since the side chains of asparagine and glutamine contain amide bonds, the acid used to cleave the peptide bonds of the protein also converts asparagine to aspartic acid and glutamine to glutamic acid. When acid hydrolysis is used, the combined total of glutamate and glutamine is designated by the abbreviation Glx or Z, and the combined total of aspartate and asparagine is designated by Asx or B, as in the chromatogram shown in Figure 3.15. Other limitations of the acid hydrolysis method include small losses of serine, threonine, and tyrosine. In addition, the side chain of tryptophan is almost totally destroyed by acid hydrolysis.

Using various analytical techniques, the complete amino acid compositions of many proteins have been determined. Dramatic differences in composition have been found, illustrating the tremendous potential for diversity based on different combinations of the 20 amino acids. The amino acid compositions of five relatively small proteins are given in Table 3.3. Note that proteins need not contain all 20 of the common amino acids.

The last column in Table 3.3 shows the average frequency of amino acid residues in more than 1000 proteins that have been sequenced. The most common amino acids are leucine and alanine, followed by serine, valine, and glutamate. Cysteine and tryptophan are the least abundant amino acids in proteins.

3.8 Determining the Sequence of Amino Acid Residues

Amino acid analysis provides information on the composition of a protein but not its primary structure (sequence of residues). In 1950 Pehr Edman developed a technique that permits removal and identification of one residue at a time from the N-terminus of a protein. The **Edman degradation procedure** involves treating a protein at pH 9.0 with PITC, also known as the Edman reagent. (Recall that PITC can also be used in the measurement of free amino acids, as shown in Figure 3.14.) PITC reacts with the free N-terminus of the chain to form a phenylthiocarbamoyl derivative, or PTC-peptide (Figure 3.16). When the PTC-peptide is treated with an anhydrous acid, such as trifluoroacetic acid, the peptide bond of the N-terminal residue is selectively cleaved, releasing an anilinothiazolinone derivative of the residue. This derivative can be extracted with an organic solvent, such as butyl chloride, leaving the remaining peptide in the aqueous phase. The unstable anilinothiazolinone derivative is then treated with aqueous acid, which converts it to a stable phenylthiohydantoin derivative of the amino acid that had been the N-terminal residue (PTH–amino acid). The polypeptide chain in the aqueous phase, now one residue shorter (residue 2 of the original protein is now the N-terminus), can be adjusted back to pH 9.0 and treated again with PITC. The entire procedure can be repeated serially using an automated instrument known as a sequenator. Each cycle yields a PTH–amino acid that can be identified chromatographically, usually by HPLC.

When a protein contains one or more cystine residues, the disulfide bonds must be cleaved to permit release of the cysteine residues as PTH–amino acids during the appropriate cycles of Edman degradation. Thiol compounds, such as 2-mercaptoethanol,

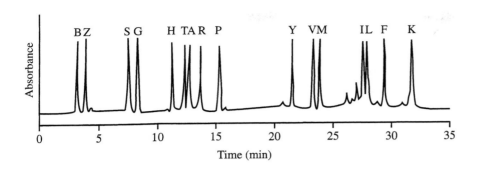

◀ **Figure 3.15**
Chromatogram obtained from HPLC separation of PTC–amino acids. PTC–amino acids in the column eluate are detected by their absorbance at 254 nm. Peaks are labeled with one-letter abbreviations. The letters B and Z indicate totals of asparagine + aspartate, and glutamine + glutamate, respectively. [Adapted from Hunkapiller, M. W., Strickler, J. E., and Wilson, K. J. (1984). Contemporary methodology for protein structure determination. *Science* 226:304–311.]

TABLE 3.3   Amino acid compositions of several proteins

Amino acid	Number of residues per molecule of protein					
	Lysozyme (hen egg white)	Cytochrome *c* (human)	Ferredoxin (spinach)	Insulin (bovine)	Hemoglobin α chain (human)	Frequency in proteins[a] (%)
Highly hydrophobic						
Ile (I)	6	8	4	1	0	5.2
Val (V)	6	3	7	5	13	6.6
Leu (L)	8	6	8	6	18	9.0
Phe (F)	3	3	2	3	7	3.9
Met (M)	2	3	0	0	2	2.4
Less hydrophobic						
Ala (A)	12	6	9	3	21	8.3
Gly (G)	12	13	6	4	7	7.2
Cys (C)	8	2	5	6	1	1.7
Trp (W)	6	1	1	0	1	1.3
Tyr (Y)	3	5	4	4	3	3.2
Pro (P)	2	4	4	1	7	5.1
Thr (T)	7	7	8	1	9	5.8
Ser (S)	10	2	7	3	11	6.9
Highly hydrophilic						
Asn (N)	13	5	2	3	4	4.4
Gln (Q)	3	2	4	3	1	4.0
Acidic						
Asp (D)	8	3	11	0	8	5.3
Glu (E)	2	8	9	4	4	6.2
Basic						
His (H)	1	3	1	2	10	2.2
Lys (K)	6	18	4	1	11	5.7
Arg (R)	11	2	1	1	3	5.7
Total residues	129	104	97	51	141	—

[a]From McCaldon, P., and Argos, P. (1988). *Proteins* 4, 99–122.

Chemistry for Biologists

Figure 3.16 ▶

Edman degradation procedure. The N-terminal residue of a polypeptide chain reacts with phenylisothiocyanate to give a phenylthiocarbamoyl-peptide. Treating this derivative with trifluoroacetic acid (F_3CCOOH) releases an anilinothiazolinone derivative of the N-terminal amino acid residue. The anilinothiazolinone is extracted and treated with aqueous acid, which re-arranges the derivative to a stable phenyl-thiohydantoin derivative that can then be identified chromatographically. The remainder of the polypeptide chain, whose new N-terminal residue was formerly in the second position, is subjected to the next cycle of Edman degradation.

Phenylisothiocyanate
(Edman reagent)

N-terminal residue
of polypeptide

pH = 9.0

Phenylthiocarbamoyl-peptide

F_3CCOOH

Anilinothiazolinone derivative

Polypeptide chain with
$n-1$ amino acid residues

Aqueous acid

Returned to alkaline conditions
for reaction with additional
phenylisothiocyanate in the
next cycle of Edman degradation

Phenylthiohydantoin derivative
of extracted N-terminal amino acid

Amino acid identified
chromatographically

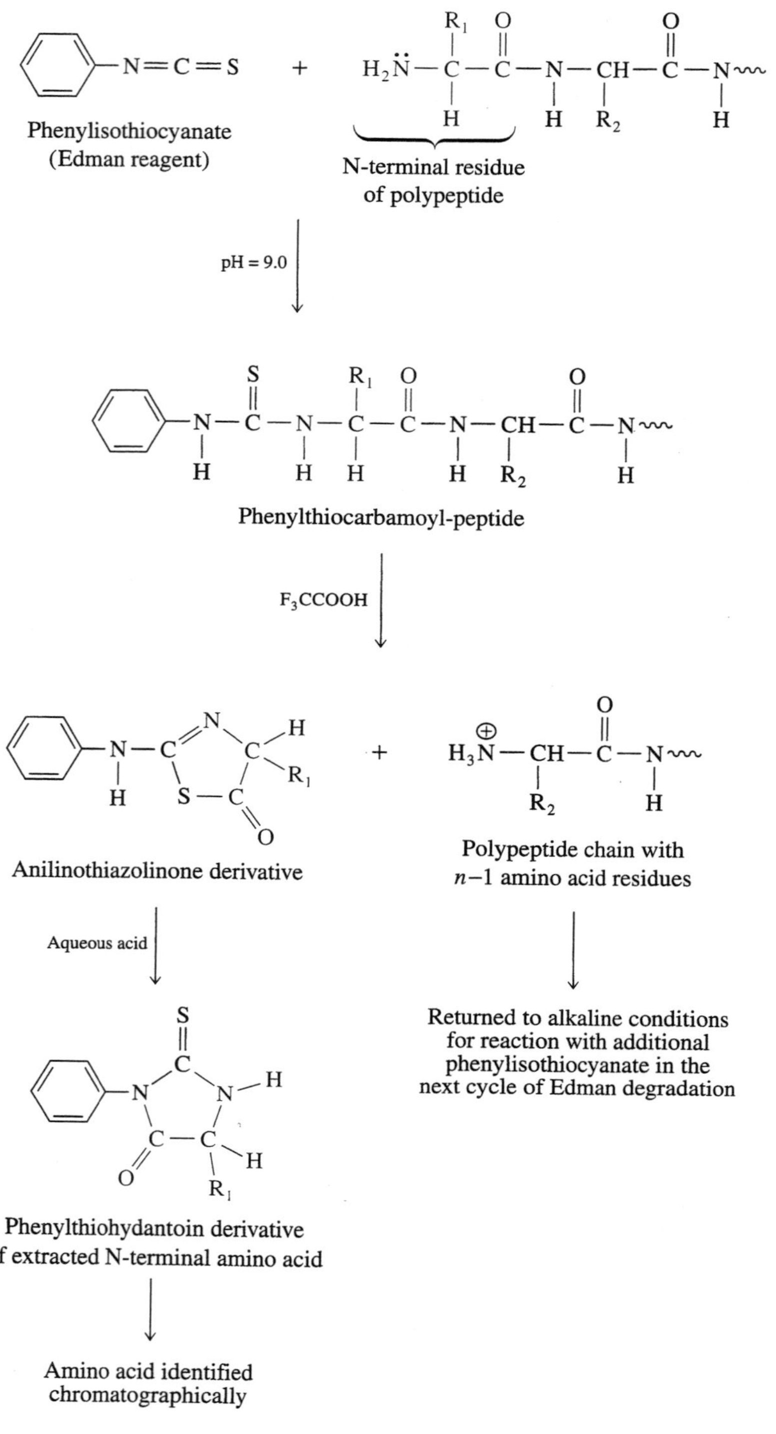

are often used to cleave disulfide bonds. Thiols reduce cystine residues to pairs of cysteine residues (Figure 3.17a). The reactive sulfhydryl groups of the cysteine residues are then blocked by treatment with an alkylating agent, such as iodoacetate, which converts oxidizable cysteine residues to stable *S*-carboxymethylcysteine residues, thereby preventing the re-formation of disulfide bonds in the presence of oxygen (Figure 3.17b).

The yield of the Edman degradation procedure under carefully controlled conditions approaches 100%, and a few picomoles of sample protein can yield sequences of 30 residues or more before further measurement is obscured by the increasing concentration of unrecovered sample from previous cycles of the procedure. For ex-

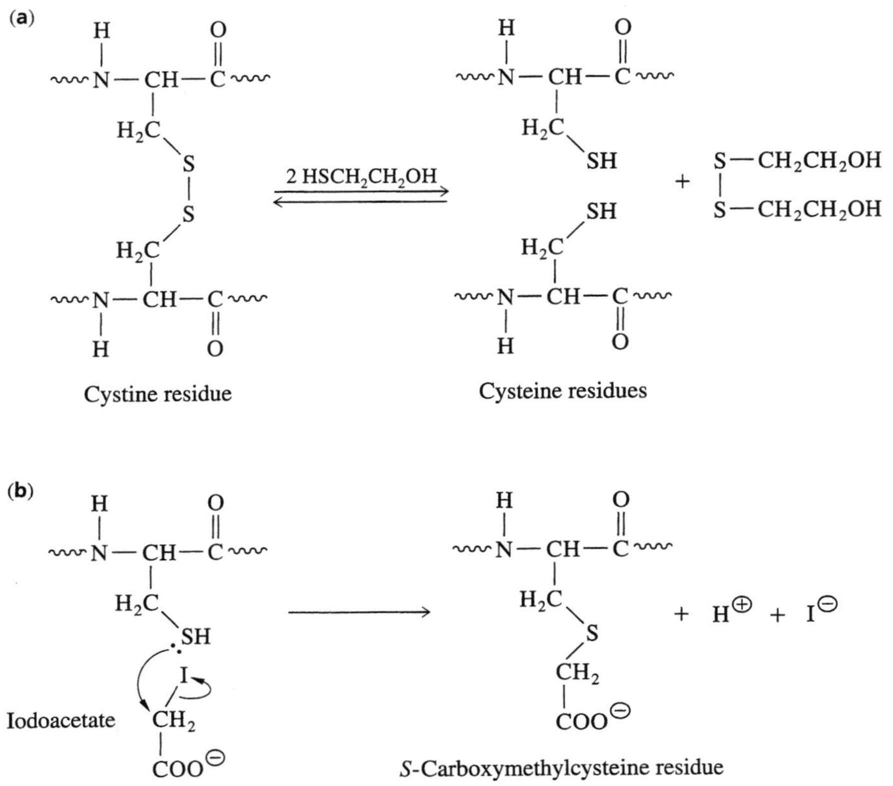

(a)

Cystine residue

Cysteine residues

(b)

Iodoacetate

S-Carboxymethylcysteine residue

◄ **Figure 3.17**
Cleaving and blocking disulfide bonds.
(a) When a protein is treated with excess
2-mercaptoethanol ($HSCH_2CH_2OH$), a disulfide-exchange reaction occurs in which each
cystine residue is reduced to two cysteine
residues and 2-mercaptoethanol is oxidized
to a disulfide. **(b)** Treating the reduced protein with the alkylating agent iodoacetate
converts all free cysteine residues to stable
S-carboxymethylcysteine residues, thus preventing the re-formation of disulfide bonds
in the presence of oxygen.

ample, if the Edman degradation procedure had an efficiency of 98%, the cumulative yield at the 30th cycle would be 0.98^{30}, or 0.55. In other words, only about half
of the PTH–amino acids generated in the 30th cycle would be derived from the 30th
residue from the N-terminus.

3.9 Protein Sequencing Strategies

Most proteins contain too many residues to be completely sequenced by Edman degradation proceeding only from the N-terminus. Therefore, proteases (enzymes that catalyze the hydrolysis of peptide bonds in proteins) or certain chemical reagents are used
to selectively cleave some of the peptide bonds of a protein. The smaller peptides formed
are then isolated and subjected to sequencing by the Edman degradation procedure.

The chemical reagent cyanogen bromide (BrCN) reacts specifically with methionine residues to produce peptides with C-terminal homoserine lactone residues
and new N-terminal residues (Figure 3.18). Since most proteins contain relatively few
methionine residues, treatment with BrCN usually produces only a few peptide fragments. For example, reaction of BrCN with a polypeptide chain containing three internal methionine residues should generate four peptide fragments. Each fragment
can then be sequenced from its N-terminus.

Many different proteases can be used to generate fragments for protein sequencing. For example, trypsin specifically catalyzes the hydrolysis of peptide bonds
on the carbonyl side of lysine and arginine residues, both of which bear positively
charged side chains (Figure 3.19a). *Staphylococcus aureus* V8 protease catalyzes
the cleavage of peptide bonds on the carbonyl side of negatively charged residues
(glutamate and aspartate); under appropriate conditions (50 mM ammonium bicarbonate), it cleaves only glutamyl bonds. Chymotrypsin, a less specific protease, preferentially catalyzes the hydrolysis of peptide bonds on the carbonyl side of uncharged
residues with aromatic or bulky hydrophobic side chains, such as phenylalanine, tyrosine, and tryptophan (Figure 3.19b).

Chemistry for Biologists

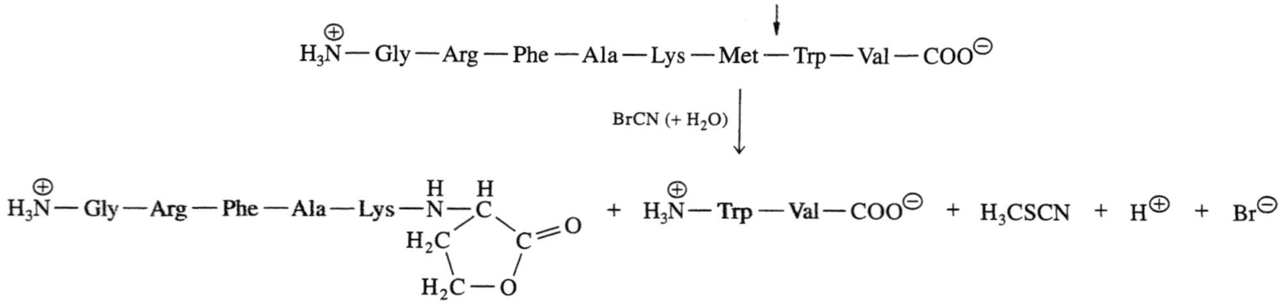

$$\overset{\oplus}{H_3N}-Gly-Arg-Phe-Ala-Lys-\underset{\downarrow}{Met}-Trp-Val-COO^{\ominus}$$

$$\Big\downarrow BrCN\;(+\,H_2O)$$

$$\overset{\oplus}{H_3N}-Gly-Arg-Phe-Ala-Lys-\text{(Peptidyl homoserine lactone)} \;+\; \overset{\oplus}{H_3N}-Trp-Val-COO^{\ominus} \;+\; H_3CSCN \;+\; H^{\oplus} \;+\; Br^{\ominus}$$

Peptidyl homoserine lactone

Figure 3.18 ▲
Protein cleavage by cyanogen bromide (BrCN). Cyanogen bromide cleaves polypeptide chains at the C-terminal side of methionine residues. The reaction produces a peptidyl homoserine lactone and generates a new N-terminus.

By judicious application of cyanogen bromide, trypsin, *S. aureus* V8 protease, and chymotrypsin to individual samples of a large protein, one can generate many peptide fragments of various sizes. These fragments can then be separated and sequenced by Edman degradation. In the final stage of sequence determination, the amino acid sequence of a large polypeptide chain can be deduced by lining up matching sequences of overlapping peptide fragments, as illustrated in Figure 3.19c. When referring to an amino acid residue whose position in the sequence is known, it is customary to follow the residue abbreviation with

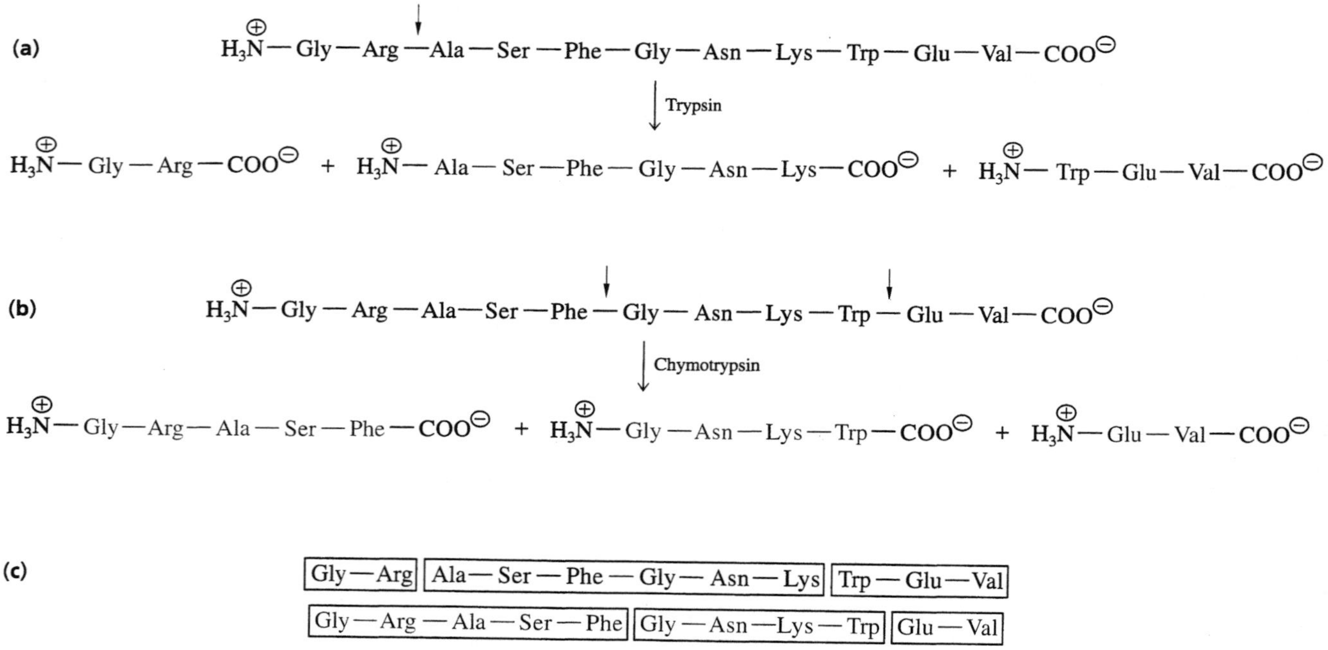

(a)
$$\overset{\oplus}{H_3N}-Gly-Arg-\underset{\downarrow}{Ala}-Ser-Phe-Gly-Asn-Lys-Trp-Glu-Val-COO^{\ominus}$$

$$\Big\downarrow Trypsin$$

$$\overset{\oplus}{H_3N}-Gly-Arg-COO^{\ominus} \;+\; \overset{\oplus}{H_3N}-Ala-Ser-Phe-Gly-Asn-Lys-COO^{\ominus} \;+\; \overset{\oplus}{H_3N}-Trp-Glu-Val-COO^{\ominus}$$

(b)
$$\overset{\oplus}{H_3N}-Gly-Arg-Ala-Ser-\underset{\downarrow}{Phe}-Gly-Asn-Lys-\underset{\downarrow}{Trp}-Glu-Val-COO^{\ominus}$$

$$\Big\downarrow Chymotrypsin$$

$$\overset{\oplus}{H_3N}-Gly-Arg-Ala-Ser-Phe-COO^{\ominus} \;+\; \overset{\oplus}{H_3N}-Gly-Asn-Lys-Trp-COO^{\ominus} \;+\; \overset{\oplus}{H_3N}-Glu-Val-COO^{\ominus}$$

(c)

| Gly—Arg | Ala—Ser—Phe—Gly—Asn—Lys | Trp—Glu—Val |

| Gly—Arg—Ala—Ser—Phe | Gly—Asn—Lys—Trp | Glu—Val |

Figure 3.19 ▲
Cleavage and sequencing of an oligopeptide. **(a)** Trypsin catalyzes cleavage of peptides on the carbonyl side of the basic residues arginine and lysine. **(b)** Chymotrypsin catalyzes cleavage of peptides on the carbonyl side of uncharged residues with aromatic or bulky hydrophobic side chains, including phenylalanine, tyrosine, and tryptophan. **(c)** By using the Edman degradation procedure to determine the sequence of each fragment (highlighted in boxes) and then lining up the matching sequences of overlapping fragments, one can determine the order of the fragments and thus deduce the sequence of the entire oligopeptide.

DNA ⌐⌐ ⌐⌐ ⌐⌐ ⌐⌐ ⌐⌐
∿∿ A A G A G T G A A C C T G T C ∿∿

Protein ∿∿∿ Lys — Ser — Glu — Pro — Val ∿∿∿

◀ **Figure 3.20**
Sequences of DNA and protein. The amino acid sequence of a protein can be deduced from the sequence of nucleotides in the corresponding gene. A sequence of three nucleotides specifies one amino acid. A, C, G, and T represent nucleotide residues of DNA.

its sequence number. For example, the third residue of the peptide shown in Figure 3.19 is called Ala-3.

The process of generating and sequencing peptide fragments is especially important in obtaining information about the sequences of proteins whose N-termini are blocked. For example, the N-terminal α-amino groups of many bacterial proteins are formylated and do not react at all when subjected to the Edman degradation procedure. Peptide fragments with unblocked N-termini can be produced by selective cleavage and then separated and sequenced so that at least some of the internal sequence of the protein can be obtained.

For proteins that contain disulfide bonds, the complete covalent structure is not fully resolved until the positions of the disulfide bonds have been established. The positions of the disulfide cross-links can be determined by fragmenting the intact protein, isolating the peptide fragments, and determining which fragments contain cystine residues. The task of determining the positions of the cross-links becomes quite complicated when the protein contains several disulfide bonds.

In recent years, it has become relatively easy to deduce the amino acid sequence of a protein by determining the sequence of nucleotides in the gene that encodes the protein (Figure 3.20). In some cases, especially when a protein is difficult to purify or very scarce, it is more efficient to isolate and sequence its gene. Often the gene is inserted into bacterial cells, where it can be expressed at high levels, making protein purification easier. DNA sequences sometimes settle uncertainties in protein sequences caused by limitations of the Edman degradation procedure. However, direct protein sequencing retains its importance because DNA sequences do not reveal the locations of disulfide bonds or amino acid residues that are removed or modified after synthesis of a protein.

In 1953 Frederick Sanger was the first scientist to determine the complete sequence of a protein (insulin). In 1956 he was awarded a Nobel Prize for this work. Twenty-four years later, Sanger won a second Nobel Prize for pioneering the sequencing of nucleic acids. Today we know the amino acid sequences of thousands of different proteins. These sequences not only reveal details of the structure of individual proteins but also allow researchers to identify families of related proteins and to predict the three-dimensional structure, and sometimes the function, of newly discovered proteins.

Frederick Sanger (1918–). ▶
Sanger won two Nobel Prizes for his work on sequencing proteins and nucleic acids.

	10	20	30	40	50	60	70	80	90	100	
Human	GDVEKGKKIF	IMKCSQCHTV	EKGGKHKTGP	NLHGLFGRKT	GQAPGYSYTA	ANKNKGIIWG	EDTLMEYLEN	PKKYIPGTKM	IFVGIKKKEE	RADLIAYLKK	ATNE
Chimpanzee	GDVEKGKKIF	IMKCSQCHTV	EKGGKHKTGP	NLHGLFGRKT	GQAPGYSYTA	ANKNKGIIWG	EDTLMEYLEN	PKKYIPGTKM	IFVGIKKKEE	RADLIAYLKK	ATNE
Spider monkey	GDVFKGKRIF	IMKCSQCHTV	EKGGKHKTGP	NLHGLFGRKT	GQASGFTYTE	ANKNKGIIWG	EDTLMEYLEN	PKKYIPGTKM	IFVGIKKKEE	RADLIAYLKK	ATNE
Macaque	GDVEKGKKIF	IMKCSQCHTV	EKGGKHKTGP	NLHGLFGRKT	GQAPGYSYTA	ANKNKGITWG	EDTLMEYLEN	PKKYIPGTKM	IFVGIKKKEE	RADLIAYLKK	ATNE
Cow	GDVEKGKKIF	VQKCAQCHTV	EKGGKHKTGP	NLHGLFGRKT	GQAPGFSYTD	ANKNKGITWG	EETLMEYLEN	PKKYIPGTKM	IFAGIKKKGE	REDLIAYLKK	ATNE
Dog	GDVEKGKKIF	VQKCAQCHTV	EKGGKHKTGP	NLHGLFGRKT	GQAPGFSYTD	ANKNKGITWG	EETLMEYLEN	PKKYIPGTKM	IFAGIKKTGE	RADLIAYLKK	ATKE
Gray whale	GDVEKGKKIF	VQKCAQCHTV	EKGGKHKTGP	NLHGLFGRKT	GQAVGFSYTD	ANKNKGITWG	EETLMEYLEN	PKKYIPGTKM	IFAGIKKKGE	RADLIAYLKK	ATNE
Horse	GDVEKGKKIF	VQKCAQCHTV	EKGGKHKTGP	NLHGLFGRKT	GQAPGFTYTD	ANKNKGITWK	EETLMEYLEN	PKKYIPGTKM	IFAGIKKKTE	REDLIAYLKK	ATNE
Zebra	GDVEKGKKIF	VQKCAQCHTV	EKGGKHKTGP	NLHGLFGRKT	GQAPGFSYTD	ANKNKGITWK	EETLMEYLEN	PKKYIPGTKM	IFAGIKKKTE	REDLIAYLKK	ATNE
Rabbit	GDVEKGKKIF	VQKCAQCHTV	EKGGKHKTGP	NLHGLFGRKT	GQAVGFSYTD	ANKNKGIIWG	EDTLMEYLEN	PKKYIPGTKM	IFAGIKKKDE	RADLIAYLKK	ATNE
Kangaroo	GDVEKGKKIF	VQKCAQCHTV	EKGGKHKTGP	NLHGIFGRKT	GQAPGFTYTD	ANKNKGIIWG	EDTLMEYLEN	PKKYIPGTKM	IFAGIKKKGE	RADLIAYLKK	ATNE
Duck	GDVEKGKKIF	VQKCSQCHTV	EKGGKHKTGP	NLHGLFGRKT	GQAEGFSYTD	ANKNKGITWG	EDTLMEYLEN	PKKYIPGTKM	IFAGIKKKSE	RADLIAYLKD	ATAK
Turkey	GDIEKGKKIF	VQKCSQCHTV	EKGGKHKTGP	NLHGLFGRKT	GQAEGFSYTD	ANKNKGITWG	EDTLMEYLEN	PKKYIPGTKM	IFAGIKKKSE	RVDLIAYLKD	ATSK
Chicken	GDIEKGKKIF	VQKCSQCHTV	EKGGKHKTGP	NLHGLFGRKT	GQAEGFSYTD	ANKNKGITWG	EDTLMEYLEN	PKKYIPGTKM	IFAGIKKKSE	RVDLIAYLKD	ATSK
Pigeon	GDIEKGKKIF	VQKCSQCHTV	EKGGKHKTGP	NLHGLFGRKT	GQAEGFSYTD	ANKNKGITWG	EDTLMEYLEN	PKKYIPGTKM	IFAGIKKKAE	RADLIAYLKQ	ATAK
King penguin	GDIEKGKKIF	VQKCSQCHTV	EKGGKHKTGP	NLHGIFGRKT	GQAEGFSYTD	ANKNKGIIWG	EDTLMEYLEN	PKKYIPGTKM	IFAGIKKKSE	RGDLIAYLKS	AITK
Snapping turtle	GDVEKGKKIF	VQKCAQCHTV	EKGGKHKTGP	NLNGLIGRKT	GQAEGFSYTE	ANKNKGITWG	EETLMEYLEN	PKKYIPGTKM	IFAGIKKKAE	RADLIAYLKE	ATSN
Alligator	GDVEKGKKIF	VQKCAQCHTV	EKGGKHKTGP	NLHGLIGRKT	GQAPGFSYTE	ANKNKGITWG	EETLMEYLEN	PKKYIPGTKM	IFAGIKKKPE	RADLIAYLKE	ATA
Bull frog	GDVEKGKKIF	VQKCAQCHTV	EKGGKHKVGP	NLYGLIGRKT	GQAAGFSYTD	ANKNKGITWG	EDTLMEYLEN	PKKYIPGTKM	IFAGIKKKGE	RADLIAYLKE	ATA
Tuna	GDVAKGKKTF	VQKCAQCHTV	ENGGKHKVGP	NLWGLFGRKT	GQAEGYSYTD	ANKSKGIVWN	ENTLMEYLEN	PKKYIPGTKM	IFAGIKKKGE	RQDLIAYLKS	ACSK
Dogfish	GDVEKGKKVF	VQKCAQCHTV	ENGGKHKTGP	NLSGLFGRKT	GQAQGFSYTD	ANKSKGITWQ	QETLRIYLEN	PKKYIPGTKM	IFAGIKKKSE	RQDLVAYLKS	ATS
Starfish	GQVEKGKKIF	VQRCAQCHTV	EKAGKHKTGP	NLNGILGRKT	GQAAGFSYTD	ANRNKGITWK	NETLFEYLEN	PKKYIPGTKM	VFAGLKKKQE	RQDLIAYLEA	TAAS
Fruit fly	GDVEKGKKLF	VQRCAQCHTV	EAGGKHKVGP	NLHGLIGRKT	GQAAGFAYTD	ANKAKGITWN	EDTLFEYLEN	PKKYIPGTKM	IFAGLKKPNE	RGDLIAYLKS	ATK
Silkmoth	GNAENGKKIF	VQRCAQCHTV	EAGGKHKVGP	NLHGFYGRKT	GQAPGFSYSN	ANKAKGITWG	DDTLFEYLEN	PKKYIPGTKM	VFAGLKKANE	RADLIAYLKE	STK
Pumpkin	GNSKAGEKIF	KTKCAQCHTV	DKGAGHKQGP	NLNGLFGRQS	GTTPGYSYSA	ANKNRAVIWE	EKTLYDYLLN	PKKYIPGTKM	VFPGLKKPQD	RADLIAYLKE	STA
Tomato	GNPKAGEKIF	KTKCAQCHTV	EKGAGHKEGP	NLNGLFGRQS	GTTAGYSYSA	ANKNMAVNWG	ENTLYDYLLN	PKKYIPGTKM	VFPGLKKPQE	RADLIAYLKE	ATA
Arabidopsis	GDAKKGANLF	KTRCAQCHTL	KAGEGNKIGP	ELHGLFGRKT	GSVAGYSYTD	ANKQKGIEWK	DDTLFEYLEN	PKKYIPGTKM	AFGGLKKPKD	RNDLITFLEE	ETK
Mung bean	GNSKSGEKIF	KTKCAQCHTV	DKGAGHKQGP	NLNGLIGRQS	GTTAGYSYST	ANKNMAVIWE	EKTLYDYLLN	PKKYIPGTKM	VFPGLKKPQD	RADVIAYLKQ	STA
Wheat	GNPDAGAKIF	KTKCAQCHTV	DAGAGHKQGP	NLHGLFGRQS	GTTAGYSYSA	ANKNKAVEWE	ENTLYDYLLN	PKKYIPGTKM	VFPGLKKPQD	RADLIAYLKS	ATSS
Sunflower	GNPTTGEKIF	KTKCAQCHTV	EKGAGHKQGP	NLNGLFGRQS	GTTAGYSYSA	GNKNKAVIWE	ENTLYDYLLN	PKKYIPGTKM	VFPGLKKPQE	RADLIAYLKT	STA
Yeast	GSAKKGATLF	KTRCLQCHTV	EKGGPHKVGP	NLHGIFGRHS	GQAEGYSYTD	ANIKKNVLWD	ENNMSEYLTN	PKKYIPGTKM	AFGGLKKEKD	RNDLITYLKK	ACE
Debaryomyces	GSEKKGANLF	KTRCLQCHTV	EKGGPHKVGP	NLHGVVGRTS	GQAQGFSYTD	ANKKKGVEWT	EQDLSDYLEN	PKKYIPGTKM	AFGGLKKAKD	RNDLITYLVK	ATK
Candida	GSEKKGATLF	KTRCLQCHTV	EKGGPHKVGP	NLHGVFGRKS	GLAEGYSYTD	ANKKKGVEWT	EQTMSDYLEN	PKKYIPGTKM	AFGGLKKGKE	RNDLVTYLKK	ATS
Aspergillus	GDAK-GAKLF	QTRCAQCHTV	EAGGPHKVGP	NLHGLFGRKT	GQSEGYAYTD	ANKQAGVTWD	ENTLFSYLEN	PKKFIPGTKM	AFGGLKKPKD	RNDLITYLKE	STA
Rhodomicrobium	GDPVKGEQVF	KQ-CKICHQV	GPTAKNGVGP	EQNDVFGQKA	GARPGFNYSD	AMKNSGLTWD	EATLDKYLEN	PKAVPGTKM	VFVGLKNPQD	RADVIAYLKQ	LSGK
Nitrobacter	GDVEAGKAAF	NK-CKACHEI	GESAKNKVGP	ELDGLDGRHS	GAVEGYAYSP	ANKASGITWT	EAEFKEYIKD	PKAKVPGTKM	VFAGIKKDSE	LDNLWAYVSQ	FDKD
Agrobacterium	GDVAKGEAAF	KR-CSACHAI	GEGAKNKVGP	QLNGIIGRTA	GGDPDYNYSN	AMKKAGLVWT	PQELRDFLSA	PKKKIPGNKM	ALAGISKPEE	LDNLIAYLIF	SASSK
Rhodopila	GDPVEGKHLF	HTICLICHT-	DIKGRNKVGP	SLYGVVGRHS	GIEPGYNYSE	ANIKSGIVWT	PDVLFKYIEH	PQKIVPGTKM	GYPG-QPDQK	RADI1AYLET	1K

3.10 Comparisons of the Primary Structures of Proteins Reveal Evolutionary Relationships

In many cases, workers have sequenced the same protein from many species. The results show that closely related species contain proteins with very similar amino acid sequences and that proteins from distantly related species are much less similar in sequence. The differences reflect evolutionary change from a common ancestral protein sequence.

The protein cytochrome *c*, which consists of a single polypeptide chain of about 104 residues, provides us with an excellent example of evolution at the molecular level. Cytochrome *c* is found in all aerobic organisms, and the protein sequences from distantly related species, such as mammals and bacteria, are similar enough to confidently conclude that the proteins are homologous. (Proteins and genes are homologous if they have descended from a common ancestor. The evidence for homology is based on sequence similarity.)

The first step in revealing evolutionary relationships is to align the amino acid sequences of proteins from a number of species. An example of such an alignment for cytochrome *c* is shown in Figure 3.21. The alignment reveals a remarkable conservation of residues at certain positions. For example, every sequence contains a proline at position 30 and a methionine at position 80. In general, conserved residues contribute to the structural stability of the protein or are essential for its function.

There is selection against any changes at these invariant positions. In addition, there are sites where only a limited number of substitutions are observed. In most cases, the allowed substitutions are amino acid residues with similar properties. For example, position 98 can be occupied by leucine, isoleucine, or valine—these are all hydrophobic residues. Similarly, many sites can be occupied by a number of different polar residues. Other positions are highly variable; residues at these sites contribute very little to the structure and function of the protein, and substitutions during evolution are due to random genetic drift.

The cytochrome *c* sequences of humans and chimpanzees are identical. This is a reflection of their close evolutionary relationship. The monkey and macaque sequences are very similar to the human and chimpanzee sequences, as expected, since all four species are primates. Similarly, the sequences of the plant cytochrome *c* molecules resemble each other much more than they resemble any of the other sequences.

Figure 3.22 illustrates the similarities between cytochrome *c* sequences in different species by depicting them as a tree whose branches are proportional in length to the number of differences in the amino acid sequences of the protein. Species that are closely related cluster together on the same branches of the tree because their proteins are very similar. At great evolutionary distances, the number of differences may be very large. For example, the bacterial sequences differ substantially from the eukaryotic sequences, reflecting divergence from a common ancestor that lived several billion years ago. The tree clearly reveals the three main kingdoms of eukaryotes: fungi, animals, and plants. (Protist sequences are not included in this tree in order to make it less complicated.)

Phylogenetic trees derived from sequence data generally agree closely with those constructed by evolutionary biologists using morphological data. They provide independent evidence of common descent.

◀ **Figure 3.21**
Cytochrome c sequences. The sequences of cytochrome c proteins from various species are aligned to show their similarities. In some cases, gaps (signified by hyphens) have been introduced to improve the alignment. The gaps represent deletions and insertions in the genes that encode these proteins. For some species, additional residues at the ends of the sequence have been omitted. Hydrophobic residues are blue and polar residues are red.

Chemistry for Biologists

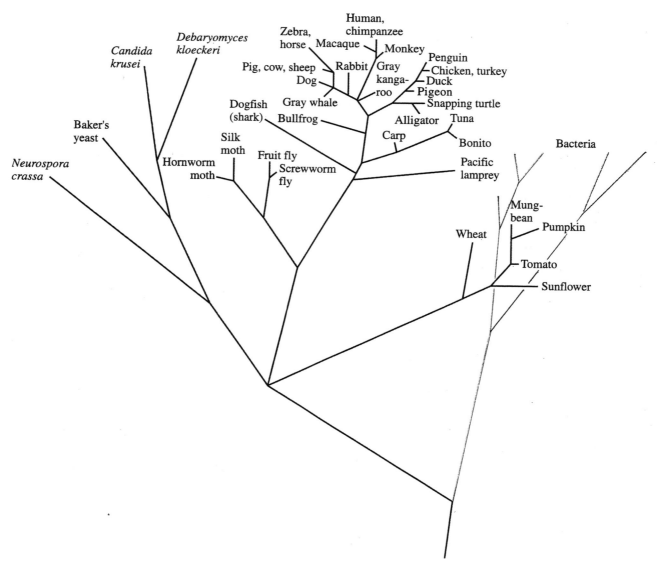

Figure 3.22 ▲
Phylogenetic tree for cytochrome *c*. The length of the branches reflects the number of differences between the sequences shown in Figure 3.21. [Adapted from Schwartz, R. M., and Dayhoff, M. O. (1978). Origins of prokaryotes, eukaryotes, mitochondria, and chloroplasts. *Science* 199:395–403.]

Summary

1. Proteins are made from 20 standard amino acids, each of which contains an amino group, a carboxyl group, and a side chain, or R group. Except for glycine, which has no chiral carbon, all amino acids in proteins are of the L configuration.

2. The side chains of amino acids can be classified according to their chemical structures: aliphatic, aromatic, sulfur-containing, alcohols, bases, acids, and amides. Some amino acids are further classified as having highly hydrophobic or highly hydrophilic side chains. The properties of the side chains of amino acids are important determinants of protein structure and function.

3. Cells contain additional amino acids that are not used in protein synthesis. Some amino acids can be chemically modified to produce compounds that act as hormones or neurotransmitters. Some amino acids are modified after incorporation into polypeptides.

4. At pH 7, the α-carboxyl group of an amino acid is negatively charged (—COO$^{\ominus}$), and the α-amino group is positively charged (—NH$_3^{\oplus}$). The charges of ionizable side chains depend on both the pH and their pK_a values.

5. Amino acid residues in proteins are linked by peptide bonds. The sequence of residues is called the primary structure of the protein.

Problems

1. Draw and label the stereochemical structures of (a) D- and L-phenylalanine, and (b) D- and L-cysteine. Indicate the *R* or *S* designation of the α-carbon in each case and explain your reasoning.

2. Show that the Fischer projection of the common form of threonine (Figure 3.4) corresponds to (2*S*,3*R*)-threonine.

3. Histamine dihydrochloride is administered to melanoma (skin cancer) patients in combination with anticancer drugs because it makes the cancer cells more receptive to the drugs. Draw the chemical structure of histamine dihydrochloride.

4. Dried fish treated with salt and nitrates has been found to contain the mutagen 2-chloro-4-methylthiobutanoic acid (CMBA). From what amino acid is CMBA derived?

$$H_3C-S \diagdown_{CH_2} \diagup^{CH_2} \diagdown_{\underset{Cl}{CH}} \diagup^{C} \overset{O}{\diagdown_{OH}}$$

5. For each of the following modified amino acid side chains, identify the amino acid from which it was derived and the type of chemical modification that has occurred.
(a) $-CH_2OPO_3^{2-}$
(b) $-CH_2CH(COO^-)_2$
(c) $-(CH_2)_4-NH-C(O)CH_3$

6. The tripeptide glutathione (GSH) (γ-Glu-Cys-Gly) serves a protective function in animals by destroying toxic peroxides that are generated during aerobic metabolic processes. Draw the chemical structure of glutathione. Note: the γ symbol indicates that the peptide bond between Glu and Cys is formed between the γ-carboxyl of Glu and the amino group of Cys.

7. Melittin is a 26-residue polypeptide found in bee venom. In its monomeric form, melittin is thought to insert into lipid-rich membrane structures. Explain how the amino acid sequence of melittin accounts for this property.

$$\overset{+}{H_3N}-\overset{1}{Gly}-Ile-Gly-Ala-Val-Leu-Lys-Val-Leu-Thr-$$
$$Gly-Leu-Pro-Ala-Leu-Ile-Ser-Trp-Ile-Lys-Arg-Lys-$$
$$Arg-Gln-\underset{26}{Gln}-NH_2$$

8. Calculate the isoelectric points of (a) arginine and (b) glutamate.

9. Oxytocin is a nonapeptide (a nine-residue peptide) hormone involved in the milk-releasing response in lactating mammals. The sequence of a synthetic version of oxytocin is shown below. What is the net charge of this peptide at (a) pH 2.0, (b) pH 8.5, and (c) pH 10.7? Assume that the ionizable groups have the pK_a values listed in Table 3.2. The disulfide bond is stable at pH 2.0, pH 8.5, and pH 10.7. Note that the C-terminus is amidated.

$$\overset{1}{Cys}-Phe-Ile-Glu-Asn-Cys-Pro-His-Gly-NH_2$$
$$\underset{\textstyle \vert_____S-S_____\vert}{}$$

10. The titration curve for histidine is shown below. The pK_a values are 1.8 (—COOH), 6.0 (side chain), and 9.3 (—NH$_3^+$).

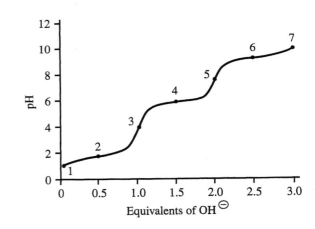

(a) Draw the structure of histidine at each stage of ionization.
(b) Identify the points on the titration curve that correspond to the four ionic species.
(c) Identify the points at which the average net charge is +2, +0.5, 0, and −1.
(d) Identify the point at which the pH equals the pK_a of the side chain.
(e) Identify the point that indicates complete titration of the side chain.
(f) In what pH ranges would histidine be a good buffer?

11. Draw the following structures for compounds that would occur during the Edman peptide degradation procedure: (a) PTC-Leu-Ala, (b) PTH-Ser, (c) PTH-Pro.

12. Predict the fragments that will be generated from the treatment of the following peptide with: (a) trypsin, (b) chymotrypsin, and (c) *S. aureus* V8 protease.

Gly-Ala-Trp-Arg-Asp-Ala-Lys-Glu-Phe-Gly-Gln

13. You have isolated a decapeptide (a 10-residue peptide) called FP, which has anticancer activity. Determine the sequence of the peptide from the following information. (Note that amino acids are separated by commas when their sequence is not known.)

(a) One cycle of Edman degradation of intact FP yields 2 mol of PTH-aspartate per mole of FP.

(b) Treatment of a solution of FP with 2-mercaptoethanol followed by the addition of trypsin yields three peptides with the composition (Ala, Cys, Phe), (Arg, Asp), and (Asp, Cys, Gly, Met, Phe). The intact (Ala, Cys, Phe) peptide yields PTH-cysteine in the first cycle of Edman degradation.

(c) Treatment of 1 mol of FP with carboxypeptidase (which cleaves the C-terminal residue from peptides) yields 2 mol of phenylalanine.

(d) Treatment of the intact pentapeptide (Asp, Cys, Gly, Met, Phe) with BrCN yields two peptides with the composition (homoserine lactone, Asp) and (Cys, Gly, Phe). The (Cys, Gly, Phe) peptide yields PTH-glycine in the first cycle of Edman degradation.

Selected Readings

General

Creighton, T. E. (1993). *Proteins: Structures and Molecular Principles*, 2nd ed. (New York: W. H. Freeman), pp. 1–48. This section of Creighton's monograph presents an excellent description of the chemistry of polypeptides.

Greenstein, J. P., and Winitz, M. (1961). *Chemistry of the Amino Acids* (New York: John Wiley & Sons).

Kreil, G. (1997). D-Amino Acids in Animal Peptides. *Annu. Rev. Biochem.* 66:337–345.

Meister, A. (1965). *Biochemistry of the Amino Acids*, 2nd ed. (New York: Academic Press). Volume I of this two-volume set is the standard reference for the properties of amino acids.

Protein Purification

Hearn, M. T. W. (1987). General strategies in the separation of proteins by high-performance liquid chromatographic methods. *J. Chromatogr.* 418:3–26. Discusses general parameters of protein purification as well as the use of HPLC.

Sherman, L. S., and Goodrich, J. A. (1985). The historical development of sodium dodecyl sulphate-polyacrylamide gel electrophoresis. *Chem. Soc. Rev.* 14:225–236.

Stellwagen, E. (1990). Gel filtration. *Methods Enzymol.* 182:317–328.

Amino Acid Analysis

Ozols, J. (1990). Amino acid analysis. *Methods Enzymol.* 182:587–601.

Amino Acid Sequencing

Doolittle, R. F. (1989). Similar amino acid sequences revisited. *Trends Biochem. Sci.* 14:244–245. A description of Darwin's notion of "descent with modification" in terms of similarities of amino acid sequences.

Han, K. -K., Belaiche, D., Moreau, O., and Briand, G. (1985). Current developments in stepwise Edman degradation of peptides and proteins. *Int. J. Biochem.* 17:429–445.

Hunkapiller, M. W., Strickler, J. E., and Wilson, K. J. (1984). Contemporary methodology for protein structure determination. *Science* 226:304–311.

Sanger, F. (1988). Sequences, sequences, and sequences. *Annu. Rev. Biochem.* 57:1–28. The story of the sequencing of protein, RNA, and DNA.

Proteins: Three-Dimensional Structure and Function

We saw in the previous chapter that a protein can be described as a chain of amino acids joined by peptide bonds in a specific sequence. However, polypeptide chains are not simply linear but are also folded into compact shapes that contain coils, zigzags, turns, and loops. Over the last 50 years, the three-dimensional shapes, or conformations, of more than a thousand proteins have been elucidated. A **conformation** is a spatial arrangement of atoms that depends on the rotation of a bond or bonds. The *conformation* of a molecule, such as a protein, can change without breaking covalent bonds, whereas the various *configurations* of a molecule can be changed only by breaking and re-forming covalent bonds. (Recall that the L and D forms of amino acids represent different configurations.) Since each amino acid residue has a number of possible conformations and since there are many residues in a protein, each protein has an astronomical number of potential conformations. Nevertheless, under physiological conditions, each protein folds into a single stable shape known as its native conformation. A number of factors constrain rotation around the covalent bonds in a polypeptide chain in its native conformation. These include the presence of hydrogen bonds and other weak interactions between amino acid residues. The biological function of a protein depends completely on its native conformation.

A protein may be a single polypeptide chain or it may be composed of several polypeptide chains bound to each other by weak interactions. As a general rule, each polypeptide chain is encoded by a single gene, although there are some interesting exceptions to this rule. The size of genes and the polypeptides they encode can vary by more than an order of magnitude. Some polypeptides contain only 100 amino acid residues with a relative molecular mass of about 11 000 ($M_r = 11\,000$). (The average relative molecular mass of an amino acid residue of a protein is 110.) On the other hand, some very large polypeptide chains contain more than 2000 amino acid residues ($M_r = 222\,000$).

Top: Bighorn sheep. The skin, wool, and horns are composed largely of fibrous proteins.

81

▶ *Escherichia coli* proteins. Proteins from *E. coli* cells are separated by two-dimensional gel electrophoresis. In the first dimension, the proteins are separated by a pH gradient where each protein migrates to its isoelectric point. The second dimension separates proteins by size on an SDS-poly-acrylamide gel. Each spot corresponds to a single polypeptide. There are about 4000 different proteins in *E. coli*, but some of them are present in very small quantities and can't be seen on this 2-D gel. This figure is from the Swiss-2D PAGE database. You can visit this site and click on any one of the spots to find out more about a particular protein.

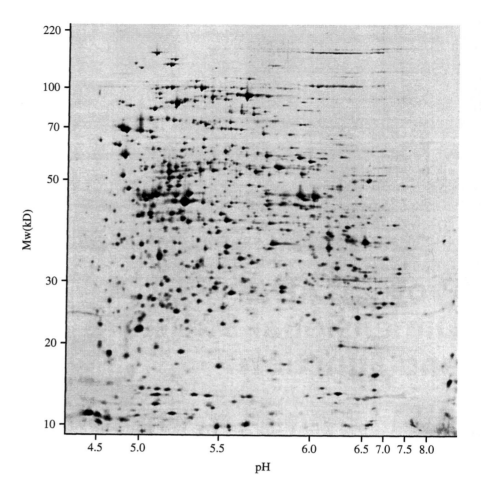

In some species, the size and sequence of every polypeptide can be determined from the sequence of the genome. There are about 4000 different polypeptides in the bacterium *Escherichia coli* with an average size of about 300 amino acid residues ($M_r = 33\,000$). The fruit fly *Drosophila melanogaster* contains about 16 000 different polypeptides with an average size about the same as that in bacteria. Humans and other mammals have about 40 000 different polypeptides. The study of large sets of proteins, such as the entire complement of proteins produced by a cell, is part of an emerging field called **proteomics**.

Proteins come in a variety of shapes. Many are water-soluble, compact, roughly spherical macromolecules whose polypeptide chains are tightly folded. These globular proteins characteristically have a hydrophobic interior and a hydrophilic surface. They possess indentations or clefts that specifically recognize and transiently bind other compounds. By selectively binding other molecules, these proteins serve as dynamic agents of biological action. Many globular proteins are enzymes, which are the biochemical catalysts of cells. About 31% of the polypeptides in *E. coli* are classical metabolic enzymes, such as those described in the next few chapters. Other types of globular proteins include various factors, carrier proteins, and regulatory proteins; 12% of the known proteins in *E. coli* fall into these categories.

Polypeptides can also be components of large subcellular or extracellular structures such as ribosomes, flagella and cilia, muscle, and chromatin. Fibrous proteins are a particular class of structural proteins that provide mechanical support to cells or organisms. Fibrous proteins are typically assembled into large cables or threads. Examples of fibrous proteins are α-keratin, the major component of hair and nails, and collagen, the major protein component of tendons, skin, bones, and teeth. Other examples of structural proteins include those that make up the protein components of viruses, bacteriophages, spores, and pollen.

Many proteins are either integral components of membranes or membrane-associated proteins. This category accounts for at least 16% of the known polypeptides in *E. coli* and a much higher percentage in eukaryotic cells.

This chapter describes the molecular architecture of proteins. We will explore the conformation of the peptide bond and will see that two simple shapes, the α helix and the β sheet, are common structural elements of all classes of proteins. We will describe higher levels of protein structure and discuss protein folding and stabilization. Finally, we will examine how protein structure is related to function, using as examples collagen, myoglobin and hemoglobin, and antibodies. Above all, we will learn that proteins have properties beyond those of free amino acids. Chapters 5 and 6 describe the role of proteins as enzymes. The structures of membrane proteins are examined in more detail in Chapter 9 and proteins that bind nucleic acids are covered in Chapters 20 to 23.

4.1 There Are Four Levels of Protein Structure

Individual protein molecules can be described by up to four levels of structure (Figure 4.1). As noted in Chapter 3, primary structure describes the linear sequence of amino acid residues in a protein. Recall that amino acid sequences are always written from the amino terminus (N-terminus) to the carboxyl terminus (C-terminus). The three-dimensional structure of a protein is described by three additional levels: secondary structure, tertiary structure, and quaternary structure. The forces responsible for maintaining, or stabilizing, these three levels are primarily noncovalent. **Secondary structure** refers to regularities in local conformations, maintained by hydrogen bonds between amide hydrogens and carbonyl oxygens of the peptide backbone. The major secondary structures are α helices and β strands (including β sheets). Cartoons showing the structures of folded proteins usually represent α-helical regions by helices, and β strands by broad arrows pointing in the N-terminal to C-terminal direction. **Tertiary structure** describes the completely

(a) Primary structure

– Ala – Glu – Val – Thr – Asp – Pro – Gly –

(b) Secondary structure

α helix

β sheet

◀ Figure 4.1
Levels of protein structure. **(a)** The linear sequence of amino acid residues defines the primary structure. **(b)** Secondary structure consists of regions of regularly repeating conformations of the peptide chain, such as α helices and β sheets. **(c)** Tertiary structure describes the shape of the fully folded polypeptide chain. The example shown has two domains. **(d)** Quaternary structure refers to the arrangement of two or more polypeptide chains into a multisubunit molecule.

(c) Tertiary structure

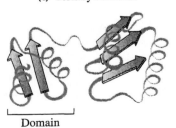

Domain

(d) Quaternary structure

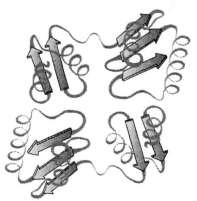

Chemistry for Biologists

▲ Dorothy Crowfoot Hodgkin (1910–1994). Hodgkin received the Nobel Prize in 1964 for determining the structure of vitamin B_{12}. The structure of insulin was published in 1969.

folded and compacted polypeptide chain. Many folded polypeptides consist of several distinct globular units linked by a short stretch of amino acid residues as shown in Figure 4.1c. Such units are called **domains**. Tertiary structures are stabilized by the interactions of amino acid side chains in nonneighboring regions of the polypeptide chain. The formation of tertiary structure brings distant portions of the primary and secondary structures close together. Some proteins possess **quaternary structure**, which involves the association of two or more polypeptide chains into a multisubunit, or oligomeric, protein. The polypeptide chains of an oligomeric protein may be identical or different.

4.2 Methods for Determining Protein Structure

As we saw in Chapter 3, the amino acid sequence of polypeptides (i.e., primary structure) can be determined directly by chemical methods such as Edman degradation or indirectly from the sequence of the gene. The usual technique for determining the three-dimensional conformation of a protein is X-ray crystallography. In this technique, a beam of collimated, or parallel, X rays is aimed at a crystal of protein molecules. Electrons in the crystal diffract the X rays, which are then recorded on film or by an electronic detector (Figure 4.2). Mathematical analysis of the diffraction pattern produces an image of the electron clouds surrounding atoms in the crystal. This electron density map reveals the overall shape of the molecule and the positions of each of the atoms in three-dimensional space. By combining these data with the principles of chemical bonding, it is possible to deduce the location of all the bonds in a molecule, and hence its overall structure. The technique of X-ray crystallography has developed to the point where it is possible to determine the structure of a protein without precise knowledge of the amino acid sequence. In practice, knowledge of the primary structure makes fitting of the electron density map much easier at the stage where chemical bonds between atoms are determined.

Initially, X-ray crystallography was used to study the simple repeating units of fibrous proteins and the structures of small biological molecules. Dorothy Crowfoot Hodgkin was one of the early pioneers in the application of X-ray crystallography to biological molecules. She solved the structure of penicillin in 1947 and devel-

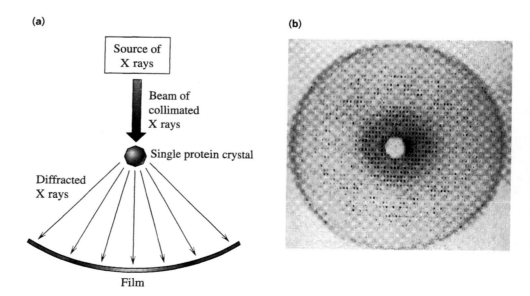

Figure 4.2 ▲
X-ray crystallography. **(a)** Diagram of X rays diffracted by a protein crystal. **(b)** X-ray diffraction pattern of a crystal of adult human deoxyhemoglobin. The location and intensity of the spots are used to determine the three-dimensional structure of the protein.

Visit the website for information on how to view three-dimensional structures and retrieve data files.

(a)

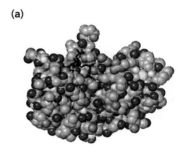

(b)

(c)

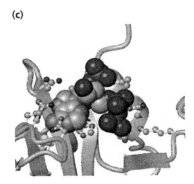

oped many of the techniques used in the study of large proteins. Hodgkin received the Nobel Prize in 1964 for determining the structure of vitamin B_{12}, and she later published the structure of insulin. The chief impediment to determining the three-dimensional structure of an entire protein, containing thousands of atoms, was the difficulty of calculating atomic positions from the positions and intensities of diffracted X-ray beams. Not surprisingly, the development of X-ray crystallography of macromolecules closely followed the development of computers. By 1962 John C. Kendrew and Max Perutz had elucidated the structures of the proteins myoglobin and hemoglobin, respectively. Their results provided the first insights into the nature of the tertiary structures of proteins and earned them a Nobel Prize in 1962. Since then, the structures of many proteins have been revealed by X-ray crystallography. In recent years, there have been significant advances in the technology due to the availability of high-speed computers and improvements in producing focused beams of X rays. The determination of protein structures is now limited mainly by the difficulty of preparing crystals of a quality suitable for X-ray diffraction.

A protein crystal contains a large number of water molecules, and it is often possible to diffuse small ligands such as substrate or inhibitor molecules into the crystal. In many cases, the proteins within the crystal retain their ability to bind these ligands, and they often exhibit catalytic activity. The catalytic activity of enzymes in the crystalline state demonstrates that the proteins crystallize in their in vivo native conformations.

Once the three-dimensional coordinates of the atoms of a macromolecule have been determined, they are deposited in a data bank where they are available to other scientists. Biochemists were among the early pioneers in exploiting the internet to share data with researchers around the world. The first public domain databases of biomolecular structures and sequences were established in the late 1970s. Many of the images in this text were created using data files from the Protein Data Bank (PDB). We will list the PDB filename, or accession number, for every protein structure shown in this text so that you can view the three-dimensional structure on your own computer.

There are many ways of showing the three-dimensional structure of proteins. Space-filling models (Figure 4.3a) depict each atom as a solid sphere. Such images reveal the dense, closely packed nature of folded polypeptide chains. Space-filling models of structures are used to illustrate the overall shape of a protein and the surface exposed to aqueous solvent. One can easily appreciate that the interior of folded proteins is nearly impenetrable, even by small molecules such as water.

Figure 4.3 ▲
Bovine (*Bos taurus*) ribonuclease A. Ribonuclease A is a secreted enzyme that hydrolyzes RNA during digestion. **(a)** Space-filling model showing a bound substrate analog in black. **(b)** Cartoon ribbon model of the polypeptide chain showing secondary structure. **(c)** View of the substrate-binding site. The substrate analog (5′-diphospho-adenosine-3′-phosphate) is depicted as a space-filling model and the side chains of amino acid residues are shown as ball-and-stick models. [PDB 1AFK].

◄ Figure 4.4
Bovine ribonuclease A NMR structure. The figure combines a set of very similar structures that satisfy the data on atomic interactions. Only the backbone of the polypeptide chain is shown. Compare this structure with that in Figure 4.3b. Note the presence of disulfide bridges (yellow), which are not shown in the images derived from the X-ray crystal structure. [PDB 2AAS].

The structure of a protein can also be depicted as a simplified cartoon that emphasizes the backbone of the polypeptide chain (Figure 4.3b). In these models, the amino acid side chains have been eliminated, making it easier to see how the polypeptide folds into a three-dimensional structure. Such models have the advantage of allowing us to see into the interior of the protein, and they also reveal elements of secondary structure such as α helices and β strands. By comparing the structures of different proteins it is possible to recognize common folds and patterns that can't be seen in space-filling models.

The most detailed models are those that emphasize the structures of the amino acid side chains and the various covalent bonds and weak interactions between atoms (Figure 4.3c). Such detailed models are especially important in understanding how a substrate binds in the active site of an enzyme. In Figure 4.3c the backbone is shown in the same orientation as in Figure 4.3b.

Another technique for analyzing the macromolecular structure of proteins is nuclear magnetic resonance (NMR) spectroscopy. This method permits the study of proteins in solution and therefore does not require the painstaking preparation of crystals. In NMR spectroscopy, a sample of protein is placed in a magnetic field. Certain atomic nuclei absorb electromagnetic radiation as the applied magnetic field is varied. Because absorbance is influenced by neighboring atoms, interactions between atoms that are close together can be recorded. By combining these results with the amino acid sequence and known structural constraints, it is possible to calculate a number of structures that satisfy the observed interactions.

Figure 4.4 depicts the complete set of structures for bovine ribonuclease A—the same protein whose X-ray crystal structure is shown in Figure 4.3. Note that the possible structures are very similar and the overall shape of the molecule is easily seen. In some cases, the set of NMR structures may represent fluctuations, or "breathing," of the protein in solution. The similarity of the NMR and X-ray crystal structures indicates that the protein structures found in crystals accurately represent the structure of the protein in solution. In general, the NMR spectra for small proteins such as ribonuclease A can be easily solved, but the spectrum of a large molecule can be extremely complex. For this reason, it is very difficult to determine the structure of larger proteins, but the technique is very powerful for smaller proteins.

4.3 The Conformation of the Peptide Group

Our detailed study of protein structure begins with the structure of the peptide bonds that link amino acids in a polypeptide chain. The two atoms involved in the peptide bond along with their four substituents (the carbonyl oxygen atom, the amide hydrogen atom, and the two adjacent α-carbon atoms) constitute the peptide group. X-ray crystallographic analyses of small peptides reveal that the bond between the carbonyl carbon and the nitrogen is shorter than typical C—N single bonds but longer than typical C=N double bonds. In addition, the bond between the carbonyl carbon and the oxygen is slightly longer than typical C=O double bonds. These measurements reveal that peptide bonds have some double-bond properties and can best be represented as a resonance hybrid (Figure 4.5).

Note that the peptide group is polar. The carbonyl oxygen has a partial negative charge and can serve as a hydrogen acceptor in hydrogen bonds. The nitrogen has a partial positive charge, and the —NH group can serve as a hydrogen donor in hydrogen bonds. Electron delocalization and the partial double-bond character of the peptide bond prevent free rotation around the bond. As a result, the atoms of the peptide group lie in the same plane (Figure 4.6). However, rotation is possible around each N—C$_\alpha$ bond and each C$_\alpha$—C bond in the repeating N—C$_\alpha$—C backbone of proteins. As we will see, restrictions on free rotation around these two additional bonds ultimately determine the three-dimensional conformation of a protein.

Because of the double-bond nature of the peptide bond, the conformation of the peptide group is restricted to one of two possible conformations, either *trans* or *cis* (Figure 4.7). In the *trans* conformation, the two α-carbons of adjacent amino acid residues are on opposite sides of the peptide bond and at opposite corners of the rectangle formed by the planar peptide group. In the *cis* conformation, the two α-carbons are on the same side of the peptide bond and are closer together. The *cis* and *trans* conformations arise during protein synthesis when the peptide bond is formed by joining amino acids to the growing polypeptide chain. The two conformations cannot be interconverted by rotation around the peptide bond once it has formed. The *cis* conformation is less favorable than the extended *trans* conformation because of steric interference between the side chains attached to the two α-carbon atoms. Consequently, nearly all peptide groups in proteins are in the *trans* conformation. Rare exceptions occur, usually at bonds involving the amide nitrogen of proline, for which the *cis* conformation creates only slightly more steric interference than the *trans* conformation.

Specific enzymes, called peptidyl prolyl *cis/trans* isomerases, can catalyze the interconversion of *cis* and *trans* conformations at proline residues by transiently destabilizing the resonance hybrid structure of the peptide bond and allowing rotation. Human peptidyl prolyl *cis/trans* isomerase is the target of the immunosuppressive drug cyclosporin A, which is used with transplant patients to prevent rejection of the donated organ. (It's now known that there is no connection between the *cis/trans* isomerase activity of the enzyme and immunosuppression. Instead, the enzyme acts as a carrier of cyclosporin A and interacts with other proteins that are inhibited by the drug.) The structure of human peptidyl prolyl *cis/trans* isomerase is shown in Figure 4.24e.

Figure 4.5 ▲
Resonance structure of the peptide bond. **(a)** In this resonance form, the peptide bond is shown as a single C—N bond. **(b)** In this resonance form, the peptide bond is shown as a double bond. **(c)** The actual structure is best represented as a hybrid of the two resonance forms in which electrons are delocalized over the carbonyl oxygen, the carbonyl carbon, and the amide nitrogen. Rotation around the C—N bond is restricted due to the double-bond nature of the resonance hybrid form.

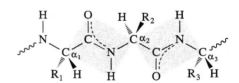

Figure 4.6 ▲
Planar peptide groups in a polypeptide chain. A peptide group consists of the N—H and C=O groups involved in formation of the peptide bond, as well as the α-carbons on each side of the peptide bond. Two peptide groups are highlighted in this diagram.

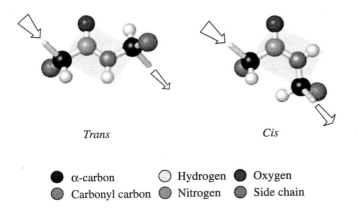

Trans   *Cis*

● α-carbon	○ Hydrogen	● Oxygen
● Carbonyl carbon	● Nitrogen	● Side chain

◀ **Figure 4.7**
Trans and *cis* conformations of a peptide group. Nearly all peptide groups in proteins are in the *trans* conformation, which minimizes steric interference between adjacent side chains. The arrows indicate the direction from the N– to the C-terminus.

Chemistry for Biologists

Figure 4.8 ▶
Rotation around the N—C$_\alpha$ and C$_\alpha$—C bonds that link peptide groups in a polypeptide chain. **(a)** Peptide groups in an extended conformation. **(b)** Peptide groups in an unstable conformation caused by steric interference between carbonyl oxygens of adjacent residues. The van der Waals radii of the carbonyl oxygen atoms are shown by the dashed lines. The rotation angle around the N—C$_\alpha$ bond is called φ (phi), and that around the C$_\alpha$—C bond is called ψ (psi). The substituents of the outer α-carbons have been omitted for clarity.

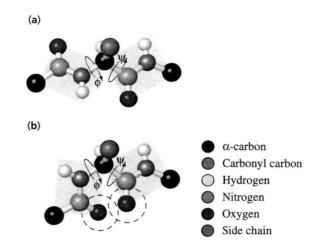

(a)

(b)

- ● α-carbon
- ● Carbonyl carbon
- ○ Hydrogen
- ● Nitrogen
- ● Oxygen
- ● Side chain

Note that even though the atoms of the peptide group lie in a plane, rotation is possible about the N—C$_\alpha$ and C$_\alpha$—C bonds in the repeating N—C$_\alpha$—C backbone. However, this rotation is also restricted by steric interference between main-chain and side-chain atoms of adjacent residues (Figure 4.8). The rotation angle around the N—C$_\alpha$ bond of a peptide group is designated φ (phi), and that around the C$_\alpha$—C bond is designated ψ (psi). In the case of proline, rotation around the N—C$_\alpha$ bond is constrained by its inclusion in the pyrrolidine ring of the side chain.

Because rotation around peptide bonds is hindered by their double-bond character, most of the conformation of the backbone of a polypeptide can be described by φ and ψ. Each of these angles is defined by the relative positions of four atoms of the backbone. Clockwise angles are positive, and counterclockwise angles are negative, with each having a 180° sweep. Thus, each of the rotation angles can range from −180° to +180°.

The biophysicist G. N. Ramachandran and his colleagues constructed space-filling models of peptides and made calculations to determine which values of φ and ψ are sterically permitted in a polypeptide chain. Permissible angles are shown as shaded regions in Ramachandran plots of φ versus ψ. Figure 4.9a shows the results of theoretical calculations—the dark, shaded regions represent permissible angles for most residues, and the lighter areas cover the φ and ψ values for smaller amino acid residues where the R groups don't restrict rotation. Blank areas on a Ramachandran plot are nonpermissible areas, due largely to steric hindrance. The conformations of several types of ideal secondary structure fall within the shaded areas, as expected.

Another version of a Ramachandran plot is shown in Figure 4.9b. This plot is based on the observed φ and ψ angles of hundreds of proteins whose structure is known. The enclosed inner regions represent angles that are found very frequently, and the outer enclosed regions represent angles that are less frequent. Typical observed angles for α helices, β sheets, and other structures in a protein are plotted. The most important difference between the theoretical and observed Ramachandran plots is in the region around 0° ψ, −90° φ. This region should not be permitted according to the modeling studies, but there are many examples of residues with these angles. It turns out that steric clashes are prevented in these regions by allowing minor distortions of the peptide bond. The peptide group is not exactly planar—a little bit of wiggle is permitted!

Some bulky amino acid residues have smaller permitted areas. Proline is restricted to a φ value of about −60° to −77° because its N—C$_\alpha$ bond is constrained by inclusion in the pyrrolidine ring of the side chain. In contrast, glycine is exempt from many steric restrictions because it lacks a β-carbon. Thus, glycine residues have greater conformational freedom than other residues and have φ and ψ values that often fall outside the shaded regions of the Ramachandran plot.

(a)

(b)

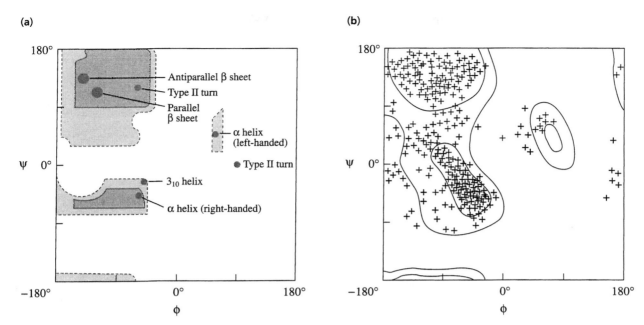

Figure 4.9 ▲
Ramachandran plot. **(a)** Solid lines indicate the range of permissible ϕ and ψ values based on molecular models. Dashed lines give the outer limits for an alanine residue. Large blue dots correspond to values of ϕ and ψ that produce recognizable conformations such as the α helix and β sheets. The positions shown for the type II turn are for the second and third residues. The white portions of the plot correspond to values of ϕ and ψ that were predicted to occur rarely. **(b)** Observed ϕ and ψ values in known structures. Crosses indicate values for typical residues in a single protein. Residues in an α helix are shown in red, β-strand residues are blue, and others are green.

4.4 The α Helix

The α-helical conformation was proposed in 1950 by Linus Pauling and Robert Corey. They considered the dimensions of peptide groups, possible steric constraints, and opportunities for stabilization by formation of hydrogen bonds. Their model accounted for the major repeat observed in the structure of the fibrous protein α-keratin. This repeat of 0.50 to 0.55 nm turned out to be the pitch (the axial distance per turn) of the α helix. Max Perutz added additional support for the structure when he observed a secondary repeating unit of 0.15 nm in the X-ray diffraction pattern of α-keratin. The 0.15 nm repeat corresponds to the rise of the α helix (the distance each residue advances the helix along its axis). Perutz also showed that the α helix was present in hemoglobin, confirming that this conformation was present in more complex globular proteins.

In theory, an α helix can be either a right- or a left-handed screw. The α helices found in proteins are almost always right-handed, as shown in Figure 4.10. In an ideal α helix, the pitch is 0.54 nm, the rise is 0.15 nm, and the number of amino acid residues required for one complete turn is 3.6 (i.e., approximately 3 2/3 residues: one carbonyl group, three N—C$_\alpha$—C units, and one nitrogen). Although α helices may be slightly distorted in proteins, they generally have 3.5 to 3.7 residues per turn.

Within an α helix, each carbonyl oxygen (residue *n*) of the polypeptide backbone is hydrogen-bonded to the backbone amide hydrogen of the fourth residue further toward the C-terminus (residue *n* + 4). (The three amino groups at one end of the helix and the three carbonyl groups at the other end lack hydrogen-bonding partners within the helix.) Each hydrogen bond closes a loop containing 13 atoms—the carbonyl oxygen, 11 backbone atoms, and the amide hydrogen. This α helix can also be called a 3.6$_{13}$ helix, based on its pitch and hydrogen-bonded loop size. The hydrogen bonds that stabilize the helix are nearly parallel to the long axis of the helix.

▲ Linus Pauling (1901–1994), winner of the Nobel Prize in chemistry in 1954.

85

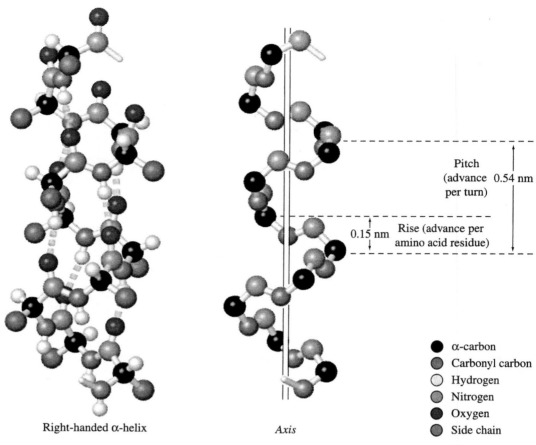

Right-handed α-helix   Axis

● α-carbon
◐ Carbonyl carbon
○ Hydrogen
◑ Nitrogen
● Oxygen
◐ Side chain

Figure 4.10 ▲

α Helix. A region of α-helical secondary structure is shown with the N-terminus at the bottom and the C-terminus at the top of the figure. Each carbonyl oxygen forms a hydrogen bond with the amide hydrogen of the fourth residue further toward the C-terminus of the polypeptide chain. The hydrogen bonds are approximately parallel to the long axis of the helix. Note that all the carbonyl groups point toward the C-terminus. In an ideal α helix, equivalent positions recur every 0.54 nm (the pitch of the helix), each amino acid residue advances the helix by 0.15 nm along the long axis of the helix (the rise), and there are 3.6 amino acid residues per turn. The arrows at the ends of the helix indicate the direction from the N- to the C-terminus. In a right-handed helix, the backbone turns in a clockwise direction when viewed along the axis from its N-terminus. If you imagine that the right-handed helix is a spiral staircase, you will be turning to the right as you walk down the staircase.

Pitch (advance 0.54 nm per turn)

0.15 nm   Rise (advance per amino acid residue)

The ϕ and ψ angles of each residue in an α helix are similar. They cluster around a stable region of the Ramachandran plot centered at a ϕ value of $-57°$ and a ψ value of $-47°$ (Figure 4.9). The similarity of these values is what gives the α helix a regular, repeating structure. The intramolecular hydrogen bonds between residues n and $n + 4$ tend to "lock in" rotation around the N—C_α and C_α—C bonds, restricting the ϕ and ψ angles to a relatively narrow range.

A single intrahelical hydrogen bond would not provide appreciable structural stability, but the cumulative effect of many hydrogen bonds within an α helix stabilizes this conformation. Hydrogen bonds between amino acid residues are especially stable in the hydrophobic interior of a protein, where water molecules do not enter and therefore cannot compete for hydrogen bonding. All the carbonyl groups point toward the C-terminus. Since each peptide group is polar and all the hydrogen bonds point in the same direction, the entire helix is a dipole with a positive N-terminus and a negative C-terminus.

The side chains of the amino acids in an α helix point outward from the cylinder of the helix (Figure 4.11). The stability of an α helix is affected by the identity of the side chains. Some amino acid residues are found in α-helical conformations more often than others. For example, alanine has a small, uncharged side chain and fits well into the α-helical conformation. Alanine residues are prevalent in the α helices of all classes of proteins. In contrast, tyrosine and asparagine with their bulky side chains are less common in α helices. Glycine, whose side chain is a single hydrogen atom, destabilizes α-helical structures since rotation around its α-carbon is so unconstrained. For this reason, many α helices begin or end with glycine residues. Proline is the least common residue in an α helix because its rigid cyclic side chain disrupts the right-handed helical conformation by occupying space that a neighboring residue of the helix would otherwise occupy. In addition, because it lacks a hy-

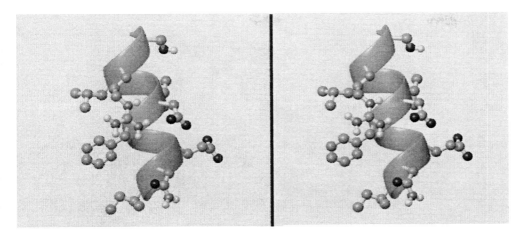

Figure 4.11 ▲
Stereo view of a right-handed α helix. The blue ribbon indicates the shape of the polypeptide backbone. All the side chains, shown as ball-and-stick models, project outward from the helix axis. This example is from residues Ile-355 (bottom) to Gly-365 (top) of horse liver alcohol dehydrogenase. Some hydrogen atoms are not shown. [PDB 1ADF].

drogen atom on its amide nitrogen, proline cannot fully participate in intrahelical hydrogen bonding. For these reasons, proline residues are found more often at the ends of α helices than in the interior.

Proteins vary in their α-helical content. In some, most of the residues are in α helices. Other proteins contain very little α-helical structure. The average content of α helix in the proteins that have been examined is 26%. The length of a helix in a protein can range from about 4 or 5 residues to more than 40, but the average is about 12.

Many α helices have hydrophilic amino acids on one face of the helix cylinder and hydrophobic amino acids on the opposite face. The amphipathic nature of the helix is easy to see when the amino acid sequence is drawn as a spiral, called a helical wheel. For example, the α helix shown in Figure 4.11 can be drawn as a helical wheel representing the helix viewed along its axis. Because there are 3.6 residues per turn of the helix, the residues are plotted every 100° along the spiral (Figure 4.12). Note that the helix is a right-handed screw and it is terminated by a glycine residue at the C-terminal end.

Amphipathic helices are often located on the surface of a protein, with the hydrophilic side chains facing outward (toward the aqueous solvent) and the hydrophobic side chains facing inward (toward the hydrophobic interior). For example, the helix shown in Figures 4.11 and 4.12 is on the surface of the water-soluble liver enzyme alcohol

◀ **Figure 4.12**
Helix in horse liver alcohol dehydrogenase. Highly hydrophobic residues are blue, less hydrophobic residues are green, and highly hydrophilic residues are red. **(a)** Sequence of amino acids. **(b)** Helical wheel diagram.

(a)

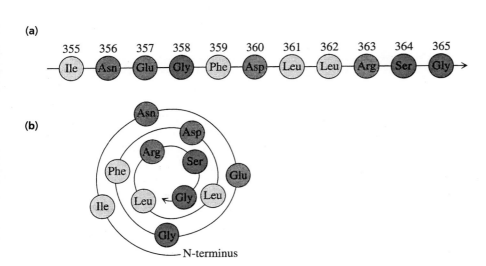

(b)

Figure 4.13 ▶
Horse liver alcohol dehydrogenase. The amphipathic α helix is highlighted. The side chains of highly hydrophobic residues are shown in blue, less hydrophobic residues are green, and charged residues are shown in red. Note that the side chains of the hydrophobic residues are directed toward the interior of the protein and that the side chains of charged residues are exposed to the surface. [PDB 1ADF].

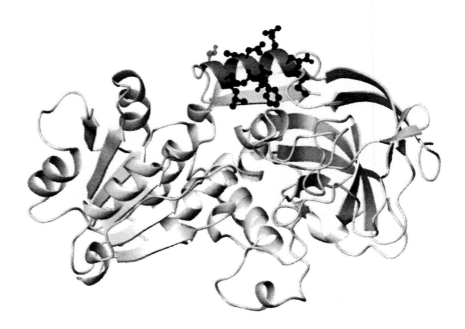

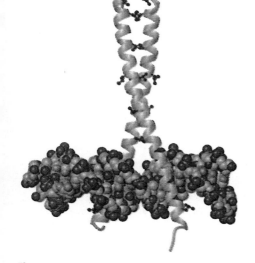

Figure 4.14 ▲
Leucine zipper region of yeast (*Saccharomyces cerevisiae*) GCN4 protein bound to DNA. GCN4 is a transcription regulatory protein that binds to specific DNA sequences. The DNA-binding region consists of two amphipathic α helices, one from each of the two subunits of the protein. The side chains of leucine residues are shown in a darker blue than the ribbon. Only the leucine zipper region of the protein is shown in the figure. [PDB 1YSA].

dehydrogenase, with the side chains of the first, fifth, and eighth residues (isoleucine, phenylalanine, and leucine, respectively) buried in the protein interior (Figure 4.13).

There are many examples of two amphipathic α helices that interact to produce an extended coiled-coil structure where the two α helices wrap around each other with their hydrophobic faces in contact and their hydrophilic faces exposed to solvent. A common structure in DNA-binding proteins is called a leucine zipper (Figure 4.14). The name refers to the fact that two α helices are "zippered" together by the hydrophobic interactions of leucine residues (and other hydrophobic residues) on one side of an amphipathic helix. In leucine zipper structures, the α helices have only a slight tendency to coil, and the ends of the helices form the DNA-binding region of the protein.

Some proteins contain a few short regions of a 3_{10} helix. Like the α helix, the 3_{10} helix is right-handed. The carbonyl oxygen of a 3_{10} helix forms a hydrogen bond with the amide hydrogen of residue $n + 3$ (as opposed to residue $n + 4$ in an α helix), so the 3_{10} helix has a tighter hydrogen-bonded ring structure than the α helix—10 atoms rather than 13—and has fewer residues per turn (3.0) and a longer pitch (0.60 nm). The 3_{10} helix is also slightly less stable than the α helix because of steric hindrances and the awkward geometry of its hydrogen bonds. When a 3_{10} helix occurs, it is usually only a few residues in length and often is the last turn at the C-terminal end of an α helix. Because of its different geometry, the ϕ and ψ angles of residues in a 3_{10} helix occupy a different region of the Ramachandran plot than the residues of an α helix.

4.5 β Strands and β Sheets

The other common secondary structure is called β structure, a class that includes β strands and β sheets. **β Strands** are portions of the polypeptide chain that are almost fully extended. Each residue in a β strand accounts for about 0.32 to 0.34 nm of the overall length, in contrast to the compact coil of an α helix where each residue corresponds to 0.15 nm of the overall length. When multiple β strands are arranged side-by-side, they form **β sheets**, a structure originally proposed by Pauling and Corey at the same time that they developed a theoretical model of the α helix.

Proteins rarely contain isolated β strands because the structure by itself is not significantly more stable than other conformations. However, β sheets are stabilized by hydrogen bonds between carbonyl oxygens and amide hydrogens on ad-

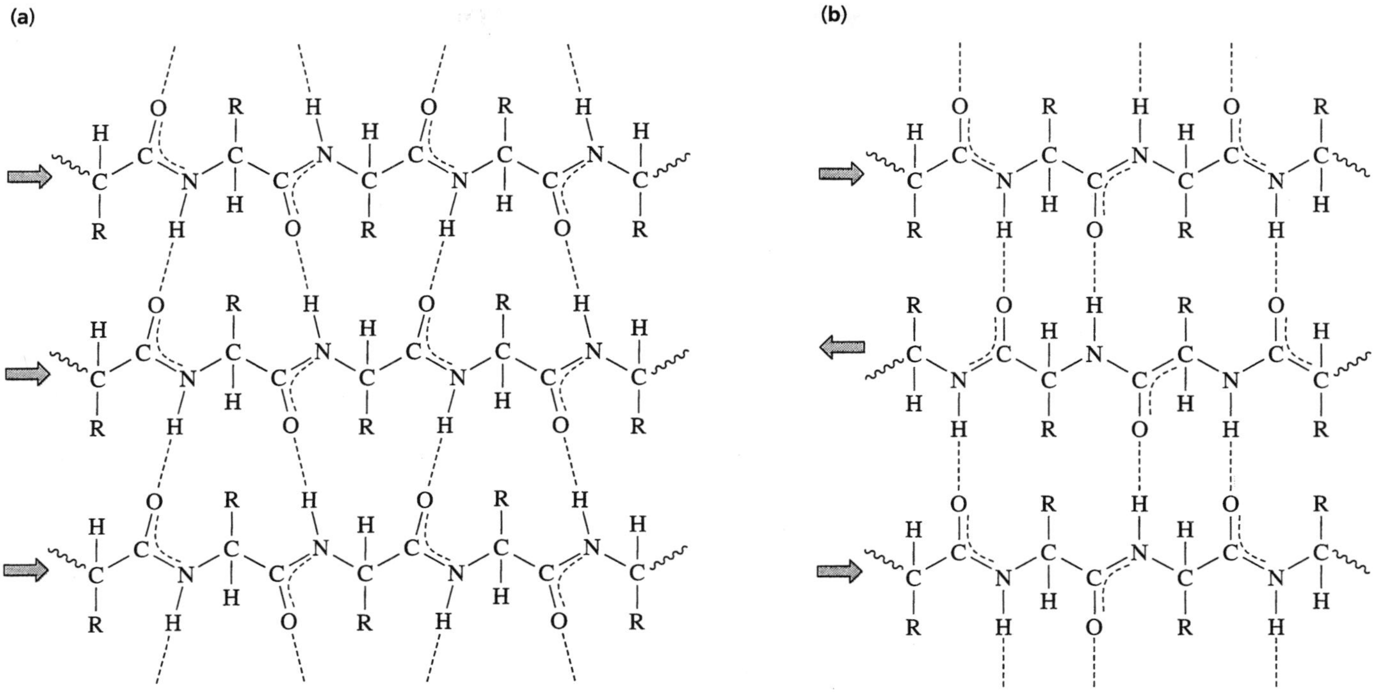

(a)

(b)

Figure 4.15 ▲
β Sheets. Arrows indicate the N- to C-terminal direction of the peptide chain. **(a)** Parallel β sheet. The hydrogen bonds are evenly spaced but slanted. **(b)** Antiparallel β sheet. The hydrogen bonds are essentially perpendicular to the β strands, and the space between hydrogen-bonded pairs is alternately wide and narrow.

jacent β strands. Thus, in proteins, the regions of β structure are almost always found in sheets. The hydrogen-bonded β strands can be on separate polypeptide chains or on different segments of the same chain. The β strands in a sheet can be either parallel (running in the same N- to C-terminal direction) (Figure 4.15a) or antiparallel (running in opposite N- to C-terminal directions) (Figure 4.15b). When the β strands are antiparallel, the hydrogen bonds are nearly perpendicular to the extended polypeptide chains. Note that in the antiparallel β sheet the carbonyl oxygen and the amide hydrogen atoms of one residue form hydrogen bonds with the amide hydrogen and carbonyl oxygen of a single residue in the other strand. In the parallel arrangement, the hydrogen bonds are not perpendicular to the extended chains, and each residue forms hydrogen bonds with the carbonyl and amide groups of two different residues on the adjacent strand.

Parallel sheets are less stable than antiparallel sheets, possibly because the hydrogen bonds are distorted in the parallel arrangement. The β sheet is sometimes called a **β pleated sheet** since the planar peptide groups meet each other at angles, like the folds of an accordion. As a result of the bond angles between peptide groups, the amino acid side chains point alternately above and below the plane of the sheet. A typical β sheet contains from 2 to as many as 15 individual β strands. Each strand has an average of six amino acid residues.

Some proteins are almost entirely β sheets but most proteins have a much lower β-strand content. As in α helices, the side of a β sheet facing the protein interior tends to be hydrophobic, and the side facing the solvent tends to be hydrophilic. Parallel β sheets are usually hydrophobic on both sides and are buried in the interior of a protein.

In most proteins, the β strands that make up β sheets are twisted and the sheet is distorted and buckled. The three-dimensional view of the β sheet of ribonuclease A (Figure 4.3) shows a more realistic view of β sheets than the idealized structures in Figure 4.15. A stereo view of two strands of a β sheet is shown in Figure 4.16. Note that the side chains of the amino acid residues in the front strand alternately project to the left and to the right of (i.e., above and below) the β strand as described above. Typically, β strands twist slightly in a right-hand direction; that is, they twist clockwise as you look along one strand.

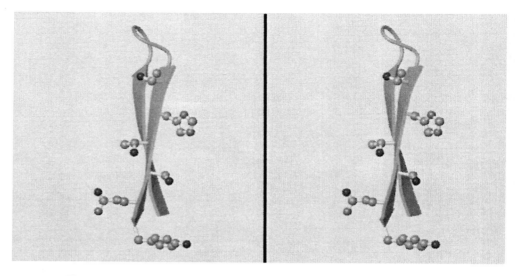

Figure 4.16 ▲
Stereo view of two strands of an antiparallel β sheet from influenza virus A neuraminidase. Only the side chains of the front β strand are shown. The side chains alternate from one side of the β strand to the other side. Both strands have a right-handed twist. [PDB 1BJI]

The φ and ψ angles of the bonds in a β strand are restricted to a broad range of values occupying a large, stable region in the upper left-hand corner of the Ramachandran plot. The typical angles for residues in parallel and antiparallel strands are not identical (see Figure 4.9). Because most β strands are twisted, the φ and ψ angles exhibit a broader range of values than those seen in the more regular α helix.

Although we usually think of β sheets as examples of secondary structure, this is not, strictly speaking, correct. In many cases, the individual β strands are located in different regions of the protein and only come together to form the β sheet when the protein adopts its final tertiary conformation. In some cases, the quaternary structure of a protein gives rise to a large β sheet.

In the previous section we noted that amphipathic α helices have hydrophobic side chains that project outward on one side of the helix. This is the side that interacts with the rest of the protein, creating a series of hydrophobic interactions that help stabilize the tertiary structure. In the case of β sheets, the side chains project alternately above and below the plane of the β strands. One surface may consist of hydrophobic side chains that allow the β sheet to lie on top of other hydrophobic residues in the interior of the protein.

An example of such hydrophobic interactions between two β sheets is seen in the structure of the coat protein of grass pollen grains (Figure 4.17a). This protein is the major allergen affecting people who are allergic to grass pollen. One surface of each β sheet contains hydrophobic side chains and the opposite surface has hydrophilic side chains. The two hydrophobic surfaces interact to form the hydrophobic core of the protein and the hydrophilic surfaces are exposed to solvent as shown in the stereo image (Figure 4.17b). This is an example of a β sandwich, one of several arrangements of secondary structural elements that are covered in more detail in the section on tertiary structure (Section 4.7).

4.6 Loops and Turns

In addition to regions where consecutive residues have a single repeating conformation, such as an α helix or a β strand, proteins contain stretches of nonrepetitive three-dimensional structure. Most of these regions of secondary structure can be characterized as loops or turns since they cause directional changes in the polypep-

(a)

(b)

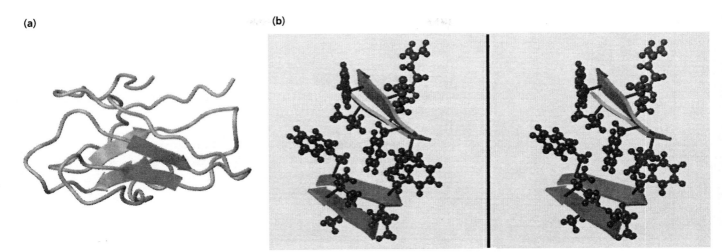

Figure 4.17 ▲

Structure of PHL P2 from Timothy grass (*Phleum pratense*) pollen. **(a)** The two short two-stranded antiparallel β sheets are highlighted in blue and purple to show their orientation within the protein. **(b)** Stereo view of the β-sandwich structure in a different orientation showing hydrophobic residues (blue) and polar residues (red). A number of hydrophobic interactions connect the two β sheets. [PDB 1BMW].

tide backbone. As in repetitive regions, the conformations of peptide groups in nonrepetitive regions are constrained. They have φ and ψ values that are usually well within the permitted regions of the Ramachandran plot and often close to the values of residues that form α helices or β strands.

Loops and turns connect α helices and β strands and allow the polypeptide chain to fold back on itself, producing the compact three-dimensional shape seen in the native structure. As much as one-third of the amino acid residues in a typical protein are found in such nonrepetitive structures. **Loops** often contain hydrophilic residues and are usually found on the surfaces of proteins, where they are exposed to solvent and form hydrogen bonds with water. As shown in many examples in this chapter, some loops can consist of many residues of extended nonrepetitive structure. About 10% of the residues can be found in such regions.

Loops containing only a few (up to five) residues are referred to as **turns**. The most common types of tight turns are called **reverse turns**, or **β turns**, because they usually connect different antiparallel β strands. (Recall that in order to create a β sheet, the polypeptide must fold so that two or more regions of β strand are adjacent to one another as shown in Figure 4.16.)

There are two common types of β turn, designated type I and type II. Both types of turn contain four amino acid residues and are stabilized by hydrogen bonding between the carbonyl oxygen of the first residue and the amide hydrogen of the fourth residue (Figure 4.18). Both type I and type II turns produce an abrupt (usually about 180°)

Figure 4.18 ▼

Reverse turns. **(a)** Type I β turn. The structure is stabilized by a hydrogen bond between the carbonyl oxygen of the first N-terminal residue (Phe) and the amide hydrogen of the fourth residue (Gly). Note the proline residue at position *n* + 1. **(b)** Type II β turn. This turn is also stabilized by a hydrogen bond between the carbonyl oxygen of the first N-terminal residue (Val) and the amide hydrogen of the fourth residue (Asn). Note the glycine residue at position *n* + 2. [PDB 1AHL (giant sea anemone neurotoxin)].

(a)   **(b)**

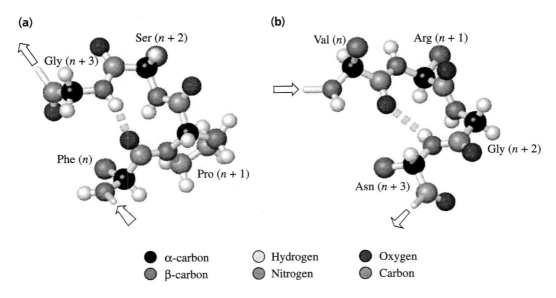

● α-carbon	○ Hydrogen	● Oxygen
● β-carbon	○ Nitrogen	○ Carbon

change in the direction of the polypeptide chain. In type II turns, the third residue is glycine about 60% of the time; in both types of turns, proline is often the second residue.

Many other types of turn are found in proteins. They all have internal hydrogen bonds that stabilize the structure, which is why they can be considered a form of secondary structure. In many proteins, turns make up a significant proportion of the structure. Some of the bonds in turn residues have ϕ and ψ angles that lie outside the "permitted" regions of a typical Ramachandran plot (Figure 4.9). This is especially true of residues in the third position of type II turns where there is an abrupt change in the direction of the backbone. Since this residue is often glycine, the bond angles can adopt a wider range of values without causing steric clashes between the side-chain atoms and the backbone atoms. Ramachandran plots usually show only the permitted regions for all residues except glycine, which is why type II turns appear to lie in a restricted area.

4.7 Tertiary Structure of Proteins

Tertiary structure results from the folding of a polypeptide (which may already possess some regions of α helix and β structure) into a closely packed three-dimensional structure. An important feature of tertiary structure is that amino acid residues that are far apart in the primary structure are brought together, permitting interactions among their side chains. Whereas secondary structure is stabilized by hydrogen bonding between amide hydrogens and carbonyl oxygens of the polypeptide backbone, tertiary structure is stabilized primarily by noncovalent interactions (mostly the hydrophobic effect) between the side chains of amino acid residues. Disulfide bridges, though covalent, are also elements of tertiary structure (they are not part of the primary structure since they form only after the protein folds).

A. Supersecondary Structures

Supersecondary structures, or **motifs**, are recognizable combinations of α helices, β strands, and loops that appear in a number of different proteins. Sometimes motifs are associated with a particular function, although structurally similar motifs may have different functions in different proteins. Some common motifs are shown in Figure 4.19.

One of the simplest motifs is the helix-loop-helix (Figure 4.19a). This structure occurs in a number of calcium-binding proteins. Glutamate and aspartate residues in the loop of these proteins form part of the calcium-binding site. In certain DNA-binding proteins a version of this supersecondary structure is called a helix-turn-helix since the residues that connect the helices form a reverse turn. In these proteins, the residues of the α helices bind DNA.

The coiled-coil motif consists of two amphipathic α helices that interact through their hydrophobic edges (Figure 4.19b), as in the leucine zipper example (Figure 4.14). Several α helices can associate to form a helix bundle (Figure 4.19c). In this case, the individual α helices have opposite orientations, whereas they are parallel in the coiled-coil motif.

The $\beta\alpha\beta$ unit consists of two parallel β strands linked to an intervening α helix by two loops (Figure 4.19d). The helix connects the C-terminal end of one β strand to the N-terminal end of the next and often runs parallel to the two strands. A hairpin consists of two adjacent antiparallel β strands connected by a β turn (Figure 4.19e). (A stereo view of a hairpin motif is shown in Figure 4.16.)

The β-meander motif (Figure 4.19f) is an antiparallel β sheet composed of sequential β strands connected by loops or turns. In the β meander the order of strands in the β sheet is the same as their order in the sequence of the polypeptide chain. The sheet may contain one or more hairpins but, more typically, the strands are joined by larger loops. The Greek key motif takes its name from a design found on classical Greek pottery. This is a β-sheet motif linking four antiparallel β strands such that strands 3 and 4 form the outer edges of the sheet and strands 1 and 2 are in the

(a) Helix-loop-helix   **(b)** Coiled coil   **(c)** Helix bundle

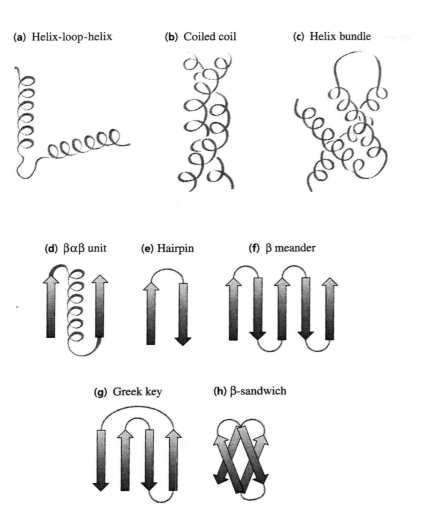

◀ **Figure 4.19**
Common motifs. In folded proteins α helices
and β strands are commonly connected by
loops and turns to form supersecondary
structures, shown here as two-dimensional
representations. Arrows indicate the N- to C-
terminal direction of the peptide chain.

(d) βαβ unit   **(e)** Hairpin   **(f)** β meander

(g) Greek key   **(h)** β-sandwich

middle of the sheet. The β-sandwich motif is formed when β strands or sheets stack on top of one another (Figure 4.19h). The figure shows an example of a β sandwich where the β strands are connected by short loops and turns, but β sandwiches can also be formed by the interaction of two β sheets in different regions of the polypeptide chain as seen in Figure 4.17.

B. Domains

Many proteins are composed of several discrete, independently folded, compact units called **domains**. Domains may consist of combinations of motifs. The size of a domain varies from about 25 to 30 amino acid residues to about 300, with an average of about 100. An example of a protein with multiple domains is shown in Figure 4.20. Note that each domain is a distinct compact unit consisting of various elements of secondary structure. Domains are usually connected by loops, but they are also bound to each other through weak interactions formed by the amino acid side chains on the surface of each domain. In the case of pyruvate kinase, the top domain in Figure 4.20 contains residues 116 to 219, the central domain contains residues 1 to 115 plus 220 to 388, and the bottom domain contains residues 389 to 530. In general, domains consist of a contiguous stretch of amino acid residues as in the top and bottom domains of pyruvate kinase, but in some cases a single domain may contain two or more different regions of the polypeptide chain as in the middle domain.

The evolutionary conservation of protein structure is one of the most important observations that have emerged from the study of proteins in the past few decades. This conservation is most easily seen in the case of single-domain homologous

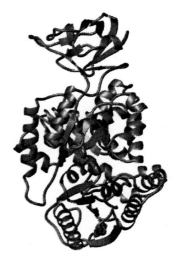

Figure 4.20 ▲
Pyruvate kinase from cat (*Felis domesticus*).
The main polypeptide chain of this common
enzyme folds into three distinct domains.
[PDB 1PKM].

Figure 4.21 ▶
Cytochrome c. **(a)** Tuna (*Thunnus alalunga*)
cytochrome c bound to heme [PDB 5CYT].
(b) Tuna cytochrome c polypeptide chain.
(c) Rice (*Oryza sativa*) cytochrome c [PDB
1CCR]. **(d)** Yeast (*Saccharomyces cerevisiae*)
cytochrome c [PDB 1YCC]. **(e)** Bacterial
(*Rhodopila globiformis*) cytochrome c
[PDB 1HRO].

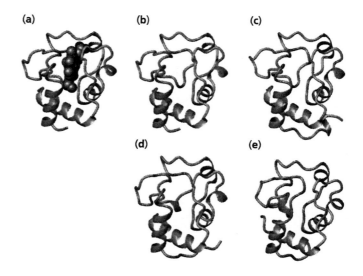

proteins from different species. For example, in Chapter 3 we examined the sequence
similarity of cytochrome *c* and showed that the similarities in primary structure could
be used to construct a phylogenetic tree that reveals the evolutionary relationships
of the proteins from different species (Section 3.10). The tertiary structures of cytochrome *c*'s are also highly conserved (Figure 4.21). Cytochrome *c* is an example
of a protein that contains a heme prosthetic group. The conservation of protein structure is a reflection of its interaction with heme and its conserved function as an electron transport protein in diverse species.

Some domain structures occur in many different proteins while others are unique.
In general, proteins can be grouped into families according to similarities in domain
structures and amino acid sequence. All of the members of a family have descended from a common ancestral protein. Some biochemists believe that there may be
only a few thousand families, suggesting that all modern proteins are descended
from only a few thousand proteins that were present in the most primitive organisms
that lived 3 billion years ago.

Lactate dehydrogenase and malate dehydrogenase are different enzymes that
belong to the same family of proteins. Their structures are very similar, as shown in
Figure 4.22. In spite of the obvious similarity in structure, the sequences of the proteins are only 23% identical. Nevertheless, this level of sequence similarity is significant enough to conclude that the two proteins are homologous. They descend
from a common ancestral gene that duplicated billions of years ago, before the last
common ancestor of all extant species of bacteria. Both lactate dehydrogenase and
malate dehydrogenase are present in the same species, which is why they are mem-

The enzymatic activities of lactate dehydrogenase and malate dehydrogenase
are compared in Box 7.1.

Figure 4.22 ▶
Structural similarity of lactate and malate
dehydrogenase. **(a)** *Bacillus stereother-
mophilus* lactate dehydrogenase [PDB
1LDN]. **(b)** *Escherichia coli* malate dehydrogenase [PDB 1EMD].

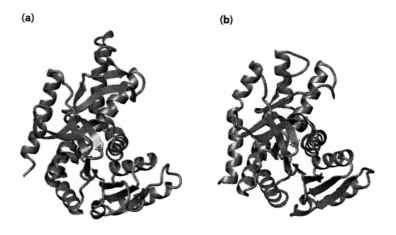

bers of a family of related proteins. (Families contain related proteins that are present in the same species. The cytochrome *c*'s shown in Figure 4.21 are homologous proteins, but, strictly speaking, they are not members of a family of proteins because there is only one of them in each species. Families of proteins arise from gene duplication events.)

Protein domains can be classified by their structures. One commonly used classification scheme groups domains into four categories. The all-α category contains domains that consist almost entirely of α helices and loops. All-β domains contain only β sheets and nonrepetitive structures that link β strands. The other two categories contain domains that have a mixture of α helices and β strands. Domains in the α/β class have supersecondary structures such as the βαβ motif and others, in which regions of α helix and β strand alternate in the polypeptide chain. In the α + β category the domains consist of local clusters of α helices and β sheet where each type of secondary structure arises from separate contiguous regions of the polypeptide chain.

Within each of the four main structural categories, protein domains can be further classified by the presence of characteristic folds. A **fold** is a combination of secondary structures that form the core of a domain. Some domains have easily recognizable folds such as the β meander, which contains antiparallel β strands connected by hairpin loops (Figure 4.19f), or helix bundles (Figure 4.19c). Other folds are more complex (Figure 4.23). Figure 4.24 shows selected examples of proteins from each of the main categories and illustrates a number of common domain folds.

(a) Parallel twisted sheet   **(b)** β barrel

◀ **Figure 4.23**
Common domain folds.

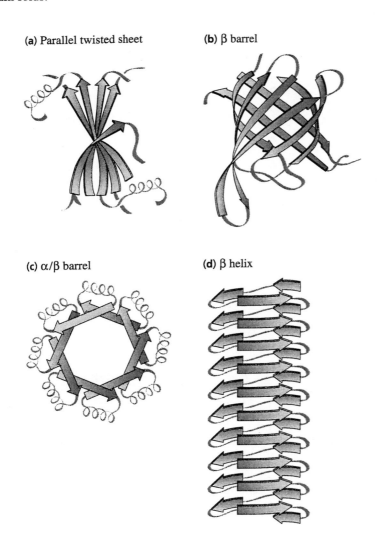

(c) α/β barrel   **(d)** β helix

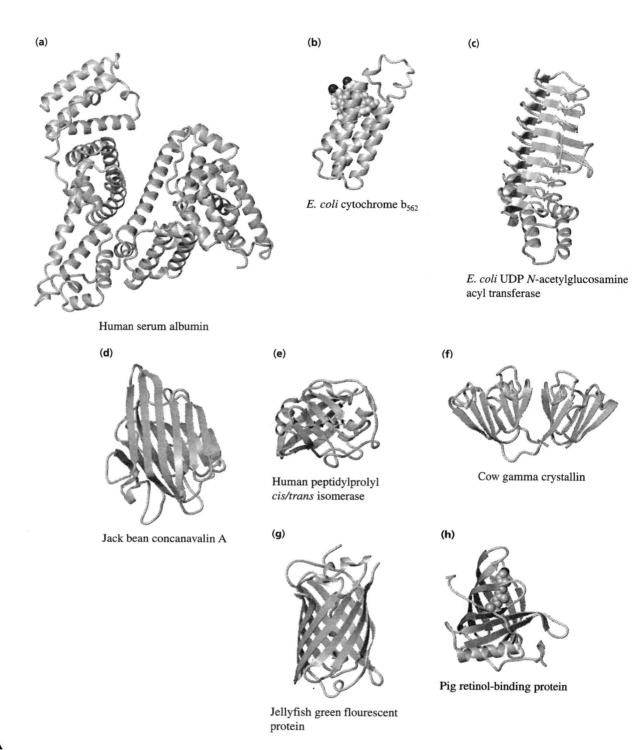

(a)

Human serum albumin

(b)

E. coli cytochrome b$_{562}$

(c)

E. coli UDP *N*-acetylglucosamine
acyl transferase

(d)

Jack bean concanavalin A

(e)

Human peptidylprolyl
cis/trans isomerase

(f)

Cow gamma crystallin

(g)

Jellyfish green flourescent
protein

(h)

Pig retinol-binding protein

Figure 4.24 ▲
Examples of tertiary structure in selected proteins. **(a)** Human (*Homo sapiens*) serum albumin [PDB 1BJ5] (class: all-α). This protein has several domains consisting of layered α helices and helix bundles. **(b)** *Escherichia coli* cytochrome b$_{562}$ [PDB 1QPU] (class: all-α). This is a heme-binding protein consisting of a single four-helix bundle domain. **(c)** *Escherichia coli* UDP *N*-acetylglucosamine acyl transferase [PDB 1LXA] (class: all-β). The structure of this enzyme shows a classic example of a β-helix domain. **(d)** Jack bean (*Canavalia ensiformis*) concanavalin A [PDB 1CON] (class: all-β). This carbohydrate-binding protein (lectin) is a single-domain protein made up of a large β-sandwich fold. **(e)** Human (*Homo sapiens*) peptidylprolyl *cis/trans* isomerase [PDB 1VBS] (class: all-β). The dominant feature of the structure is a β-sandwich fold. **(f)** Cow (*Bos taurus* γ-crystallin) [PDB 1A45] (class: all-β) This protein contains two β-barrel domains. **(g)** Jellyfish (*Aequorea victoria*) green fluorescent protein [PDB 1GFL] (class: all-β). This is a β-barrel structure with a central α helix. The strands of the sheet are antiparallel. **(h)** Pig (*Sus scrofa*) retinol-binding protein [PDB 1AQB] (class: all-β). Retinol binds in the interior of a β-barrel fold. **(i)** Brewer's yeast (*Saccharomyces carlsburgensis*) old yellow enzyme (FMN oxidoreductase) [PDB 1OYA] (class: α/β). The central fold is an α/β barrel with parallel β strands connected by α helices. Two of the connecting α-helical regions are highlighted in yellow. **(j)** *Escherichia coli* enzyme required for tryptophan biosynthesis [PDB 1PII] (class: α/β). This is a bifunctional enzyme containing two distinct domains. Each domain is an example of an α/β barrel. The left-hand domain contains the in-

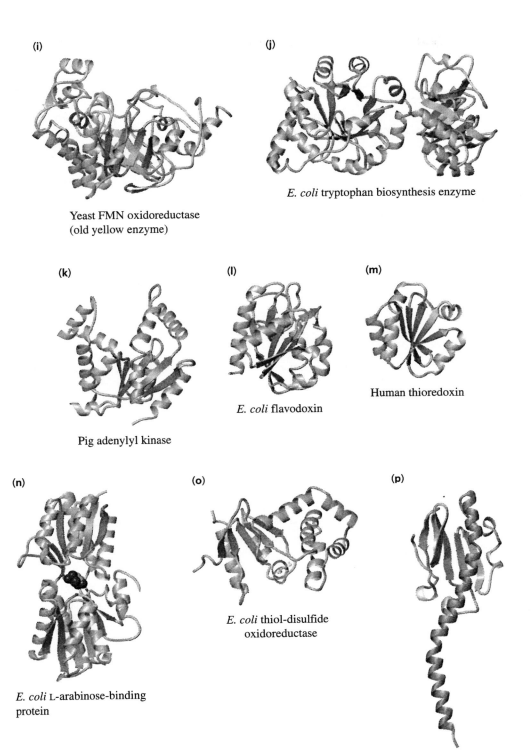

(i) Yeast FMN oxidoreductase (old yellow enzyme)

(j) *E. coli* tryptophan biosynthesis enzyme

(k) Pig adenylyl kinase

(l) *E. coli* flavodoxin

(m) Human thioredoxin

(n) *E. coli* L-arabinose-binding protein

(o) *E. coli* thiol-disulfide oxidoreductase

(p) *Neisseria gonorrhea* pilin

dolglycerol phosphate synthetase activity, and the right-hand domain contains the phosphoribosylanthranilate isomerase activity. **(k)** Pig (*Sus scrofa*) adenylyl kinase [PDB 3ADK] (class: α/β). This single-domain protein consists of a five-stranded parallel β sheet with layers of α helices above and below the sheet. The substrate binds in the prominent groove between α helices. **(l)** *Escherichia coli* flavodoxin [PDB 1AHN] (class: α/β). The fold is a five-stranded parallel twisted sheet surrounded by α helices. **(m)** Human (*Homo sapiens*) thioredoxin [PDB 1ERU] (class: α/β). The structure of this protein is very similar to that of *E. coli* flavodoxin except that the five-stranded twisted sheet in the thioredoxin fold contains a single antiparallel strand. **(n)** *Escherichia coli* L-arabinose-binding protein [PDB 1ABE] (class: α/β). This is a two-domain protein where each domain is similar to that in *E. coli* flavodoxin. The sugar L-arabinose binds in the cavity between the two domains. **(o)** *Escherichia coli* DsbA (thiol-disulfide oxidoreductase/disulfide isomerase) [PDB 1A23] (class: α/β). The predominant feature of this structure is a (mostly) antiparallel β sheet sandwiched between α helices. Cysteine side chains at the end of one of the α helices are shown (sulfur atoms are yellow). **(p)** *Neisseria gonorrhea* pilin [PDB 2PIL] (class: α + β). This polypeptide is one of the subunits of the pili on the surface of the bacteria responsible for gonorrhea. There are two distinct regions of the structure: a β sheet and a long α helix.

C. Domain Structure and Function

The relationship between domain structure and function is complex. Often a single domain has a particular function, such as binding small molecules or catalyzing a single reaction. However, in many cases, binding of small molecules and the formation of the active site of an enzyme take place at the interface between two separate domains. These interfaces often form crevices, grooves, and pockets that are accessible on the surface of the protein. In multifunctional enzymes, each catalytic activity can be associated with one of several domains found in a single polypeptide chain (Figure 4.24j). The extent of contact between domains varies from protein to protein.

The unique shapes of proteins, with their indentations, interdomain interfaces, and other crevices, allow them to fulfill dynamic functions by selectively and transiently binding other molecules. This property is best exemplified by the highly specific binding of reactants (substrates) to substrate-binding sites, or active sites, of enzymes. Because many binding sites are positioned toward the interior of a protein, they are relatively free of water. When substrates bind, they fit so well that some of the few water molecules in the binding site are displaced.

4.8 Quaternary Structure

Many proteins exhibit an additional level of organization called quaternary structure. Quaternary structure refers to the organization and arrangement of subunits in a protein with multiple subunits. Each subunit is a separate polypeptide chain. A multisubunit protein is referred to as an oligomer (proteins with only one polypeptide chain are monomers). The subunits within an oligomeric protein always have a defined stoichiometry, and the arrangement of the subunits gives rise to a stable structure. The subunits of a multisubunit protein may be identical or different. When the subunits are identical, dimers and tetramers predominate. When the subunits differ, each type often has a different function. A common shorthand method for describing oligomeric proteins uses Greek letters to identify types of subunits, and subscript numerals to indicate numbers of subunits. For example, an $\alpha_2\beta\gamma$ protein contains two subunits designated α and one each of subunits designated β and γ.

The subunits of oligomeric proteins are usually held together by weak noncovalent interactions. Hydrophobic interactions are the principal forces involved, although electrostatic forces may contribute to the proper alignment of the subunits. Because intersubunit forces are usually rather weak, the subunits of an oligomeric protein can often be separated in the laboratory. In vivo, however, the subunits usually remain tightly associated. Examples of several multisubunit proteins are shown in Figure 4.25.

In the case of triose phosphate isomerase (Figure 4.25a) and HIV protease (Figure 4.25b), the identical subunits associate through weak interactions between the side chains found mainly in loop regions. Similar interactions are responsible for the formation of the MS2 capsid protein, which consists of a trimer of identical subunits. In this case, the trimer units assemble into a more complex structure—the bacteriophage particle. The enzyme HGPRT (Figure 4.25e) is a tetramer formed from the association of two pairs of nonidentical subunits. Each of the subunits is a recognizable domain.

The potassium channel protein (Figure 4.25c) is an example of a tetramer of identical subunits where the subunits interact to form a membrane-spanning region consisting of an eight-helix bundle. The subunits do not form separate domains within the protein. The bacterial photosynthetic reaction center shown in Figure 4.25f is a complex example of quaternary structure. It contains four different subunits that bind various heme and chlorophyll prosthetic groups. Three of the subunits contribute to a large membrane-bound helix bundle while the fourth subunit (a cytochrome) sits on the exterior surface of the membrane.

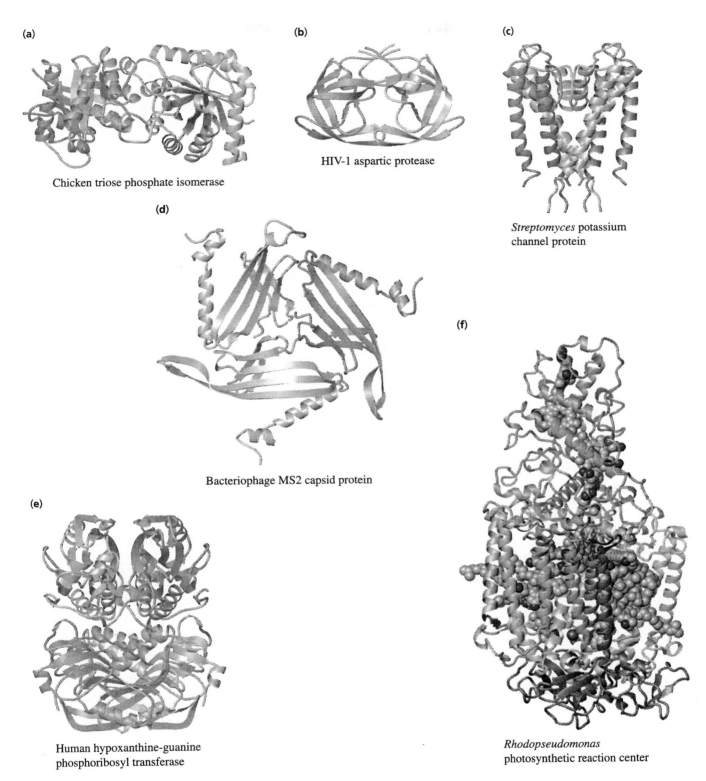

(a) Chicken triose phosphate isomerase

(b) HIV-1 aspartic protease

(c) *Streptomyces* potassium channel protein

(d) Bacteriophage MS2 capsid protein

(e) Human hypoxanthine-guanine phosphoribosyl transferase

(f) *Rhodopseudomonas* photosynthetic reaction center

Figure 4.25 ▲

Quaternary structure. **(a)** Chicken (*Gallus gallus*) triose phosphate isomerase [PDB 1TIM]. This protein has two identical subunits with α/β barrel folds. **(b)** HIV-1 aspartic protease [PDB 1DIF]. This protein has two identical all-β subunits that bind symmetrically. HIV protease is the target of many new drugs designed to treat AIDS patients. **(c)** *Streptomyces lividans* potassium channel protein [PDB 1BL8]. This membrane-bound protein has four identical subunits, each of which contributes to a membrane-spanning eight-helix bundle. **(d)** Bacteriophage MS2 capsid protein [PDB 2MS2]. The basic unit of the MS2 capsid is a trimer of identical subunits with a large β sheet. **(e)** Human (*Homo sapiens*) hypoxanthine-guanine phosphoribosyl transferase (HGPRT) [PDB 1BZY]. HGPRT is a tetrameric protein containing two different types of subunit. **(f)** *Rhodopseudomonas viridis* photosynthetic reaction center [PDB 1PRC]. This complex, membrane-bound protein has two identical subunits (orange, blue) and two other subunits (purple, green) bound to several molecules of photosynthetic pigments.

Determination of the subunit composition of an oligomeric protein is an essential step in the physical description of a protein. Typically, the molecular weight of the native oligomer is estimated by gel-filtration chromatography, and then the molecular weight of each chain is determined by SDS–polyacrylamide gel electrophoresis (Section 3.6). For a protein having only one type of chain, the ratio of the two values provides the number of chains per oligomer.

The fact that a large proportion of proteins consist of multiple subunits is probably related to several factors:

1. Oligomers are usually more stable than their dissociated subunits, suggesting that quaternary structure prolongs the life of a protein in vivo.

2. The active sites of some oligomeric enzymes are formed by residues from adjacent polypeptide chains.

3. The three-dimensional structures of many oligomeric proteins change when the proteins bind ligands. Both the tertiary structures of the subunits and the quaternary structures (i.e., the contacts between subunits) may be altered. Such changes are key elements in the regulation of the biological activity of certain oligomeric proteins.

4. Different proteins can share the same subunits. Since many subunits have a defined function (e.g., ligand binding), evolution has favored selection for different combinations of subunits to carry out related functions. This is more efficient than selection for an entirely new monomeric protein that duplicates part of the function.

4.9 Protein Denaturation and Renaturation

Environmental changes or chemical treatments may cause a disruption in the native conformation of a protein, with concomitant loss of biological activity. Such a disruption is called **denaturation**. The amount of energy needed to cause denaturation is often small, perhaps equivalent to that needed for the disruption of three or four hydrogen bonds. Although some proteins may unfold completely when denatured to form a random coil (a fluctuating chain considered to be totally disordered), most denatured proteins retain considerable internal structure. It is sometimes possible to find conditions under which small denatured proteins can renature, or refold, following denaturation.

Proteins are commonly denatured by heating. Under the appropriate conditions, a modest increase in temperature will result in unfolding and loss of secondary and tertiary structure. An example of thermal denaturation is shown in Figure 4.26. In this experiment, a solution containing bovine ribonuclease A is heated slowly and the structure of the protein is monitored by various techniques that measure changes in conformation. All three techniques detect a change when denaturation occurs. In the case of bovine ribonuclease A, thermal denaturation requires a reducing agent that disrupts internal disulfide bridges, allowing the protein to unfold. (The structure of native ribonuclease A is shown in Figure 4.3.)

Denaturation takes place over a relatively small range of temperature. This indicates that unfolding is a cooperative process: the destabilization of just a few weak interactions leads to almost complete loss of native conformation. Most proteins have a characteristic "melting" temperature (T_m) that corresponds to the temperature at the midpoint of the transition between the native and denatured forms. The T_m depends on pH and the ionic strength of the solution.

Under physiological conditions, most proteins are stable at temperatures up to 50° to 60°C. However, some species of bacteria, such as those that inhabit hot springs and the vicinity of deep ocean thermal vents, thrive at temperatures well above this range. Proteins in these species have very high T_m's, as expected. Biochemists actively study these proteins in order to determine how they resist denaturation.

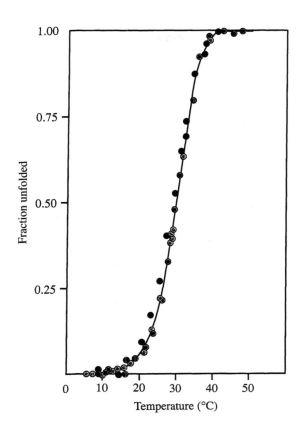

◀ Figure 4.26
Heat denaturation of ribonuclease A. A solution of ribonuclease A in 0.02 M KCl at pH 2.1 was heated. Unfolding was monitored by changes in ultraviolet absorbance (blue), viscosity (red), and optical rotation (green). [Adapted from Ginsburg, A. and Carroll, W. R. (1965). Some specific ion effects on the conformation and thermal stability of ribonuclease. *Biochemistry* 4:2159–2174.]

Proteins can also be denatured by two types of chemicals—chaotropic agents and detergents (Section 2.4). High concentrations of chaotropic agents, such as urea and guanidinium salts (Figure 4.27), denature proteins by allowing water molecules to solvate nonpolar groups in the interior of proteins. The water molecules disrupt the hydrophobic interactions that normally stabilize the native conformation. The hydrophobic tails of detergents, such as sodium dodecyl sulfate (Figure 2.8), also denature proteins by penetrating the protein interior and disrupting hydrophobic interactions.

The native conformation of some proteins (e.g., ribonuclease A) is stabilized by disulfide bonds. Disulfide bonds are not generally found in intracellular proteins but are sometimes found in proteins that are secreted from cells. The presence of disulfide bonds makes the proteins less susceptible to unfolding and subsequent degradation when they leave the intracellular environment. Disulfide bond formation does not drive protein folding; instead, the bonds form where two cysteine residues are appropriately located once the protein has folded. Formation of a disulfide bond requires oxidation of the thiol groups of the cysteine residues (Figure 3.4), probably by disulfide-exchange reactions involving oxidized glutathione, a cysteine-containing tripeptide.

Figure 4.28a shows the locations of the disulfide bridges in ribonuclease A. (Compare this orientation of the protein with that shown in Figure 4.3.) There are four disulfide bridges. They can link adjacent β strands, β strands to α helices, or β strands to loops. Figure 4.28b is a stereo view of the disulfide bridge between a cysteine residue in an α helix (Cys-26) and a cysteine residue in a β strand (Cys-84). Note that the S—S bond does not align with the cysteine side chains. Disulfide bridges will form whenever the two cysteine sulfhydryl groups are in close proximity in the native conformation.

Complete denaturation of proteins that contain disulfide bonds requires cleavage of these bonds in addition to disruption of hydrophobic interactions and hydrogen bonds. 2-Mercaptoethanol or other thiol reagents can be added to a denaturing medium in order to reduce any disulfide bonds to sulfhydryl groups (see Figure 3.17).

Urea

Guanidinium chloride

Figure 4.27 ▲
Urea and guanidinium chloride.

(a)

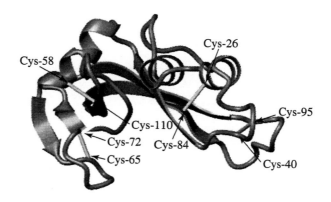

(b)

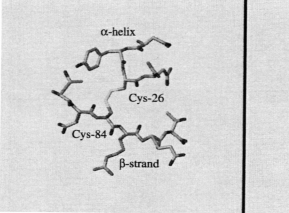 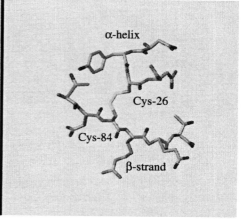

Figure 4.28 ▲
Disulfide bridges in bovine ribonuclease A. **(a)** Location of disulfide bridges in the native protein. **(b)** Stereo view of the disulfide bridge between Cys-26 and Cys-84.

▲ Christian B. Anfinsen (1916–1995). Anfinsen was awarded the Nobel Prize in Chemistry in 1972 for his work on the refolding of proteins.

Reduction of the disulfide bonds of a protein is accompanied by oxidation of the thiol reagent.

Christian B. Anfinsen and his coworkers studied the renaturation pathway of ribonuclease A that had been denatured in the presence of thiol reducing agents. Since ribonuclease A is a relatively small protein (124 amino acid residues), it refolds (renatures) quickly once it is returned to conditions where the native form is stable (e.g., cooled below the melting temperature or removed from a solution containing chaotropic agents). Anfinsen was among the first to show that denatured proteins can refold spontaneously to their native conformation. This indicates that the information required for the native three-dimensional conformation is contained in the amino acid sequence of the polypeptide chain. In other words, the primary structure determines the tertiary structure.

Denaturation of ribonuclease A with 8 M urea containing 2-mercaptoethanol results in complete loss of tertiary structure and enzymatic activity and yields a polypeptide chain containing eight sulfhydryl groups. When 2-mercaptoethanol is removed and oxidation is allowed to occur in the presence of urea, the sulfhydryl groups pair randomly, so that only about 1% of the protein population forms the correct four disulfide bonds and recovers its original enzymatic activity. (If the eight sulfhydryl groups pair randomly, 105 disulfide-bonded structures are possible—7 possible pairings for the first bond, 5 for the second, 3 for the third, and 1 for the fourth; $7 \times 5 \times 3 \times 1 = 105$—but only one of these structures is correct.) However, when urea and 2-

mercaptoethanol are removed simultaneously and dilute solutions of the reduced protein are then exposed to air, ribonuclease A spontaneously regains its native conformation, its correct set of disulfide bonds, and its full enzymatic activity (Figure 4.29). The inactive proteins containing randomly formed disulfide bonds can be renatured if urea is removed, a small amount of 2-mercaptoethanol is added, and the solution gently warmed. Anfinsen's experiments demonstrate that the correct disulfide bonds can form only after the protein folds into its native conformation. Anfinsen concluded that the renaturation of ribonuclease A is spontaneous, driven entirely by the free energy gained in changing to the stable physiological conformation. This conformation is determined by the primary structure.

When proteins fold inside a cell, they occasionally adopt a nonnative conformation and form inappropriate disulfide bridges. Anfinsen discovered an enzyme, called protein disulfide isomerase (PDI), that catalyzes reduction of these incorrect bonds. All living cells contain such an activity. The structure of the reduced form of *E. coli* disulfide isomerase (DsbA) is shown in Figure 4.24o. The enzyme contains two reduced cysteine residues positioned in the active site where the misfolded protein binds. The enzyme catalyzes a disulfide-exchange reaction where the disulfide in the misfolded protein is reduced and a new disulfide bridge is created between the two cysteine residues in the enzyme. The misfolded protein is then released, and it can refold into the low-energy native conformation.

4.10 Protein Folding and Stability

New polypeptides are synthesized in the cell by a translation complex that includes ribosomes, mRNA, and various factors (Chapter 21). As the newly synthesized polypeptide emerges from the ribosome, it folds into its characteristic three-dimensional shape.

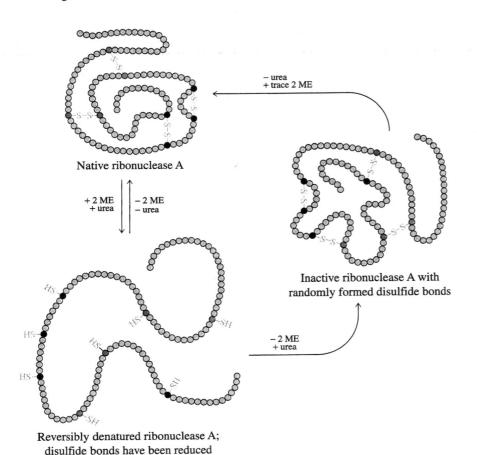

Native ribonuclease A

+ 2 ME
+ urea

− 2 ME
− urea

Reversibly denatured ribonuclease A;
disulfide bonds have been reduced

− urea
+ trace 2 ME

− 2 ME
+ urea

Inactive ribonuclease A with
randomly formed disulfide bonds

◄ Figure 4.29
Denaturation and renaturation of ribonuclease A. Treatment of native ribonuclease A (top) with urea in the presence of 2-mercaptoethanol unfolds the protein and disrupts disulfide bonds to produce reduced, reversibly denatured ribonuclease A (bottom). When the denatured protein is returned to physiological conditions in the absence of 2-mercaptoethanol, it refolds into its native conformation and the correct disulfide bonds form. However, when 2-mercaptoethanol alone is removed, ribonuclease A reoxidizes in the presence of air, but the disulfide bonds form randomly, producing inactive protein (such as the form shown on the right). When urea is removed, a trace of 2-mercaptoethanol is added to the randomly reoxidized protein, and the solution is warmed gently, the disulfide bonds break and re-form correctly to produce native ribonuclease A.

Figure 4.30 ▶
Energy well of protein folding. The funnels represent the free-energy potential of folding proteins. **(a)** A simplified funnel showing two possible pathways to the low-energy native protein. In path B the polypeptide enters a local low-energy minimum as it folds. **(b)** A more realistic version of the possible free-energy forms of a folding protein with many local peaks and dips.

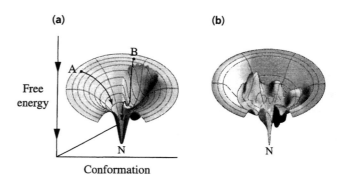

Folded proteins occupy a low-energy well that makes the native structure much more stable than alternative conformations (Figure 4.30). The in vitro experiments of Anfinsen and many other biochemists demonstrate that many proteins can fold spontaneously to reach this low-energy conformation.

It is thought that as a protein folds, the first few interactions initiate subsequent interactions by assisting in the alignment of groups. This process is known as cooperativity of folding—the phenomenon whereby the formation of one part of a structure leads to the formation of the remaining parts of the structure. As the protein begins to fold, it adopts lower and lower energies and begins to fall into the energy well shown in Figure 4.30. The protein may become temporarily trapped in a local energy well (shown as small dips in the energy diagram), but eventually it reaches the energy minimum at the bottom of the well. In its final, stable, conformation, the native protein is much less sensitive to degradation than an extended, unfolded polypeptide chain. Thus, native proteins can have half-lives of many cell generations, and some molecules may last for decades.

Folding is extremely rapid; in most cases the native conformation is reached in less than a second. Protein folding and stabilization depend on several noncovalent forces, including the hydrophobic effect, hydrogen bonding, van der Waals interactions, and charge-charge interactions. Although noncovalent interactions are weak individually, collectively they account for the stability of the native conformations of proteins. The weakness of each noncovalent interaction gives proteins the resilience and flexibility to undergo small conformational changes. (Covalent disulfide bonds also contribute to the stability of certain proteins.)

No actual protein-folding pathway has yet been described in detail, but current research is focused on intermediates in the folding pathways of a number of proteins. Several hypothetical folding pathways are shown in Figure 4.31. During protein folding, the polypeptide collapses upon itself due to the hydrophobic effect, and elements of secondary structure begin to form. This intermediate is called a molten globule. Subsequent steps involve rearrangement of the backbone chain to form characteristic motifs and, finally, the stable native conformation. Each domain in a multidomain protein folds independently.

The mechanism of protein folding is one of the most challenging problems in biochemistry. The process is spontaneous and must be largely determined by the primary structure (sequence) of the polypeptide. Biochemists would like to be able to predict the tertiary structure of a protein from knowledge of its sequence. Much progress has been made in recent years by modeling folding using fast computers. In the remainder of this section, we examine the forces that stabilize protein structure and the role of chaperones in protein folding.

A. The Hydrophobic Effect

Proteins are more stable in water when their hydrophobic side chains are aggregated in the protein interior rather than solvated by the aqueous medium. Because water molecules interact more strongly with each other than with the nonpolar side chains

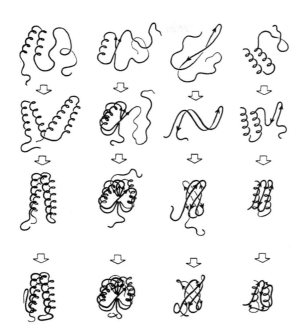

◀ **Figure 4.31**
Hypothetical protein-folding pathways. The initially extended polypeptide chains form partial secondary structures, then approximate tertiary structures, and finally the unique native conformations. The arrows within the structures indicate the direction from the N- to the C-terminus.

of a protein, the side chains are forced to associate with one another, causing the polypeptide chain to collapse into a more compact molten globule. The decrease in entropy of the polypeptide is more than offset by the increase in solvent entropy; this overall increase in entropy provides the major driving force for protein folding. Whereas nonpolar side chains are driven into the interior of the protein, most polar side chains remain in contact with water on the surface of the protein. The sections of the polar backbone that are forced into the interior of a protein neutralize their polarity by hydrogen bonding to each other, often generating secondary structures. Thus, the hydrophobic nature of the interior not only accounts for the association of hydrophobic residues but also contributes to the stability of helices and sheets. Studies of folding pathways indicate that hydrophobic collapse and formation of secondary structures occur simultaneously.

Localized examples of this hydrophobic effect are the interactions of the hydrophobic side of an amphipathic α helix with the protein core (Section 4.4) and the hydrophobic region between β sheets in the β-sandwich structure (Section 4.5). Most of the examples shown in Figures 4.24 and 4.25 contain juxtaposed regions of secondary structure that are stabilized by hydrophobic interactions between the side chains of hydrophobic amino acid residues.

B. Hydrogen Bonding

Hydrogen bonds contribute to the cooperativity of folding and help stabilize the native conformations of proteins. The hydrogen bonds in α helices, β sheets, and turns are the first to form, giving rise to defined regions of secondary structure. The final native structure also contains hydrogen bonds between the polypeptide backbone and water, between the polypeptide backbone and polar side chains, between two polar side chains, and between polar side chains and water. Table 4.1 shows some of the many types of hydrogen bonds found in proteins, along with their typical bond lengths. Most hydrogen bonds in proteins are of the N—H------O type. The distance between the donor and acceptor atoms varies from 0.26 to 0.34 nm, and the bonds may deviate from linearity by up to 40°. Recall that hydrogen bonds within the hydrophobic core of a protein are much more stable than those that form near the surface because the internal hydrogen bonds don't compete with water molecules.

TABLE 4.1 Examples of Hydrogen Bonds in Proteins

Type of hydrogen bond		Typical distance between donor and acceptor atom (nm)
Hydroxyl-hydroxyl	$-O-H\text{------}O-$ $\quad\quad\quad\quad\quad / $ $\quad\quad\quad\quad\quad H$	0.28
Hydroxyl-carbonyl	$-O-H\text{------}O=C$	0.28
Amide-carbonyl	$N-H\text{------}O=C$	0.29
Amide-hydroxyl	$N-H\text{------}O-$ $\quad\quad\quad\quad\quad H$	0.30
Amide-imidazole nitrogen	$N-H\text{------}N\diagdown NH$	0.31

C. Van der Waals Interactions and Charge-Charge Interactions

Van der Waals contacts between nonpolar side chains also contribute to the stability of proteins. The extent of stabilization due to optimized van der Waals interactions cannot yet be assessed, but because the interior of a protein is closely packed, the magnitude may be considerable.

Charge-charge interactions between oppositely charged side chains may make a small contribution to the stability of proteins. Most ionic side chains are found on the surfaces, where they are solvated and can contribute only minimally to the overall stabilization of the protein. However, two oppositely charged ions occasionally form an ion pair in the interior of a protein. Such ion pairs are much stronger than those exposed to water.

D. Protein Folding Is Assisted by Chaperones

Studies of protein folding have led to two general observations regarding the folding of polypeptide chains into biologically active proteins. First, protein folding does not involve a random search in three-dimensional space for the native conformation. Rather, protein folding appears to be a cooperative, sequential process in which formation of the first few structural elements assists in the alignment of subsequent structural features. [The need for cooperativity is illustrated by a calculation made by Cyrus Levinthal. Consider a polypeptide of 100 residues. If each residue had three possible conformations, a random search of all possible conformations for the complete polypeptide would take 10^{87} seconds—many times the estimated age of the universe (6×10^{17} seconds)!]

Second, the folding pattern and the final conformation of a protein depend on its primary structure. As we saw in the case of ribonuclease A, simple proteins may fold spontaneously into their native conformations in a test tube, without any energy input or assistance. However, larger protein chains may adopt incorrect conformations (corresponding to the local energy wells in Figure 4.30) unless certain proteins called **molecular chaperones** are present.

Chaperones are proteins that increase the rate of correct folding of some proteins by binding newly synthesized polypeptides before they are completely folded. Chaperones prevent the formation of incorrectly folded intermediates that may trap the polypeptide in an aberrant form. Chaperones can also bind to unassembled protein subunits to prevent them from aggregating incorrectly and precipitating before they are assembled into a complete multisubunit protein.

There are many different chaperones. Most chaperones are **heat shock proteins**— proteins that are synthesized in response to temperature increases (heat shock) or other changes that cause protein denaturation in vivo. The role of heat shock proteins, now recognized as chaperones, is to repair the damage caused by heat shock by binding to denatured proteins and helping them to refold rapidly into their native conformation.

The major heat shock protein is HSP70 (heat shock protein, $M_r \sim 70\,000$). This protein is present in every species except some species of archaebacteria. In bacteria, it is also called DnaK. The normal role of the chaperone HSP70 is to bind to nascent proteins while they are being synthesized and prevent aggregation or entrapment in a local low-energy well. The binding and release of nascent polypeptides is coupled to the hydrolysis of ATP and usually requires additional accessory proteins. HSP70/DnaK is one of the most highly conserved proteins known, indicating that chaperone-assisted protein folding is an ancient and essential requirement for efficient synthesis of proteins with the correct three-dimensional structure.

Another important and ubiquitous chaperone is called chaperonin (also called GroE in bacteria). Chaperonin is also a heat shock protein (Hsp60), but it plays an important role in assisting normal protein folding.

E. coli chaperonin is a complex multisubunit protein. The core structure consists of two rings containing seven identical GroEL subunits. Each subunit can bind a molecule of ATP (Figure 4.32a). A simplified version of chaperonin-assisted

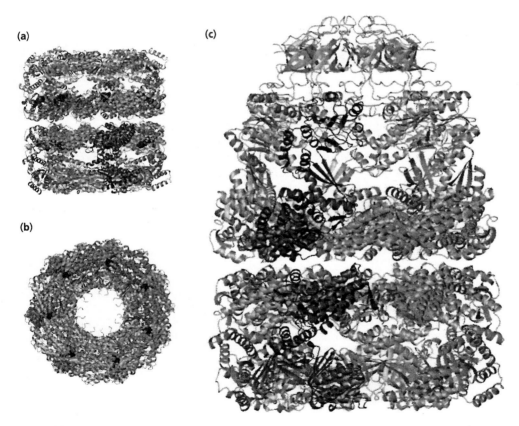

(a)

(b)

(c)

Figure 4.32 ▲
Escherichia coli chaperonin (GroE). The core structure consists of two identical rings composed of seven GroEL subunits. Unfolded proteins bind to the central cavity. Bound ATP molecules can be identified by their red oxygen atoms. (a) Side view. (b) Top view showing the central cavity. [PDB 1DER]. (c) During folding the size of the cental cavity of one of the rings increases and the end is capped by a protein containing seven GroES subunits. [PDB 1AON].

Figure 4.33 ▶
Chaperonin-assisted protein folding. The unfolded polypeptide enters the central cavity
of chaperonin, where it folds. The hydrolysis
of several ATP molecules is required for
chaperonin function.

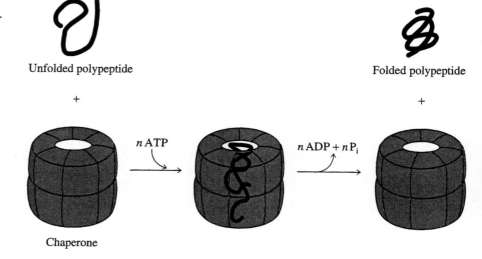

Figure 4.33 ▶
Chaperonin-assisted protein folding. The unfolded polypeptide enters the central cavity
of chaperonin, where it folds. The hydrolysis
of several ATP molecules is required for
chaperonin function.

folding is shown in Figure 4.33. Unfolded proteins bind to the hydrophobic central cavity enclosed by the rings. When folding is complete, the protein is released
by hydrolysis of the bound ATP molecules. The actual pathway is more complicated
and requires an additional component that serves as a cap, sealing one end of the
central cavity while the folding process takes place. The cap contains seven GroES
subunits forming an additional ring (Figure 4.32c). The conformation of the GroEL
ring can be altered during folding to increase the size of the cavity, and the role of
the cap is to prevent the unfolded protein from being released prematurely.

The central cavity of chaperonin is large enough to accommodate a polypeptide
chain of about 630 amino acid residues ($M_r \sim 70\,000$). Thus, the folding of most
small and medium-sized proteins potentially can be assisted by chaperonin. However,
only about 5% to 10% of *E. coli* proteins (i.e., about 300 different proteins) appear
to interact with chaperonin during protein synthesis. Medium-sized proteins, and
those of the α/β structural class, are more likely to require chaperonin-assisted folding. Smaller proteins are able to fold quickly on their own. Many of the remaining
proteins in the cell may require other chaperones, such as HSP70/DnaK.

Chaperones appear to inhibit incorrect folding and assembly pathways by forming stable complexes with surfaces on polypeptide chains that are exposed only during synthesis, folding, and assembly. Even in the presence of chaperones, protein
folding is spontaneous; for this reason, chaperone-assisted protein folding has been
described as assisted self-assembly.

4.11 Collagen, a Fibrous Protein

To conclude our examination of the three-dimensional structure of proteins, we examine several proteins to see how their structures are related to their biological functions. The proteins selected for more detailed study are the structural protein collagen,
the oxygen-binding proteins myoglobin and hemoglobin (Sections 4.12 to 4.13),
and antibodies (Section 4.14).

Collagen is the major protein component of the connective tissue of vertebrates;
it constitutes about 25% to 35% of the total protein in mammals. Collagen molecules
have remarkably diverse forms and functions. For example, collagen in tendons
forms stiff, ropelike fibers of tremendous tensile strength; in skin, collagen takes
the form of loosely woven fibers, permitting expansion in all directions.

Collagen consists of three left-handed helical chains coiled around each other
to form a right-handed supercoil. Each left-handed helix in collagen has 3.0 amino
acid residues per turn and a pitch of 0.94 nm, giving a rise of 0.31 nm per residue.

Consequently, a collagen helix is more extended than an α helix, and the coiled-coil structure of collagen is not the same as the coiled-coil motif discussed in Section 4.7. (Several proteins unrelated to collagen also form similar three-chain supercoils.)

The collagen triple helix is stabilized by interchain hydrogen bonds. The sequence of the protein in the helical region consists of multiple repeats of the form –Gly–X–Y–, where X is often proline and Y is often a modified proline called 4-hydroxyproline (Figure 4.34). The glycine residues are located along the central axis of the triple helix, where tight packing of the protein strands can accommodate no other residue. For each –Gly–X–Y– triplet, one hydrogen bond forms between the amide hydrogen atom of glycine in one chain and the carbonyl oxygen atom of residue X in an adjacent chain (Figure 4.35). Unlike the more common α helix, the collagen helix has no intrachain hydrogen bonds (Figure 4.36).

In addition to hydroxyproline, collagen contains an additional modified amino acid residue called 5-hydroxylysine (Figure 4.37). Some hydroxylysine residues are covalently bonded to carbohydrate residues, making collagen a glycoprotein. The role of this glycosylation is not known.

Hydroxyproline and hydroxylysine residues are formed when specific proline and lysine residues are hydroxylated after incorporation into the polypeptide chains of collagen. The hydroxylation reactions are catalyzed by enzymes and require ascorbic acid (vitamin C). Hydroxylation is impaired in the absence of vitamin C, and the triple helix of collagen is not assembled properly. People deprived of vitamin C develop scurvy, a disease whose symptoms include skin lesions, fragile blood vessels, loose teeth, and bleeding gums. Humans are unusual mammals because they have lost the ability to synthesize vitamin C. One of the genes required for vitamin C synthesis is mutated in humans, making us dependent on fruit and other exogenous sources of this key vitamin.

The limited conformational flexibility of proline and hydroxyproline residues prevents the formation of α helices in collagen chains and also makes collagen somewhat rigid. (Recall that proline is almost never found in α helices.) The presence of glycine residues at every third position allows collagen chains to form a tightly wound left-handed helix that accommodates the proline residues. (Recall that the flexibility of glycine residues tends to disrupt the right-handed α helix.) Hydrogen bonds involving the hydroxyl group of hydroxyproline may also stabilize the collagen triple helix.

Figure 4.34 ▲
4-Hydroxyproline residue. 4-Hydroxyproline residues are formed by enzyme-catalyzed hydroxylation of proline residues.

Figure 4.35 ▲
Interchain hydrogen bonding in collagen. The amide hydrogen of a glycine residue in one chain is hydrogen-bonded to the carbonyl oxygen of a residue, often proline, in an adjacent chain.

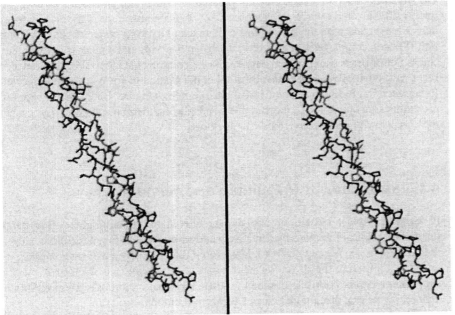

Figure 4.36 ▲
Stereo view of the human type III collagen triple helix. The extended region of collagen contains three identical subunits (purple, light blue, and green). Three left-handed collagen helices are coiled around one another to form a right-handed supercoil. [PDB 1BKV]

Figure 4.37 ▲
5-Hydroxylysine residue. 5-Hydroxylysine residues are formed by enzyme-catalyzed hydroxylation of lysine residues.

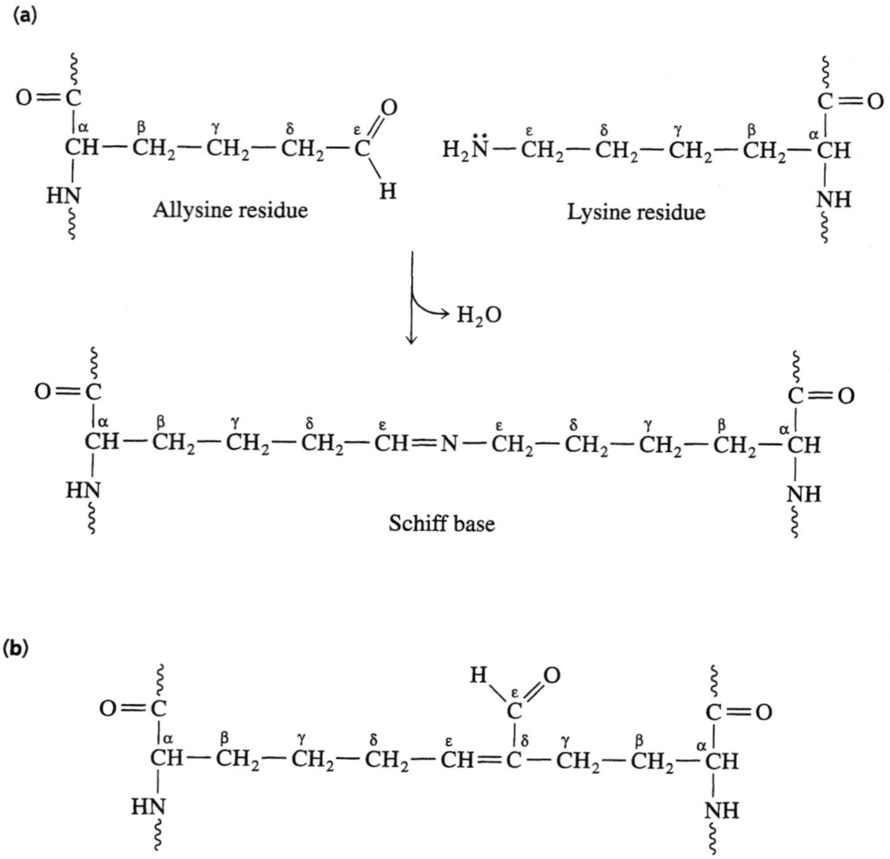

Figure 4.38 ▶
Covalent cross-links in collagen. **(a)** An allysine residue condenses with a lysine residue to form an intermolecular Schiff-base cross-link. **(b)** Two allysine residues condense to form an intramolecular cross-link.

(a)

(b)

Collagen triple helices aggregate in a staggered fashion to form strong, insoluble fibers. The strength and rigidity of collagen fibers result in part from covalent cross-links. The $—CH_2NH_3^{\oplus}$ groups of the side chains of some lysine and hydroxylysine residues are converted enzymatically to aldehyde groups ($—CHO$), producing allysine and hydroxyallysine residues. Allysine residues (and their hydroxy derivatives) react with the side chains of lysine and hydroxylysine residues to form **Schiff bases**, complexes formed between carbonyl groups and amines (Figure 4.38a). These Schiff bases usually form between collagen molecules. Allysine residues also react with other allysine residues by aldol condensation to form cross-links, usually between the individual strands of the triple helix (Figure 4.38b). Both types of cross-links are converted to more stable bonds during the maturation of tissues, but the chemistry of these conversions is unknown.

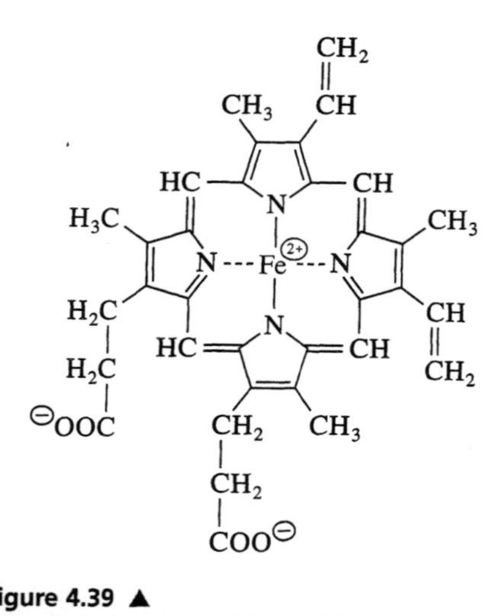

4.12 Structures of Myoglobin and Hemoglobin

Like most proteins, myoglobin (Mb) and the related protein hemoglobin (Hb) carry out their biological functions by selectively and reversibly binding other molecules—in this case, molecular oxygen (O_2). Myoglobin is a relatively small monomeric protein that facilitates the diffusion of oxygen in vertebrates. It is responsible for supplying oxygen to muscle tissue in reptiles, birds, and mammals. Hemoglobin is a larger tetrameric protein that carries oxygen in blood.

The red color associated with the oxygenated forms of myoglobin and hemoglobin (e.g., the red color of oxygenated blood) is due to a heme prosthetic group (Figure 4.39). (A prosthetic group is a protein-bound organic molecule essential for the activity of the protein.) Heme consists of a tetrapyrrole ring system called pro-

Figure 4.39 ▲
Chemical structure of the Fe(II)-protoporphyrin IX heme group in myoglobin and hemoglobin. The porphyrin ring provides four of the six ligands that surround the iron

toporphyrin IX complexed with iron. The four pyrrole rings of this system are linked by methene (—CH=) bridges, so that the unsaturated porphyrin is highly conjugated and planar. The bound iron is in the ferrous, or Fe(II), oxidation state; it forms a complex with six ligands, four of which are the nitrogen atoms of protoporphyrin IX. (Other proteins, such as cytochrome *a* and cytochrome *c*, contain different porphyrin/heme groups.)

The polypeptide component of myoglobin is a member of a family of proteins called globins. The tertiary structure of sperm whale myoglobin shows that the protein consists of a bundle of eight α helices (Figure 4.40). It is a member of the all-α structural category. The globin fold has several groups of α helices that form a layered structure. Adjacent helices in each layer are tilted at an angle that allows the side chains of the amino acid residues to interdigitate.

The interior of myoglobin is made up almost exclusively of hydrophobic amino acid residues, particularly those that are highly hydrophobic—valine, leucine, isoleucine, phenylalanine, and methionine. The surface of the protein contains both hydrophilic and hydrophobic residues. As is the case with most proteins, the tertiary structure of myoglobin is stabilized by hydrophobic interactions within the core. Folding of the polypeptide chain is driven by the energy minimization that results from formation of this hydrophobic core.

The heme prosthetic group of myoglobin occupies a hydrophobic cleft formed by three α helices and two loops. The binding of the porphyrin moiety to the polypeptide is due to a number of weak interactions, including hydrophobic interactions, van der Waals contacts, and hydrogen bonds. There are no covalent bonds between the porphyrin and the amino acid side chains of myoglobin. The iron atom of heme is the site of oxygen binding as shown in Figure 4.40. Two histidine residues interact with the iron atom and the bound oxygen. Accessibility of the heme group to molecular oxygen depends on slight movement of nearby amino acid side chains. We will see later that the hydrophobic crevices of myoglobin and hemoglobin are essential for the reversible binding of oxygen.

In vertebrates, O_2 is bound to molecules of hemoglobin for transport in red blood cells, or erythrocytes. Viewed under a microscope, a mature mammalian erythrocyte is a biconcave disk that lacks a nucleus or other internal membrane-enclosed compartments (Figure 4.41). A typical human erythrocyte is filled with approximately 3×10^8 hemoglobin molecules.

Hemoglobin is more complex than myoglobin because it possesses quaternary structure. In adult mammals, hemoglobin contains two different globin subunits called α-globin and β-globin. Hemoglobin is an $\alpha_2\beta_2$ tetramer, which indicates that it contains two α-globin chains and two β-globin chains. Each of these globin subunits is similar in structure and sequence to myoglobin, reflecting their evolution from a common ancestral globin gene in primitive chordates.

Each of the four globin chains contains a heme prosthetic group identical to that found in myoglobin. The α and β chains face each other across a central cavity (Figure 4.42). The tertiary structure of each of the four chains is almost identical

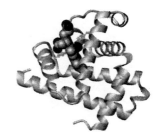

Figure 4.40 ▲
Sperm whale (*Physeter catodon*) oxymyoglobin. Myoglobin consists of **eight** α helices. The heme prosthetic group binds oxygen (red). His-64 (green) forms a hydrogen bond with oxygen, and His-93 (green) is complexed to the iron atom of the heme. [PDB 1A6M].

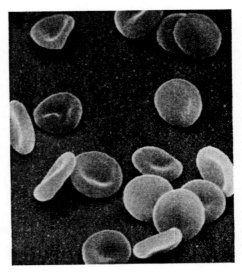

Figure 4.41 ▲
Scanning electron micrograph of mammalian erythrocytes. Each cell contains approximately 300 million hemoglobin molecules.

(a)

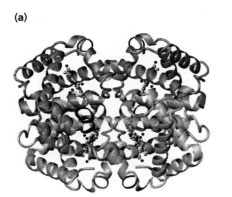

(b)

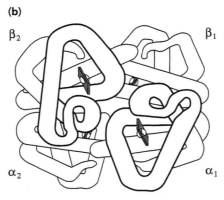

◀ **Figure 4.42**
Human (*Homo sapiens*) oxyhemoglobin. **(a)** Structure of human oxyhemoglobin showing two α and two β subunits. Heme groups are shown as stick models. [PDB 1 HND]. **(b)** Schematic diagram of the hemoglobin tetramer. The heme groups are red.

Figure 4.43 ▲
Tertiary structure of myoglobin, α-globin, and β-globin. The orientations of the individual α-globin and β-globin subunits of hemoglobin have been shifted in order to reveal the similarities in tertiary structure. Heme groups have been removed and the three structures have been superimposed. All of the structures are from the oxygenated forms shown in Figures 4.40 and 4.42. Color code: α-globin (blue), β-globin (purple), myoglobin (green).

to that of myoglobin (Figure 4.43). The α chain has seven α helices, and the β chain has eight. (Two short α helices found in β-globin and myoglobin are fused into one larger one in α-globin.) Hemoglobin, however, is not simply a tetramer of myoglobin molecules. Each α chain interacts extensively with a β chain, so hemoglobin is actually a dimer of αβ subunits. We will see in the following section that the presence of quaternary structure is responsible for oxygen-binding properties not possible with single-chain myoglobin.

4.13 Oxygen Binding to Myoglobin and Hemoglobin

The oxygen-binding activity of myoglobin and hemoglobin provides an excellent example of how protein structure relates to physiological function. These proteins are among the most intensely studied proteins in biochemistry. They were the first complex proteins whose structure was determined by X-ray crystallography (Section 4.2). A number of the principles described here for oxygen-binding proteins also hold true for the enzymes that we will study in the next two chapters. In this section, we examine the chemistry of oxygen binding to heme, the physiology of oxygen binding to myoglobin and hemoglobin, and the regulatory properties of hemoglobin.

A. Oxygen Binds Reversibly to Heme

We will use myoglobin as an example of oxygen binding to the heme prosthetic group, although the same principles apply to hemoglobin. The reversible binding of oxygen is termed **oxygenation**. Oxygen-free myoglobin is called deoxymyoglobin, and the oxygen-bearing molecule is called oxymyoglobin. (The two forms of hemoglobin are called deoxyhemoglobin and oxyhemoglobin.)

Some substituents of the heme prosthetic group are hydrophobic; this feature allows the prosthetic group to be partially buried in the hydrophobic interior of the myoglobin molecule. Recall from Figure 4.40 that there are two polar residues, His-64 and His-93, situated near the heme group. In oxymyoglobin, six ligands are coordinated to the ferrous iron, with the ligands in octahedral geometry around the metal cation (Figures 4.44 and 4.45). Four of the ligands are the nitrogen atoms of the tetrapyrrole ring system; the fifth ligand is an imidazole nitrogen from His-93 (called the proximal histidine); and the sixth ligand is molecular oxygen bound between the iron and the imidazole side chain of His-64 (called the distal histidine). In deoxymyoglobin, the iron is coordinated to only five ligands since oxygen is not present. The nonpolar side chains of Val-68 and Phe-43, shown in Figure 4.45, contribute to the hydrophobicity of the oxygen-binding pocket and help hold the heme group in place. Several side chains block the entrance to the heme-containing pocket in both oxymyoglobin and deoxymyoglobin. The protein structure in this region must vibrate, or breathe, rapidly to allow oxygen to bind and dissociate.

The hydrophobic crevice of the globin polypeptide holds the key to the ability of myoglobin and hemoglobin to suitably bind and release oxygen. In aqueous solution, free heme does not reversibly bind oxygen; instead, the Fe(II) of the heme is almost instantly oxidized to Fe(III). The structure of myoglobin and hemoglobin prevents formal transfer of an electron and precludes irreversible oxidation, thereby ensuring the reversible binding of molecular oxygen for transport. In fact, the ferrous iron atom of heme in hemoglobin is partially oxidized when O_2 is bound. An electron is transferred toward the oxygen atom that is attached to the iron, so that the molecule of dioxygen is partially reduced. If the electron were transferred completely to the oxygen, the complex would be $Fe^{3+}\text{------}O_2^{-}$ (a superoxide anion attached to ferric iron). The globin crevice prevents complete electron transfer and enforces return of the electron to the iron atom when O_2 dissociates.

His-64

Heme

His-93

Figure 4.44 ▲
Oxygen-binding site of sperm whale oxymyoglobin. The heme prosthetic group is represented by a parallelogram with a nitrogen atom at each corner. The blue dashed lines illustrate the octahedral geometry of the coordination complex.

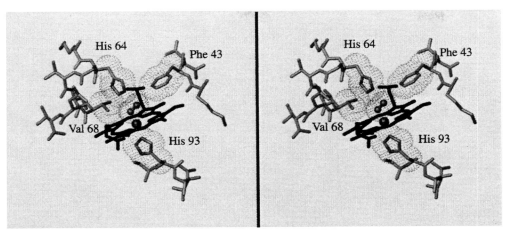

Figure 4.45 ▲
Stereo view of the oxygen-binding site in sperm whale myoglobin. Fe(II) (orange) lies in the plane of the heme group. Oxygen (green) is bound to the iron atom and the amino acid side chain of His-64. Val-68 and Phe-43 contribute to the hydrophobic environment of the oxygen-binding site. [PDB 1AGM].

B. Oxygen-Binding Curves of Myoglobin and Hemoglobin

The extent of reversible binding of oxygen to myoglobin and hemoglobin at equilibrium is depicted by oxygen-binding curves. In these figures, the fractional saturation (Y) is plotted against the concentration of oxygen (measured as the partial pressure of gaseous oxygen, pO_2). The fractional saturation of myoglobin or hemoglobin is the fraction of the total number of molecules that are oxygenated.

$$Y = \frac{[MbO_2]}{[MbO_2] + [Mb]}$$ **(4.1)**

The oxygen-binding curve of myoglobin is hyperbolic (Figure 4.46), indicating that there is a single equilibrium constant for the binding of O_2 to the macromolecule. The binding of more than one molecule of ligand to a macromolecule often produces a sigmoidal (S-shaped) binding curve. Up to four molecules of O_2 bind to hemoglobin, one per heme group of the tetrameric protein, and the curve depicting oxygen binding to hemoglobin is sigmoidal (Figure 4.46). The shape of the curve indicates that the oxygen-binding sites of hemoglobin interact such that the binding of one molecule of oxygen to one heme group facilitates binding of oxygen molecules to the other hemes. The oxygen affinity of hemoglobin increases as each oxygen molecule is bound. This interactive binding phenomenon is termed **positive cooperativity of binding**.

The partial pressure at half-saturation (P_{50}) is a measure of the affinity of the protein for O_2. A low P_{50} indicates a high affinity for oxygen since the protein is half-saturated with oxygen at a low oxygen concentration; similarly, a high P_{50} signifies a low affinity. Myoglobin molecules are half-saturated at a pO_2 of 2.8 torr (1 atmosphere = 760 torr). The P_{50} for hemoglobin is much higher (26 torr), reflecting its lower affinity for oxygen. The heme prosthetic groups of myoglobin and hemoglobin are identical, but the affinities of these groups for oxygen differ because the microenvironments provided by the proteins are slightly different. Oxygen affinity is an intrinsic property of the protein. It is similar to the equilibrium binding/dissociation constants that are commonly used to describe the binding of ligands to other proteins and enzymes.

As Figure 4.46 shows, at the high pO_2 found in the lungs (about 100 torr), both myoglobin and hemoglobin are nearly saturated. However, at pO_2 values below about 50 torr, myoglobin is still almost fully saturated, whereas hemoglobin is only partially saturated. Within the capillaries of tissues, where pO_2 is low (20 to 40 torr), much of the oxygen carried by hemoglobin in erythrocytes is released. Myoglobin

Figure 4.46 ▶
Oxygen-binding curves of myoglobin and hemoglobin. **(a)** Comparison of myoglobin and hemoglobin. The fractional saturation, (Y) of each protein is plotted against the partial pressure of oxygen (pO_2). The oxygen-binding curve of myoglobin is hyperbolic, with half-saturation ($Y = 0.5$) at an oxygen pressure of 2.8 torr. The oxygen-binding curve of hemoglobin in whole blood is sigmoidal, with half-saturation at an oxygen pressure of 26 torr. Myoglobin has a greater affinity than hemoglobin for oxygen at all oxygen pressures. In the lungs, where the partial pressure of oxygen is high, hemoglobin is nearly saturated with oxygen. In tissues, where the partial pressure of oxygen is low, oxygen is released from oxygenated hemoglobin and transferred to myoglobin. **(b)** O_2 binding by the different states of hemoglobin. The oxy (R, or high-affinity) state of hemoglobin has a hyperbolic binding curve. The deoxy (T, or low-affinity) state of hemoglobin would also have a hyperbolic binding curve but with a much higher concentration for half-saturation. Solutions of hemoglobin containing mixtures of low- and high-affinity forms show sigmoidal binding curves with intermediate oxygen affinities.

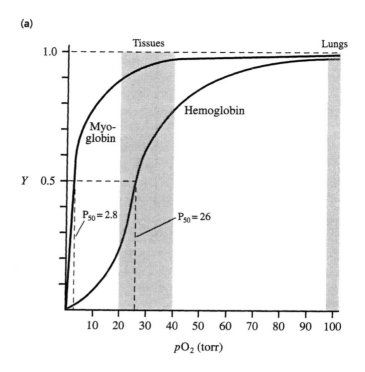
(a)

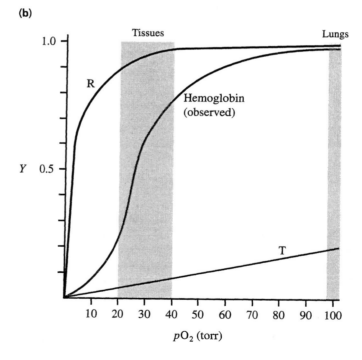
(b)

in muscle tissue then binds oxygen released from hemoglobin. The differential affinities of myoglobin and hemoglobin for oxygen thus lead to an efficient system for oxygen delivery from the lungs to muscle.

The cooperative binding of oxygen by hemoglobin can be related to changes in the protein conformation that occur on oxygenation. Deoxyhemoglobin is stabilized by several intra- and intersubunit ion pairs. When oxygen binds to one of the subunits, it causes a movement that disrupts these ion pairs and favors a slightly different conformation. The movement is triggered by the reactivity of the heme iron atom (Figure 4.47). In deoxyhemoglobin, the iron atom is bound to only five

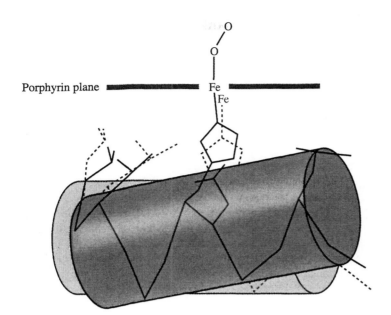

Porphyrin plane

◀ **Figure 4.47**
Conformational changes in a hemoglobin chain induced by oxygenation. When the heme iron of a hemoglobin subunit is oxygenated (red), the proximal histidine residue is pulled toward the porphyrin ring. The helix containing the histidine also shifts position, disrupting ion pairs that cross-link the subunits of deoxyhemoglobin (blue).

ligands (as in myoglobin). It is slightly larger than the cavity within the porphyrin ring and lies above the plane of the ring. When O_2—the sixth ligand—binds to the iron atom, the electronic structure of the iron changes, its diameter decreases, and it moves into the plane of the porphyrin ring, pulling the helix that contains the proximal histidine. The change in tertiary structure results in a slight change in quaternary structure, and this allows the remaining subunits to bind oxygen more readily. The entire tetramer appears to shift from the deoxy to the oxy conformation only after at least one oxygen molecule binds to each αβ dimer. (For further discussion see Section 5.10C.)

The conformational change of hemoglobin is responsible for the positive co-operativity of binding seen in the binding curve (Figure 4.46a). The shape of the curve is due to the combined effect of the two conformations (Figure 4.46b). The completely deoxygenated form of hemoglobin has a low affinity for oxygen and thus exhibits a hyperbolic binding curve with a very high concentration of half-saturation. Only a small amount of hemoglobin is saturated at low oxygen concentrations. As the concentration of oxygen increases, some of the hemoglobin molecules bind a molecule of oxygen, and this increases their affinity for oxygen so that they are more likely to bind additional oxygen. This causes the sigmoidal curve and also a sharp rise in binding. More molecules of hemoglobin are in the oxy conformation. If all of the hemoglobin molecules were in the oxy conformation, a solution would exhibit a hyperbolic binding curve. Release of the oxygen molecules allows the hemoglobin molecule to re-form the ion pairs and resume the deoxy conformation.

The two conformations of hemoglobin are called the T (tense) and R (relaxed) states, using the standard terminology for such conformational changes. In hemoglobin, the deoxy conformation, which resists oxygen binding, is considered the inactive (T) state, and the oxy conformation, which facilitates oxygen binding, is considered the active (R) state. The R and T states are in dynamic equilibrium.

C. Hemoglobin Is an Allosteric Protein

The binding and release of oxygen by hemoglobin are regulated by **allosteric interactions** (from the Greek *allos*, other). In this respect, hemoglobin—a carrier protein, not an enzyme—resembles certain regulatory enzymes (Section 5.10). Allosteric interactions occur when a specific small molecule, called an **allosteric modulator**, or **allosteric effector**, binds to a protein (usually an enzyme) and modulates its activity. The allosteric modulator binds reversibly at a site separate from the functional binding

Figure 4.48 ▲
2,3-Bisphospho-D-glycerate (2,3BPG).

site of the protein. An effector molecule may be an activator or an inhibitor. A protein whose activity is modulated by allosteric effectors is called an **allosteric protein**.

Allosteric modulation is accomplished by small but significant changes in the conformations of allosteric proteins. It involves cooperativity of binding that is regulated by binding of the allosteric effector to a distinct site that doesn't overlap the normal binding site of a substrate, product, or transported molecule such as oxygen. An allosteric protein is in an equilibrium in which its active shape (R state) and its inactive shape (T state) are rapidly interconverting. A substrate, which obviously binds at the active site (to heme in hemoglobin), binds most avidly when the protein is in the R state. An allosteric inhibitor, which binds at an allosteric or regulatory site, binds most avidly to the T state. The binding of an allosteric inhibitor to its own site causes the allosteric protein to change rapidly from the R state to the T state. The binding of a substrate to the active site (or an allosteric activator to the allosteric site) causes the reverse change. The change in conformation of an allosteric protein caused by binding or release of an effector extends from the allosteric site to the functional binding site (the active site). The activity level of an allosteric protein depends on the relative proportions of molecules in the R and T forms, and these in turn depend on the relative concentrations of the substrates and modulators that bind to each form.

The molecule 2,3-bisphospho-D-glycerate (2,3BPG), shown in Figure 4.48, is an allosteric effector of mammalian hemoglobin. The presence of 2,3BPG in erythrocytes raises the P_{50} for binding of oxygen to adult hemoglobin to about 26 torr—much higher than the P_{50} for oxygen binding to purified hemoglobin in aqueous solution, about 12 torr. In other words, 2,3BPG in erythrocytes substantially lowers the affinity of deoxyhemoglobin for oxygen. The concentrations of 2,3BPG and hemoglobin within erythrocytes are nearly equal (about 4.7 mM).

In the central cavity of hemoglobin, between the two β subunits, there are six positively charged side chains and the N-terminal α-amino group of each β chain. These form a cationic binding site (Figure 4.49). In deoxyhemoglobin, these positively charged groups can interact electrostatically with the five negative charges of 2,3BPG. When 2,3BPG is bound, the deoxy conformation (the T state, which has a low affinity for O_2) is stabilized, and conversion to the oxy conformation (the R or high-affinity state) is inhibited. In oxyhemoglobin, the β chains are closer together,

Figure 4.49 ▶
Binding of 2,3BPG to deoxyhemoglobin. The central cavity of deoxyhemoglobin is lined with positively charged groups that are complementary to the carboxylate and phosphate groups of 2,3BPG. Both 2,3BPG and the ion pairs shown help stabilize the deoxy conformation. The α subunits are shown in pink, the β subunits in blue, and the heme prosthetic groups in red.

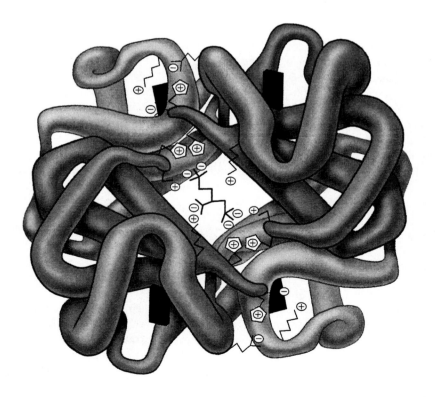

and the allosteric binding site is too small to accommodate 2,3BPG. The reversibly bound ligands O_2 and 2,3BPG have opposite effects on the $R \rightleftharpoons T$ equilibrium. Oxygen binding increases the proportion of hemoglobin molecules in the oxy (R) conformation, and 2,3BPG binding increases the proportion of hemoglobin molecules in the deoxy (T) conformation. Because oxygen and 2,3BPG have different binding sites, 2,3BPG is an allosteric effector.

In the absence of 2,3BPG, hemoglobin is nearly saturated at an oxygen pressure of about 20 torr. Thus, at the low partial pressure of oxygen that prevails in the tissues (20 to 40 torr), hemoglobin without 2,3BPG would not unload its oxygen. In the presence of equimolar 2,3BPG, however, hemoglobin is only about one-third saturated at 20 torr. The allosteric effect of 2,3BPG causes hemoglobin to release oxygen at the low partial pressures of oxygen in the tissues. In muscle, myoglobin can bind some of the oxygen that is released.

Additional regulation of the binding of oxygen to hemoglobin involves carbon dioxide and protons; both are products of aerobic metabolism. CO_2 decreases the affinity of hemoglobin for O_2 by lowering the pH inside red blood cells. Enzyme-catalyzed hydration of CO_2 in erythrocytes produces carbonic acid (H_2CO_3), which dissociates to form bicarbonate and a proton, thereby lowering the pH.

$$CO_2 + H_2O \rightleftharpoons H_2CO_3 \rightleftharpoons H^{\oplus} + HCO_3^{\ominus} \tag{4.2}$$

The lower pH leads to protonation of several groups in hemoglobin. These groups then form ion pairs that help stabilize the deoxy conformation. The increase in the concentration of CO_2 and the concomitant decrease in pH raise the P_{50} of hemoglobin (Figure 4.50). This phenomenon, called the Bohr effect, increases the efficiency of the oxygen delivery system: in inhaling lungs, where the CO_2 level is low, O_2 is readily picked up by hemoglobin; in metabolizing tissues, where the CO_2 level is relatively high and the pH is relatively low, O_2 is readily unloaded from oxyhemoglobin.

Carbon dioxide is transported from the tissues to the lungs in two ways. Most CO_2 produced by metabolism is transported as dissolved bicarbonate ions. Some carbon dioxide, however, is carried via hemoglobin itself, in the form of carbamate adducts (Figure 4.51). At the pH of red blood cells (7.2) and at high concentrations of CO_2, the unprotonated amino groups of the four N-terminal residues of deoxyhemoglobin (pK_a values between 7 and 8) can react reversibly with CO_2 to form carbamate adducts. The carbamates of oxyhemoglobin are less stable than those of deoxyhemoglobin. When hemoglobin reaches the lungs, where the partial pressure of CO_2 is low and the partial pressure of O_2 is high, hemoglobin is converted to its oxygenated state, and the CO_2 that was bound is released.

4.14 Antibodies Bind Specific Antigens

Vertebrates possess a complex immune system that eliminates foreign substances, including infectious bacteria and viruses. As part of this defense system, vertebrates synthesize proteins called **antibodies** (also known as immunoglobulins) that specifically recognize and bind **antigens**. Many different types of foreign compounds can serve as antigens that produce an immune response. Antibodies are synthesized by white blood cells called lymphocytes; each lymphocyte and its descendants synthesize the same antibody. Because animals are exposed to many foreign substances over their lifetimes, they develop a huge array of antibody-producing lymphocytes that persist at low levels for many years and can later respond to the antigen during reinfection. The memory of the immune system is the reason certain infections do not recur in an individual despite repeated exposure. Vaccines (inactivated pathogens or analogs of toxins) administered to children are effective because immunity established in childhood lasts through adulthood.

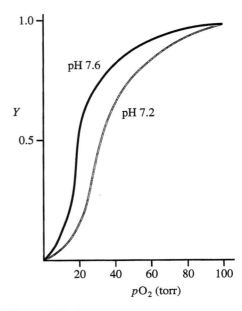

Figure 4.50 ▲
Bohr effect. Lowering the pH decreases the affinity of hemoglobin for oxygen.

Figure 4.51 ▲
Carbamate adduct. Carbon dioxide produced by metabolizing tissues can react reversibly with the N-terminal residues of the globin chains of hemoglobin, converting them to carbamate adducts.

(a)

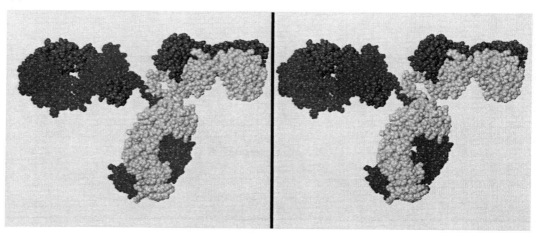

(b)

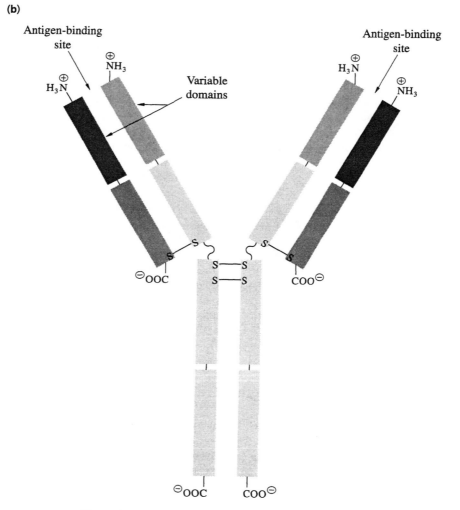

Figure 4.52 ▲
Human antibody structure. **(a)** Structure. **(b)** Diagram. Two heavy chains (blue) and two light chains (red) of antibodies of the immunoglobulin G class are joined by disulfide bonds (yellow). The variable domains of both the light and heavy chains (where antigen binds) are colored more darkly.

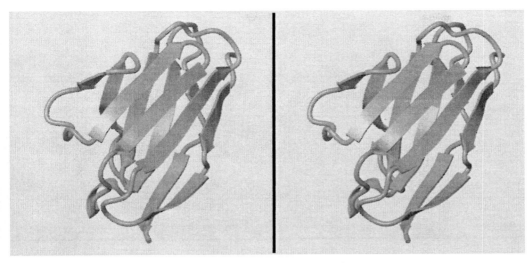

Figure 4.53 ▲
Stereo view of the immunoglobulin fold. The domain consists of a sandwich of two antiparallel β sheets. [PDB 1REI].

When an antigen—either novel or previously encountered—binds to the surface of lymphocytes, these cells are stimulated to proliferate and produce soluble antibodies for secretion into the bloodstream. The soluble antibodies bind to the foreign organism or substance, forming antibody-antigen complexes that precipitate and mark the antigen for destruction by a series of interacting proteases or by lymphocytes that engulf the antigen and digest it intracellularly.

The most abundant antibodies in the bloodstream are of the immunoglobulin G class (IgG). These are Y-shaped oligomers composed of two identical light chains and two identical heavy chains connected by disulfide bonds (Figure 4.52). Immunoglobulins are glycoproteins; they contain covalently bound carbohydrates attached to the heavy chains. The N-termini of pairs of light and heavy chains are close together. Light chains contain two domains, and heavy chains contain four domains. All the domains consist of about 110 residues assembled into a common motif termed the immunoglobulin fold. The characteristic feature of the immunoglobulin fold is a sandwich composed of two antiparallel β sheets (Figure 4.53). This domain structure is found in many other proteins of the immune system.

The N-terminal domains of antibodies, called the variable domains because of their sequence diversity, determine the specificity of antigen binding. X-ray crystallographic studies have shown that the antigen-binding site of a variable domain consists of three loops, called hypervariable regions, that differ widely in size and sequence. The loops from a light chain and a heavy chain combine to form a barrel, the upper surface of which is complementary to the shape and polarity of a specific antigen. The match between the antigen and antibody is so close that there is no space for water molecules between the two. The forces that stabilize the interaction of antigen with antibody are primarily hydrogen bonds and electrostatic interactions. An example of the interaction of antibodies with a protein antigen is shown in Figure 4.54.

Because of their remarkable antigen-binding specificity, antibodies are used in the laboratory for the detection of small quantities of various substances. In a common type of immunoassay, fluid containing an unknown amount of antigen is mixed with a solution of labeled antibody, and the amount of antibody-antigen complex formed is measured. The sensitivity of these assays can be enhanced in a variety of ways to make them suitable for diagnostic tests.

Figure 4.54 ▶
Binding of three different antibodies to an antigen (the protein lysozyme). The structures of the three antigen-antibody complexes have been determined by X-ray crystallography. This composite view, in which the antigen and antibodies have been separated, shows the surfaces of the antigen and antibodies that interact. Only parts of the three antibodies are shown.

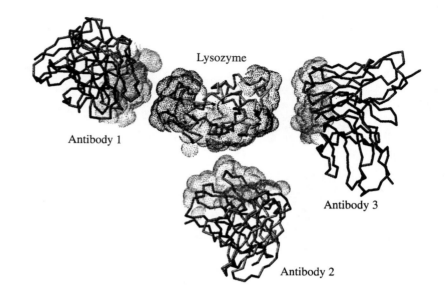

Summary

1. Globular proteins are water-soluble, roughly spherical, and tightly folded. Fibrous proteins are generally water-insoluble and provide mechanical support to cells and tissues. Membrane proteins are integral components of membranes or are associated with membranes.

2. There are four levels of protein structure: primary (sequence of amino acid residues), secondary (regular local conformation, stabilized by hydrogen bonds), tertiary (compacted shape of the entire polypeptide chain), and quaternary (assembly of two or more polypeptide chains into a multisubunit protein).

3. The three-dimensional structures of biopolymers, such as proteins, can be determined by X-ray crystallography and NMR spectroscopy.

4. The peptide group is polar and planar. Rotation around the $N—C_\alpha$ and $C_\alpha—C$ bonds is described by ϕ and ψ.

5. The α helix, a common secondary structure, is a coil containing approximately 3.6 amino acid residues per turn. Hydrogen bonds between amide hydrogens and carbonyl oxygens are roughly parallel to the helix axis.

6. The other common type of secondary structure, β structure, often consists of either parallel or antiparallel β strands that are hydrogen-bonded to each other to form β sheets.

7. Most proteins include stretches of nonrepeating conformation, including turns and loops that connect α helices and β strands. Recognizable combinations of secondary structural elements are called motifs.

8. The tertiary structure of proteins consists of one or more domains, which may have recognizable structures and may be associated with particular functions.

9. In proteins that possess quaternary structure, subunits are usually held together by noncovalent interactions.

10. The native conformation of a protein can be disrupted by the addition of denaturing agents. Renaturation may be possible under certain conditions.

11. Folding of a protein into its biologically active state is a sequential, cooperative process driven primarily by the hydrophobic effect. Folding can be assisted by chaperones.

12. Collagen is the major fibrous protein of connective tissues. The three left-handed helical chains of collagen form a right-handed supercoil.

13. The compact, folded structures of proteins allow them to selectively bind other molecules. The heme-containing proteins myoglobin and hemoglobin bind and release oxygen. Oxygen binding to hemoglobin is characterized by positive cooperativity and allosteric regulation.

14. Antibodies are multidomain proteins that bind foreign substances, or antigens, marking them for destruction. The variable domains at the ends of the heavy and light chains interact with the antigen.

Problems

1. Examine the following tripeptide:

(a) Label the α-carbon atoms and draw boxes around the atoms of each peptide group.

(b) What do the R groups represent?

(c) Why is there no free rotation around the carbonyl $C=O$ to N amide bonds?

(d) Assuming that the chemical structure represents the correct conformation of the peptide linkage, are the peptide groups in the *cis* or the *trans* conformation?

(e) Which bonds allow rotation of peptide groups with respect to each other?

2. (a) Characterize the hydrogen-bonding pattern of: (1) an α-helix, and (2) a collagen triple helix.

(b) Explain how the amino acid side chains are arranged in each of these helices.

3. Explain why (1) glycine and (2) proline residues are not commonly found in α helices.

4. A synthetic 20 amino acid polypeptide named Betanova was designed as a small soluble molecule that would theoretically form stable β-sheet structures in the absence of disulfide bonds. NMR of Betanova in solution indicates that it does, in fact, form a three-stranded antiparallel β sheet. Given the sequence of Betanova below:

(a) Draw a ribbon diagram for Betanova indicating likely residues for each hairpin turn between the β strands.

(b) Show the interactions that are expected to stabilize this β-sheet structure.

    Betanova   RGWSVQNGKYTNNGKTTEGR

5. Each member of an important family of 250 different DNA-binding proteins is composed of a dimer with a common protein motif. This motif permits each DNA-binding protein to recognize and bind to specific DNA sequences. What is the common protein motif in the structure below?

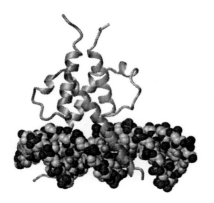

6. Refer to Figure 4.20 to answer the following questions.

(a) To which of the four major domain categories does the middle domain of pyruvate kinase (PK) belong (all α, all β, α/β, α + β)?

(b) Describe any characteristic domain "fold" that is prominent in this middle domain of PK.

(c) Identify two other proteins that have the same fold as the middle domain of pyruvate kinase.

7. Myoglobin contains eight α helices, one of which has the following sequence:

    –Gln–Gly–Ala–Met–Asn–Lys–Ala–Leu–Glu–
      His–Phe–Arg–Lys–Asp–Ile–Ala–Ala–

Which side chains are likely to be on the side of the helix that faces the interior of the protein? Which are likely to be facing the aqueous solvent? Account for the spacing of the residues facing the interior.

8. Protein disulfide isomerase (PDI) markedly increases the rate of correct refolding of the inactive ribonuclease form with random disulfide bonds (Figure 4.21). Show the mechanism for the PDI-catalyzed rearrangement of a nonnative (inactive) protein with incorrect disulfide bonds to the native (active) protein with correct disulfide bonds.

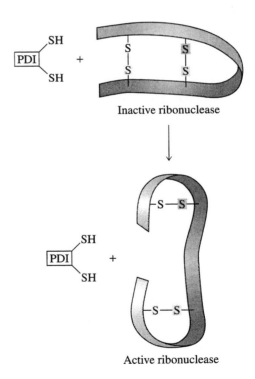

Inactive ribonuclease

Active ribonuclease

9. Homocysteine is an α-amino acid containing one more methylene group in its side chain than cysteine (side chain = —CH$_2$CH$_2$SH). Homocysteinuria is a genetic disease characterized by elevated levels of homocysteine in plasma and urine, as well as skeletal deformities due to defects in collagen structure. Homocysteine reacts readily with allysine under physiological conditions. Show this reaction and suggest how it might lead to defective cross-linking in collagen.

10. The larval form of the parasite *Schistosoma mansoni* infects humans by penetrating the skin. The larva secretes enzymes that catalyze the cleavage of peptide bonds between residues X and Y in the sequence –Gly–Pro–X–Y– (X and Y can be any of several amino acids). Why is this enzyme activity important for the parasite?

11. (a) How does the reaction of carbon dioxide with water help explain the Bohr effect? Include the equation for the formation of bicarbonate ion from CO$_2$ and water, and explain the effects of H$^{\oplus}$ and CO$_2$ on hemoglobin oxygenation.
    (b) Explain the physiological basis for the intravenous administration of bicarbonate to shock victims.

12. Fetal hemoglobin (Hb F) contains serine in place of the cationic histidine at position 143 of the β chains of adult hemoglobin (Hb A). Residue 143 faces the central cavity between the β chains.
    (a) Why does 2,3BPG bind more tightly to deoxy Hb A than to deoxy Hb F?
    (b) How does the decreased affinity of Hb F for 2,3BPG affect the affinity of Hb F for O$_2$?
    (c) The P_{50} for Hb F is 18 torr, and the P_{50} for Hb A is 26 torr. How do these values explain the efficient transfer of oxygen from maternal blood to the fetus?

13. Amino acid substitutions at the αβ subunit interfaces of hemoglobin may interfere with the R $\rightleftarrows$ T quaternary structural changes that take place on oxygen binding. In the hemoglobin variant Hb$_{\text{Yakima}}$, the R form is stabilized relative to the T form, and $P_{50} = 12$ torr. Explain why the mutant hemoglobin is less efficient than normal hemoglobin ($P_{50} = 26$ torr) in delivering oxygen to working muscle, where pO$_2$ may be as low as 10 to 20 torr.

Selected Readings

General

Creighton, T. E. (1993). *Proteins: Structures and Molecular Properties*, 2nd ed. (New York: W. H. Freeman). Chapters 4–7.

Fersht, A. (1998). *Structure and Mechanism in Protein Structure* (New York: W. H. Freeman).

Goodsell, D., and Olson, A. J. (1993). Soluble proteins: size, shape, and function. *Trends Biochem. Sci.* 18:65–68.

Kyte, J. (1995). *Structure in Protein Chemistry* (New York: Garland).

Protein Structure

Branden, C., and Tooze, J. (1991). *Introduction to Protein Structure* (New York: Garland). A comprehensive discussion of three-dimensional structures of proteins, based on X-ray crystallographic analyses.

Chothia, C., Hubbard, T., Brenner, S., Barns, H., and Murzin, A. (1997). Protein folds in the all-β and all-α classes. *Annu. Rev. Biophys. Biomol. Struct.* 26:597–627.

Harper, E. T., and Rose, G. D. (1993). Helix stop signals in proteins and peptides: the capping box. *Biochemistry* 32:7605–7609.

Rhodes, G. (1993). *Crystallography Made Crystal Clear* (San Diego: Academic Press). An introduction to X-ray crystallography and a guide for using crystallographic models.

Richardson, J. S., and Richardson, D. C. (1989). Principles and patterns of protein conformation. In *Prediction of Protein Structure and the*

Principles of Protein Conformation, G. D. Fasman, ed. (New York: Plenum), pp. 1–98. An excellent review of secondary and tertiary structures of globular proteins.

Protein Folding and Stability

Anfinsen, C. B. (1973). Principles that govern the folding of protein chains. *Science* 181:223–230. Describes the self-assembly of ribonuclease.

Baldwin, R. L., and Rose, G. D. (1999). Is protein folding hierarchic? I. Local structure and peptide folding. *Trends Biochem. Sci.* 24:26–33.

Baldwin, R. L., and Rose, G. D. (1999). Is protein folding hierarchic? II. Folding intermediates and transition states. *Trends Biochem. Sci.* 24:26–33.

Dill, K. A. (1990). Dominant forces in protein folding. *Biochemistry* 29:7133–7155.

Ellis, R. J. (2000). Chaperone substrates inside the cell. *Trends Biochem. Sci.* 25:210–212.

Feldman, D. E., and Frydman, J. (2000). Protein folding *in vivo*: the importance of molecular chaperones. *Curr. Opin. Struct. Biol.* 10:26–33.

Gething, M. J., and Sambrook, J. (1992). Protein folding in the cell. *Nature* 355:33–45.

Matthews, B. W. (1993). Structural and genetic analysis of protein stability. *Annu. Rev. Biochem.* 62:139–160.

Richards, F. M. (1991). The protein folding problem. *Sci. Am.* 264(1):54–63.

Sigler, P. B., Xu, Z., Rye, H. S., Burston, S. G., Fenton, W. A., and Horwich, A. L. (1998). Structure and function in GroEL-mediated protein folding. *Annu. Rev. Biochem.* 67:581–608.

Specific Proteins

Ackers, G. K., Doyle, M. L., Myers, D., and Daugherty, M. A. (1992). Molecular code for cooperativity in hemoglobin. *Science* 255:54–63.

Davies, D. R., Padlan, E. A., and Sheriff, S. (1990). Antibody-antigen complexes. *Annu. Rev. Biochem.* 59:439–473. Describes the three-dimensional structures of antibody-antigen complexes.

Eaton, W. A., Henry, E. R., Hofrichter, J., and Mozzarelli, A. (1999). Is cooperative binding by hemoglobin really understood? *Nature Struct. Biol.* 6(4):351–357.

Kadler, K. (1994). Extracellular matrix 1: fibril-forming collagens. *Protein Profile* 1:519–549.

Perutz, M. F. (1978). Hemoglobin structure and respiratory transport. *Sci. Am.* 239(6):92–125.

Perutz, M. F., Wilkinson, A. J., Paoli, M., and Dodson, G. G. (1998). The stereochemical mechanism of the cooperative effects in hemoglobin revisited. *Annu. Rev. Biophys. Biomol. Struct.* 27:1–34.

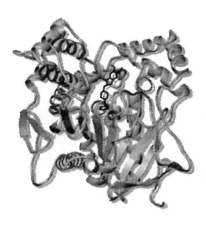

CHAPTER

5

Properties
of Enzymes

e have seen how the three-dimensional shapes of proteins allow them to
serve structural and transport roles. We now discuss their functions as enzymes. Enzymes are extraordinarily efficient, selective biological catalysts. Every living cell has hundreds of different enzymes catalyzing the reactions
essential for life. Even the simplest living organisms contain multiple copies of hundreds of different enzymes. In multicellular organisms, the complement of enzymes
present differentiates one cell type from another. Most enzymes discussed in this
book are among the several hundred common to virtually all cells. These enzymes
catalyze the reactions of the central metabolic pathways necessary for the mainte-
nance of life.

Most reactions catalyzed by enzymes do not proceed at significant rates under
physiological conditions in the absence of the enzymes. Enzyme-catalyzed reactions, or **enzymatic reactions**, are 10^3 to 10^{17} times faster than the corresponding uncatalyzed reactions.

A **catalyst** is a substance that speeds up the attainment of an equilibrium.
Although it may be changed during the reaction, it is unchanged in the overall
process, as it recycles to participate again. Reactants bind to a catalyst, and products
dissociate from it. A catalyst does not change the position of the reaction's equilibrium (i.e., it does not make an unfavorable reaction favorable). Rather, it lowers the
amount of energy needed for the reaction. A catalyst converts a one- or two-step
process into several smaller steps, each needing less energy than the uncatalyzed
reaction. The next chapter describes the details of how enzymes act as catalysts.

Enzymes are highly specific for the reactants, or **substrates**, they act on, and the degree of substrate specificity varies. Some enzymes act on a group of related substrates,
and others on only a single compound. Many enzymes exhibit **stereospecificity**, meaning that they act on only a single stereoisomer of the substrate. Perhaps the most important

---

Top: The enzyme acetylcholinesterase with the reversible inhibitor donepezil hydrochloride (Aricept; shown in
red) occupying the active site. Aricept is used to improve mental functioning in patients with Alzheimer's disease;
it is thought to act by inhibiting the breakdown of the neurotransmitter acetylcholine in the brain, thus
prolonging the neurotransmitter effects. (It does not, however, affect the course of the disease.) [PDB 1EVE].

Chemistry for Biologists

aspect of enzyme specificity is **reaction specificity**, that is, the lack of formation of wasteful by-products. Reaction specificity is reflected in the exceptional purity of product (essentially 100%)—much higher than the purity of products of typical catalyzed reactions in organic chemistry. The specificity of enzymes not only saves energy for cells but also precludes the buildup of potentially toxic metabolic by-products.

Some enzymatic reactions function as control points in metabolism. As we will see, metabolism is regulated in a variety of ways, including alterations in the concentrations of enzymes, substrates, and enzyme inhibitors, and modulation of the activity levels of certain enzymes.

The name *enzyme* is derived from a Greek word meaning "in yeast." It indicates that these catalysts are present inside cells. In the late 1800s, scientists studied the fermentation of sugars by yeast cells. Vitalists (who maintained that organic compounds could be made only by living cells) said that intact cells were needed for fermentation. Mechanists claimed that enzymes in yeast cells catalyze the reactions of fermentation. The latter conclusion was supported by the observation that cell-free extracts of yeast can catalyze fermentation. This finding was soon followed by the identification of individual reactions and the enzymes that catalyze them.

A generation later, in 1926, James B. Sumner crystallized the first enzyme (urease) and proved that it is a protein. In the next decade, five more enzymes [pepsin, trypsin, chymotrypsin, carboxypeptidase, and Old Yellow enzyme, a flavoprotein NADPH (reduced nicotinamide adenine dinucleotide phosphate) oxidase] were purified and also found to be proteins. Since then, almost all enzymes have been shown to be proteins or proteins plus cofactors. Certain RNA molecules also exhibit catalytic activity, but they are not usually referred to as enzymes.

The enzymes described in this chapter are proteins and therefore possess the main functional characteristic of proteins—the ability to specifically bind one or several molecules. Substrate molecules are bound in a somewhat hydrophobic cleft known as the active site, which is often located in an indentation such as a pocket at one end of the protein, or between two protein domains (or sometimes between subunits). Enzymes whose activity is regulated, called regulatory enzymes, generally have a more complex structure than unregulated enzymes. With few exceptions, regulatory enzymes are oligomeric molecules that have separate binding sites for substrates and modulators, the compounds that act as regulatory signals.

In this chapter, we describe enzymes and their properties, starting with their classification and nomenclature. Next, we discuss kinetic analysis (measurements of reaction rates), emphasizing how kinetic experiments can reveal the properties of an enzyme and the nature of the complexes it forms with substrates and inhibitors. Finally, we describe the principles of inhibition and activation of regulatory enzymes. Chapter 6 explains how enzymes work at the chemical level and uses serine proteases to illustrate the relationship between protein structure and enzymatic function. Chapter 7 is devoted to the biochemistry of coenzymes, the organic molecules that assist some enzymes in their catalytic roles by providing reactive groups not found on amino acid side chains.

Catalytic RNA molecules are discussed in Chapters 21 and 22.

5.1 The Six Classes of Enzymes

Most of the classical metabolic enzymes are named by adding the suffix -*ase* to the name of their substrates or to a descriptive term for the reactions they catalyze. For example, urease has urea as a substrate. Alcohol dehydrogenase catalyzes the removal of hydrogen from alcohols (i.e., the oxidation of alcohols). A few enzymes, such as trypsin and amylase, are known by their historic names. Many newly discovered enzymes are named after their genes or for some nondescriptive characteristic. For example, Rec A is named after the *rec*A gene and HSP70 is a heat shock protein; both catalyze the hydrolysis of ATP.

Chemistry for Biologists

A committee of the International Union of Biochemistry and Molecular Biology (IUBMB) maintains a classification scheme that categorizes enzymes according to the general class of organic chemical reaction catalyzed. The six categories—oxidoreductases, transferases, hydrolases, lyases, isomerases, and ligases—are defined below, with an example of each. The IUBMB classification scheme assigns a unique number, a systematic name, and a shorter, common name to each enzyme. This book usually refers to enzymes by their common names.

1. **Oxidoreductases** catalyze oxidation-reduction reactions. Most of these enzymes are referred to as **dehydrogenases**, but some are called oxidases, peroxidases, oxygenases, or reductases.

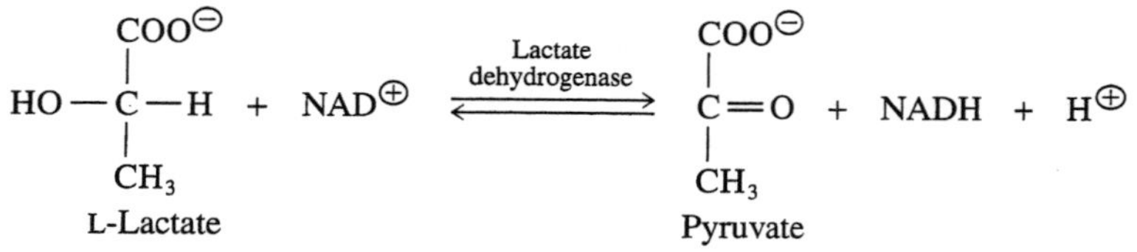

$$\text{L-Lactate} + NAD^{\oplus} \underset{\text{dehydrogenase}}{\overset{\text{Lactate}}{\rightleftharpoons}} \text{Pyruvate} + NADH + H^{\oplus} \qquad (5.1)$$

This reaction requires the coenzyme nicotinamide adenine dinucleotide (NAD).

2. **Transferases** catalyze group-transfer reactions, and many require the presence of coenzymes. In group-transfer reactions, a portion of the substrate molecule usually binds covalently to the enzyme or its coenzyme. This group includes kinases, enzymes that catalyze the transfer of a phosphoryl group from ATP.

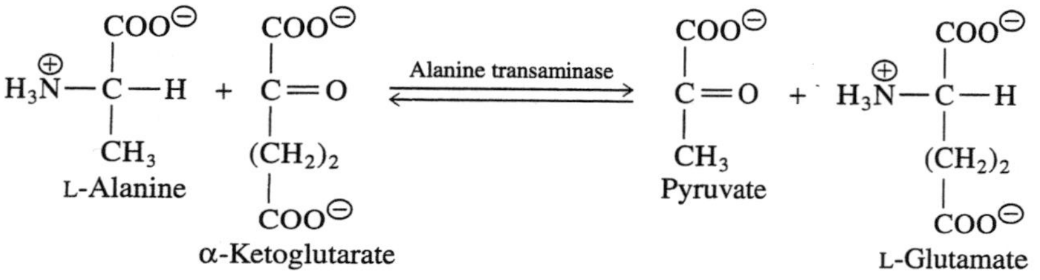

$$\text{L-Alanine} + \alpha\text{-Ketoglutarate} \overset{\text{Alanine transaminase}}{\rightleftharpoons} \text{Pyruvate} + \text{L-Glutamate} \qquad (5.2)$$

3. **Hydrolases** catalyze hydrolysis. They are a special class of transferases, with water serving as the acceptor of the group transferred.

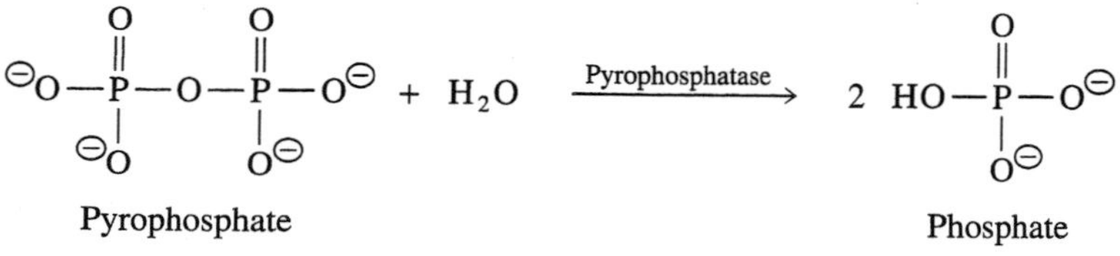

$$\text{Pyrophosphate} + H_2O \overset{\text{Pyrophosphatase}}{\longrightarrow} 2 \ \text{Phosphate} \qquad (5.3)$$

4. **Lyases** catalyze lysis of a substrate, generating a double bond; these are non-hydrolytic, nonoxidative elimination reactions. In the reverse direction, lyases catalyze the addition of one substrate to a double bond of a second substrate. A lyase that catalyzes an addition reaction in cells is often termed a **synthase**.

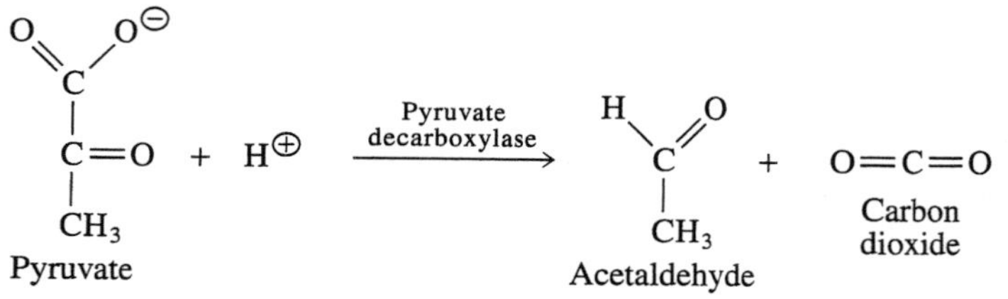

$$\text{Pyruvate} + H^{\oplus} \overset{\text{Pyruvate decarboxylase}}{\longrightarrow} \text{Acetaldehyde} + O=C=O \ \text{(Carbon dioxide)} \qquad (5.4)$$

5. **Isomerases** catalyze structural change within a single molecule (isomerization reactions). Because these reactions have only one substrate and one product, they are among the simplest enzymatic reactions.

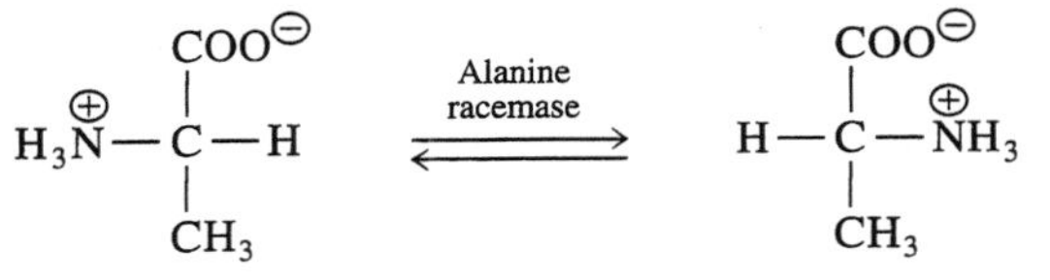

$$\text{L-Alanine} \xrightarrow[\text{racemase}]{\text{Alanine}} \text{D-Alanine} \qquad (5.5)$$

6. **Ligases** catalyze ligation, or joining, of two substrates. These reactions require the input of the chemical potential energy of a nucleoside triphosphate such as ATP. Ligases are usually referred to as **synthetases**.

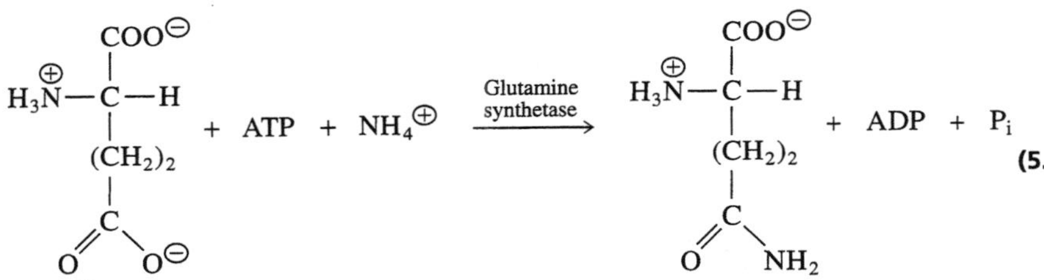

$$\text{L-Glutamate} + \text{ATP} + \text{NH}_4^{\oplus} \xrightarrow[\text{synthetase}]{\text{Glutamine}} \text{L-Glutamine} + \text{ADP} + \text{P}_i \qquad (5.6)$$

Note from the examples given above that most enzymes have more than one substrate; the second substrate may be only a molecule of water. Note also that although enzymes catalyze both forward and reverse reactions, one-way arrows are used when the equilibrium favors a great excess of product over substrate. At equilibrium, an enzyme catalyzes both the forward and reverse reactions at the same rate.

5.2 Kinetic Experiments Reveal Enzyme Properties

Enzyme kinetics is the study of the rates of enzyme-catalyzed reactions. Such studies provide indirect information concerning the specificities and catalytic mechanisms of enzymes. Clinically, kinetic assays are used to detect alterations in the concentrations or activities of enzymes; these alterations may be symptomatic of a disease.

For the first half of the 20th century, most enzyme research was limited to kinetic experiments. This research revealed how the rates of reactions are affected by variations in experimental conditions or in the concentration of enzyme or substrate. Before discussing enzyme kinetics in depth, we review the principles of kinetics for nonenzymatic chemical systems. These principles are then applied to enzymatic reactions.

A. Chemical Kinetics

Kinetic experiments examine the relationship between the amount of **product** (P) formed in a unit of time ($\Delta[P]/\Delta t$) and the experimental conditions under which the reaction takes place. The basis of most kinetic measurements is the observation that the rate, or **velocity** (v), of a reaction varies directly with the concentration of each reactant, whether substrate or catalyst. This observation is expressed in a **rate equation**. For example, the rate equation for the nonenzymatic conversion of substrate (S) to product in an isomerization reaction is written as

> Recall that concentrations are indicated by square brackets: [P] signifies the concentration of product, [E] the concentration of enzyme, and so on.

$$\frac{\Delta[P]}{\Delta t} = v = k[S] \qquad (5.7)$$

Chemistry for Biologists

127

The symbol k is the rate constant and indicates the speed or efficiency of a reaction. Each reaction has a different rate constant. A graph of velocity versus [S] for this reaction is a straight line that increases with the concentration of substrate. The overall **kinetic order** of a reaction, which is the sum of the exponents in the rate equation, indicates how many molecules react in the slowest step of the reaction. Equation 5.7 is the rate equation for a first-order reaction, a reaction in which only one component reacts. The rate constant for a first-order reaction is expressed in reciprocal time units (s^{-1}).

For a more complicated single-step reaction, such as the reaction $S_1 + S_2 \rightarrow P_1 + P_2$, the rate is determined by the concentrations of both substrates. If both substrates are present at similar concentrations, the rate equation is

$$v = k[S_1]^1[S_2]^1 \tag{5.8}$$

This reaction is first order with respect to each reactant, and since the sum of the exponents is 2, the reaction is second order overall. The reaction is also termed bimolecular because two molecules react to form the products. The rate constants for second-order reactions have the units $M^{-1} s^{-1}$. Reactions with more than two reactants are often studied, but because the calculations can become quite complex, experimental conditions are arranged so that the reactions proceed in several steps, with each step being either first order or second order.

When the concentration of one reactant is so high that it remains essentially constant during the reaction, the reaction is said to be zero order with respect to that reactant, and the term for the reactant is eliminated from the rate equation. The reaction then becomes an artificial, or pseudo, first-order reaction.

$$v = k[S_1]^1[S_2]^0 = k'[S_1] \tag{5.9}$$

An example of a pseudo first-order reaction is the nonenzymatic hydrolysis of the glycosidic bond of sucrose (table sugar) in aqueous acid solution. Sucrose is a disaccharide composed of one residue each of the sugars glucose and fructose.

$$\text{Sucrose} + \text{Water} \longrightarrow \text{Glucose} + \text{Fructose} \tag{5.10}$$
$$(C_{12}H_{22}O_{11}) \quad (H_2O) \quad (C_6H_{12}O_6) \quad (C_6H_{12}O_6)$$

The concentration of water, which is both solvent and substrate, is so high that it remains effectively constant during the reaction. Under these reaction conditions, the reaction rate depends on only the concentration of sucrose. To prove that the original reaction is not truly first order, the concentration of water can be made a limiting factor by replacing most of the water with a nonreacting solvent.

B. Enzyme Kinetics

One of the first great advances in biochemistry, the discovery that enzymes bind substrates transiently, resulted from the investigation of enzyme kinetics. In 1894 Emil Fischer proposed that an enzyme is a rigid template, or lock, and that the substrate is a matching key. Only specific substrates can fit into a given enzyme. Early studies of enzyme kinetics confirmed that an enzyme (E) binds a substrate to form an **enzyme-substrate complex** (ES). (This is an example of a bimolecular reaction.) ES complexes are formed when ligands bind noncovalently in their proper places in the active site. The substrate reacts transiently with the protein catalyst (and with other substrates in a multisubstrate reaction) to form the product of the reaction.

Let us now consider a simple enzymatic reaction, the conversion of a substrate to a product, catalyzed by an enzyme. Although most enzymatic reactions have two or more substrates, the general principles of enzyme kinetics can be elucidated by assuming the simple case of one substrate and one product.

$$E + S \longrightarrow ES \longrightarrow E + P \qquad \qquad \textbf{(5.11)}$$

The rate of an enzymatic reaction depends on the concentrations of both the substrate and the catalyst (enzyme). When the amount of enzyme is much less than the amount of substrate, the reaction is pseudo first order. The straight line in Figure 5.1 illustrates the effect of enzyme concentration on the reaction velocity in a pseudo first-order reaction. The more enzyme present, the faster the reaction.

Pseudo first-order conditions are used in analyses called **enzyme assays**, which determine the concentrations of enzymes. The concentration of enzyme in a test sample can be easily determined by comparing its activity to a reference curve similar to the model curve in Figure 5.1. Under these experimental conditions, there are sufficient numbers of substrate molecules so that every enzyme molecule binds a molecule of substrate to form an ES complex, a condition called **saturation** of E with S. Enzyme assays measure the amount of product formed in a given time period. In some assay methods, a recording spectrophotometer can be used to record data continuously; in other methods, samples are removed and analyzed at intervals. The assay is performed at a constant pH and temperature, generally chosen for optimal enzyme activity or for approximation to physiological conditions.

At the beginning of an enzyme-catalyzed reaction, the amount of product formed is negligible, and the reaction can be described by

$$E + S \underset{k_{-1}}{\overset{k_1}{\rightleftharpoons}} ES \overset{k_2}{\longrightarrow} E + P \qquad \qquad \textbf{(5.12)}$$

The rate constants k_1 and k_{-1} in Equation 5.12 govern the rates of association of S with E and dissociation of S from ES, respectively. The rate constant for the second step is k_2, the rate of formation of product from ES. Note that conversion of the ES complex to free enzyme and product is shown by a one-way arrow. During the initial period when measurements are made, little product has been formed, so the rate of the reverse reaction (E + P → EP) is negligible. The velocity measured during this short period is called the **initial velocity** (v_0). The use of v_0 measurements simplifies the interpretation of kinetic data and avoids complications that may arise as the reaction progresses, such as product inhibition and slow denaturation of the enzyme. The formation and dissociation of ES complexes are usually very rapid reactions because only noncovalent bonds are formed and broken. In contrast, the conversion of substrate to product is usually rate-limiting. It is during this step that the substrate is chemically altered.

Initial velocities are obtained from progress curves, graphs of either the increase in product concentration or the decrease in substrate concentration over time (Figure 5.2). The initial velocity is the slope ($\Delta[P]/\Delta t$) at the origin of a progress curve.

5.3 The Michaelis-Menten Equation

Enzyme-catalyzed reactions, like any chemical reaction, can be described mathematically by rate equations. Several constants in the equations indicate the efficiency and specificity of an enzyme and are therefore useful for comparing the activities of several enzymes or for assessing the physiological importance of a given enzyme. The first rate equations were derived in the early 1900s by examining the effects of variations in substrate concentration. Most workers used extracts

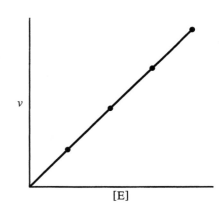

Figure 5.1 ▲
Effect of enzyme concentration ([E]), on the velocity (*v*) of an enzyme-catalyzed reaction at a fixed, saturating [S]. Because the reaction rate is affected by the concentration of enzyme but not by the concentration of the other reactant, S, the bimolecular reaction is pseudo first order.

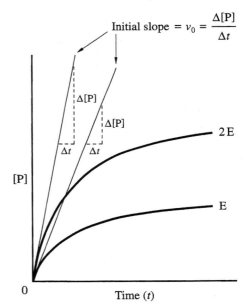

Figure 5.2 ▲
Progress curve for an enzyme-catalyzed reaction. [P], the concentration of product, increases as the reaction proceeds. The initial velocity of the reaction (v_0) is the slope of the initial linear portion of the curve. Note that the rate of the reaction doubles when twice as much enzyme (2E, upper curve) is added to an otherwise identical reaction mixture.

(a)

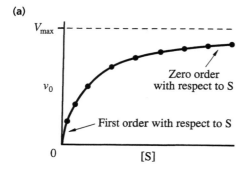

(b)

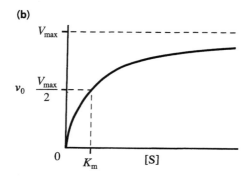

Figure 5.3 ▲
Plots of initial velocity (v_0) versus substrate concentration ([S]) for an enzyme-catalyzed reaction. **(a)** Each experimental point is obtained from a separate progress curve using the same concentration of enzyme. The shape of the curve is hyperbolic. At low substrate concentrations, the curve approximates a straight line that rises steeply. In this region of the curve, the reaction is first order with respect to substrate. At high concentrations of substrate, the enzyme is saturated, and the reaction is zero order with respect to substrate. **(b)** The concentration of substrate that corresponds to half-maximum velocity is called the Michaelis constant (K_m). The enzyme is half-saturated when [S] = K_m.

of yeast to catalyze the hydrolysis of sucrose to glucose and fructose (Equation 5.10). Two major observations supported a theory involving the formation of ES complexes. First, at high concentrations of substrate, E is saturated with S, and the reaction rate is independent of the concentration of substrate. The value of v_0 for a solution of E saturated with S is called the **maximum velocity** (V_{max}). Second, at low concentrations of substrate, the reaction is first order with respect to substrate (making the reaction second order overall: first order with respect to S and first order with respect to E). Under intermediate substrate concentrations, the order with respect to S is fractional, decreasing from first order toward zero order as [S] increases. The shape of the v_0 versus [S] curve from low to high [S] is a rectangular hyperbola (Figure 5.3a). Hyperbolic curves are indicative of processes involving simple dissociation, as we saw for the dissociation of oxygen from oxymyoglobin (Section 4.13B). These observations indicate that the simple reaction under study is bimolecular, involving the association of E and S to form an ES complex.

The equation for a rectangular hyperbola is

$$y = \frac{ax}{b + x} \qquad \textbf{(5.13)}$$

where a is the asymptote of the curve (the value of y at an infinite value of x) and b is the point on the x axis corresponding to a value of $a/2$. We can obtain the rate equation for the simple bimolecular reaction shown in Equation 5.12 by substituting a kinetic variable and constant terms into the general equation for a rectangular hyperbola. Three of the terms have already been introduced: $y = v_0$, $x = $ [S], and $a = V_{max}$. The fourth term, b in the general equation, is the **Michaelis constant** (K_m), defined as the concentration of substrate when v_0 is equal to one-half V_{max} (Figure 5.3b). The complete rate equation is

$$v_0 = \frac{v_{max}[S]}{K_m + [S]} \qquad \textbf{(5.14)}$$

This is called the **Michaelis-Menten equation**, named after Leonor Michaelis and Maud Menten. In the following section, we derive the Michaelis-Menten equation by a kinetic approach and then consider the meaning of the various constants.

(a) Leonor Michaelis (1875–1949) and ▶
(b) Maud Menten (1879–1960), pioneers in enzyme kinetics.

(a)

(b)

A. Derivation of the Michaelis-Menten Equation

One common derivation of the Michaelis-Menten equation, provided by George E. Briggs and J. B. S. Haldane, is termed the steady-state derivation. This derivation postulates that there is a period of time (called the steady state) during which the ES complex is formed at the same rate that it decomposes, so that the concentration of ES is constant. The steady state coincides with the initial-velocity phase, so v_0 is used in the steady-state derivation. The steady state is a common condition for metabolic reactions in cells.

The velocity of an enzyme-catalyzed reaction depends on the rate of conversion of ES to E + P.

$$v_0 = k_2[ES] \tag{5.15}$$

The steady-state derivation solves Equation 5.15 for [ES] using terms that can be measured, such as the rate constant, total enzyme concentration ($[E]_{total}$), and substrate concentration ([S]). [S] is assumed to be greater than $[E]_{total}$ but not necessarily saturating. For example, soon after a small amount of enzyme is mixed with substrate, [ES] becomes constant because the overall rate of decomposition of ES (the sum of the rates of conversion of ES to E + S and to E + P) is equal to the rate of formation of the ES complex from E + S. The rate of formation of ES from E + S depends on the concentration of free enzyme (enzyme molecules not in the form of ES), which is $[E]_{total} -$ [ES]. The concentration of the ES complex remains constant until consumption of S causes [S] to approach $[E]_{total}$. Algebraic expression of these statements about the steady state provides this equivalence.

$$\text{Rate of ES formation} = \text{Rate of ES decomposition} \tag{5.16}$$

$$k_1([E]_{total} - [ES])[S] = (k_{-1} + k_2)[ES]$$

Equation 5.16 is rearranged to collect the rate constants, and the ratio of constants obtained defines the Michaelis constant (K_m).

$$\frac{k_{-1} + k_2}{k_1} = K_m = \frac{([E]_{total} - [ES])[S]}{[ES]} \tag{5.17}$$

Next, this equation is solved for [ES] in several steps.

$$[ES]K_m = ([E]_{total} - [ES])[S] \tag{5.18}$$

Expanding,

$$[ES]K_m = ([E]_{total}[S]) - ([ES][S]) \tag{5.19}$$

Collecting [ES] terms,

$$[ES](K_m + [S]) = [E]_{total}[S] \tag{5.20}$$

and

$$[ES] = \frac{[E]_{total}[S]}{K_m + [S]} \tag{5.21}$$

Chemistry for Biologists

Since the velocity of an enzymatic reaction is the rate of formation of E + P from ES (Equation 5.15),

$$v_0 = k_2[\text{ES}] \tag{5.22}$$

The velocity, and hence the rate equation, can be obtained by substituting the value of [ES] from Equation 5.21 into Equation 5.22

$$v_0 = \frac{k_2[\text{E}]_{\text{total}}[\text{S}]}{K_m + [\text{S}]} \tag{5.23}$$

As indicated by Figure 5.3a, when the concentration of S is very high, the enzyme is saturated, and essentially all the molecules of E are present as ES. Adding more S has virtually no effect on the reaction velocity; only the addition of more enzyme can increase the velocity. Thus, the reaction velocity approaches the maximum velocity (V_{max}). Equation 5.22 thus becomes

$$V_{\text{max}} = k_2[\text{E}]_{\text{total}} \tag{5.24}$$

Substituting this in Equation 5.23 gives the most familiar form of the Michaelis-Menten equation.

$$v_0 = \frac{V_{\text{max}}[\text{S}]}{K_m + [\text{S}]} \tag{5.25}$$

The rate constant observed under these saturating conditions is the **catalytic constant** or turnover number (k_{cat}) defined as

$$k_{\text{cat}} = \frac{V_{\text{max}}}{[\text{E}]_{\text{total}}} \tag{5.26}$$

k_{cat} represents the number of moles of substrate converted to product per second per mole of enzyme (or per mole of active site for an oligomeric enzyme) under saturating conditions. In other words, k_{cat} indicates the maximum number of substrate molecules converted to product each second by each active site. The catalytic constant is thus a measure of how quickly a given enzyme can catalyze a specific reaction. The unit for k_{cat} is s^{-1}, and the reciprocal of k_{cat} is the time required for one catalytic event. Note that to obtain k_{cat}, the enzyme concentration must be known.

For a simple reaction such as Equation 5.12, the limiting step is ES $\rightarrow$ E + P. Thus, $k_{\text{cat}} = k_2$. Many biochemical reactions, however, consist of several steps. If one step is clearly rate-limiting, its rate constant is the k_{cat} for that reaction. For mechanisms more complicated than Equation 5.12, k_{cat} may be a complex function.

B. The Meanings of K_m

The Michaelis constant has a number of meanings. As we saw in Figure 5.3b, K_m is the initial concentration of substrate at half-maximum velocity, or at half-saturation of E with S. This can be verified by substituting K_m for [S] in Equation 5.25; v_0 is found to be $V_{max}/2$.

Equation 5.17 defined K_m as the ratio of the combined constants for the breakdown of ES divided by the constant for its formation. If the rate constant for product formation (k_{cat}) is much smaller than either k_1 or k_{-1}, as is often the case, k_{cat} can be neglected and K_m becomes k_{-1}/k_1, the equilibrium constant for dissociation of the ES complex to E + S. Thus, K_m is a measure of the affinity of E for S. The lower the value of K_m, the more tightly the substrate is bound. K_m values are sometimes used to distinguish between different enzymes that catalyze the same reaction. For example, there are several different forms of lactate dehydrogenase in mammals, each with distinct K_m values. For many enzymes, however, K_m is a complex function of the rate constants; this is especially true when the reaction occurs in more than two steps.

The K_m of an enzyme for a substrate is often near the concentration of that substrate in a cell. Because the K_m value is just above the steeply rising portion of the rate curve for any enzyme, an enzyme for which $K_m \geq$ [S] is most able to respond proportionally to changes in [S] (Figure 5.4). Physiologically, this can help prevent the accumulation of substrate under changing metabolic conditions.

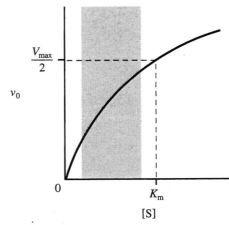

Figure 5.4 ▲
K_m and physiological substrate concentration. K_m values for enzymes are typically just above the concentrations of substrates in cells (pink area), so enzymatic rates are sensitive to small changes in substrate concentrations.

5.4 Kinetic Constants Indicate Enzyme Activity and Specificity

The kinetic constants K_m and k_{cat} can be used to gauge the relative activities of enzymes and substrates. K_m is a measure of the stability of the ES complex. k_{cat} is the first-order rate constant for the conversion of ES to E + P and describes the rate when the substrate is not limiting (region A in Figure 5.5). It is a measure of the catalytic activity of an enzyme, indicating how many reactions a molecule of enzyme can catalyze per second.

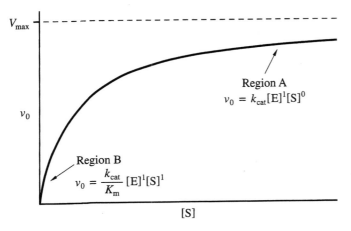

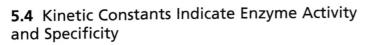

◄ Figure 5.5
Meanings of k_{cat} and k_{cat}/K_m. The catalytic constant (k_{cat}) is the first-order rate constant for conversion of the ES complex to E + P. It is measured most easily when the enzyme is saturated with substrate (region A on the Michaelis-Menten curve shown). The ratio k_{cat}/K_m is the second-order rate constant for the conversion of E + S to E + P at very low concentrations of substrate (region B). The reactions measured by these rate constants are summarized below the graph.

TABLE 5.1   Examples of catalytic constants

Enzyme	k_{cat} (s^{-1})*
Papain	10
Ribonuclease	10^2
Carboxypeptidase	10^2
Trypsin	10^2 (to 10^3)
Acetylcholinesterase	10^3
Kinases	10^3
Dehydrogenases	10^3
Transaminases	10^3
Carbonic anhydrase	10^6
Superoxide dismutase	10^6
Catalase	10^7

*The catalytic constants are given only as orders of magnitude. [Most values obtained from Eigen, M., and Hammes, G. G. (1963). Elementary steps in enzyme reactions (as studied by relaxation spectrometry). *Adv. Enzymol.* 25:1–38.]

Representative values of k_{cat} are listed in Table 5.1. Most enzymes are potent catalysts with k_{cat} values of 10^2 to 10^3 s^{-1}. Evolution has produced a few extremely rapid catalysts with k_{cat} values of 10^6 s^{-1} or greater. Mammalian carbonic anhydrase, for example, must act very rapidly in order to maintain equilibrium between aqueous CO_2 and bicarbonate (Section 2.10). As we will see in Section 6.4B, superoxide dismutase and catalase are responsible for rapid decomposition of the toxic oxygen metabolites superoxide anion and hydrogen peroxide, respectively.

In region B of the hyperbolic curve in Figure 5.5, the concentration of S is very low and the curve approximates a straight line. Under these conditions, the reaction is second order: first order with respect to S, and first order with respect to E. The rate equation for this region is

$$v_0 = k[E][S] \tag{5.27}$$

When Michaelis and Menten first wrote the full rate equation, they used the form that included $k_{cat}[E]_{total}$ (Equation 5.23) rather than V_{max}. If we consider only the region of the Michaelis-Menten curve at a very low [S], Equation 5.23 can be simplified by neglecting the [S] in the denominator since [S] is much less than K_m.

$$v_0 = \frac{k_{cat}}{K_m}[E][S] \tag{5.28}$$

Therefore, the rate constant for Equation 5.27 is k_{cat}/K_m.

The ratio k_{cat}/K_m is an apparent second-order rate constant for the formation of E + P from E + S when the overall reaction is limited by the encounter of S with E. This constant approaches 10^8 to 10^9 M^{-1} s^{-1}, the fastest rate at which two uncharged solutes can approach each other by diffusion at physiological temperature. Enzymes that can catalyze reactions at this extremely rapid rate are discussed in Section 6.4.

The ratio k_{cat}/K_m is a measure of the specificity of an enzyme, or its preference for different substrates. Suppose that two different substrates, A and B, are competing for binding and catalysis by the same enzyme. When the concentrations of A and B are equal, the ratio of the rates of their conversion to product by the enzyme is equal to the ratio of their k_{cat}/K_m values. For this reason, the ratio k_{cat}/K_m is often called the specificity constant.

The rate constants k_{cat} and k_{cat}/K_m are useful for comparing the activities of different enzymes. It is also possible to assess the efficiency of an enzyme by measuring the **rate acceleration** that it provides. This value is the ratio of the rate constant for a reaction in the presence of the enzyme (k_{cat}) divided by the rate constant for the same reaction in the absence of the enzyme (k_n). Surprisingly few rate acceleration values are known because most cellular reactions occur extremely slowly in the absence of enzymes—so slowly that their nonenzymatic rates are almost impossible to measure.

Several examples of rate acceleration are provided in Table 5.2. Typical values range from 10^8 to 10^{12}, but some are quite a bit higher (up to 10^{17}). The difficulty in obtaining rate constants for nonenzymatic reactions is exemplified by the half-time for the deamination of adenosine at 20°C and pH 7, about 20 000 years! Because the nonenzymatic rate of this reaction is so slow, adenosine deaminase has an extraordinarily high rate acceleration despite a moderate k_{cat} of 4×10^2 M^{-1} s^{-1}.

5.5 Measurement of K_m and V_{max}

The kinetic parameters of an enzymatic reaction can provide valuable information about the specificity and mechanism of the reaction. The key parameters are K_m and V_{max} because k_{cat} can be calculated if V_{max} is known.

TABLE 5.2   Rate accelerations of some enzymes

	Nonenzymatic rate constant (k_n in s^{-1})	Enzymatic rate constant (k_{cat} in s^{-1})	Rate acceleration (k_{cat}/k_n)
Carbonic anhydrase	10^{-1}	10^6	8×10^6
Chymotrypsin	4×10^{-9}	4×10^{-2}	10^7
Lysozyme	3×10^{-9}	5×10^{-1}	2×10^8
Triose phosphate isomerase	4×10^{-6}	4×10^3	10^9
Fumarase	2×10^{-8}	2×10^3	10^{11}
β-Amylase	3×10^{-9}	10^3	3×10^{11}
Adenosine deaminase	2×10^{-10}	4×10^2	2×10^{12}
Urease	3×10^{-10}	3×10^4	10^{14}
Mandelate racemase	3×10^{-13}	5×10^2	1.7×10^{15}
Alkaline phosphatase	10^{-15}	10^2	10^{17}
Orotidine 5'-phosphate decarboxylase	3×10^{-16}	4×10	10^{17}

K_m and V_{max} for an enzyme-catalyzed reaction can be measured in several ways. Both values can be obtained by the analysis of initial velocities at a series of substrate concentrations and a fixed concentration of enzyme. In order to obtain reliable values for the kinetic constants, the [S] points must be spread out both below and above K_m to produce a hyperbola. It is difficult to determine either K_m or V_{max} directly from a graph of initial velocity versus concentration because the curve approaches V_{max} asymptotically. However, accurate values can be determined by using a suitable computer program to fit the experimental results to the equation for the hyperbola.

The Michaelis-Menten equation can be rewritten in order to obtain values for V_{max} and K_m from straight lines on graphs. The most commonly used transformation is the double-reciprocal, or Lineweaver-Burk, plot, in which the values of $1/v_0$ are plotted against $1/[S]$ (Figure 5.6). The absolute value of $1/K_m$ is obtained from the intercept of the line at the x axis, and the value of $1/V_{max}$ is obtained from the y intercept. Although double-reciprocal plots are not the most accurate methods for determining kinetic constants, they are easily understood and provide recognizable patterns for the study of enzyme inhibition, an extremely important aspect of enzymology that we will examine shortly.

Values of k_{cat} can be obtained from measurements of V_{max} only when the absolute concentration of the enzyme is known. Values of K_m can be determined even when enzymes have not been purified, provided that only one enzyme in the impure preparation can catalyze the observed reaction.

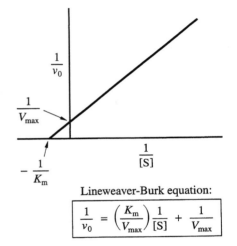

Lineweaver-Burk equation:

$$\frac{1}{v_0} = \left(\frac{K_m}{V_{max}}\right)\frac{1}{[S]} + \frac{1}{V_{max}}$$

Figure 5.6 ▲
Double-reciprocal (Lineweaver-Burk) plot. This plot is derived from a linear transformation of the Michaelis-Menten equation. Values of $1/v_0$ are plotted as a function of $1/[S]$ values.

5.6 Kinetics of Multisubstrate Reactions

Kinetic measurements for multisubstrate reactions are a little more complicated than simple one-substrate enzyme kinetics. However, for many purposes, such as designing an enzyme assay, it is sufficient simply to determine the K_m for each substrate in the presence of saturating amounts of each of the other substrates. Furthermore, the simple enzyme kinetics discussed in this chapter can be extended to distinguish among several mechanistic possibilities for multisubstrate reactions, such as group-transfer reactions. This is done by measuring the effect of variations in the concentration of one substrate on the kinetic results obtained for the other.

Multisubstrate reactions can occur by several different kinetic schemes, called **kinetic mechanisms** because they are derived entirely from kinetic experiments.

Figure 5.7 ▶
Notation for bisubstrate reactions. **(a)** In sequential reactions, all substrates are bound before a product is released. The binding of substrates may be either ordered or random. **(b)** In ping-pong reactions, one substrate is bound and a product is released, leaving a substituted enzyme. A second substrate is then bound and a second product released, restoring the enzyme to its original form.

(a) Sequential reactions

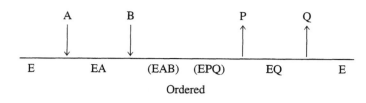

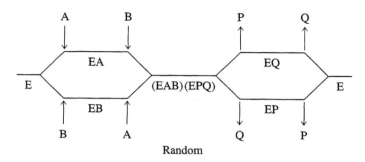

(b) Ping-pong reaction

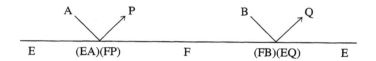

Kinetic mechanisms are commonly represented using the notation introduced by W. W. Cleland. As shown in Figure 5.7, the sequence of steps proceeds from left to right. The addition of substrate molecules (A, B, C, . . .) to the enzyme and the release of products (P, Q, R, . . .) from the enzyme are indicated by arrows pointing toward (substrate binding) or from (product release) the line. The various forms of the enzyme (free E, ES complexes, or EP complexes) are written under a horizontal line. The ES complexes that undergo chemical transformation when the active site is filled are shown in parentheses. **Sequential reactions** (Figure 5.7a) require all the substrates to be present before any product is released. Sequential reactions can be either **ordered**, with an obligatory order for the addition of substrates and release of products, or **random**, with no obligatory order of binding or release. In **ping-pong reactions** (Figure 5.7b), a product is released before all the substrates are bound. In a bisubstrate ping-pong reaction, the first substrate is bound, the enzyme is altered by substitution, and the first product is released, after which the second substrate is bound, the altered enzyme is restored to its original form, and the second product is released. Because of the covalent binding of a portion of a substrate to the enzyme, a ping-pong mechanism is sometimes called a substituted-enzyme mechanism. The binding and release of ligands in a ping-pong mechanism are usually indicated by slanted lines. The two forms of the enzyme are represented by E (unsubstituted) and F (substituted).

5.7 Reversible Enzyme Inhibition

An **inhibitor** (I) is a compound that binds to an enzyme and interferes with its activity by preventing either the formation of the ES complex or its breakdown to E + P. Natural inhibitors regulate metabolism, and many drugs are enzyme inhibitors. Inhibitors also are used experimentally to investigate enzyme mechanisms and to decipher metabolic pathways.

Inhibition can be either irreversible or reversible. Irreversible inhibitors are bound to enzymes by covalent bonds. Reversible inhibitors are bound to enzymes by the same noncovalent forces that bind substrates and products. Reversible inhibitors can be distinguished from irreversible inhibitors by their easy removal from solutions of enzyme by a method such as dialysis or gel filtration (Section 3.6). The constant for the dissociation of I from the EI complex, called the **inhibition constant** (K_i), is described by the equation

$$K_i = \frac{[E][I]}{[EI]} \qquad \textbf{(5.29)}$$

Irreversible inhibitors are described in Section 5.8.

The basic types of reversible inhibition are competitive, uncompetitive, and noncompetitive. These can be distinguished experimentally by their effects on the kinetic behavior of enzymes, which are summarized in Table 5.3. Figure 5.8 shows diagrams representing modes of reversible enzyme inhibition.

A. Competitive Inhibition

Competitive inhibitors are the most commonly encountered inhibitors in biochemistry. In competitive inhibition, the inhibitor can bind only to enzyme molecules that have not bound any substrate. Competitive inhibition is illustrated by Figure 5.8a and 5.8b and by the kinetic scheme in Figure 5.9a. In this scheme, only ES can lead to the formation of product.

When a competitive inhibitor is bound to an enzyme molecule, a substrate molecule cannot bind to that enzyme molecule. Conversely, the binding of substrate to an enzyme molecule prevents the binding of an inhibitor; that is, S and I compete for binding to the enzyme molecule. Most commonly, S and I bind at the same site on the enzyme, the active site. This type of inhibition (Figure 5.8a) is termed classical competitive inhibition. However, with some allosteric enzymes, inhibitors bind at a different site than substrates do (Figure 5.8b), although the inhibition exhibits competitive characteristics. This type of inhibition is called nonclassical competitive inhibition. When both I and S are present in a solution, the proportion of the enzyme that is able to form ES complexes depends on the relative affinities of the enzyme for S and I and the amount of each present.

The formation of EI can be reversed by increasing the concentration of S. At sufficiently high [S], S can still saturate E. Therefore, the maximum velocity is the same in the presence or in the absence of an inhibitor. The more competitive inhibitor present, the more substrate needed for half-saturation. We have shown that the concentration of substrate at half-saturation is K_m. Thus, in the presence of increasing concentrations of a competitive inhibitor, K_m increases. The new value is usually referred to as the apparent K_m (K_m^{app}). On a double-reciprocal plot, adding a competitive inhibitor shows as a decrease in the absolute value of the intercept at the x axis ($1/K_m$), whereas the y intercept ($1/V_{max}$) remains the same (Figure 5.9b).

TABLE 5.3	Effects of reversible inhibitors on kinetic constants
Type of inhibitor	**Effect**
Competitive (I binds to E only)	Raises K_m V_{max} remains unchanged
Uncompetitive (I binds to ES only)	Lowers V_{max} and K_m Ratio of V_{max}/K_m remains unchanged
Noncompetitive (I binds to E or ES)	Lowers V_{max} K_m remains unchanged

Figure 5.8 ▶
Diagrams of reversible enzyme inhibition. In this scheme, catalytically competent enzymes are green and inactive enzymes are red. **(a)** Classical competitive inhibition. S and I bind to the active site in a mutually exclusive manner. **(b)** Nonclassical competitive inhibition. The binding of S at the active site prevents the binding of I at a separate site, and vice versa. **(c)** Uncompetitive inhibition. I binds only to the ES complex. The enzyme becomes inactive when I binds. **(d)** Noncompetitive inhibition. I can bind to either E or ES. The enzyme becomes inactive when I binds. Although the EI complex can still bind S, no product is formed.

(a) Classical competitive inhibition

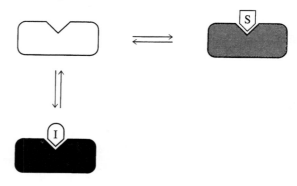

(b) Nonclassical competitive inhibition

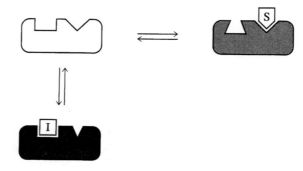

(c) Uncompetitive inhibition

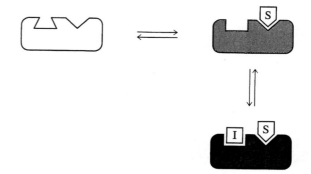

(d) Noncompetitive inhibition

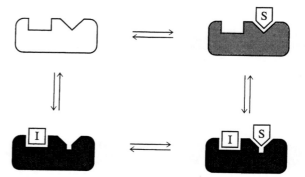

(a)

$$E + S \underset{k_{-1}}{\overset{k_1}{\rightleftharpoons}} ES \xrightarrow{k_{cat}} E + P$$
$$+$$
$$I$$
$$K_i \Updownarrow$$
$$EI$$

(b)

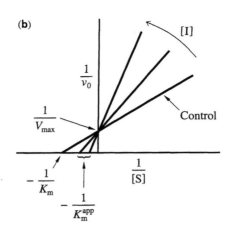

◄ **Figure 5.9**
Competitive inhibition. **(a)** Kinetic scheme illustrating the binding of I to E. Note that this is an expansion of Equation 5.12 that includes formation of the EI complex.
(b) Double-reciprocal plot. In competitive inhibition, V_{max} remains unchanged and K_m increases. The black line labeled "Control" is the result in the absence of inhibitor. The red lines are the results in the presence of inhibitor, with the arrow showing the direction of increasing [I].

Figure 5.10 ►
Benzamidine and arginine. Benzamidine competes with arginine residues for binding to trypsin.

Many classical competitive inhibitors are substrate analogs, compounds that are structurally similar to substrates. The analogs bind to the enzyme but do not react. For example, benzamidine is a competitive inhibitor of trypsin (Figure 5.10). Trypsin catalyzes hydrolysis of peptide bonds whose carbonyl groups are contributed by arginine and lysine residues, and benzamidine is an analog of the alkylguanidyl side chain of arginine. Benzamidine acts as a competitive inhibitor by competing with arginine residues of peptides for the binding pocket of trypsin.

B. Uncompetitive Inhibition

Uncompetitive inhibitors bind only to ES, not to free enzyme (Figures 5.8c and 5.11a). In uncompetitive inhibition, V_{max} is decreased ($1/V_{max}$ is increased) by the conversion of some molecules of E to the inactive form ESI. Since it is the ES complex that binds I, the decrease in V_{max} is not reversed by the addition of more substrate. Uncompetitive inhibitors also decrease the K_m (seen as an increase in the absolute value of $1/K_m$ on a double-reciprocal plot) because the equilibria for the formation of both ES and ESI are shifted toward the complexes by the binding of I.

(a)

$$E + S \rightleftharpoons ES \longrightarrow E + P$$
$$+$$
$$I$$
$$K_i \Updownarrow$$
$$ESI$$

(b)

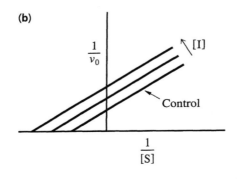

◄ **Figure 5.11**
Uncompetitive inhibition. **(a)** Kinetic scheme illustrating the binding of I to ES.
(b) Double-reciprocal plot. In uncompetitive inhibition, both V_{max} and K_m decrease (i.e., the absolute values of both $1/V_{max}$ and $1/K_m$, obtained from the y and x intercepts, respectively, increase). The ratio V_{max}/K_m remains unchanged.

Figure 5.12 ▶
Noncompetitive inhibition. **(a)** Kinetic scheme illustrating the binding of I to E or ES. **(b)** Double-reciprocal plot. V_{max} decreases, but K_m remains the same.

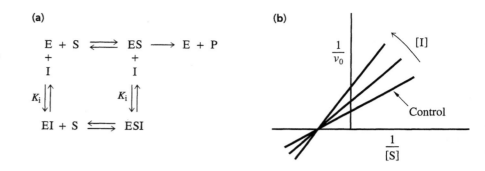

(a)

$$E + S \rightleftharpoons ES \longrightarrow E + P$$

(b)

Experimentally, the lines on a double-reciprocal plot representing varying concentrations of an uncompetitive inhibitor all have the same slope, indicating proportionally decreased values for K_m and V_{max} (Figure 5.11b). This type of inhibition usually occurs only with multisubstrate reactions.

C. Noncompetitive Inhibition

Noncompetitive inhibitors can bind to E or ES, forming inactive EI or ESI complexes, respectively (Figures 5.8d and 5.12a). These inhibitors are not substrate analogs and do not bind at the same site as S. Noncompetitive inhibition is characterized by an apparent decrease in V_{max} ($1/V_{max}$ appears to increase) with no change in K_m. On a double-reciprocal plot, the lines for noncompetitive inhibition intersect at a point on the x axis (Figure 5.12b). The effect of noncompetitive inhibition is to reversibly titrate E and ES with I, in essence removing active enzyme molecules from solution. This inhibition cannot be overcome by the addition of S. Noncompetitive inhibition is rare, but examples are known among allosteric enzymes. In these cases, the noncompetitive inhibitor probably alters the conformation of the enzyme to a shape that can still bind S but cannot catalyze any reaction.

D. Uses of Enzyme Inhibition

Reversible enzyme inhibition provides a powerful tool for probing enzyme activity and for altering it in the treatment of disease. Information about the shape and chemical reactivity of the active site of an enzyme can be obtained from experiments involving a series of competitive inhibitors with systematically altered structures.

The pharmaceutical industry uses enzyme inhibition studies to design clinically useful drugs. In many cases, a naturally occurring enzyme inhibitor is used as the starting point for drug design. Instead of using mass synthesis and testing of potential inhibitors, some investigators are turning to a more efficient approach known as rational drug design. Theoretically, with the greatly expanded bank of knowledge about enzyme structure, inhibitors can now be rationally designed to fit the active site of a target enzyme. The effects of a synthetic compound are tested first on isolated enzymes and then in biological systems. Even if a compound has suitable inhibitory activity, other problems may be encountered. For example, the drug may not enter the target cells, may be rapidly metabolized to an inactive compound, or may be toxic to the host organism, or the target cell may develop resistance to the drug.

The advances made in drug synthesis are exemplified by the design of a series of inhibitors of the enzyme purine nucleoside phosphorylase. This enzyme catalyzes a degradative reaction between phosphate and the nucleoside guanosine, whose structure is shown in Figure 5.13a. With computer modeling, the structures of potential inhibitors were designed and fitted into the active site of the enzyme. One such compound (Figure 5.13b) was synthesized and found to be 100 times more inhibitory than any compound made by the traditional trial-and-error approach. Researchers hope that the rational-design approach will produce a drug suitable for treating autoimmune disorders such as rheumatoid arthritis and multiple sclerosis.

(a)

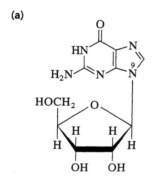

(b)

Figure 5.13 ▲
Comparison of a substrate and a designed inhibitor of purine nucleoside phosphorylase. The two substrates of this enzyme are guanosine and inorganic phosphate. **(a)** Guanosine. **(b)** A potent inhibitor of the enzyme. N-9 of guanosine has been replaced by a carbon atom. The chlorinated benzene ring binds to the sugar-binding site of the enzyme, and the acetate side chain binds to the phosphate-binding site.

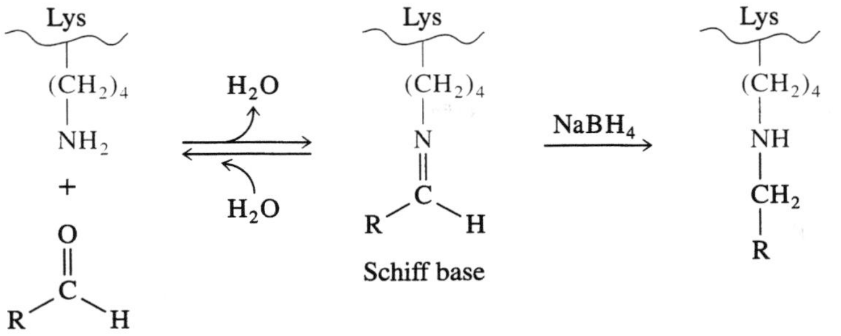

Figure 5.14 ▲
Reaction of the ε-amino group of a lysine residue with an aldehyde. Reduction of the Schiff base with sodium borohydride (NaBH₄) forms a stable substituted enzyme.

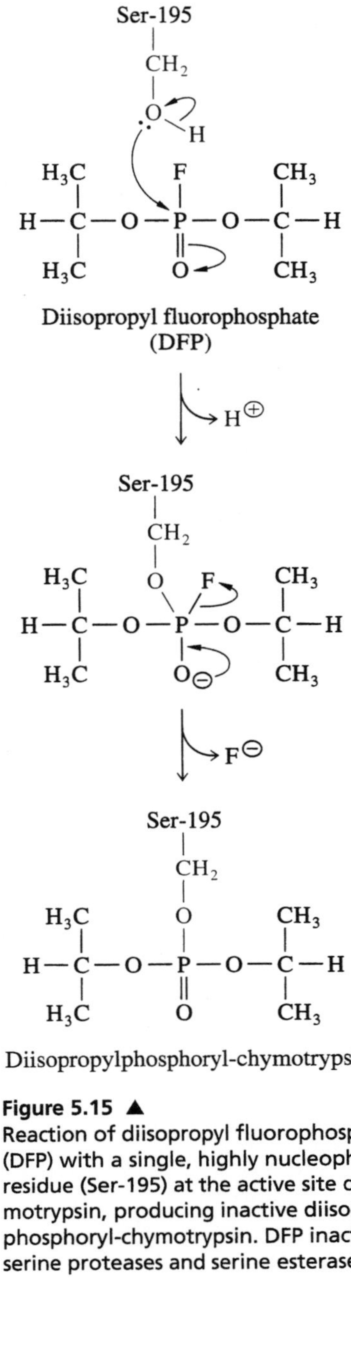

5.8 Irreversible Enzyme Inhibition

In contrast to a reversible enzyme inhibitor, an irreversible enzyme inhibitor forms a stable covalent bond with an enzyme molecule, thus removing active molecules from the enzyme population. Irreversible inhibition typically occurs by alkylation or acylation of the side chain of an active-site amino acid residue. There are many naturally occurring irreversible inhibitors, as well as the synthetic examples described here.

An important use of irreversible inhibitors is the identification of amino acid residues at the active site by specific substitution of their reactive side chains. In this process, an irreversible inhibitor that reacts with only one type of amino acid is incubated with a solution of enzyme, which is then tested for loss of activity. Ionizable side chains are modified by acylation or alkylation reactions. For example, free amino groups such as the ε-amino group of lysine react with an aldehyde to form a Schiff base, which can be stabilized by reduction with sodium borohydride (NaBH₄) (Figure 5.14).

The nerve gas diisopropyl fluorophosphate (DFP) is one of a group of organic phosphorus compounds that inactivate hydrolases with a reactive serine as part of the active site. These enzymes are called serine proteases or serine esterases, depending on their reaction specificity. The serine protease chymotrypsin, an important digestive enzyme, is inhibited irreversibly by DFP (Figure 5.15). DFP reacts with the serine residue at chymotrypsin's active site (Ser-195) to produce diisopropylphosphoryl-chymotrypsin. Some organophosphorus inhibitors are used in agriculture as insecticides; others, such as DFP, are useful reagents for enzyme research. The original organophosphorus nerve gases are extremely toxic poisons developed for military use. The major biological action of these poisons is irreversible inhibition of the serine esterase acetylcholinesterase, which catalyzes hydrolysis of the neurotransmitter acetylcholine. When acetylcholine released from an activated nerve cell binds to its receptor on a second nerve cell, it triggers a nerve impulse. The action of acetylcholinesterase restores the cell to its resting state. Inhibition of this enzyme can cause paralysis.

More useful than general substituting reagents are irreversible inhibitors with structures that allow them to bind specifically to an active site. These inhibitors are referred to as active site–directed reagents, or **affinity labels**. Bromohydroxyacetone phosphate is an affinity label for triose phosphate isomerase, which catalyzes the interconversion of dihydroxyacetone phosphate and glyceraldehyde 3-phosphate. This inhibitor reacts with the side chain of a glutamate residue of the enzyme (Figure 5.16). Experiments such as this identified Glu-165 as a component of the active site of triose phosphate isomerase. An affinity label that inhibits chymotrypsin is described in Section 6.11.

Diisopropylphosphoryl-chymotrypsin

Figure 5.15 ▲
Reaction of diisopropyl fluorophosphate (DFP) with a single, highly nucleophilic serine residue (Ser-195) at the active site of chymotrypsin, producing inactive diisopropylphosphoryl-chymotrypsin. DFP inactivates serine proteases and serine esterases.

Section 6.4A gives the details of this isomerase reaction.

Chemistry for Biologists

Figure 5.16 ▶
Irreversible inhibition of triose phosphate isomerase. The 1-bromo analog of dihydroxy-acetone phosphate reacts with the side chain of the active-site glutamate residue. Reduction of the carbonyl group of the substituent by $NaBH_4$ prevents migration of the affinity label to another group.

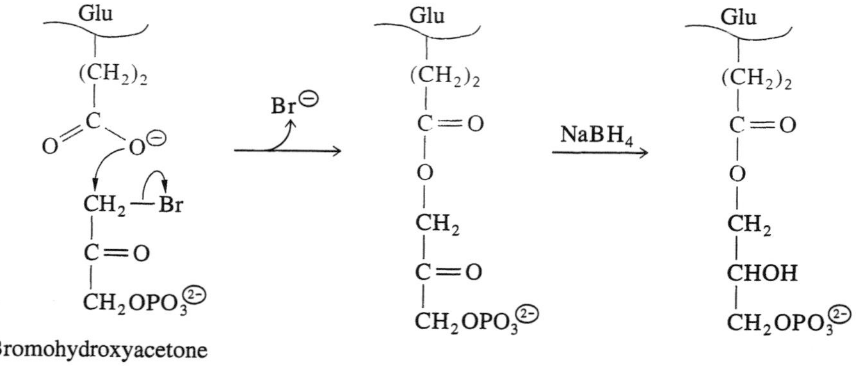

Bromohydroxyacetone phosphate

Recombinant DNA technology is described in Chapter 23.

5.9 Site-Directed Mutagenesis Modifies Enzymes

With the technique of **site-directed mutagenesis** (Section 23.10), it is possible to test the functions of the amino acid side chains of an enzyme. Mutagenesis is more specific than traditional irreversible inhibition and also allows the testing of amino acids for which there are no specific chemical inhibitors. In this procedure, one amino acid is specifically replaced by another through the biosynthesis of a modified enzyme. To begin, the gene that encodes an enzyme is isolated, sequenced, and inserted into a suitable vector used to transform bacteria. The enzyme can then be synthesized in the transformed bacterial cells. After verification that the unmodified (wild-type) enzyme is synthesized by the bacteria, the experiment is repeated using DNA that has been mutated in vitro at specific sites. The bacteria, transformed by the new DNA, synthesize the mutant protein, which is then isolated and tested for enzymatic activity.

A successful example of site-directed mutagenesis is the alteration of the peptidase subtilisin from *Bacillus subtilis* to make it more resistant to chemical oxidation. Subtilisin is added to detergent powders to help remove protein stains such as chocolate and blood. It has a methionine residue in the active-site cleft (Met-222) that is readily oxidized, leading to inactivation of the enzyme. Resistance to oxidation would increase the suitability of subtilisin as a detergent additive. In a series of mutagenic experiments, Met-222 was systematically replaced by each of the other common amino acids. All 19 possible mutant subtilisins were isolated and tested, and most had greatly diminished peptidase activity. The Cys-222 mutant had high activity but was also subject to oxidation. The Ala-222 and Ser-222 mutants, with nonoxidizable side chains, were not inactivated by oxidation and had relatively high activity. They were the only active, oxygen-stable mutant subtilisin variants.

Site-directed mutagenesis has been performed to alter 8 of the 319 amino acid residues of a bacterial protease. The wild-type protease is moderately stable when heated, but the suitably mutated enzyme is stable and can function at 100°C. Its denaturation is prevented by groups, such as a disulfide bridge, that stabilize its conformation. Experiments of this type may enable production of enzymes that can be stored at room temperature for long periods of time. Several studies of active sites by site-directed mutagenesis are discussed in later chapters.

5.10 Regulation of Enzyme Activity

A number of mechanisms, including the regulation of specific enzymes, coordinate and control the metabolism of a cell. The amount of an enzyme can be controlled by regulating the rate of its synthesis or degradation. This mode of control occurs in all species, but it often takes many minutes or hours to synthesize new or degrade existing enzymes. In all organisms, rapid control—on the scale of seconds or less—

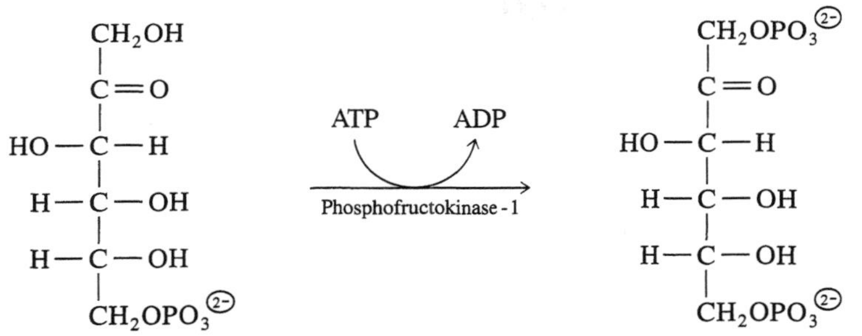

$$CH_2OH$$
$$|$$
$$C=O$$
$$|$$
$$HO-C-H$$
$$|$$
$$H-C-OH$$
$$|$$
$$H-C-OH$$
$$|$$
$$CH_2OPO_3^{2-}$$

Fructose 6-phosphate

ATP   ADP

Phosphofructokinase - 1

$$CH_2OPO_3^{2-}$$
$$|$$
$$C=O$$
$$|$$
$$HO-C-H$$
$$|$$
$$H-C-OH$$
$$|$$
$$H-C-OH$$
$$|$$
$$CH_2OPO_3^{2-}$$

Fructose 1,6-*bis*phosphate

◄ **Figure 5.17**
Reaction catalyzed by phosphofructokinase-1.

can be accomplished through reversible modulation of the activity of **regulatory enzymes**. Most of these enzymes are located at the first step unique to a metabolic pathway, called the first committed step of the pathway. The activity of a regulatory enzyme changes in response to environmental signals, allowing the cell to respond to changing conditions by adjusting the rates of its metabolic processes. Regulatory enzymes become more active catalysts when the concentrations of their substrates increase, or when the concentrations of the products of their metabolic pathways decrease. They become less active when the concentrations of their substrates decrease, or when the products of their metabolic pathways accumulate. Inhibition of the first enzyme unique to a pathway conserves both material and energy by preventing the accumulation of intermediates and the ultimate end product. Regulatory enzymes may be classified by the method of their modulation: noncovalent allosteric modulation or covalent modification.

Allosteric phenomena are responsible for the reversible control of many regulatory enzymes. In Section 4.13C, we saw how the conformation of hemoglobin and its affinity for oxygen change when 2,3-bisphosphoglycerate is bound. Many regulatory enzymes also undergo allosteric transitions between active (R) states and inactive (T) states. These enzymes have a second ligand-binding site away from their catalytic centers. This second site is called the **regulatory site** or allosteric site. An allosteric inhibitor or activator, also called an allosteric modulator or allosteric effector, binds to the regulatory site and causes a conformational change in the regulatory enzyme. This conformational change is transmitted to the active site of the enzyme, which changes shape sufficiently to alter its activity. The regulatory and catalytic sites are physically distinct regions of the protein—usually located on separate domains and sometimes on separate subunits. Regulatory enzymes are often larger than other enzymes.

First, we examine an enzyme that undergoes allosteric (noncovalent) regulation, and then we list some general properties of such enzymes. Next, we describe two theories proposed to explain allosteric regulation in terms of changes in the conformation of regulatory enzymes. Finally, we discuss a closely related group of regulatory enzymes, those subject to covalent modification.

A. Phosphofructokinase Is an Allosteric Enzyme

Phosphofructokinase-1 of the bacterium *Escherichia coli* provides a good example of allosteric inhibition and activation in the regulation of a metabolic pathway. Phosphofructokinase-1 catalyzes the ATP-dependent phosphorylation of fructose 6-phosphate to produce fructose 1,6-*bis*phosphate and ADP (Figure 5.17). This reaction is one of the first steps of glycolysis, an ATP-generating pathway for glucose degradation (described in detail in Chapter 11). Phosphoenolpyruvate (Figure 5.18), an intermediate near the end of the glycolytic pathway, is an allosteric inhibitor of *E. coli* phosphofructokinase-1. ADP is an allosteric activator of the enzyme. When the ratio of [phosphoenolpyruvate] to [ADP] is high, flux through the glycolytic

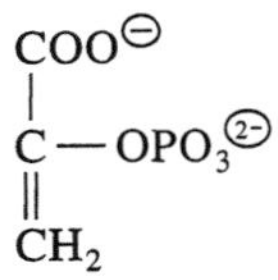

Aspartate transcarbamoylase (ATCase), another well-characterized allosteric enzyme, is described in Chapter 18.

$$COO^-$$
$$|$$
$$C-OPO_3^{2-}$$
$$||$$
$$CH_2$$

Figure 5.18 ▲
Phosphoenolpyruvate, an intermediate of glycolysis and an allosteric inhibitor of phosphofructokinase-1 from *Escherichia coli*.

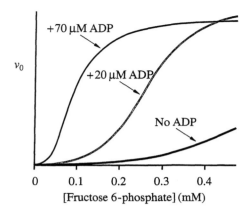

Figure 5.19 ▲
Plots of initial velocity versus [fructose 6-phosphate] for phosphofructokinase-1 from *E. coli*. Increasing the concentration of ADP decreases the apparent K_m without affecting V_{max}. The concentration of ATP is 10^{-4} M. [Adapted from Blangy, D., Buc, H., and Monod, J. (1968). Kinetics of the allosteric interactions of phosphofructokinase from *Escherichia coli. J. Mol. Biol.* 31:13–35.]

pathway decreases at the phosphofructokinase-catalyzed step. When the ratio is low, phosphofructokinase is activated and glycolysis proceeds more rapidly, resulting in the formation of more ATP from ADP. In other words, the concentrations of phosphoenolpyruvate and ADP act through phosphofructokinase-1 to regulate the activity of the entire pathway.

Both phosphoenolpyruvate and ADP affect the binding of the substrate fructose 6-phosphate to phosphofructokinase-1. A plot of initial velocity versus [fructose 6-phosphate] for the reaction catalyzed by phosphofructokinase-1 does not produce the hyperbola typical of Michaelis-Menten kinetics. Instead, the curve is sigmoidal or S-shaped (Figure 5.19). A sigmoidal saturation curve is caused by cooperativity of substrate binding, as we saw for oxygen binding to hemoglobin (Section 4.13B). When ADP is included in the reaction mixture, the curve is shifted to the left, indicating activation of phosphofructokinase-1 by ADP. Increasing the concentration of ADP lowers the apparent K_m for fructose 6-phosphate without markedly affecting V_{max}. Phosphoenolpyruvate raises the K_m, also without changing V_{max}.

Kinetic experiments have shown that there are four binding sites on phosphofructokinase-1 for fructose 6-phosphate, and structural experiments have confirmed that *E. coli* phosphofructokinase-1 (M_r 140 000) is a tetramer consisting of four identical subunits. Figure 5.20 shows the structure of the enzyme complexed with its products, fructose 1,6-*bis*phosphate and ADP, and a second molecule of ADP, an allosteric activator. The four elongated chains associate symmetrically to form two dimers in the native oligomer. The two products are bound in the active site, which is located between two domains of each chain—ADP is bound to the large domain, and fructose 1,6-*bis*phosphate is bound mostly to the small domain.

A notable feature of the structure of phosphofructokinase-1 (and a general feature of regulatory enzymes) is the physical separation of the active site and the regulatory site on each subunit. (In some regulatory enzymes, the active sites and regulatory sites are on different subunits.) The activator ADP binds at a distance from the active site, in a deep hole between the subunits. When ADP is bound to the regulatory site, phosphofructokinase-1 assumes the R conformation, which has a high affinity for fructose 6-phosphate. When the smaller compound phosphoenolpyruvate is bound to the same regulatory site, the enzyme assumes a different conformation, the T conformation, which has a lower affinity for fructose 6-phosphate. The transition between conformations is accomplished by a slight rotation of one rigid dimer relative to the other. The cooperativity of substrate binding is tied to the concerted movement of an arginine residue in each of the four fructose 6-phosphate-binding sites, near the interface between the dimers. Movement of the side chain of this arginine from the active site lowers the affinity for fructose 6-phosphate. In many organisms phosphofructokinase-1 is larger and is subject to more complex allosteric regulation than in *E. coli*, as you will see in Chapter 11.

B. General Properties of Allosteric Enzymes

Examination of the kinetic and physical properties of allosteric enzymes has shown that they have a number of general features.

1. The activities of allosteric regulatory enzymes are changed by metabolic inhibitors and activators. These allosteric modulators seldom resemble the substrates or products of the enzyme. For example, phosphoenolpyruvate (Figure 5.18) resembles neither the substrate nor the product (Figure 5.17) of phosphofructokinase. Consideration of the structural differences between substrates and metabolic inhibitors originally led to the conclusion that allosteric modulators are bound to regulatory sites separate from catalytic sites.

2. Allosteric modulators bind noncovalently to the enzymes they regulate. (There is a special group of regulatory enzymes whose activities are controlled by covalent modification, described in Section 5.10D.) Many modulators alter the

(a)

(b)

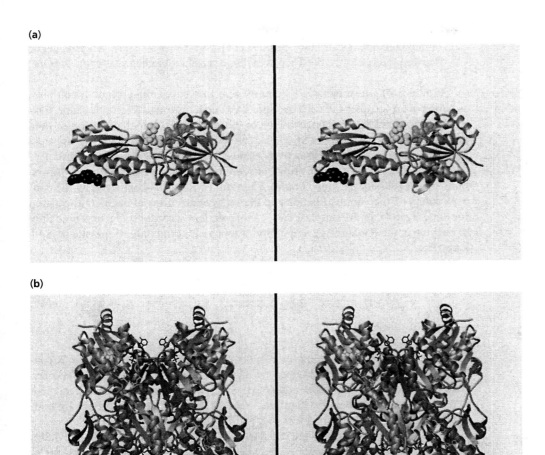

Figure 5.20 ▲
Stereo views of the R conformation of phosphofructokinase-1 from *E. coli*. The enzyme is a tetramer of identical chains. **(a)** Single subunit, shown as a ribbon. The products, fructose 1,6-*bis*phosphate (yellow) and ADP (green), are bound in the active site. The allosteric activator ADP (red) is bound in the regulatory site. **(b)** Tetramer. Two are blue, and two are purple. The products, fructose 1,6-*bis*phosphate (yellow) and ADP (green), are bound in the four active sites. The allosteric activator ADP (red) is bound in the four regulatory sites, at the interface of the subunits. [PDB 1PFK].

K_m of the enzyme for a substrate, others the V_{max} of the enzyme. We have just seen that phosphoenolpyruvate changes the apparent K_m of phosphofructokinase-1 for fructose 6-phosphate. Modulators themselves are not altered chemically by the enzyme.

3. With few exceptions, regulatory enzymes possess quaternary structure. (Not all enzymes composed of subunits are regulatory enzymes, however.) The individual polypeptide chains of a regulatory enzyme may be identical or different. For those with identical subunits (such as phosphofructokinase-1 from *E. coli*), each polypeptide chain can contain both the catalytic and regulatory sites, and the oligomer is a symmetric complex, most often possessing two or four protein chains. Regulatory enzymes composed of nonidentical subunits have more complex but usually symmetric arrangements.

4. A regulatory enzyme usually has at least one substrate for which the v_0 versus [S] curve is sigmoidal rather than hyperbolic. Phosphofructokinase-1 exhibits Michaelis-Menten (hyperbolic) kinetics with respect to one substrate, ATP, but

sigmoidal kinetics with respect to its other substrate, fructose 6-phosphate. A sigmoidal curve is caused by positive cooperativity of substrate binding, which is made possible by the presence of multiple substrate-binding sites in the enzyme.

Figure 5.21 illustrates the regulatory role that cooperative binding can play. Addition of an activator can shift the sigmoidal curve toward a hyperbolic shape, lowering the apparent K_m (the concentration of substrate required for half-saturation) and raising the activity at a given [S]. The addition of an inhibitor can raise the apparent K_m of the enzyme and lower its activity at any particular concentration of substrate.

The allosteric R $\rightleftarrows$ T transition between the active and the inactive conformations of a regulatory enzyme is rapid. The ratio of R to T is controlled by the concentrations of the various ligands and the relative affinities of each conformation for these ligands. In the simplest cases, substrate and activator molecules bind only to enzyme in the R state (E_R), and inhibitor molecules bind only to enzyme in the T state (E_T).

$$E_T\!\!-\!\!I \;\underset{I}{\overset{I}{\rightleftharpoons}}\; E_T \;\overset{\text{Allosteric transition}}{\rightleftharpoons}\; E_R \;\underset{S}{\overset{S}{\rightleftharpoons}}\; E_R\!\!-\!\!S \qquad\qquad (5.30)$$

The addition of S leads to an increase in the concentration of enzyme in the R conformation. Conversely, the addition of I increases the proportion of the T species. Activator molecules bind preferentially to the R conformation, leading to an increase in the R/T ratio. Note that this simplified scheme does not show that there are multiple interacting binding sites for both S and I.

Some allosteric inhibitors are nonclassical competitive inhibitors (Figure 5.8b). For example, Figure 5.21 describes an enzyme that has a higher apparent K_m for its substrate in the presence of the allosteric inhibitor but an unaltered V_{max}. Therefore, the allosteric modulator is a competitive inhibitor.

Some regulatory enzymes exhibit noncompetitive inhibition patterns (Figure 5.8d). Binding of a modulator at the regulatory site does not prevent substrate from binding, but it appears to distort the conformation of the active site sufficiently to decrease the activity of the enzyme.

C. Two Theories of Allosteric Regulation

Two models that account for the cooperativity of binding of ligands to oligomeric proteins have gained general recognition. Both the concerted theory and the sequential theory describe the cooperative transitions in simple quantitative terms. The latter is a more general theory; the former is adequate to explain many allosteric enzymes.

Figure 5.21 ▶
Role of cooperativity of binding in regulation. The activity of an allosteric enzyme with a sigmoidal binding curve can be altered markedly when either an activator or an inhibitor is bound to the enzyme. Addition of an activator can lower the apparent K_m, raising the activity at a given [S]. Conversely, addition of an inhibitor can raise the apparent K_m, producing less activity at a given [S].

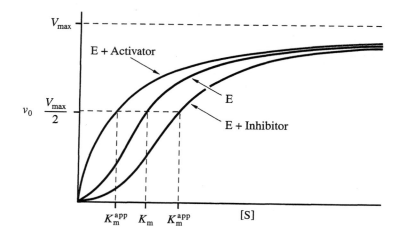

The **concerted theory**, or symmetry-driven theory, was devised to explain the cooperative binding of identical ligands, such as substrates. It assumes that there is one binding site per subunit for each ligand, that the conformation of each subunit is constrained by its association with other subunits, and that when the protein changes conformation, it retains its molecular symmetry (Figure 5.22a). Thus, there are two conformations in equilibrium, R (with a high affinity for the substrate) and T (with a low affinity for the substrate). The binding of substrate shifts the equilibrium. When the conformation of the protein changes, the affinity of its ligand-binding sites also changes. The concerted theory was extended to include the binding of allosteric modulators, and it can be simplified by assuming that the substrate binds only to the R state and the allosteric inhibitor binds only to the T state. The concerted theory is based on the observed structural symmetry of regulatory enzymes. It suggests that all subunits of a given protein molecule have the same conformation, either all R or all T; that is, they retain their symmetry when they shift from the T to the R state. Experimental data obtained with a number of enzymes can be explained by this simple theory. For example, many of the properties of phosphofructokinase-1 from *E. coli* fit the concerted theory. In almost all cases, however, not all observations can be explained by the concerted theory, so their allosteric behavior probably is more complex than that suggested by this simple two-state model.

The **sequential theory**, or ligand-induced theory, is a more general proposal. It is based on the idea that a ligand may induce a change in the tertiary structure of the subunit to which it binds. This subunit-ligand complex may change the conformations of neighboring subunits to varying extents. Like the concerted theory, the sequential theory assumes that only one shape has a high affinity for the ligand, but it differs from the concerted theory in allowing the existence of both high- and low-affinity subunits in an oligomeric molecule with fractional saturation (Figure 5.22b). The sequential theory can account for negative cooperativity—a decrease in affinity

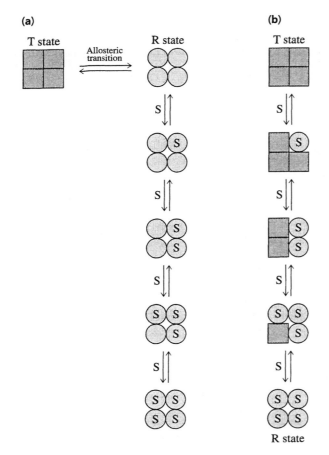

(a)

(b)

◀ **Figure 5.22**
Two models for cooperativity of binding of substrate (S) to a tetrameric protein. **(a)** In the simplified concerted model, all subunits are either in the R or the T state, and S binds only to the R state. **(b)** In the sequential model, binding of S to a subunit converts only that subunit to the R conformation. Neighboring subunits might remain in the T state or might assume conformations between T and R.

Deoxyhemoglobin
(quaternary T state)

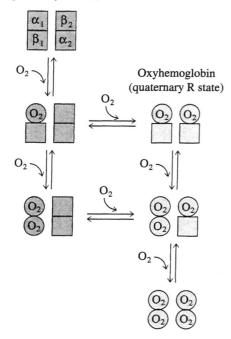

Oxyhemoglobin
(quaternary R state)

Figure 5.23 ▲
Conformational changes during oxygen binding to hemoglobin. The tertiary structure of a single chain changes as oxygen is bound. The quaternary structure of hemoglobin changes from the T state to the R state only when at least one subunit on each αβ dimer is oxygenated. Only four of the eight possible partially oxygenated species are shown (e.g., oxygen could bind initially to either an α or a β chain, and so on). [Adapted from Ackers, G. K., Doyle, M. L., Myers, D., and Daugherty, M. A. (1992). Molecular code for cooperativity in hemoglobin. *Science* 255:54–63.]

as subsequent molecules of ligand are bound to an oligomer. Negative cooperativity occurs with a relatively small number of enzymes. The sequential theory treats the concerted theory, with its symmetry requirement, as a limiting and simple case.

Extensive tests of the concerted and sequential theories have been made using the oxygen-binding protein hemoglobin. Recall that hemoglobin is not a simple tetramer but rather a dimer of αβ dimers because each α subunit interacts with a specific β subunit (Section 4.12). Recall also that O_2 binds weakly to the T state of hemoglobin, and more tightly to the R state (Section 4.13). The composite results from many types of experiments indicate that the tertiary structure of a hemoglobin subunit changes when it binds oxygen. The quaternary structure of the oligomer remains unchanged until oxygen has bound to at least one subunit in each αβ dimer. The binding of an oxygen molecule to the second dimer causes a change in quaternary structure, the relative movement of the αβ dimers described in Section 4.13B. The changes in tertiary and quaternary structure are modeled in Figure 5.23. The process of oxygen binding to hemoglobin has aspects of both the sequential and concerted theories: independent alteration of tertiary structure within subunits and a concerted transition in quaternary structure.

D. Regulation by Covalent Modification

Frequently, a cell's response to extracellular modulators includes covalent modification of intracellular enzymes. Regulation by covalent modification is slightly slower than the allosteric regulation described above. The covalent modification of regulatory enzymes is reversible, but it usually requires one enzyme for activation and another for inactivation. Enzymes controlled by covalent modification, termed **interconvertible enzymes**, are believed to generally undergo R ⇌ T transitions. They may be frozen in one conformation or the other by a covalent substitution. The substitution reaction is catalyzed by an accessory enzyme called a **converter enzyme**, and release of the substituent is catalyzed by another converter enzyme (Figure 5.24). Converter enzymes are usually controlled by allosteric modulators, although in some cases, converter enzymes within a regulatory sequence are themselves subject to covalent modification, with the entire sequence under allosteric control.

The most common type of covalent modification is phosphorylation of one or more specific serine residues of an interconvertible enzyme, although in some cases threonine, tyrosine, or histidine residues are phosphorylated. An enzyme called a protein kinase, a member of a diverse family of enzymes, catalyzes the transfer of the terminal phosphoryl group from ATP to the appropriate serine residue of the regulated enzyme. The activity of each protein kinase is itself regulated, commonly by interaction with hormone-elicited compounds called second messengers (Section 9.12). The phosphoserine of the interconvertible enzyme is hydrolyzed by the activity of a protein phosphatase, releasing phosphate and returning the interconvertible enzyme to its dephosphorylated state. Individual enzymes differ as to whether it is their phospho or dephospho forms that are active.

The reactions involved in the regulation of mammalian pyruvate dehydrogenase by covalent modification are shown in Figure 5.25. Pyruvate dehydrogenase catalyzes a reaction that connects the pathway of glycolysis to the citric acid cycle. Phosphorylation of pyruvate dehydrogenase, catalyzed by the allosteric enzyme pyruvate dehydrogenase kinase, inactivates the dehydrogenase. The kinase can be activated by any of several metabolites. Phosphorylated pyruvate dehydrogenase is reactivated under different metabolic conditions by hydrolysis of its phosphoserine residue, catalyzed by pyruvate dehydrogenase phosphatase. This phosphatase is allosterically activated by Ca^{2+}.

There are too few X-ray crystallographic structures of the phospho and dephospho forms of interconvertible enzymes to provide a general molecular explanation of how covalent modification alters catalytic activity. In several cases, modification stabilizes one conformation (either the R or the T state) of the interconvertible enzyme. In one case, phosphorylation directly alters the binding site for a substrate.

5.11 Multienzyme Complexes and Multifunctional Enzymes

In some cases, different enzymes that catalyze sequential reactions in the same pathway are bound together in a multienzyme complex. In other cases, different activities may be found on a single multifunctional polypeptide chain. The presence of multiple activities on a single polypeptide chain is usually the result of a gene fusion event.

Some multienzyme complexes are quite stable. We will encounter several of these complexes in other chapters, for example, when we discuss the biosynthesis of fatty acids and nucleic acids. In other multienzyme complexes, proteins may be associated more weakly, mainly by steric and electrostatic complementarity and hydrophobic binding. Because such complexes dissociate easily, it has been difficult to demonstrate their existence and importance. Attachment to membranes or cytoskeletal components is another way that enzymes may be associated.

The metabolic advantages of multienzyme complexes and multifunctional enzymes include the possibility of **metabolite channeling**. Channeling of reactants between active sites can occur when the product of one reaction is transferred directly to the next active site without entering the bulk solvent. Channeling can vastly increase the rate of a reaction sequence by decreasing transit times for intermediates between enzymes and by producing local high concentrations of intermediates. Channeling can also protect chemically labile intermediates from degradation by the solvent.

One of the best-characterized examples of channeling involves the bienzyme tryptophan synthase, which catalyzes the last two steps in the biosynthesis of tryptophan (Section 18.5C). Tryptophan synthase has a tunnel that conducts a reactant between its two active sites. The structure of the enzyme not only prevents the loss of the reactant to the bulk solvent but also provides allosteric control to keep the reactions occurring at the two active sites in phase. Several other enzymes have two or three active sites connected by a molecular tunnel. Another mechanism for metabolite channeling is guidance along a path of basic amino acid side chains on the surface of coupled enzymes. The metabolites (most of which are negatively charged) are directed between active sites by the electrostatically positive surface path. The search for enzyme complexes and the evaluation of their catalytic and regulatory roles is an extremely active area of research in enzyme chemistry.

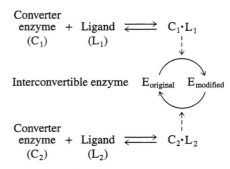

Figure 5.24 ▲
General scheme for covalent modification of interconvertible enzymes. Two allosterically controlled converter enzymes, C_1 and C_2, catalyze modifications of the interconvertible enzyme, E. The interconvertible enzyme exists in two forms, original and modified. C_1 and C_2 are activated when they bind their respective modulator ligands, L_1 and L_2.

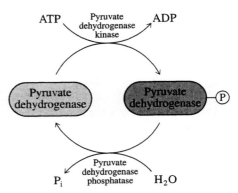

Figure 5.25 ▲
Regulation of mammalian pyruvate dehydrogenase. Pyruvate dehydrogenase, an interconvertible enzyme, is inactivated by phosphorylation catalyzed by pyruvate dehydrogenase kinase. It is reactivated by hydrolysis of its phosphoserine residue, catalyzed by an allosteric hydrolase called pyruvate dehydrogenase phosphatase.

Summary

1. Enzymes, the catalysts of living organisms, are remarkable for their catalytic efficiency and their substrate and reaction specificity. With few exceptions, enzymes are proteins or proteins plus cofactors. Enzymes are grouped into six classes according to the nature of the reactions they catalyze.

2. The kinetics of a chemical reaction can be described by a rate equation. Kinetic order is the sum of the exponents in the equation.

3. Enzymes and substrates form noncovalent enzyme-substrate complexes. Consequently, enzymatic reactions are characteristically first order with respect to enzyme concentration and typically show hyperbolic dependence on substrate concentration. The hyperbola is described by the Michaelis-Menten equation.

4. Maximum velocity (V_{max}) is reached when the substrate concentration is saturating. The Michaelis constant (K_m) is equal to the substrate concentration at half-maximal reaction velocity, that is, at half-saturation of E with S.

5. The catalytic constant (k_{cat}), or turnover number, for an enzyme is the maximum number of molecules of substrate that can be transformed into product per molecule of enzyme (or per active site) per second. The ratio k_{cat}/K_m is an apparent second-order rate constant that governs the reaction of an enzyme when the substrate is dilute and nonsaturating. k_{cat}/K_m provides a measure of the substrate specificity of an enzyme.

6. K_m and V_{max} can be obtained from plots of initial velocity at a series of substrate concentrations and at a fixed enzyme concentration.

7. Multisubstrate reactions may follow a sequential mechanism, with binding and release events being ordered or random, or a ping-pong mechanism.

8. Inhibitors decrease the rates of enzyme-catalyzed reactions. Reversible inhibitors may be competitive (increasing the apparent value of K_m without changing V_{max}), uncompetitive (appearing to decrease K_m and V_{max} proportionally), or noncompetitive (appearing to decrease V_{max} without changing K_m). Irreversible enzyme inhibitors form covalent bonds with the enzyme.

9. Site-directed mutagenesis can be used to change the identity of a single amino acid residue within a protein, generating a new protein whose properties may reveal the role of the original amino acid residue.

10. Allosteric modulators bind to enzymes at a site other than the active site and alter enzyme activity. Two models, the concerted model and the sequential model, describe the cooperativity of allosteric enzymes. Covalent modification, usually phosphorylation, of certain regulatory enzymes can also regulate enzyme activity.

11. Multienzyme complexes and multifunctional enzymes offer the advantage of metabolite channeling.

Problems

1. Use the Michaelis-Menten equation (Equation 5.14) to demonstrate the following:
   (a) v_0 becomes independent of [S] when $[S] \gg K_m$.
   (b) The reaction is first order with respect to S when $[S] \ll K_m$.
   (c) $[S] = K_m$ when v_0 is one-half V_{max}.

2. Initial velocities have been measured for the reaction of α-chymotrypsin with tyrosine benzyl ester [S] at six different substrate concentrations. Use the data below to make a reasonable estimate of the V_{max} and K_m value for this substrate.

mM [S]	0.00125	0.10	0.04	0.10	2.0	10
v_0 (mM/min)	14	35	56	66	69	70

3. (a) Why is the k_{cat}/K_m value (specificity constant) used to measure the preference of an enzyme for different substrates?
   (b) What are the upper limits for k_{cat}/K_m values for enzymes?
   (c) Enzymes with k_{cat}/K_m values approaching these upper limits are said to have reached "catalytic perfection." Explain.

4. Carbonic anhydrase (CA) has a 25 000-fold higher activity ($k_{cat} = 10^6$ s^{-1}) than orotidine monophosphate decarboxylase (OMPD) ($k_{cat} = 40$ s^{-1}). However, OMPD provides more than a 10^{10} higher "rate acceleration" than CA (Table 5.2). Explain how this is possible.

5. An enzyme that follows Michaelis-Menten kinetics has a K_m of 1 μM. The initial velocity is 0.1 μM min^{-1} at a substrate concentration of 100 μM. What is the initial velocity when [S] is equal to (a) 1 mM, (b) 1 μM, or (c) 2 μM?

6. Human immunodeficiency virus 1 (HIV-1) encodes a protease (M_r 21 500) that is essential for the assembly and maturation of the virus. The protease catalyzes the hydrolysis of a heptapeptide substrate with a k_{cat} of 1000 s^{-1} and a K_m of 0.075 M.

   (a) Calculate V_{max} for substrate hydrolysis when HIV-1 protease is present at 0.2 mg ml^{-1}.

   (b) When —C(O)NH— of the heptapeptide is replaced by —CH$_2$NH—, the resulting derivative cannot be cleaved by HIV-1 protease and acts as an inhibitor. Under the same experimental conditions as in part (a), but in the presence of 2.5 μM inhibitor, V_{max} is 9.3×10^{-3} M s^{-1}. What kind of inhibition is occurring? Is this type of inhibition expected for a molecule of this structure?

7. Draw a graph of v_0 versus [S] for a typical enzyme reaction (a) in the absence of an inhibitor, (b) in the presence of a competitive inhibitor, and (c) in the presence of a noncompetitive inhibitor.

8. Sulfonamides (sulfa drugs) such as sulfanilamide are antibacterial drugs that inhibit the enzyme dihydropteroate synthase (DS) that is required for the synthesis of folic acid in bacteria. There is no corresponding enzyme inhibition in animals, because folic acid is a required vitamin and cannot be synthesized. If *p*-aminobenzoic acid (PABA) is a substrate for DS, what type of inhibition can be predicted for the bacterial synthase enzyme in the presence of sulfonamides? Draw a double reciprocal plot for this type of inhibition with correctly labeled axes, and identify the uninhibited and inhibited lines.

Sulfonamides
(R = H, sulfanilamide)

p-Aminobenzoic acid

9. (a) Fumarase is an enzyme in the citric acid cycle that catalyzes the conversion of fumarate to L-malate. Given the fumarate (substrate) concentrations and initial velocities below, construct a Lineweaver-Burk plot and determine the V_{max} and K_m values for the fumarase catalyzed reaction.

Fumarate (mM)	Rate of product formation (mmol l^{-1}min^{-1})
2.0	2.5
3.3	3.1
5.0	3.6
10.0	4.2

   (b) Fumarase has a molecular weight of 194 000 and is composed of four identical subunits, each with an active site. If the enzyme concentration is 1×10^{-8} M for the experiment in part (a), calculate the k_{cat} value for the reaction of fumarase with fumarate. Note: the units for k_{cat} are reciprocal seconds (s^{-1}).

10. The therapeutic antiinflammatory effects of aspirin arise from its inhibition of the enzyme cyclooxygenase-2 (COX-2)—involved in the synthesis of prostaglandins, mediators of inflammation, pain, and fever. Aspirin irreversibly inhibits COX-2 by covalently transferring an acetyl group to a serine residue at the enzyme active site. However, the undesirable side effect of stomach irritation arises from the irreversible inhibition of the related intestinal enzyme cyclooxygenase-1 (COX-1) by aspirin. COX-1 is involved in the synthesis of prostaglandins that regulate secretion of gastric mucin, which protects the stomach from acid. The aspirin analog APHS was synthesized and shown to be 60 times more selective as an inhibitor of COX-2 than of COX-1, suggesting that it could be an antiinflammatory drug with far less gastrointestinal side effects. Draw the structure of the inactivated COX-2 enzyme-inhibitor complex with APHS. Since aspirin and structural analogs act at the active site of COX enzymes, will they exhibit competitive inhibition patterns?

APHS

11. Covalent enzyme regulation plays an important role in the metabolism of muscle glycogen, an energy storage molecule. The active phosphorylated form of glycogen phosphorylase (GP) catalyzes the degradation of glycogen to glucose 1-phosphate. Using pyruvate dehydrogenase as a model (Figure 5.25), fill in the boxes below for the activation and inactivation of muscle glycogen phosphorylase.

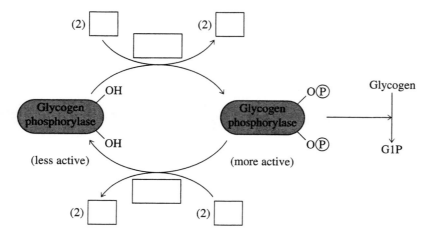

12. Regulatory enzymes in metabolic pathways are often found at the first step that is unique to that pathway. How does regulation at this point improve metabolic efficiency?

13. ATCase is a regulatory enzyme at the beginning of the pathway for the biosynthesis of pyrimidine nucleotides. ATCase exhibits positive cooperativity and is activated by ATP and inhibited by the pyrimidine nucleotide cytidine triphosphate (CTP). Both ATP and CTP affect the K_m for the substrate aspartate but not V_{max}. In the absence of ATP or CTP, the concentration of aspartate required for half-maximal velocity is about 5 mM at saturating concentrations of the second substrate, carbamoyl phosphate. Draw a v_0 versus [aspartate] plot for ATCase and indicate how CTP and ATP affect v_0 when [aspartate] = 5 mM.

Selected Readings

Enzyme Catalysis

Fersht, A. (1985). *Enzyme Structure and Mechanism*, 2nd ed. (New York: W. H. Freeman). A description of the mechanisms and functions of enzymes.

Sigman, D. S., and Boyer, P. D., eds. (1990–1992). *The Enzymes*, Vols. 19 and 20, 3rd ed. (San Diego: Academic Press). These two volumes include chapters on the basic principles of catalysis, enzyme kinetics, inhibition, and mechanisms of various enzymes.

Webb, E. C., ed. (1992). *Enzyme Nomenclature 1992: Recommendations of the Nomenclature Committee of the International Union of Biochemistry and Molecular Biology on the Nomenclature and Classification of Enzymes* (San Diego, Academic Press). A listing of the six classes of enzymes.

RNA Enzymes

Frank, D. N., and Pace, N. R. (1998). Ribonuclease P: Unity and diversity in a tRNA processing ribozyme. *Annu. Rev. Biochem.* 67:153–180.

Joyce, G. F. (1998). Nucleic acid enzymes: Playing with a fuller deck. *Proc. Natl. Acad. Sci USA* 95:5845–5847.

Enzyme Kinetics and Inhibition

Bugg, C. E., Carson, W. M., and Montgomery, J. A. (1993). Drugs by design. *Sci. Am.* 269(6):92–98.

Cleland, W. W. (1970). *Steady State Kinetics. The Enzymes*, Vol. 2, 3rd ed., P. D. Boyer, ed. (New York: Academic Press), pp. 1–65. Methods used for studying the kinetics of multisubstrate reactions.

Cornish-Bowden, A. (1999). Enzyme kinetics from a metabolic perspective. *Biochem. Soc. Trans.* 27:281–284. Suggestions of how inhibition measurements can be applied to cellular metabolism.

Radzicka, A., and Wolfenden, R. (1995). A proficient enzyme. *Science* 267:90–93. Discusses an excellent example of rate acceleration.

Segel, I. H. (1975). *Enzyme Kinetics: Behavior and Analysis of Rapid Equilibrium and Steady State Enzyme Systems* (New York: Wiley-Interscience). A comprehensive description of kinetic behavior and analysis.

Site-Directed Mutagenesis

Johnson, K. A., and Benkovic, S. J. (1990). Analysis of protein function by mutagenesis. In *The Enzymes*, Vol. 19, 3rd ed., D. S. Sigman and P. D. Boyer, eds. (San Diego: Academic Press), pp. 159–211.

Van den Burg, B., Vriend, G., Veltman, O. R., Venema, G., and Eijsink, V. G. H. (1998). Engineering an enzyme to resist boiling. *Proc. Natl. Acad. Sci USA* 95:2056–2060.

Regulatory Enzymes

Ackers, G. K., Doyle, M. L., Myers, D., and Daugherty, M. A. (1992). Molecular code for cooperativity in hemoglobin. *Science* 255:54–63.

Barford, D. (1991). Molecular mechanisms for the control of enzymic activity by protein phosphorylation. *Biochim. Biophys. Acta* 1133:55–62.

Hurley, J. H., Dean, A. M., Sohl, J. L., Koshland, D. E., Jr., and Stroud, R. M. (1990). Regulation of an enzyme by phosphorylation at the active site. *Science* 249:1012–1016. Describes control of the activity of isocitrate dehydrogenase by covalent modification of a binding residue.

Schirmer, T., and Evans, P. R. (1990). Structural basis of the allosteric behaviour of phosphofructokinase. *Nature* 343:140–145. Comparison of different structures of enzyme-ligand complexes of bacterial phosphofructokinase-1.

Metabolite Channeling

Pan, P., Woehl, E., and Dunn, M. F. (1997). Protein architecture, dynamics and allostery in tryptophan synthase channeling. *Trends Biochem. Sci.* 22:22–27.

Vélot, C., Mixon, M. B., Teige, M., and Srere, P. A. (1997) Model of a quinary structure between Krebs TCA cycle enzymes: a model for the metabolon. *Biochemistry* 36:14271–14276. Evidence that weakly attached enzymes catalyze adjacent steps in the citric acid cycle.

Carbohydrates

Carbohydrates (also called saccharides) are—on the basis of mass—the most abundant class of biological molecules on Earth. The bulk of the planet's carbohydrate is produced by photosynthesis, the process by which certain organisms, including plants, algae, and some bacteria, assimilate atmospheric carbon dioxide and convert solar energy to chemical energy. Carbohydrates, including simple monomeric sugars and their polymers, play several crucial roles in living organisms. They can be oxidized to yield energy to drive metabolic processes. In animals and plants, carbohydrate polymers act as energy storage molecules. Polymeric carbohydrates are also found in cell walls and in the protective coatings of many organisms; other carbohydrate polymers are marker molecules that allow one type of cell to recognize and interact with another type. Carbohydrate derivatives are found in a number of biological molecules, including some coenzymes (Chapter 7) and the nucleic acids DNA and RNA (Chapter 19).

Carbohydrates can be described by the number of monomeric units they contain. **Monosaccharides** are the smallest units of carbohydrate structure. The name *carbohydrate*, "hydrate of carbon," refers to their empirical formula $(CH_2O)_n$, where n is 3 or greater (n is usually 5 or 6 but can be up to 9). **Oligosaccharides** are polymers of 2 to about 20 monosaccharide residues. The most common oligosaccharides are disaccharides, which consist of two linked monosaccharide residues. **Polysaccharides** are polymers that contain many (usually more than 20) monosaccharide residues. Oligosaccharides and polysaccharides do not have the empirical formula $(CH_2O)_n$ because water is eliminated during polymer formation. The term *glycan* is a more general term for carbohydrate polymers. It can refer to a polymer of identical sugars (homoglycan) or of different sugars (heteroglycan).

Photosynthesis is described in detail in Chapter 15.

Top: Darkling beetle. The exoskeletons of insects contain chitin, a homoglycan.

Glycoconjugates are carbohydrate derivatives in which one or more carbohydrate chains are linked covalently to a peptide chain, protein, or lipid. These derivatives include proteoglycans, peptidoglycans, glycoproteins, and glycolipids.

In this chapter, we discuss nomenclature, structure, and function of monosaccharides, disaccharides, and the major homoglycans—starch, glycogen, cellulose, and chitin. We then consider proteoglycans, peptidoglycans, and glycoproteins, all of which contain heteroglycan chains.

Glycolipids are discussed in Chapter 10.

8.1 Most Monosaccharides Are Chiral Compounds

Monosaccharides are water-soluble, white, crystalline solids that have a sweet taste. Examples include glucose and fructose. Chemically, monosaccharides are polyhydroxy aldehydes or **aldoses**, or polyhydroxy ketones or **ketoses**. They are classified by their type of carbonyl group and their number of carbon atoms. As a rule, the suffix -*ose* is used in naming carbohydrates, although there are a number of exceptions. All monosaccharides contain at least three carbon atoms. One of these is the carbonyl carbon, and each of the remaining carbon atoms bears a hydroxyl group. In aldoses, the most oxidized carbon atom is designated C-1 and is drawn at the top of a Fischer projection. In ketoses, the most oxidized carbon atom is usually C-2.

You can review Fischer projections in Section 1.4B.

The smallest monosaccharides are **trioses**, or three-carbon sugars. One- or two-carbon compounds having the general formula $(CH_2O)_n$ do not have properties typical of carbohydrates (such as sweet taste and the ability to crystallize). The aldehydic triose, or aldotriose, is glyceraldehyde (Figure 8.1a). Because its central carbon, C-2, has four different groups attached to it, glyceraldehyde is chiral (Section 3.1). The ketonic triose, or ketotriose, is dihydroxyacetone (Figure 8.1b), which is achiral—it has no asymmetric carbon atom. All other monosaccharides, longer-chain versions of these two sugars, are chiral.

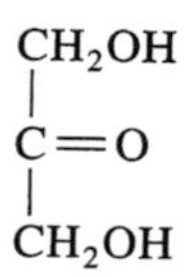

The stereoisomers D- and L-glyceraldehyde are shown as ball-and-stick models in Figure 8.2. Chiral molecules are optically active; that is, they rotate the plane of polarized light. The convention for designating D and L isomers was originally based on the optical properties of glyceraldehyde. The form of glyceraldehyde that caused rotation to the right (dextrorotatory) was designated D; the form that caused rotation to the left (levorotatory) was designated L. Structural knowledge was limited when this convention was established in the

(a)

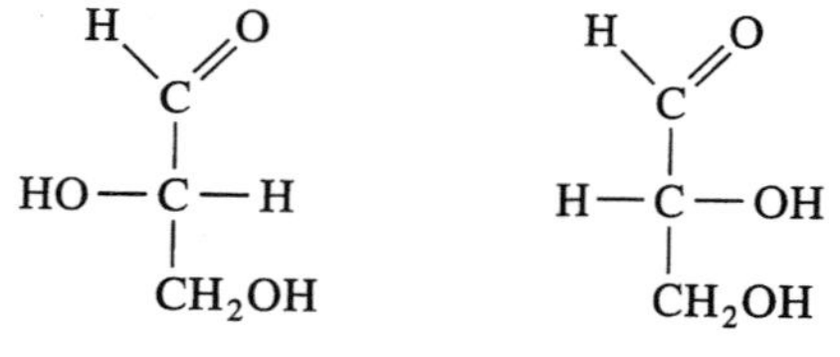

L-Glyceraldehyde   D-Glyceraldehyde

◀ **Figure 8.1**
Fischer projections of **(a)** glyceraldehyde and **(b)** dihydroxyacetone. The designations L (for left) and D (for right) for glyceraldehyde refer to the configuration of the hydroxyl group of the chiral carbon (C-2). Dihydroxyacetone is achiral.

(b)

Dihydroxyacetone

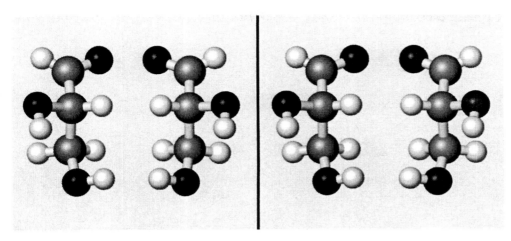

Figure 8.2 ▲
Stereo view of L-glyceraldehyde (left) and D-glyceraldehyde (right).

late 19th century, and configurations for the enantiomers of glyceraldehyde were assigned arbitrarily, with a 50% probability of error. In the mid-20th century, X-ray crystallographic experiments proved that the original structural assignments were correct.

Longer aldoses and ketoses can be regarded as extensions of glyceraldehyde and dihydroxyacetone, respectively, with chiral H—C—OH groups inserted between the carbonyl carbon and the primary alcohol group. Figure 8.3 shows the structures of the tetroses (four-carbon aldoses), pentoses (five-carbon aldoses), and hexoses (six-carbon aldoses) related to D-glyceraldehyde. Note that the carbon atoms are numbered from the aldehydic carbon, which is assigned the number 1. By convention, sugars are said to have the D configuration when the configuration of the chiral carbon with the highest number—the chiral carbon most distant from the carbonyl carbon—is the same as that of C-2 of D-glyceraldehyde (i.e., the —OH group attached to this carbon atom is on the right side in a Fischer projection). Except for glyceraldehyde (which was used as the standard), there is no predictable association between the absolute configuration of a sugar and whether it is dextrorotatory or levorotatory. The arrangement of asymmetric carbon atoms is unique for each monosaccharide, giving each its distinctive properties.

In nature, the D enantiomers of sugars predominate (in the same way that the L enantiomers of amino acids predominate). Therefore, the L enantiomers of the 15 aldoses in Figure 8.3 are not shown. Pairs of enantiomers are mirror images; in other words, the configuration at each chiral carbon is opposite. For example, the hydroxyl groups bound to carbon atoms 2, 3, 4, and 5 of D-glucose point right, left, right, and right, respectively, in the Fischer projection; those of L-glucose point left, right, left, and left (Figure 8.4).

The aldotriose glyceraldehyde, which has a single chiral carbon atom, has two stereoisomers (D- and L-glyceraldehyde). There are four stereoisomers for aldotetroses (D- and L-erythrose and D- and L-threose) because erythrose and threose each possess two chiral carbon atoms. In general, there are 2^n possible stereoisomers for a compound with n chiral carbons. Aldohexoses, which possess four chiral carbons, have a total of 2^4, or 16, stereoisomers (the eight D aldohexoses in Figure 8.3 and their L enantiomers).

Sugar molecules that differ in configuration at only one of several chiral centers are called **epimers**. For example, D-mannose and D-galactose are epimers of D-glucose (at C-2 and C-4, respectively), although they are not epimers of each other (Figure 8.3).

Longer-chain ketoses (Figure 8.5) are related to dihydroxyacetone in the same way that longer-chain aldoses are related to glyceraldehyde. Note that a ketose has one fewer chiral carbon atom than the aldose of the same empirical formula. For

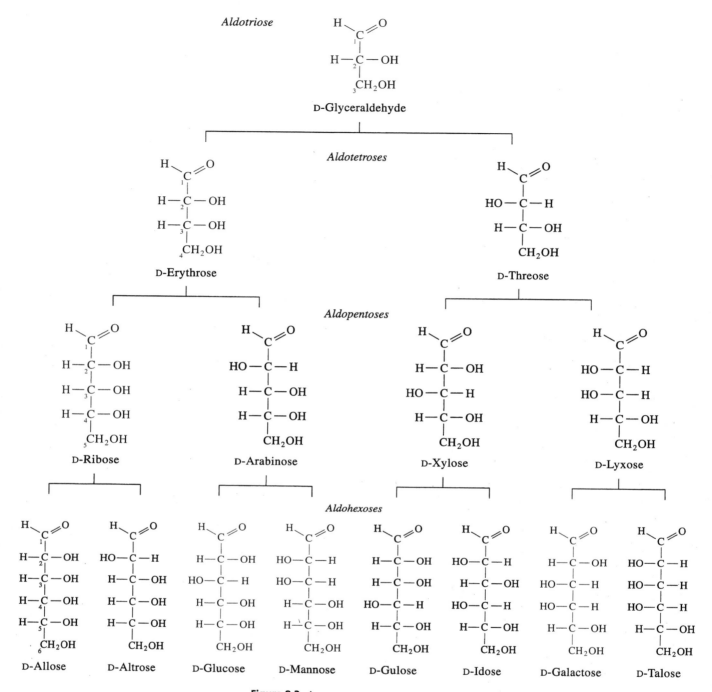

Figure 8.3 ▲
Fischer projections of the three- to six-carbon D-aldoses. The aldoses shown in blue are the most important in our study of biochemistry.

example, there are only two stereoisomers for the one ketotetrose (D- and L-erythrulose), and four stereoisomers for ketopentoses (D- and L-xylulose and D- and L-ribulose). Ketotetrose and ketopentoses are named by inserting -ul- in the name of the corresponding aldose. For example, the ketose xylulose corresponds to the aldose xylose. However, this nomenclature does not apply to ketohexoses (tagatose, sorbose, psicose, and fructose), which bear trivial names.

Figure 8.4 ▶
Fischer projections of L- and D-glucose.

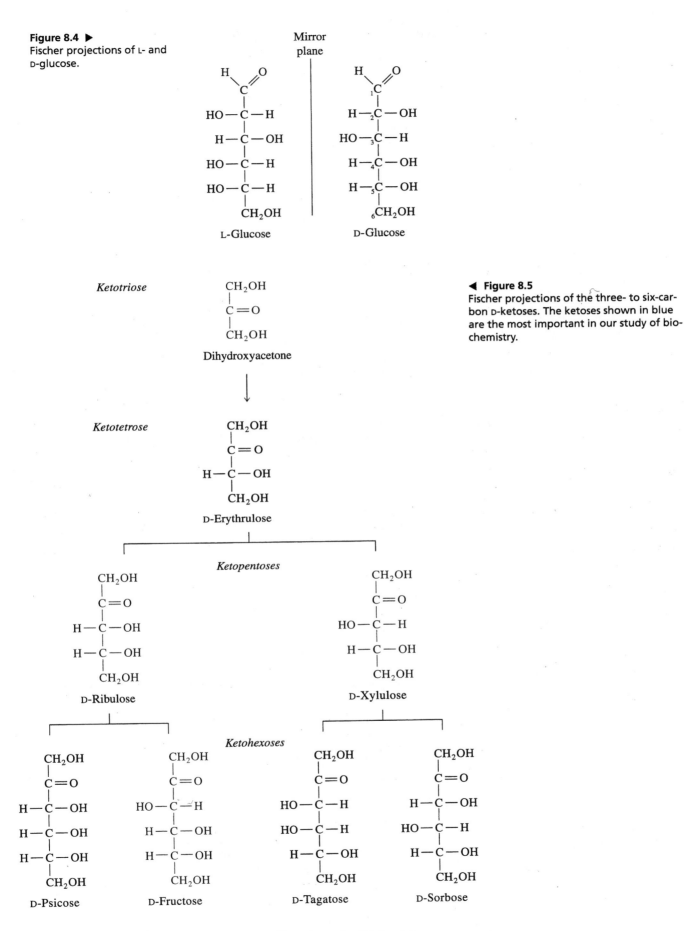

Mirror plane

L-Glucose

D-Glucose

◀ **Figure 8.5**
Fischer projections of the three- to six-carbon D-ketoses. The ketoses shown in blue are the most important in our study of biochemistry.

Ketotriose

Dihydroxyacetone

Ketotetrose

D-Erythrulose

Ketopentoses

D-Ribulose

D-Xylulose

Ketohexoses

D-Psicose

D-Fructose

D-Tagatose

D-Sorbose

Chemistry for Biologists

Figure 8.6 ▶
(a) Reaction of an alcohol with an aldehyde to form a hemiacetal. **(b)** Reaction of an alcohol with a ketone to form a hemiketal. The asterisks indicate the newly formed chiral centers.

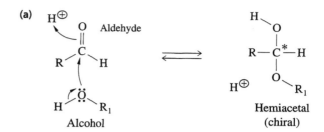

8.2 Cyclization of Aldoses and Ketoses

The optical behavior of some monosaccharides suggests that they have one more chiral carbon atom than is evident from the structures shown in Figures 8.3 and 8.5. D-Glucose, for example, exists in two forms that contain five (not four) asymmetric carbons. The source of this additional asymmetry is an intramolecular cyclization reaction that produces a new chiral center at the carbon atom of the carbonyl group. This cyclization resembles the reaction of an alcohol with an aldehyde (to form a hemiacetal) or with a ketone (to form a hemiketal) (Figure 8.6).

The carbonyl carbon of an aldose containing at least five carbon atoms or of a ketose containing at least six carbon atoms can react with an intramolecular hydroxyl group to form a cyclic hemiacetal or cyclic hemiketal, respectively. The oxygen atom from the reacting hydroxyl group becomes a member of the five- or six-membered ring structures.

Because it resembles the six-membered heterocyclic compound pyran (Figure 8.7a), the six-membered ring of a monosaccharide is called a **pyranose**. Similarly, because the five-membered ring of a monosaccharide resembles furan (Figure 8.7b), it is called a **furanose**. Note that, unlike pyran and furan, the rings of carbohydrates do not contain double bonds.

The most oxidized carbon of a cyclized monosaccharide, the one attached to two oxygen atoms, is referred to as the **anomeric carbon**. In ring structures, the anomeric carbon is chiral. Thus, the cyclized aldose or ketose can adopt either of two configurations (designated α or β), as illustrated for D-glucose in Figure 8.8. The α and β isomers are called anomers.

In solution, aldoses and ketoses capable of forming ring structures equilibrate among their various cyclic and open-chain forms. At 31°C, for example, D-glucose exists in an equilibrium mixture of approximately 64% β-D-glucopyranose and 36% α-D-glucopyranose, with very small amounts of the furanose and open-chain forms. Similarly, D-ribose exists as a mixture of approximately 58.5% β-D-ribopyranose, 21.5% α-D-ribopyranose, 13.5% β-D-ribofuranose, and 6.5% α-D-ribofuranose, with a tiny fraction in the open-chain form (Figure 8.9). The relative abundance of the various forms of monosaccharides at equilibrium reflects the relative stabilities of each form. Although unsubstituted D-ribose is most stable as the β-pyranose, its structure in nucleotides (Section 8.5c) is the β-furanose.

(a)

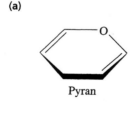

Pyran

(b)

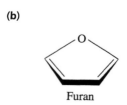

Furan

Figure 8.7 ▲
(a) Pyran and **(b)** furan.

D-Glucose
(Fischer projection)

α-D-Glucopyranose
(Haworth projection)

or

β-D-Glucopyranose
(Haworth projection)

◀ **Figure 8.8**
Cyclization of D-glucose to form glucopyranose. The Fischer projection (top left) is rearranged into a three-dimensional
representation (top right). Rotation of the
bond between C-4 and C-5 brings the C-5 hydroxyl group close to the C-1 aldehyde
group. Reaction of the C-5 hydroxyl group
with one side of C-1 gives α-D-glucopyranose; reaction of the hydroxyl group with
the other side gives β-D-glucopyranose. The
glucopyranose products are shown as
Haworth projections in which the lower
edges of the ring (thick lines) project in front
of the plane of the paper and the upper
edges project behind the plane of the paper.
In the α-D anomer of glucose, the hydroxyl
group at C-1 points down; in the
β-D anomer, it points up.

The ring drawings shown in Figures 8.8 and 8.9 are called Haworth projections, after Norman Haworth who elucidated the cyclization reactions of carbohydrates and first proposed these representations. A Haworth projection adequately indicates stereochemistry and can be easily related to a Fischer projection. A cyclic mono-saccharide is drawn so the anomeric carbon is on the right and the other carbons are numbered in a clockwise direction. Hydroxyl groups pointing down in the Haworth projection point to the right of the carbon skeleton in the Fischer projection, where-as hydroxyl groups pointing up in the Haworth projection point to the left in the Fischer projection. In a Haworth projection, the configuration of the anomeric car-bon atom is designated α if its hydroxyl group is *cis* to (on the same side of the ring as) the oxygen atom of the highest-numbered chiral carbon atom. It is β if its hy-droxyl group is *trans* to (on the opposite side of the ring from) the oxygen attached to the highest-numbered chiral carbon. With α-D-glucopyranose, the hydroxyl group at the anomeric carbon points down; with β-D-glucosopyranose it points up.

Monosaccharides are often drawn in either the α- or β-D-furanose or the α- or β-D-pyranose form. However, you should remember that the anomeric forms of five- and six-carbon sugars are in rapid equilibrium. Throughout this chapter and the rest of the book, we draw sugars in the correct anomeric form if it is known. We refer to sugars in a nonspecific way (e.g., glucose) when we are discussing an equilibrium

Norman Haworth, who elucidated the cyclization reactions of carbohydrates.

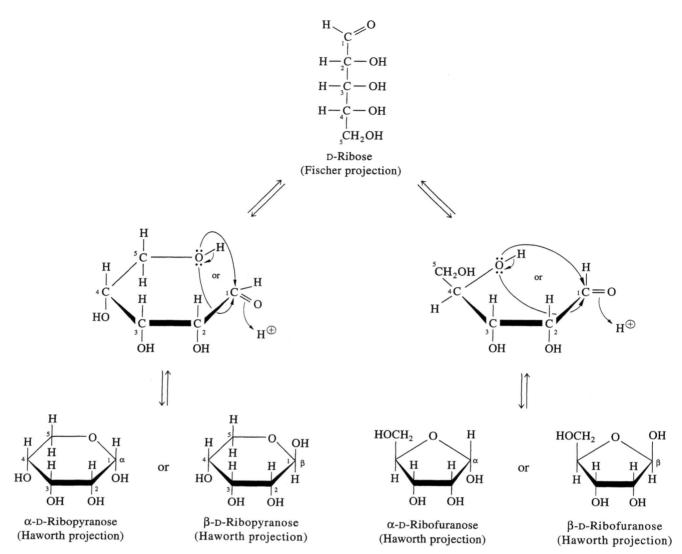

Figure 8.9 ▲
Cyclization of D-ribose to form α- and β-D-ribopyranose and α- and β-D-ribofuranose.

mixture of the various anomeric forms as well as the open-chain forms. When we are discussing a specific form of a sugar, however, we refer to it precisely (e.g., β-D-glucopyranose). Also, since the D enantiomers of carbohydrates predominate in nature, we always assume that a carbohydrate has the D configuration unless specified otherwise.

8.3 Conformations of Monosaccharides

Because of their simplicity, Haworth projections are commonly used in biochemistry. These formulas show the configuration of the atoms and groups at each carbon atom of the sugar's backbone. However, the geometry of the carbon atoms of a monosaccharide ring is tetrahedral (bond angles near 110°), so monosaccharide rings are not actually planar. They can exist in a variety of conformations (three-dimensional shapes having the same configuration). In nucleic acids, furanose rings adopt envelope conformations, in which one of the five ring atoms (either C-2 or C-3) is out-of-plane and the remaining four are approximately coplanar (Figure 8.10). Furanoses can also form twist conformations, in which two of the five ring atoms are

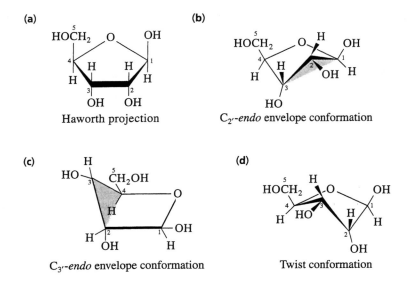

(a)
Haworth projection

(b)
$C_{2'}$-*endo* envelope conformation

(c)
$C_{3'}$-*endo* envelope conformation

(d)
Twist conformation

◄ **Figure 8.10**
Conformations of β-D-ribofuranose.
(a) Haworth projection. **(b)** $C_{2'}$-endo envelope conformation. **(c)** $C_{3'}$-endo envelope
conformation. **(d)** Twist conformation. In the
$C_{2'}$-endo conformation, C-2 lies above the
plane defined by C-1, C-3, C-4, and the ring
oxygen. In the $C_{3'}$-endo conformation, C-3
lies above the plane defined by C-1, C-2,
C-4, and the ring oxygen. In the twist conformation shown, C-3 lies above and C-2 lies
below the place defined by C-1, C-4, and
the ring oxygen. The planes are shown in
yellow.

out-of-plane, one on either side of the plane formed by the other three atoms. The
relative stability of each conformer depends on the degree of steric interference between the hydroxyl groups. The various conformers of unsubstituted monosaccharides can rapidly interconvert.

Pyranose rings tend to assume one of two conformations, the chair conformation or the boat conformation (Figure 8.11). For each pyranose, there are two distinct

(a)

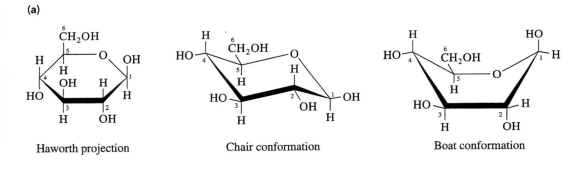

Haworth projection   Chair conformation   Boat conformation

(b)

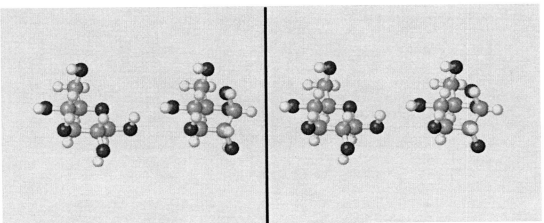

Figure 8.11 ▲
Conformations of β-D-glucopyranose. **(a)** Haworth projection, a chair conformation, and
a boat conformation. **(b)** Stereo view of a chair (left) and a boat (right) conformation.

Chemistry for Biologists

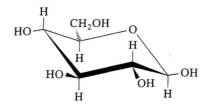

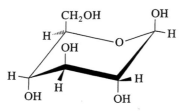

Figure 8.12 ▲
The two chair conformers of β-D-glucopyra-nose. The top conformer is more stable.

chair conformers and six distinct boat conformers. Since the chair conformations minimize steric repulsion among the ring substituents, they are generally more stable than boat conformations. Note that the substituents of a pyranose ring in the chair conformation may occupy two different positions. Axial substituents extend perpendicular to the plane of the ring, and equatorial substituents extend along the plane of the ring. In pyranoses, five substituents are axial and five are equatorial. However, whether a group is axial or equatorial depends on which carbon atom (C-1 or C-4) extends above the plane of the ring when the ring is in the chair conformation. Figure 8.12 shows the two different chair conformers of β-D-glucopyranose. The more stable conformation is the one in which the bulkiest ring substituents are equatorial (top structure). In fact, this conformation of β-D-glucose has the least steric strain of any aldohexose. Pyranose rings are occasionally forced to adopt slightly different conformations, such as the unstable half-chair adopted by a polysaccharide residue in the active site of lysozyme (Section 6.7).

8.4 Derivatives of Monosaccharides

Many derivatives of the sugars we have already described are found in biological systems. They include polymerized monosaccharides, such as oligosaccharides and polysaccharides, as well as several classes of nonpolymerized compounds. In this section, we introduce a few monosaccharide derivatives, including sugar phosphates, deoxy and amino sugars, sugar alcohols, sugar acids, and ascorbic acid (vitamin C).

Like other polymer-forming biomolecules, monosaccharides and their derivatives have abbreviations for describing their polymers easily. The accepted abbreviations contain three letters, with suffixes added in some cases. The abbreviations for some pentoses and hexoses and their major derivatives are listed in Table 8.1. We use these abbreviations later in this chapter.

A. Sugar Phosphates

Monosaccharides in metabolic pathways are often converted to phosphate esters. Figure 8.13 shows the structures of several sugar phosphates we will encounter in our study of carbohydrate metabolism. The triose phosphates, ribose 5-phosphate, and glucose 6-phosphate are simple alcohol-phosphate esters. Glucose 1-phosphate is a hemiacetal phosphate, which is more reactive than an alcohol phosphate. The ability of UDP-glucose to act as a glucosyl donor (Section 7.7) is evidence of this reactivity.

B. Deoxy Sugars

The structures of two deoxy sugars are shown in Figure 8.14. In these derivatives, a hydrogen atom replaces one of the hydroxyl groups in the parent monosaccharide. 2-Deoxy-D-ribose is an important building block for DNA. L-Fucose (6-deoxy-L-galactose) is widely distributed in plants, animals, and microorganisms. Despite its unusual L configuration, fucose is derived metabolically from D-mannose.

C. Amino Sugars

In a number of sugars, an amino group replaces one of the hydroxyl groups in the parent monosaccharide. Sometimes the amino group is acetylated. Three examples of amino sugars are shown in Figure 8.15. Amino sugars formed from glucose and galactose commonly occur in glycoconjugates. N-Acetylneuraminic acid (NeuNAc) is an acid formed from N-acetylmannosamine and pyruvate. When this compound cyclizes to form a pyranose, the carbonyl group at C-2 (from the pyruvate moiety) reacts with the hydroxyl group of C-6. NeuNAc is an important constituent of many glycoproteins and of a family of lipids called gangliosides (Section 10.5). Neuraminic acid and its derivatives, including NeuNAc, are collectively known as sialic acids.

TABLE 8.1 Abbreviations for some monosaccharides and their derivatives

Monosaccharide or derivative	Abbreviation
Pentoses	
Ribose	Rib
Xylose	Xyl
Hexoses	
Fructose	Fru
Galactose	Gal
Glucose	Glc
Mannose	Man
Deoxy sugars	
Abequose	Abe
Fucose	Fuc
Amino sugars	
Glucosamine	GlcN
Galactosamine	GalN
N-Acetylglucosamine	GlcNAc
N-Acetylgalactosamine	GalNAc
N-Acetylneuraminic acid	NeuNAc
N-Acetylmuramic acid	MurNAc
Sugar acids	
Glucuronic acid	GlcUA
Iduronic acid	IdoA

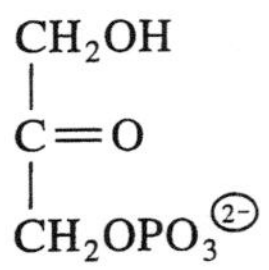

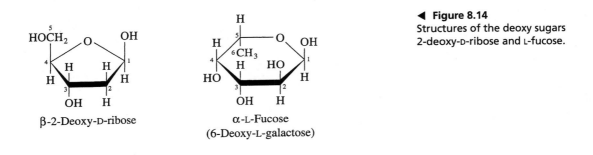

Figure 8.13 ▲
Structures of several metabolically important sugar phosphates.

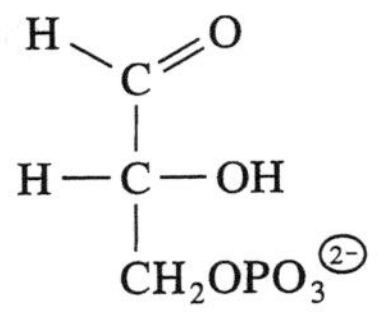

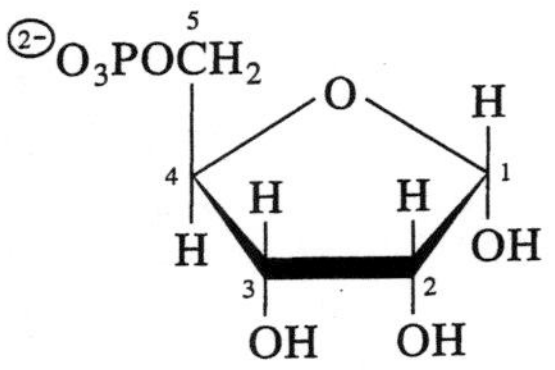

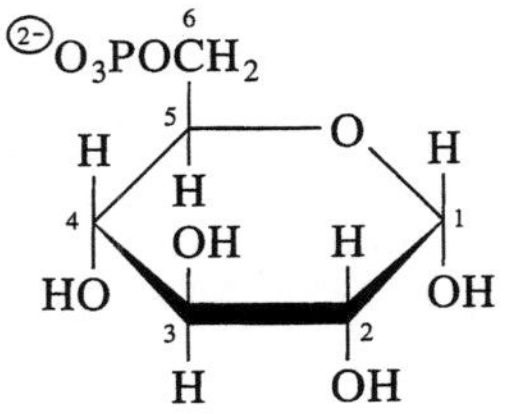

◄ Figure 8.14
Structures of the deoxy sugars
2-deoxy-D-ribose and L-fucose.

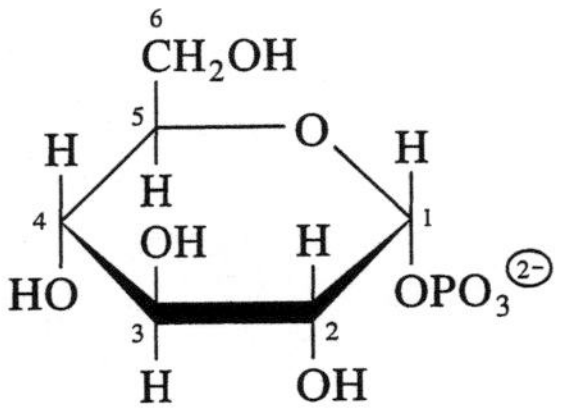

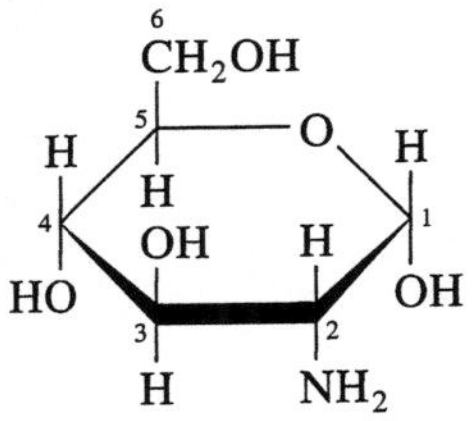

β-2-Deoxy-D-ribose

α-L-Fucose
(6-Deoxy-L-galactose)

α-D-Glucosamine

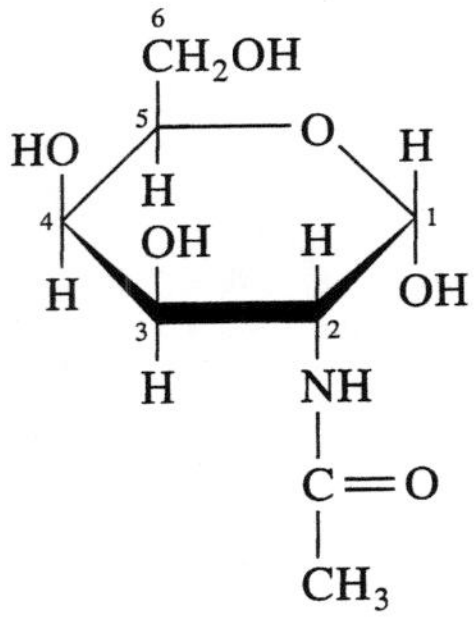

N-Acetyl-α-D-galactosamine

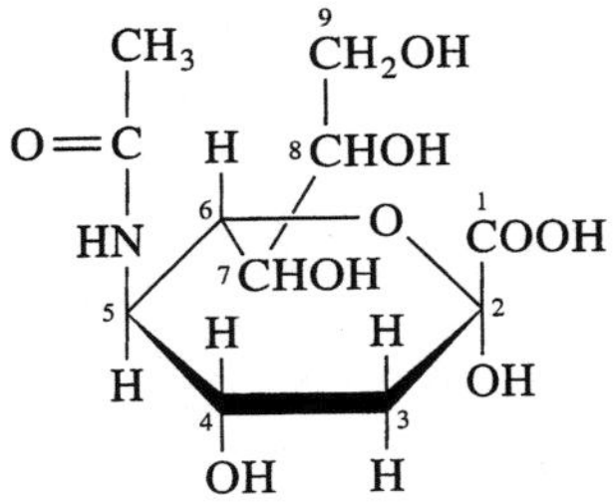

N-Acetyl-α-D-neuraminic acid

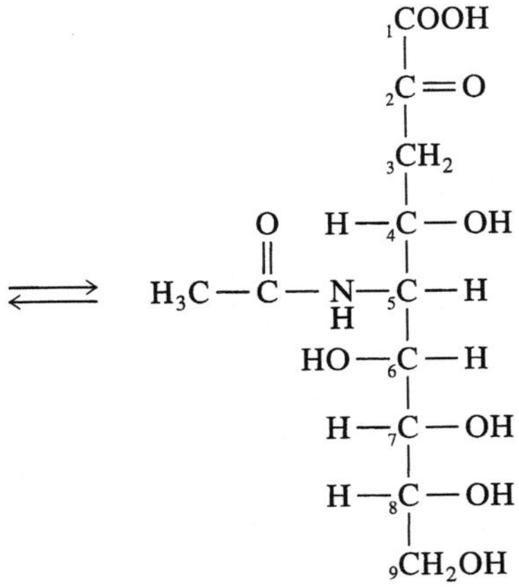

N-Acetyl-D-neuraminic acid
(open-chain form)

Figure 8.15 ▲
Structures of several amino sugars. The amino and acetylamino groups are shown in red.

Chemistry for Biologists

D. Sugar Alcohols

In a sugar alcohol, the carbonyl oxygen of the parent monosaccharide has been reduced, producing a polyhydroxy alcohol. Figure 8.16 shows three examples of sugar alcohols. Both glycerol and *myo*-inositol are important components of lipids (Section 10.4). Ribitol is a component of flavin mononucleotide (FMN) and flavin adenine dinucleotide (FAD) (Section 7.4). In general, sugar alcohols are named by replacing the suffix *-ose* of the parent monosaccharides with *-itol*.

E. Sugar Acids

Sugar acids are carboxylic acids derived from aldoses, either by oxidation of C-1 (the aldehydic carbon) to yield an aldonic acid or by oxidation of the highest-numbered carbon (the carbon bearing the primary alcohol) to yield an alduronic acid. The structures of the aldonic and alduronic derivatives of glucose—gluconate and glucuronate—are shown in Figure 8.17. Aldonic acids exist in the open-chain form in alkaline solution and form lactones (intramolecular esters) on acidification. Alduronic

Figure 8.16 ▶
Structures of several sugar alcohols. Glycerol (a reduced form of glyceraldehyde) and *myo*-inositol (metabolically derived from glucose) are important constituents of many lipids. Ribitol (a reduced form of ribose) is a constituent of the vitamin riboflavin and its coenzymes.

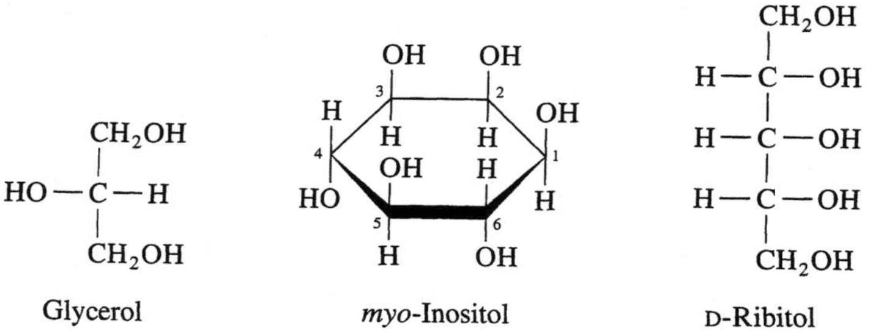

Figure 8.17 ▶
Structures of sugar acids derived from D-glucose. **(a)** Gluconate and its δ-lactone. **(b)** The open-chain and pyranose forms of glucuronate.

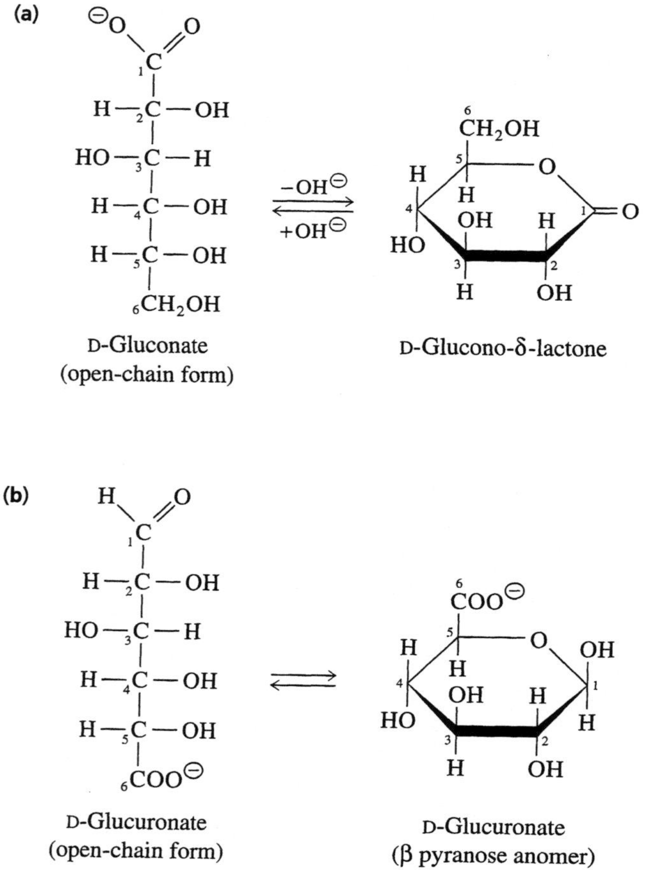

Glycerol   *myo*-Inositol   D-Ribitol

(a)

D-Gluconate
(open-chain form)

D-Glucono-δ-lactone

(b)

D-Glucuronate
(open-chain form)

D-Glucuronate
(β pyranose anomer)

acids can exist as pyranoses and therefore possess an anomeric carbon. Note that *N*-acetylneuraminic acid (Figure 8.15) is an aldonic acid as well as an amino sugar. Sugar acids are important components of many polysaccharides.

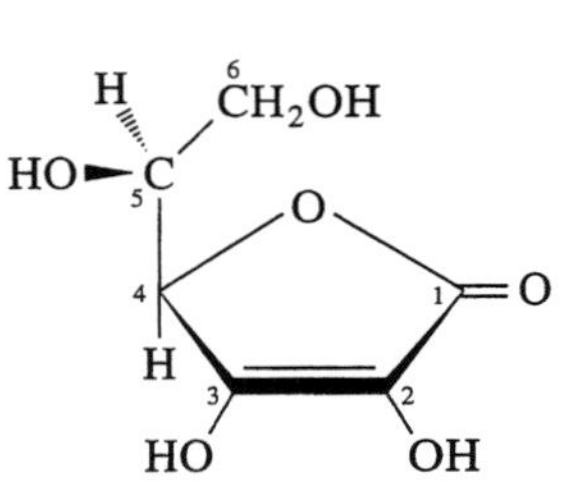

F. Ascorbic Acid

L-Ascorbic acid (Figure 8.18 and Section 7.2b), or vitamin C, is an enediol of a lactone derived from D-glucuronate. Primates cannot convert glucuronate to ascorbic acid and must therefore obtain ascorbic acid from the diet. Ascorbic acid is an essential cofactor for the enzymes that catalyze the hydroxylation of proline and lysine residues during collagen synthesis (Section 4.11).

Figure 8.18 ▲
L-Ascorbic acid (vitamin C).

See Box 7.1 for more about ascorbic acid.

8.5 Disaccharides and Other Glycosides

The **glycosidic bond** is the primary structural linkage in all polymers of monosaccharides. A glycosidic bond is an acetal linkage in which the anomeric carbon of a sugar is condensed with an alcohol, an amine, or a thiol. As a simple example, glucopyranose can react with methanol in an acidic solution to form an acetal (Figure 8.19). Compounds containing glycosidic bonds are called glycosides; if glucose supplies the anomeric carbon, they are specifically termed **glucosides**. The glycosides include disaccharides, polysaccharides, and some carbohydrate derivatives.

A. Structures of Disaccharides

In forming a disaccharide, the anomeric carbon of one sugar molecule can interact with one of several hydroxyl groups in the other sugar molecule. Thus, for disaccharides and other carbohydrate polymers, we must note both the types of monosaccharide residues that are present and the atoms that form the glycosidic bonds. In the systematic description of a disaccharide, the linking atoms, the configuration of the glycosidic bond, and the name of each monosaccharide residue (including its

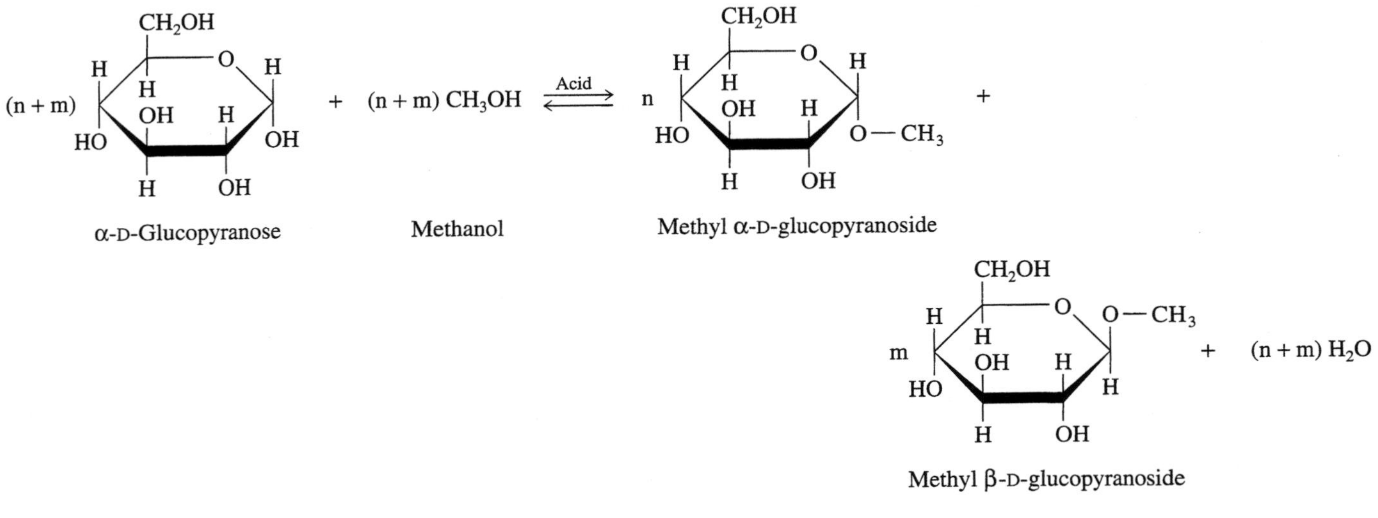

Figure 8.19 ▲
Reaction of glucopyranose with methanol produces a glycoside. In this acid-catalyzed condensation reaction, the anomeric —OH group of the hemiacetal is replaced by an —OCH₃ group, forming methyl glucoside, an acetal. The product is a mixture of the α and β anomers of methyl glucopyranoside.

designation as a pyranose or furanose) must be specified. Figure 8.20 presents the structures and nomenclature for four common disaccharides.

Maltose (Figure 8.20a) is a disaccharide released during the hydrolysis of starch, which is a polymer of glucose residues. It is present in malt, a mixture obtained from corn or grain that is used in malted milk and in brewing. Maltose is composed of two D-glucose residues joined by an α-glycosidic bond. The glycosidic bond links C-1 of one residue (on the left in Figure 8.20a) to the oxygen atom attached to C-4 of the second residue (on the right). Maltose is therefore α-D-glucopyranosyl-(1→4)-D-glucose. Note that the glucose residue on the left, whose anomeric carbon is involved in the glycosidic bond, is fixed in the α configuration, whereas the glucose residue on the right (the reducing end, as explained in Section 8.5B) freely equilibrates among the α, β, and open-chain structures. The latter is present in very small amounts. The structure shown in Figure 8.20a is the β-pyranose anomer of maltose (the anomer whose reducing end is in the β configuration, the predominant anomeric form).

Cellobiose [β-D-glucopyranosyl-(1→4)-D-glucose] is another glucose dimer (Figure 8.20b). Cellobiose is the repeating disaccharide in the structure of cellulose, a plant polysaccharide, and is released during cellulose degradation. The only difference between cellobiose and maltose is that the glycosidic linkage in cellobiose is β (it is α in maltose). The glucose residue on the right in Figure 8.20b, like the residue on the right in Figure 8.20a, equilibrates among the α, β, and open-chain structures.

Lactose [β-D-galactopyranosyl-(1→4)-D-glucose], a major carbohydrate in milk, is a disaccharide synthesized only in lactating mammary glands (Figure 8.20c). Note

(a)

β anomer of maltose
(α-D-Glucopyranosyl-(1→4)-β-D-glucopyranose)

(b)

β anomer of cellobiose
(β-D-Glucopyranosyl-(1→4)-β-D-glucopyranose)

(c)

α anomer of lactose
(β-D-Galactopyranosyl-(1→4)-α-D-glucopyranose)

(d)

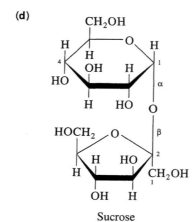

Sucrose
(α-D-Glucopyranosyl-(1→2)-β-D-fructofuranoside)

Figure 8.20 ▲
Structures of **(a)** maltose, **(b)** cellobiose, **(c)** lactose, and **(d)** sucrose. The oxygen atom of each glycosidic bond is shown in red.

that lactose is an epimer of cellobiose. The naturally occurring α anomer of lactose is sweeter and more soluble than the β anomer. The β anomer can be found in stale ice cream, where it has crystallized during storage and given a gritty texture to the ice cream.

Sucrose [α-D-glucopyranosyl-(1→2)-β-D-fructofuranoside], or table sugar, the most abundant disaccharide found in nature, is synthesized only in plants (Figure 8.20d). Sucrose is distinguished from the other three disaccharides in Figure 8.20 in that its glycosidic bond links the anomeric carbon atoms of two monosaccharide residues. Therefore, the configurations of both the glucopyranose and fructofuranose residues in sucrose are fixed, and neither residue is free to equilibrate between α and β anomers.

B. Reducing and Nonreducing Sugars

Because monosaccharides and most disaccharides are hemiacetals and therefore contain a reactive carbonyl group, they are readily oxidized to diverse products, a property often used in their analysis. Such carbohydrates, including glucose, maltose, cellobiose, and lactose, are sometimes called reducing sugars. Historically, reducing sugars were detected by their ability to reduce metal ions such as $Cu^{2\oplus}$ or $Ag^{\oplus}$ to insoluble products. Carbohydrates that are acetals, such as sucrose, which is not readily oxidized because both anomeric carbon atoms are fixed in a glycosidic linkage, are classified as nonreducing sugars.

The reducing ability of a sugar polymer is of more than analytical interest. The polymeric chains of oligosaccharides and polysaccharides show directionality, based on their reducing and nonreducing ends. In a linear polymer, there is usually one reducing-end residue (the residue containing the free anomeric carbon) and one nonreducing-end residue. All the internal glycosidic bonds of a polysaccharide involve acetals, which are not in equilibrium with open-chain forms and thus cannot reduce metal ions. A branched polysaccharide has a number of nonreducing ends but only one reducing end.

C. Nucleosides and Other Glycosides

The anomeric carbons of sugars form glycosidic linkages not only with other sugars but also with a variety of alcohols, amines, and thiols. These latter compounds are referred to as **aglycones** when they are linked to sugars. The most commonly encountered glycosides other than oligosaccharides and polysaccharides are the nucleosides and their phosphorylated derivatives, the nucleotides, in which a purine or pyrimidine aglycone is attached by its secondary amino group to a β-D-ribofuranose or β-D-deoxyribofuranose moiety. Nucleosides are called N-glycosides because a nitrogen atom of the aglycone participates in the glycosidic linkage. In the example β-D-ribofuranosylguanine (commonly called guanosine) shown in Figure 8.21a, the purine guanine is the aglycone that has substituted β-D-ribose. We have already

> There is a more complete discussion of nucleosides and nucleotides in Chapter 19.

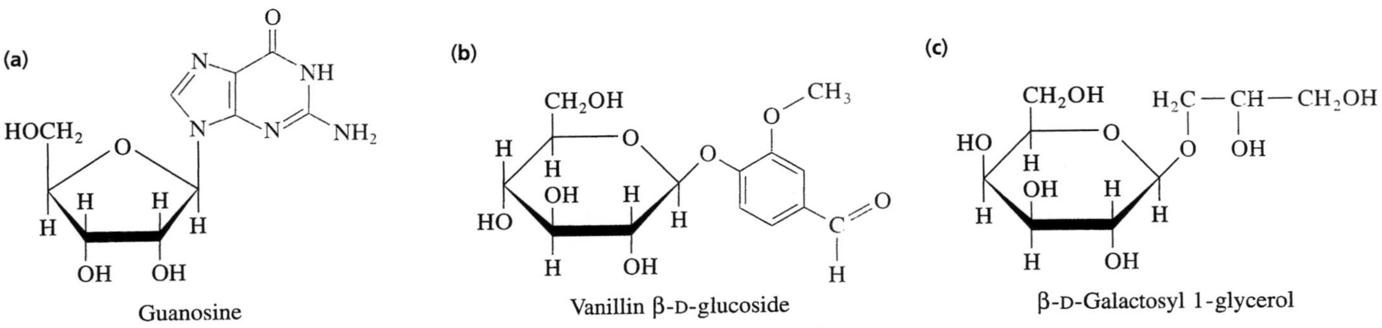

Figure 8.21 ▲
Structures of three glycosides. The aglycones are shown in blue. **(a)** Guanosine.
(b) Vanillin glucoside, the flavored compound in vanilla extract. **(c)** β-D-Galactosyl
1-glycerol, derivatives of which are common in eukaryotic cell membranes.

BOX 8.1   Nodulation Factors Are Lipo-oligosaccharides

Legumes such as alfalfa, peas, and soybeans develop organs called nodules on their roots. Certain soil bacteria (rhizobia) infect the nodules and, in a symbiosis with the plants, carry out nitrogen fixation (reduction of atmospheric nitrogen to ammonia). The symbiosis is highly species-specific: only certain combinations of legumes and bacteria can cooperate, and therefore these organisms must recognize each other. Rhizobia produce extracellular signal molecules—oligosaccharides called nodulation factors. Extremely low concentrations of these compounds can induce their plant hosts to develop the nodules that the rhizobia can infect. A host plant responds only to a nodulation factor of a characteristic composition.

All the nodulation factors studied to date are oligosaccharides that have a linear chain of β-$(1\rightarrow4)$ N-acetylglu-

cosamine (GlcNAc), the same repeating structure as in chitin (Section 8.6b). Although the number of residues can vary between three and six, most nodulation factors are sugar pentamers (see figure below). Species specificity is provided by variation in polymer length and potential substitution on five sites at the nonreducing end (R_1 to R_5) and two sites at the reducing end (R_6 and R_7). R_1, an acyl group substituting the nitrogen atom at C-2 of the nonreducing end, is a fatty acid, usually 18 carbons long. Thus, the nodulation factors are lipo-oligosaccharides. R_6, bound to the alcohol at C-6 of the reducing end, can have a wide variety of structures, including sulfate or methyl fucose. Research on these oligosaccharides, growth regulators for legumes, has stimulated the search for biological activities of other oligosaccharides.

◄ General structure of nodulation factors, lipo-oligosaccharides with an N-acetylglucosamine (GlcNAc) backbone. The number of internal residues of N-acetylglucosamine is shown by n, which is usually 3 but sometimes be 1, 2, or 4. R_1 is a fatty acyl substituent, usually 18 carbons long.

See Section 17.1 for details about nitrogen fixation.

discussed ATP and other nucleotides that are metabolite coenzymes (Section 7.2a); NAD and FAD also are nucleotides.

Two other examples of naturally occurring glycosides are shown in Figure 8.21. Vanillin glucoside (Figure 8.21b) is the flavored compound in natural vanilla extract. β-Galactosides constitute an abundant class of glycosides. In these compounds, a variety of nonsugar molecules are joined in β linkage to galactose. For example, galactocerebrosides—derivatives of β-D-galactosyl 1-glycerol (Figure 8.21c)—are glycolipids common in eukaryotic cell membranes and can be hydrolyzed readily by the action of enzymes called β-galactosidases.

8.6 Polysaccharides

Polysaccharides are frequently divided into two broad classes: **homoglycans** or homopolysaccharides, which are polymers containing residues of only one type of monosaccharide, and **heteroglycans** or heteropolysaccharides, which are polymers containing residues of more than one type of monosaccharide. Unlike proteins, whose primary structures are encoded by the genome and thus have specified lengths, polysaccharides are created without a template by the addition of particular monosaccharide and oligosaccharide residues. As a result, the lengths and compositions of polysaccharide molecules may vary within a population of these molecules. Such a population is said to be polydisperse. Some common polysaccharides and their structures are listed in Table 8.2.

TABLE 8.2   Structures of some common polysaccharides

Polysaccharide[a]	Component(s)[b]	Linkage(s)
Storage homoglycans		
Starch		
Amylose	Glc	α-(1→4)
Amylopectin	Glc	α-(1→4), α-(1→6) (branches)
Glycogen	Glc	α-(1→4), α-(1→6) (branches)
Structural homoglycans		
Cellulose	Glc	β(1→4)
Chitin	GlcNAc	β(1→4)
Heteroglycans		
Glycosaminoglycans	Disaccharides (amino sugars, sugar acids)	Various
Hyaluronic acid	GlcUA and GlcNAc	β(1→3), β(1→4)

[a]Polysaccharides are unbranched unless otherwise indicated.

[b]Glc, Glucose; GlcNAc, *N*-acetylglucosamine; GlcUA, D-glucuronate.

Most polysaccharides can also be classified according to their biological roles. For example, starch and glycogen are storage polysaccharides, and cellulose and chitin are structural polysaccharides. We will see additional examples of the variety and versatility of carbohydrates when we discuss the heteroglycans in glycoconjugates (Section 8.7).

A. Starch and Glycogen

D-Glucose, the main source of metabolic energy for many organisms, is stored intracellularly in polymeric form. The most common storage homoglycan of glucose in plants and fungi is starch, and in animals, glycogen. Both types of polysaccharides occur in bacteria.

In plant cells, starch is present as a mixture of amylose and amylopectin and is stored in granules whose diameters range from 3 to 100 μm. Amylose is an unbranched polymer of about 100 to 1000 D-glucose residues connected by α-(1→4) glycosidic linkages, specifically termed α-(1→4) glucosidic bonds because the anomeric carbons belong to glucose residues (Figure 8.22a). The same type of linkage connects glucose monomers in the disaccharide maltose (Figure 8.20a). Although it is not truly soluble in water, amylose forms hydrated micelles in water and can assume a helical structure under some conditions (Figure 8.22b).

Amylopectin is a branched version of amylose (Figure 8.23). Branches, or polymeric side chains, are attached via α-(1→6) glucosidic bonds to linear chains of residues linked by α-(1→4) glucosidic bonds. Branching occurs, on average, once every 25 residues, and the side chains contain about 15 to 25 glucose residues. Some side chains themselves are branched. Amylopectin molecules isolated from living cells may contain 300 to 6000 glucose residues.

An adult human consumes about 300 g of carbohydrate daily, much of which is in the form of starch. Raw starch granules resist enzymatic hydrolysis, but cooking causes them to absorb water and swell; the swollen starch is a substrate of two glycosidases. Dietary starch is degraded in the gastrointestinal tract by the actions of α-amylase and a debranching enzyme. α-Amylase, which is present in both animals and plants, is an endoglycosidase (it acts on internal glycosidic bonds) that catalyzes random hydrolysis of the α-(1→4) glucosidic bonds of amylose and amylopectin.

(a)

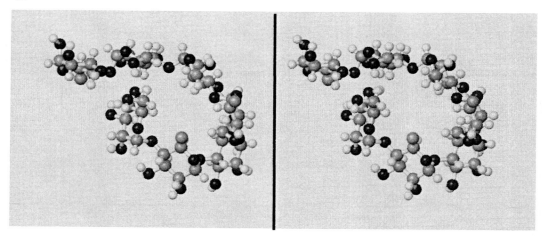

(b)

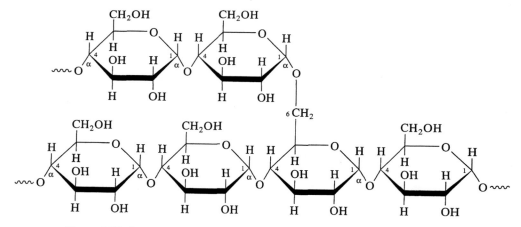

Figure 8.22 ▲
(a) Structure of amylose. Amylose, one form of starch, is a linear polymer of glucose residues linked by α-(1→4)-D-glucosidic bonds. **(b)** Stereo view of amylose. Amylose can assume a left-handed helical conformation, which is hydrated on the inside as well as on the outer surface.

Figure 8.23 ▲
Structure of amylopectin. Amylopectin, a second form of starch, is a branched polymer. The linear glucose residues of the main chain and the side chains of amylopectin are linked by α-(1→4)-D-glucosidic bonds, and the side chains are linked to the main chain by α-(1→6)-D-glucosidic bonds.

Another hydrolase, β-amylase, is found in the seeds and tubers of some higher plants. β-Amylase is an exoglycosidase (it acts on terminal glycosidic bonds) that catalyzes sequential hydrolytic release of maltose from the free, nonreducing ends of amylopectin.

Despite their α and β designations, both types of amylases act only on α-(1→4)-D-glycosidic bonds. Figure 8.24 depicts the action of α-amylase and β-amylase on amylopectin. The α-(1→6) linkages at branch points are not substrates for either α- or β-amylase. After amylase-catalyzed hydrolysis of amylopectin, highly branched cores resistant to further hydrolysis, called **limit dextrins**, remain. Limit dextrins can be further degraded only after debranching enzymes have catalyzed hydrolysis of the α-(1→6) linkages at branch points.

Glycogen, a storage polysaccharide found in animals and bacteria, is also a branched polymer of glucose residues. Glycogen contains the same types of linkages found in amylopectin, but the branches in glycogen are smaller and more frequent, occurring every 8 to 12 residues. In general, glycogen molecules are larger than starch molecules, containing up to about 50 000 glucose residues. In mammals, depending on the nutritional state, glycogen can account for up to 10% of the mass of the liver and 2% of the mass of muscle.

The branched structures of amylopectin and glycogen possess only one reducing end but many nonreducing ends. It is at these nonreducing ends that enzymatic lengthening and degradation occur.

We consider enzymes that catalyze the intracellular synthesis and breakdown of glycogen in Chapter 13.

B. Cellulose and Chitin

Plant cell walls contain a high percentage of the structural homoglycan cellulose, which accounts for more than 50% of the organic matter in the biosphere. Unlike storage polysaccharides, cellulose and other structural polysaccharides are extracellular molecules extruded by the cells in which they are synthesized. Like amylose, cellulose is a linear polymer of glucose residues, but in cellulose the glucose residues are joined by β-(1→4) linkages rather than α-(1→4) linkages. The two glucose residues of the disaccharide cellobiose also are connected by a β-(1→4) linkage (Figure 8.20b). Cellulose molecules vary greatly in size, ranging from about 300 to more than 15 000 glucose residues.

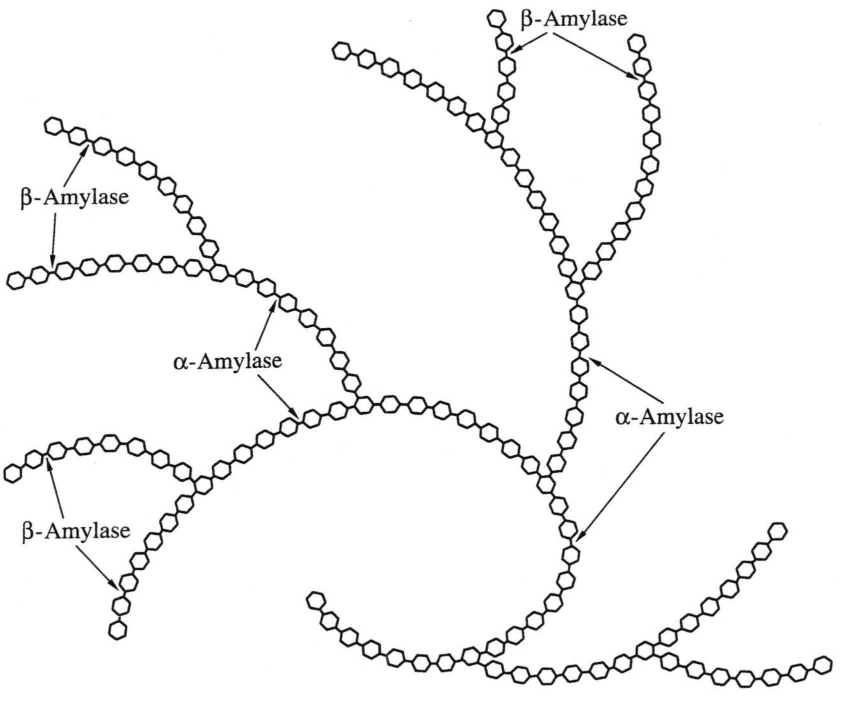

◄ **Figure 8.24**
Action of α-amylase and β-amylase on amylopectin. α-Amylase catalyzes random hydrolysis of internal α-(1→4) glucosidic bonds; β-amylase acts on the nonreducing ends. Each hexagon represents a glucose residue; the single reducing end of the branched polymer is red. (An actual amylopectin molecule contains many more glucose residues than shown here.)

The β linkages of cellulose result in a rigid extended conformation in which each glucose residue is rotated 180° relative to its neighbors (Figure 8.25). Extensive hydrogen bonding within and between cellulose chains leads to the formation of bundles, or fibrils (Figure 8.26). Cellulose fibrils are insoluble in water and are quite strong and rigid. Cotton fibers are almost entirely cellulose, and wood is about half cellulose. Because of its strength, cellulose is used for a variety of purposes and is a component of a number of synthetic materials, including cellophane and the fabric rayon.

Enzymes that catalyze the hydrolysis of α-D-glucosidic bonds (α-glucosidases, such as α- and β-amylase) do not catalyze the hydrolysis of β-D-glucosidic bonds. Similarly, β-glucosidases (such as cellulase) do not catalyze the hydrolysis of α-D-glucosidic bonds. Humans and other mammals that can metabolize starch, glycogen, lactose, and sucrose as energy sources cannot metabolize cellulose because they lack enzymes capable of catalyzing the hydrolysis of β-glucosidic linkages. Ruminants such as cows and sheep have microorganisms in their rumen (a compartment in their multichambered stomachs) that produce β-glucosidases. Thus, ruminants can obtain glucose from grass and other plants that are rich in cellulose. Because they have cellulase-producing bacteria in their digestive tracts, termites also can obtain glucose from dietary cellulose.

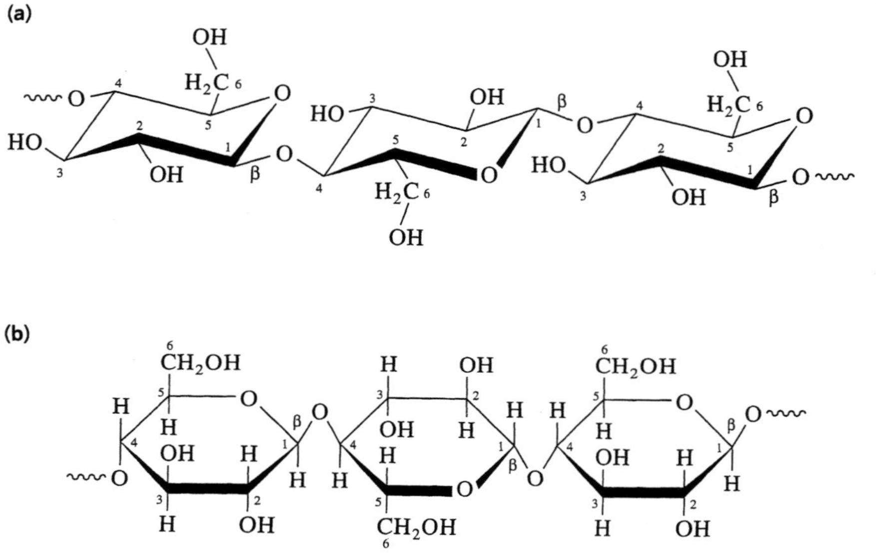

Figure 8.25 ▶
Structure of cellulose. Note the alternating orientation of successive glucose residues in the cellulose chain. **(a)** Chair conformation. **(b)** Modified Haworth projection.

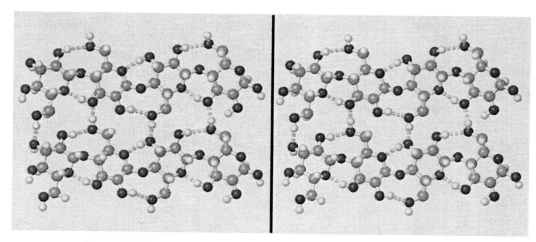

Figure 8.26 ▲
Stereo view of cellulose fibrils. Intra- and interchain hydrogen bonding gives cellulose its strength and rigidity.

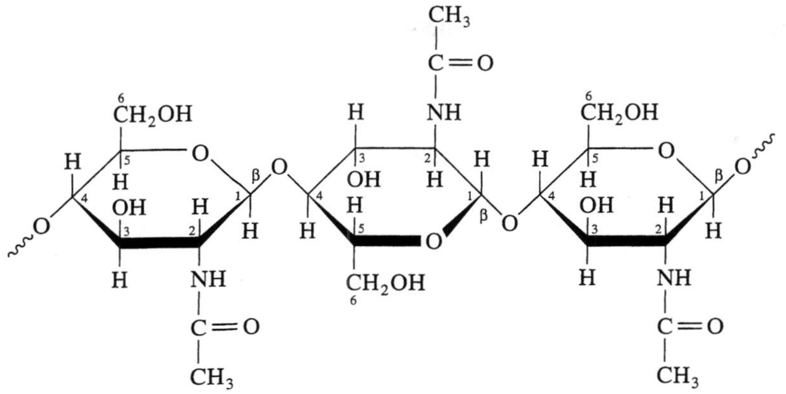

◀ Figure 8.27
Structure of chitin. The linear homoglycan chitin consists of repeating units of β-(1→4)-linked GlcNAc residues. Each residue is rotated 180° relative to its neighbors.

Chitin, probably the second most abundant organic compound on earth, is a structural homoglycan found in the exoskeletons of insects and crustaceans and also in the cell walls of most fungi and many algae. A linear polymer similar to cellulose, chitin consists of β-(1→4)-linked GlcNAc residues rather than glucose residues (Figure 8.27). Each GlcNAc residue is rotated 180° relative to its neighbors. The GlcNAc residues in adjacent strands of chitin form hydrogen bonds with each other, resulting in linear fibrils of great strength. Chitin is often closely associated with nonpolysaccharide compounds, such as proteins and inorganic material.

8.7 Glycoconjugates

Having discussed the structure, nomenclature, and function of monosaccharides, disaccharides, and homoglycans, we now turn our attention to heteroglycans. Heteroglycans appear in three types of glycoconjugates—proteoglycans, peptidoglycans, and glycoproteins. In this section, we see how the chemical and physical properties of the heteroglycans in glycoconjugates are suited to various biological functions.

A. Proteoglycans

Proteoglycans are complexes of polysaccharides called glycosaminoglycans and specific proteins. These glycoconjugates occur predominately in the extracellular matrix (connective tissue) of multicellular animals.

Glycosaminoglycans are unbranched heteroglycans of repeating disaccharide units. As the name *glycosaminoglycan* indicates, one component of the disaccharide is an amino sugar, either D-galactosamine (GalN) or D-glucosamine (GlcN). The amino group of the amino-sugar component can be acetylated, forming *N*-acetylgalactosamine (GalNAc) or GlcNAc, respectively. The other component of the repeating disaccharide is usually an alduronic acid. Specific hydroxyl and amino groups of many glycosaminoglycans are sulfated. These sulfate groups and the carboxylate groups of alduronic acids make glycosaminoglycans polyanionic.

Several types of glycosaminoglycans have been isolated and characterized. Each type has its own sugar composition, linkages, tissue distribution, and function, and each is attached to a characteristic protein. Hyaluronic acid is an example of a glycosaminoglycan; it is composed of the repeating disaccharide unit shown in Figure 8.28. Found in the synovial fluid of joints, hyaluronic acid forms a viscous solution that is an excellent lubricant. Hyaluronic acid is also a major component of cartilage.

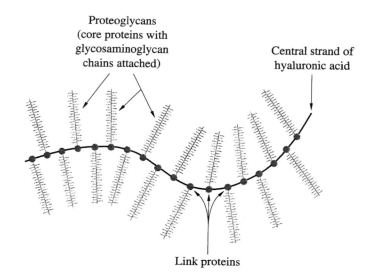

◀ **Figure 8.28**
Structure of the repeating disaccharide of hyaluronic acid. The repeating disaccharide of this glycosaminoglycan contains D-glucuronate (GlcUA) and GlcNAc. Each GlcUA residue is linked to a GlcNAc residue through a β-(1→3) linkage; each GlcNAc residue is in turn linked to the next GlcUA residue through a β-(1→4) linkage.

From 1 to more than 100 glycosaminoglycan chains can be attached to the protein of a proteoglycan. These heteroglycan chains are usually covalently bound by a glycosidic linkage to the hydroxyl oxygens of serine residues. (Not all glycosaminoglycans are found covalently linked to proteins, however.) Glycosaminoglycans can account for up to 95% of the mass of a proteoglycan.

Because glycosaminoglycans contain polar and ionic groups, proteoglycans are highly hydrated and occupy a large volume. These features confer elasticity and resistance to compression—important properties of connective tissue. For example, the flexibility of cartilage allows it to absorb shocks. Some of the water can be pressed out when cartilage is compressed, but relief from pressure allows cartilage to rehydrate. In addition to maintaining the shapes of tissues, proteoglycans can also act as extracellular sieves and help direct cell growth and migration.

Examination of the structure of cartilage shows how proteoglycans are organized in this tissue. Cartilage is a mesh of collagen fibers (Section 4.11) interspersed with large proteoglycan aggregates (M_r ~2 × 10^8). Each aggregate assumes a characteristic shape that resembles a bottle brush (Figure 8.29). These aggregates contain hyaluronic acid and several other glycosaminoglycans, as well as two types of proteins—core proteins and link proteins. A central strand of hyaluronic acid runs through the aggregate, and many proteoglycans—core proteins with glycosaminoglycan chains attached—branch from its sides. The core proteins interact noncovalently with the hyaluronic acid strand, mostly by electrostatic interactions. Using electrostatic forces, link proteins stabilize the core protein–hyaluronic acid interactions.

The major proteoglycan of cartilage is called aggrecan. The protein core of aggrecan (M_r ~220 000) carries approximately 30 molecules of keratan sulfate (a glycosaminoglycan composed chiefly of alternating N-acetylglucosamine 6-sulfate and

Figure 8.29 ▶
Proteoglycan aggregate of cartilage. Core proteins carrying glycosaminoglycan chains are associated with a central strand of a single hyaluronic acid molecule. These proteins have many covalently attached glycosaminoglycan chains (keratan sulfate and chondroitin sulfate molecules). The interactions of the core proteins with hyaluronic acid are stabilized by link proteins, which interact noncovalently with both types of molecules. The aggregate has the appearance of a bottle brush.

BOX 8.2   Decorin and Collagen

A family of structurally related proteoglycan molecules, small leucine-rich proteoglycans (SLRPs), has a diverse set of biological functions, which affect the structures of skin, teeth, bones, tendons, and the cornea of the eye. SLRPs appear to be modulators of a number of complex assembly processes.

The prototype SLRP is decorin, which is found in connective tissue. The structure of decorin includes an *N*-terminal protein domain to which one glycosaminoglycan chain is attached (at Ser-7) and a central domain that possesses 10 leucine-rich, 24-residue repeats. The core protein (M_r ~40 000) of decorin is shaped like an arch or a horseshoe. Its single glycosaminoglycan chain extends outward from the protein.

One role of decorin is regulation of the aggregation of collagen molecules into collagen fibers (Section 4.11). Although the amino acid sequence of collagen directs the formation of its fibers, other proteins—including decorin—

bind reversibly to collagen and modulate its self-assembly. In vivo, maturation of collagen fibers is accompanied by release of decorin during the development of skin, tendon, and cornea. This suggests that decorin is involved in controlling the shapes of these tissues. The horseshoe-shaped decorin, by binding electrostatically to complementary regions of the collagen triple helix (as shown in the figure below), helps control the self-assembly of collagen into fibers. The proteoglycan portion of decorin acts by properly spacing the collagen as it forms its regular networks. Laboratory animals treated so that they cannot make decorin have fragile skin; the collagen network of their skin is quite irregular. There are indications that decorin plays other roles in cells. Although other SLRPs appear to have a number of major functions in cellular development and proliferation, the mechanisms of their actions are not yet known.

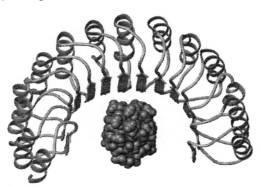

◀ Figure showing the interaction of the core protein of decorin (ribbon structure, blue) with a triple helix of collagen (space-filling structure, green). Note the β-sheets on the inner, concave surface of decorin, and the α helices on its outer surface. If the decorin protein were shown as a space-filling model, contacts with collagen could be seen.

galactose residues) and approximately 100 molecules of chondroitin sulfate (a glycosaminoglycan composed of alternating *N*-acetylgalactosamine sulfate and glucuronate residues). Aggrecan is a member of a small family of hyalectans, proteoglycans that bind to hyaluronic acid. Other hyalectans provide elasticity to blood vessel walls and modulate cell-cell interactions in the brain.

B. Peptidoglycans

The cell walls of many bacteria are made of **peptidoglycans**, which are heteroglycan chains linked to peptides. The heteroglycan component is composed of alternating residues of GlcNAc and *N*-acetylmuramic acid (MurNAc) joined by β-(1→4) linkages (Figure 8.30). MurNAc, a nine-carbon sugar specific to bacteria, consists of the three-carbon acid D-lactate joined by an ether linkage to C-3 of GlcNAc. The glycan moiety of peptidoglycans resembles chitin, except that alternating molecules of GlcNAc are modified by addition of the lactyl moiety. The antibacterial action of lysozyme (Section 6.10) results from its ability to catalyze hydrolysis of the polysaccharide chains of peptidoglycans.

The peptide component of peptidoglycans varies among bacteria. In *Staphylococcus aureus*, the peptide component is a tetrapeptide with alternating L and D amino acids: L-Ala–D-Isoglu–L-Lys–D-Ala. (Isoglu represents isoglutamate, a form of glutamate in which the γ-carboxyl group—not the α-carboxyl group—is linked to the next residue.) An amide bond links the amino group of the L-alanine

Chemistry for Biologists

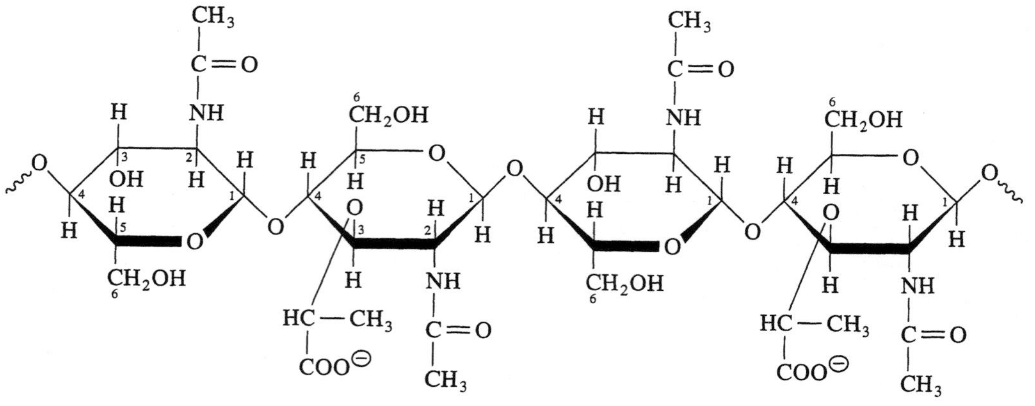

Figure 8.30 ▲
Structure of the glycan moiety of peptidoglycan. The glycan is a polymer of alternating GlcNAc and *N*-acetylmuramic acid (MurNAc) residues.

residue to the lactyl carboxylate group of a MurNAc residue of the glycan polymer (Figure 8.31). The tetrapeptide is cross-linked to another tetrapeptide on a neighboring peptidoglycan molecule by a chain of five glycine residues (pentaglycine). Pentaglycine joins the L-lysine residue of one tetrapeptide to the carboxyl group of the D-alanine residue of the other tetrapeptide. Extensive cross-linking essentially converts the peptidoglycan to one huge, rigid macromolecule that defines the shape of the bacterium and covers its delicate plasma membrane and protects it from fluctuations in osmotic pressure.

During peptidoglycan biosynthesis, a five-residue peptide—L-Ala–D-Isoglu–L-Lys–D-Ala–D-Ala—is attached to a MurNAc residue. In subsequent steps, five glycine residues are added sequentially to the ε-amino group of the lysine residue, forming the pentaglycine bridge. In the final step of synthesis, a transpeptidase catalyzes formation of a peptide linkage between the penultimate alanine residue and a terminal glycine residue of a pentaglycine bridge of a neighboring peptidoglycan strand. This reaction is driven by release of the terminal D-alanine residue. The structure of the antibiotic penicillin (Figure 8.32) resembles the terminal D-Ala–D-Ala residues of the immature peptidoglycan. Penicillin binds, probably irreversibly, to the transpeptidase active site, inhibiting the activity of the enzyme and thereby blocking further peptidoglycan synthesis. Penicillin is selectively toxic to bacteria because the reaction it affects occurs only in certain bacteria, not in eukaryotic cells.

C. Glycoproteins

Glycoproteins, like proteoglycans, are proteins that contain covalently bound oligosaccharides (i.e., proteins that are glycosylated). (In fact, proteoglycans are a type of glycoprotein.) The carbohydrate chains of a glycoprotein vary in length from 1 to more than 30 residues and can account for as much as 80% of the total mass of the molecule. Glycoproteins are an extraordinarily diverse group of proteins that includes enzymes, hormones, structural proteins, and transport proteins. They are found almost exclusively in eukaryotic cells.

Unlike glycosaminoglycans, the oligosaccharide chains of glycoproteins exhibit great variability in composition. Even among molecules of the same protein, the composition of oligosaccharide chains can vary, a phenomenon called microheterogeneity. Proteins with identical amino acid sequences but different oligosaccharide chain compositions are called **glycoforms**.

Several factors contribute to the structural diversity of the oligosaccharide chains of glycoproteins.

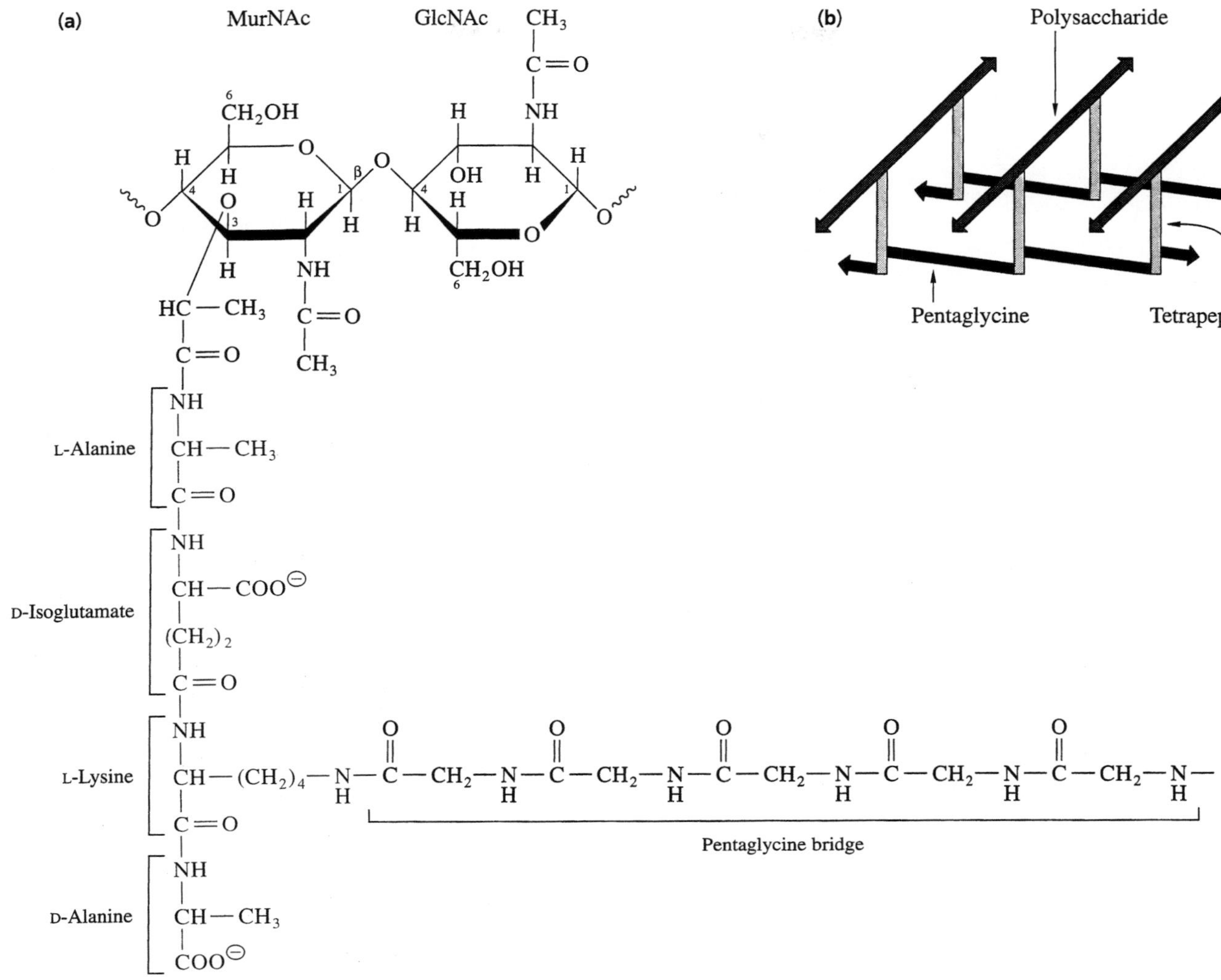

Figure 8.31 ▲
Structure of the peptidoglycan of *Staphylococcus aureus*. **(a)** Repeating disaccharide unit, tetrapeptide, and pentaglycine components. The tetrapeptide (blue) is linked to a MurNAc residue of the glycan moiety (black). The ε-amino group of the L-lysine residue of one tetrapeptide is cross-linked to the α-carboxyl group of the D-alanine residue of another tetrapeptide on a neighboring peptidoglycan molecule via a pentaglycine bridge (red). **(b)** Cross-linking of the peptidoglycan macromolecule.

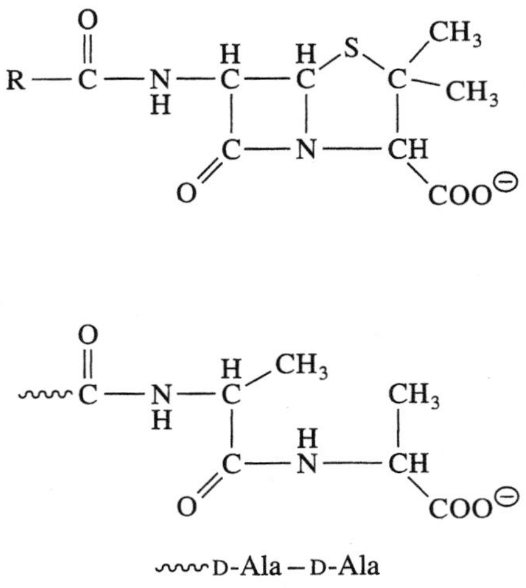

1. An oligosaccharide chain can contain several different sugars. Eight sugars predominate in eukaryotic glycoproteins: the hexoses L-fucose, D-galactose, D-glucose, and D-mannose; the hexosamines *N*-acetyl-D-galactosamine and *N*-acetyl-D-glucosamine; the nine-carbon sialic acids (usually *N*-acetylneuraminic acid); and the pentose D-xylose. Many different combinations of these sugars are possible.

2. The sugars can be joined by either α- or β-glycosidic linkages.

3. The linkages can join various carbon atoms in the sugars. In hexoses and hexosamines, the glycosidic linkages always involve C-1 of one sugar but can involve C-2, C-3, C-4, or C-6 of another hexose or C-3, C-4, or C-6 of an amino sugar (C-2 is usually *N*-acetylated in this class of sugar). C-2 of sialic acid, not C-1, is linked to other sugars.

4. Oligosaccharide chains of glycoproteins can contain up to four branches.

Figure 8.32 ▲
Structures of penicillin and –D-Ala–D-Ala. The portion of penicillin that resembles the dipeptide is shown in red. R can be a variety of substituents.

However, the astronomical number of possible oligosaccharide structures afforded by these four factors is not realized in cells because cells do not possess specific glycosyltransferases to catalyze the formation of all possible glycosidic linkages. In addition, individual glycoproteins—through their unique conformations—modulate their own interactions with the glycosylating enzymes, so that most glycoproteins possess a heterogeneous but reproducible oligosaccharide structure.

The oligosaccharide chains of most glycoproteins are either O- or N-linked. In **O-linked oligosaccharides**, a GalNAc residue is typically linked to the side chain of a serine or threonine residue. In **N-linked oligosaccharides**, a GlcNAc residue is linked to the amide nitrogen of an asparagine residue. The structures of an O-glycosidic and an N-glycosidic linkage are compared in Figure 8.33. Additional sugar residues can be attached to the GalNAc or the GlcNAc residue. An individual glycoprotein can contain both O- and N-linked oligosaccharides. Some glycoproteins contain a third type of linkage. In these glycoproteins, the protein is attached to ethanolamine, which is linked to a branched oligosaccharide to which lipid is also attached (Section 9.10).

There are four important subclasses of O-glycosidic linkages in glycoproteins.

1. The most common O-glycosidic linkage is the GalNAc-Ser/Thr linkage mentioned above. Other sugars—for example, galactose and sialic acid—are frequently linked to the GalNAc residue (Figure 8.34a).

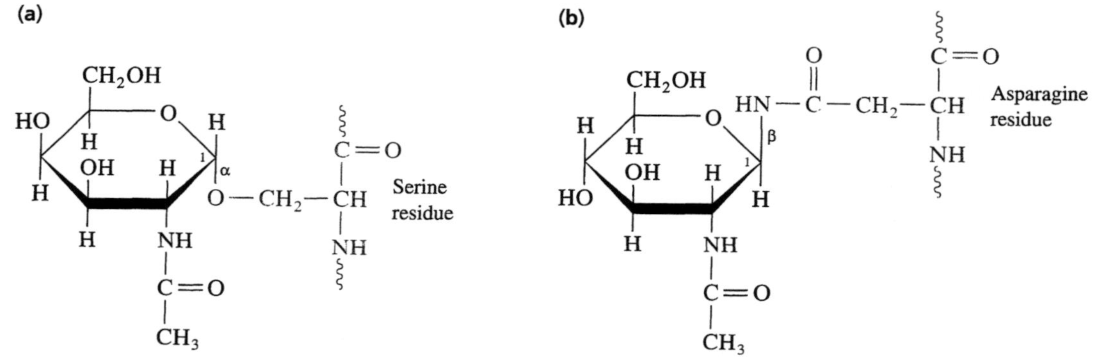

Figure 8.33 ▲
O-Glycosidic and N-glycosidic linkages. **(a)** N-Acetylgalactosamine–serine linkage, the major O-glycosidic linkage found in glycoproteins. **(b)** N-Acetylglucosamine–asparagine linkage, which characterizes N-linked glycoproteins. The O-glycosidic linkage is α, whereas the N-glycosidic linkage is β.

Figure 8.34 ▶
Four subclasses of O-glycosidic linkages.
(a) Example of a typical linkage in which N-acetylgalactosamine (GalNAc) with attached residues is linked to a serine or threonine residue. **(b)** Linkage found in collagen, where a galactose residue, usually attached to a glucose residue, is linked to hydroxylysine (Hyl). **(c)** Trisaccharide linkage found in certain proteoglycans. **(d)** GlcNAc linkage found in some proteins.

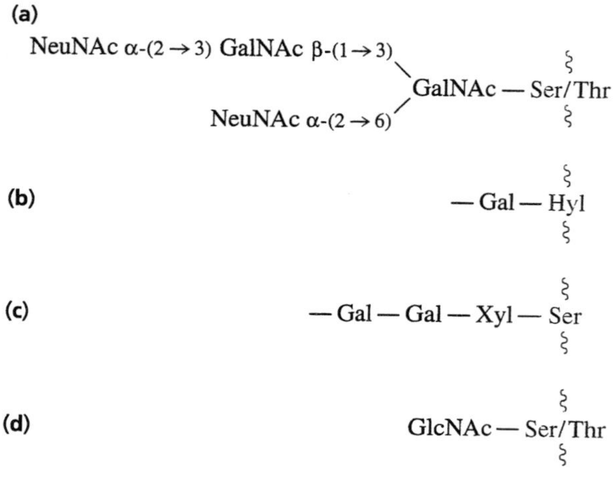

(a)

NeuNAc α-(2 → 3) GalNAc β-(1 → 3)

GalNAc — Ser/Thr

NeuNAc α-(2 → 6)

(b)

— Gal — Hyl

(c)

— Gal — Gal — Xyl — Ser

(d)

GlcNAc — Ser/Thr

2. Some of the 5-hydroxylysine (Hyl) residues of collagen (Figure 4.35) are joined to D-galactose via an *O*-glycosidic linkage (Figure 8.34b). This structure is unique to collagen.

3. The glycosaminoglycans of certain proteoglycans are joined to the core protein via a Gal–Gal–Xyl–Ser structure (Figure 8.34c).

4. In some proteins, a single residue of GlcNAc is linked to serine or threonine (Figure 8.34d).

O-Linked oligosaccharides may account for 80% of the mass of mucins. These large glycoproteins are found in mucus, the viscous fluid that protects and lubricates the epithelium of the gastrointestinal, genitourinary, and respiratory tracts. The oligosaccharide chains of mucins contain an abundance of NeuNAc residues and sulfated sugars. The negative charges of these residues are responsible in part for the extended shape of mucins, which contributes to the viscosity of solutions containing mucins.

The biosynthesis of the oligosaccharide chains of glycoproteins requires a battery of specific enzymes in distinct compartments of the cell. In the stepwise synthesis of *O*-linked oligosaccharides, glycosyltransferases catalyze the addition of glycosyl groups donated by nucleotide-sugar coenzymes. The oligosaccharide chains are assembled by addition of the first sugar molecule to the protein, followed by subsequent single-sugar additions to the nonreducing end.

N-Linked oligosaccharides, like *O*-linked oligosaccharides, exhibit great variety in sugar sequence and composition. Most *N*-linked oligosaccharides can be divided into three subclasses: high mannose, complex, and hybrid (Figure 8.35). The appearance of a common core pentasaccharide ($GlcNAc_2Man_3$) in each class reflects a common initial pathway for biosynthesis. The synthesis of *N*-linked oligosaccharides begins with the assembly of a compound consisting of a branched oligosaccharide with 14 residues (9 of which are mannose residues) linked to the lipid dolichol. The entire oligosaccharide chain is transferred to an asparagine residue of a newly synthesized protein, after which the chain is

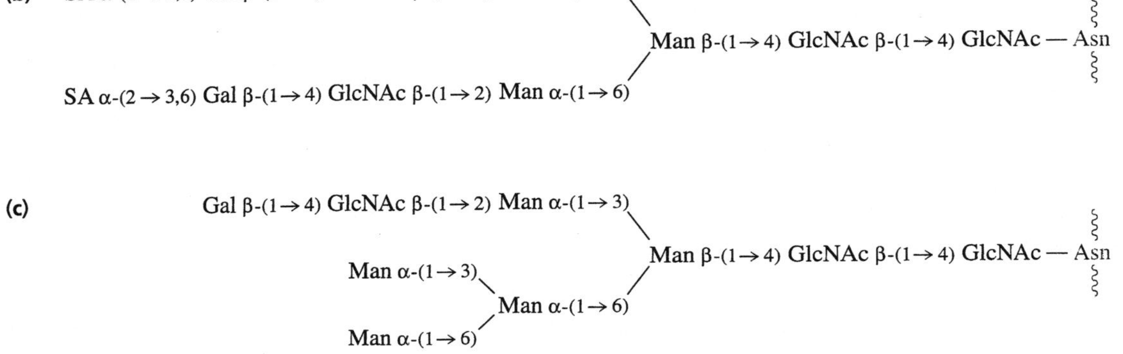

> Nucleotide sugars are discussed in Section 7.2a.

(a)

Man α-(1→2) Man α-(1→2) Man α-(1→3)

Man α-(1→2) Man α-(1→3)

Man α-(1→6)

Man α-(1→2) Man α-(1→6)

Man β-(1→4) GlcNAc β-(1→4) GlcNAc — Asn

(b)

SA α-(2→3,6) Gal β-(1→4) GlcNAc β-(1→2) Man α-(1→3)

Man β-(1→4) GlcNAc β-(1→4) GlcNAc — Asn

SA α-(2→3,6) Gal β-(1→4) GlcNAc β-(1→2) Man α-(1→6)

(c)

Gal β-(1→4) GlcNAc β-(1→2) Man α-(1→3)

Man α-(1→3)

Man α-(1→6)

Man α-(1→6)

Man β-(1→4) GlcNAc β-(1→4) GlcNAc — Asn

Figure 8.35 ▲
Structures of *N*-linked oligosaccharides. **(a)** High-mannose chain. **(b)** Complex chain. **(c)** Hybrid chain. The pentasaccharide core common to all *N*-linked structures is shown in red. SA represents sialic acid, usually NeuNAc.

trimmed by the action of glycosidases. High-mannose chains represent an early stage in the biosynthesis of *N*-linked oligosaccharides. Complex oligosaccharide chains result from further removal of sugar residues from high-mannose chains and the addition of other sugar residues, such as fucose, galactose, GlcNAc, and sialic acid (a phenomenon called oligosaccharide processing). As in the synthesis of *O*-linked oligosaccharides, these additional sugar residues are donated by nucleotide sugars in reactions catalyzed by glycosyltransferases. In certain cases, a glycoprotein can contain a hybrid oligosaccharide chain, a branched oligosaccharide in which one branch is of the high-mannose type and the other is of the complex type.

The presence of one or more oligosaccharide chains on a protein can alter its physical properties, including its size, shape, solubility, electric charge, and stability. Biological properties that can be altered include rate of secretion, half-life in the circulation, and immunogenicity. In a few cases, specific roles for the oligosaccharide chains of glycoproteins have been identified. For example, a number of mammalian hormones are dimeric glycoproteins whose oligosaccharide chains facilitate assembly of the dimer and confer resistance to proteolysis. Also, the recognition of one cell by another that occurs during cell migration or oocyte fertilization can depend in part on the binding of proteins on the surface of one cell to the carbohydrate portions of certain glycoproteins on the surface of the other cell.

The role of carbohydrates as molecular markers is illustrated by lysosomal proteases. These enzymes are synthesized in the endoplasmic reticulum and transferred to the Golgi apparatus, where they are modified by the attachment of mannose 6-phosphate. Proteins tagged with mannose 6-phosphate are specifically transported to lysosomes, whereas most other glycosylated proteins are transported to the cell surface or secreted from the cell.

Summary

1. Carbohydrates include monosaccharides, oligosaccharides, and polysaccharides. Monosaccharides are classified as aldoses or ketoses or their derivatives.

2. A monosaccharide is designated D or L, according to the configuration of the chiral carbon farthest from the carbonyl carbon atom. Each monosaccharide has 2^n possible stereoisomers, where *n* is the number of chiral carbon atoms. Enantiomers are nonsuperimposable mirror images of each other. Epimers differ in configuration at only one of several chiral centers.

3. Aldoses with at least five carbon atoms and ketoses with at least six carbon atoms exist principally as cyclic hemiacetals or hemiketals known as furanoses and pyranoses. In these ring structures, the configuration of the anomeric (carbonyl) carbon is designated either α or β. Furanoses and pyranoses can adopt several conformations.

4. Derivatives of monosaccharides include sugar phosphates, deoxy sugars, amino sugars, sugar alcohols, and sugar acids.

5. Glycosides are formed when the anomeric carbon of a sugar forms a glycosidic linkage with another molecule. Glycosides include disaccharides, polysaccharides, and some carbohydrate derivatives.

6. Homoglycans are polymers containing a single type of sugar residue. Examples of homoglycans include the storage polysaccharides starch and glycogen and the structural polysaccharides cellulose and chitin.

7. Heteroglycans, which contain more than one type of sugar residue, are found in glycoconjugates, which include proteoglycans, peptidoglycans, and glycoproteins.

8. Proteoglycans are proteins linked to glycosaminoglycans, chains of repeating disaccharides. Proteoglycans are prominent in the extracellular matrix and in connective tissues such as cartilage.

9. The cell walls of many bacteria are made of peptidoglycans, which are heteroglycan chains linked to peptides. Peptidoglycan molecules are extensively cross-linked, essentially converting peptidoglycan into a rigid macromolecule that defines the shape of a bacterium and protects the plasma membrane.

10. Glycoproteins are proteins containing covalently bound oligosaccharides. The oligosaccharide chains of most glycoproteins are either *O*-linked to serine or threonine residues or *N*-linked to asparagine residues and exhibit great variety in structure and sugar composition.

Problems

1. Identify each of the following:
   (a) Two aldoses whose configuration at carbons 3, 4, and 5 matches that of D-fructose.
   (b) The enantiomer of D-galactose.
   (c) An epimer of D-galactose that is also an epimer of D-mannose.
   (d) A ketose that has no chiral centers.
   (e) A ketose that has only one chiral center.
   (f) Monosaccharide residues of cellulose, amylose, and glycogen.
   (g) Monosaccharide residues of chitin.

2. Draw Fischer projections for (a) L-mannose, (b) L-fucose (6-deoxy-L-galactose), (c) D-xylitol, and (d) D-iduronate.

3. Honey is an emulsion of microcrystalline D-fructose and D-glucose. Although D-fructose in polysaccharides exists mainly in the furanose form, solution or crystalline D-fructose (as in honey) is a mixture of several forms with β-D-fructopyranose (67%) and β-D-fructofuranose (25%) predominating. Draw the Fischer projection for D-fructose and show how it can cyclize to form both of the cyclized forms above.

4. Sialic acid is often found in *N*-linked oligosaccharides that are involved in cell-cell interactions. Cancer cells synthesize much greater amounts of sialic acid than normal cells and derivatives of sialic acid have been proposed as anticancer agents to block cell-surface interactions between normal and cancerous cells. Answer the following questions about the structure of sialic acid.
   (a) Is it an α or a β anomeric form?
   (b) Will sialic acid mutorotate between α and β anomeric forms?
   (c) Is this a "deoxy" sugar?
   (d) Will the open chain form of sialic acid be an aldehyde or a ketone?
   (e) How many chiral carbons are there in the sugar ring?

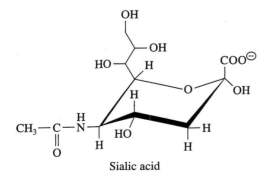
Sialic acid

5. How many stereoisomers are possible for glucopyranose and for fructofuranose? How many are D sugars in each case, and how many are L sugars?

6. Draw the structure of each of the following molecules and label each chiral carbon with an asterisk.
   (a) α-D-Glucose 1-phosphate.
   (b) 2-Deoxy-β-D-ribose 5-phosphate.
   (c) D-Glyceraldehyde 3-phosphate.
   (d) L-Glucuronate.

7. In aqueous solution, virtually all D-glucose molecules (>99%) are in the pyranose form. Other aldoses have a greater proportion of molecules in the open-chain form. D-Glucose may have evolved to be the predominant metabolic fuel because it is less likely than its isomers to react with and damage cellular proteins. Explain why D-glucose reacts less than other aldoses with the amino groups of proteins.

8. Why is the β-D-glucopyranose form of glucose more abundant than α-D-glucopyranose in aqueous solution?

9. The relative orientations of substituents on ribose rings are determined by the conformation of the ring itself, and if the ribose is part of a polymeric molecule then ring conformation will affect overall polymer structure. For example, the orientation of ribose phosphate substituents connecting monomeric nucleoside units is important in determining the overall structure of nucleic acid molecules. In one major form of DNA (B-DNA), the ribofuranose rings adopt an envelope conformation in which C-2′ carbon is above the plane defined by C-1, C-3, C-4 and the ring oxygen (C-2′ *endo* conformation). Draw the envelope structure of D-ribose 5-phosphate with a nucleoside base (B) attached in a β-anomeric position at the C-1 carbon.

10. In a procedure for testing blood glucose, a drop of blood is placed on a paper strip impregnated with the enzyme glucose oxidase and all the reagents necessary for the reaction

$$\text{β-D-Glucose} + O_2 \longrightarrow \text{D-Gluconolactone} + H_2O_2$$

The H_2O_2 produced causes a color change on the paper, which indicates how much glucose is present. Since glucose oxidase is specific for the β anomer of glucose, why can the total blood glucose be measured?

11. Draw Haworth projections for the following glycosides:
   (a) Isomaltose [α-D-glucopyranosyl-(1→6)-α-D-glucopyranose]
   (b) Amygdalin, a compound in the pits of certain fruits, which has a —CH(CN)C₆H₅ group attached to C-1 of β-D-glucopyranosyl-(1→6)-β-D-glucopyranose
   (c) The *O*-linked oligosaccharide in collagen (β-D-galactose attached to a 5-hydroxylysine residue)

12. A number of diseases result from hereditary deficiencies in specific glycosidases. In these diseases, certain glycoproteins are incompletely degraded and oligosaccharides accumulate in tissues. Which of the *N*-linked oligosaccharides in Figure 8.35 would be affected by deficiencies of the following enzymes?

(a) *N*-Acetyl-β-glucosaminyl asparagine amidase

(b) β-Galactosidase

(c) Sialidase

(d) Fucosidase

13. A carbohydrate-amino acid polymer that is a potent inhibitor of influenza virus has been synthesized. The virus is thought to be inactivated when multiple sialyl groups bind to viral surface proteins. Draw the chemical structure of the carbohydrate portion of this polymer (below, where X represents the rest of the polymer).

NeuNAc α-(2→3) Gal β-(1→4) Glu β-(1→)-X

Selected Readings

General

Collins, P. M., ed. (1987). *Carbohydrates* (London and New York: Chapman and Hall).

El Khadem, H. S. (1988). *Carbohydrate Chemistry: Monosaccharides and Their Derivatives* (Orlando, FL: Academic Press).

Nodulation Factors

Dénarié, J., and Debellé, F. (1996). Rhizobium lipo-chitooligosaccharide nodulation factors: signaling molecules mediating recognition and morphogenesis. *Annu. Rev. Biochem.* 65:503–535.

Mergaert, P., Van Montagu, M., and Holsters, M. (1997). Molecular mechanisms of Nod factor diversity. *Mol. Microbiol.* 25:811–817.

Proteoglycans

Heinegård, D., and Oldberg, Å. (1989). Structure and biology of cartilage and bone matrix noncollagenous macromolecules. *FASEB J.* 3:2042–2051.

Iozzo, R. V. (1999). The biology of the small leucine-rich proteoglycans: functional network of interactive proteins. *J. Biol. Chem.* 274:18843–18846. Discusses the functions of decorin and other SLRPs.

Iozzo, R. V., and Murdoch, A. D. (1996). Proeteoglycans of the extracellular environment: clues from the gene and protein side offer novel perspectives in molecular diversity and function. *FASEB J.* 10:598–614. Description of small leucine-rich proteoglycans and hyalectans.

Kjellén, L., and Lindahl, U. (1991). Proteoglycans: structures and interactions. *Annu. Rev. Biochem.* 60:443–475.

Glycoproteins

Drickamer, K., and Taylor, M. E. (1998). Evolving views of protein glycosylation. *Trends Biochem. Sci.* 23:321–324. Speculation on the evolution of glycosylation pathways.

Dwek, R. A., Edge, C. J., Harvey, D. J., Wormald, M. R., and Parekh, R. B. (1993). Analysis of glycoprotein-associated oligosaccharides. *Annu. Rev. Biochem.* 62:65–100.

Lechner, J., and Wieland, F. (1989). Structure and biosynthesis of prokaryotic glycoproteins. *Annu. Rev. Biochem.* 58:173–194.

Rademacher, T. W., Parekh, R. B., and Dwek, R. A. (1988). Glycobiology. *Annu. Rev. Biochem.* 57:785–838. A review of oligosaccharides linked to proteins and lipids, including changes in glycosylation in several diseases.

Rudd, P. M., and Dwek, R. A. (1997). Glycosylation: heterogeneity and the 3D structure of proteins. *Crit. Rev. Biochem. Mol. Biol.* 32:1–100. An explanation of limited heterogeneity of glycoproteins.

Strous, G. J., and Dekker, J. (1992). Mucin-type glycoproteins. *Crit. Rev. Biochem. Mol. Biol.* 27:57–92.

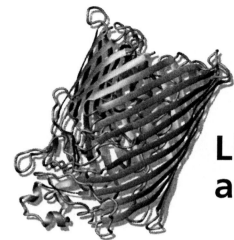

CHAPTER

9

Lipids
and Membranes

I n this chapter, we consider **lipids**, a third major class of biomolecules. Lipids (*lipo-*, fat)—like proteins and carbohydrates—are essential components of all living organisms. Unlike these other types of biomolecules, however, lipids have widely varied structures. They are often defined as water-insoluble (or only sparingly soluble) organic compounds found in biological systems. Lipids have high solubility in nonpolar organic solvents. They are either hydrophobic (nonpolar) or amphipathic (containing both nonpolar and polar regions). We begin this chapter with a discussion of the structures and functions of the different classes of lipids. In the second part of the chapter, we examine the structures and functions of biological membranes, whose properties as cellular barriers to polar solutes depend on the properties of their lipids.

9.1 Structural and Functional Diversity of Lipids

Figure 9.1 shows the major types of lipids and their structural relationships to one another. The simplest lipids, **fatty acids**, have the general formula R—COOH, where R represents a hydrocarbon chain. Fatty acids are components of many more complex types of lipids, including triacylglycerols, glycerophospholipids, and sphingolipids. Lipids containing phosphate moieties are called **phospholipids**, and lipids containing both sphingosine and carbohydrate groups are called **glycosphingolipids**.

Top: Ribbon structure of the transmembrane portion of porin FhuA from *Escherichia coli*. This porin forms a channel for the passage of protein-bound iron into the bacterium. The channel is formed from 22 antiparallel β strands. [Adapted from Locher, K. P., Rosenbusch, J. P. (1997): Oligomeric states and siderophore binding of the ligand-gated FhuA protein that forms channels across *Escherichia coli* outer membranes. *Eur. J. Biochem.* 247:770–775.] [PDB 1BY3].

264

Chemistry for Biologists

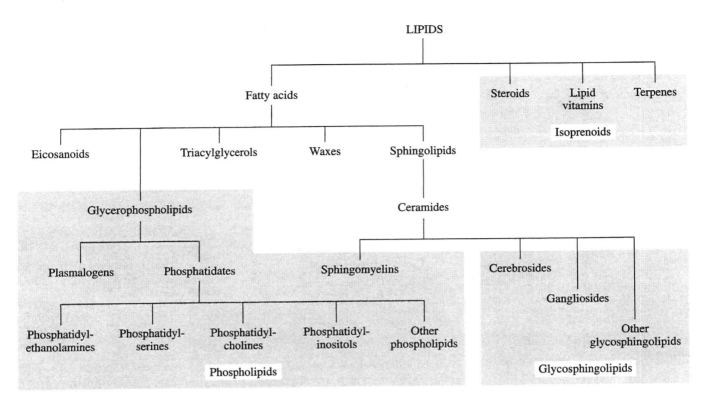

Figure 9.1 ▲
Structural relationships of the major classes of lipids. Fatty acids are the simplest lipids. Many other types of lipids either contain or are derived from fatty acids. Glycerophospholipids and sphingomyelins contain phosphate and are classified as phospholipids. Cerebrosides and gangliosides contain sphingosine and carbohydrate and are classified as glycosphingolipids. Steroids, lipid vitamins, and terpenes are called isoprenoids because they are related to the five-carbon molecule isoprene rather than to fatty acids.

Steroids, lipid vitamins, and terpenes are related to the five-carbon molecule isoprene and are therefore called **isoprenoids**. The name *terpenes* has been applied to all isoprenoids but usually is restricted to those that occur in plants.

Lipids have diverse biological functions as well as diverse structures. Biological membranes contain a variety of amphipathic lipids, including glycerophospholipids and sphingolipids. In some organisms, triacylglycerols (fats and oils) function as intracellular storage molecules for metabolic energy. Fats also provide animals with thermal insulation and padding. Waxes in cell walls, exoskeletons, and skins protect the surfaces of some organisms. Some lipids have highly specialized functions. For example, steroid hormones regulate and integrate a host of metabolic activities in animals, and eicosanoids participate in the regulation of blood pressure, body temperature, and smooth-muscle contraction in mammals. Gangliosides and other glycosphingolipids are located at the cell surface and can participate in cellular recognition.

9.2 Fatty Acids

More than 100 different fatty acids have been identified in various species. Fatty acids differ from one another in the length of their hydrocarbon tails, the degree of unsaturation (the number of carbon-carbon double bonds), and the positions of the double bonds in the chains. Some fatty acids commonly found in mammals are shown in Table 9.1. Most fatty acids have a pK_a of about 4.5 to 5.0 and are therefore

TABLE 9.1   Some common fatty acids (anionic forms)

Number of carbons	Number of double bonds	Common name	IUPAC name	Melting point, °C	Molecular formula
12	0	Laurate	Dodecanoate	44	$CH_3(CH_2)_{10}COO^{\ominus}$
14	0	Myristate	Tetradecanoate	52	$CH_3(CH_2)_{12}COO^{\ominus}$
16	0	Palmitate	Hexadecanoate	63	$CH_3(CH_2)_{14}COO^{\ominus}$
18	0	Stearate	Octadecanoate	70	$CH_3(CH_2)_{16}COO^{\ominus}$
20	0	Arachidate	Eicosanoate	75	$CH_3(CH_2)_{18}COO^{\ominus}$
22	0	Behenate	Docosanoate	81	$CH_3(CH_2)_{20}COO^{\ominus}$
24	0	Lignocerate	Tetracosanoate	84	$CH_3(CH_2)_{22}COO^{\ominus}$
16	1	Palmitoleate	cis-Δ^9-Hexadecenoate	−0.5	$CH_3(CH_2)_5CH{=}CH(CH_2)_7COO^{\ominus}$
18	1	Oleate	cis-Δ^9-Octadecenoate	13	$CH_3(CH_2)_7CH{=}CH(CH_2)_7COO^{\ominus}$
18	2	Linoleate	cis,cis-$\Delta^{9,12}$-Octadecadienoate	−9	$CH_3(CH_2)_4(CH{=}CHCH_2)_2(CH_2)_6COO^{\ominus}$
18	3	Linolenate	all cis-$\Delta^{9,12,15}$-Octadecatrienoate	−17	$CH_3CH_2(CH{=}CHCH_2)_3(CH_2)_6COO^{\ominus}$
20	4	Arachidonate	all cis-$\Delta^{5,8,11,14}$-Eicosatetraenoate	−49	$CH_3(CH_2)_4(CH{=}CHCH_2)_4(CH_2)_2COO^{\ominus}$

Fatty acid biosynthesis is discussed in Chapter 16.

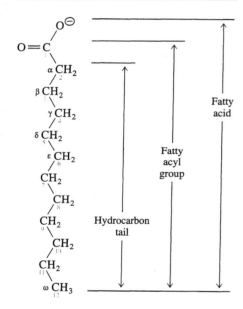

Figure 9.2 ▲
Structure and nomenclature of fatty acids. Fatty acids consist of a long hydrocarbon tail terminating with a carboxyl group. Since the pK_a of the carboxyl group is approximately 4.5 to 5.0, fatty acids are anionic at physiological pH. In IUPAC nomenclature, carbons are numbered beginning with the carboxyl carbon. In common nomenclature, the carbon atom adjacent to the carboxyl carbon is designated α, and the remaining carbons are lettered β, γ, δ, and so on. The carbon atom farthest from the carboxyl carbon is designated the ω carbon, whatever the length of the tail. The fatty acid shown, laurate (or dodecanoate), has 12 carbon atoms and contains no carbon-carbon double bonds.

ionized at physiological pH. Although—like other detergents (Section 2.4)—fatty acids have a long hydrophobic tail and a polar head, they are almost always esterified in cells. This is fortunate because otherwise high concentrations of free fatty acids could disrupt membranes. Fatty acids can be referred to by either International Union of Pure and Applied Chemistry (IUPAC) names or common names. Common names are used for the most frequently encountered fatty acids.

The number of carbon atoms in the most abundant fatty acids ranges from 12 to 20 and is almost always even since fatty acids are synthesized by the sequential addition of two-carbon units. In IUPAC nomenclature, the carboxyl carbon is labeled C-1 and the remaining carbon atoms are numbered sequentially. In common nomenclature, Greek letters are used to identify the carbon atoms. The carbon adjacent to the carboxyl carbon (C-2 in IUPAC nomenclature) is designated α, and the other carbons are lettered β, γ, δ, ε, and so on. The Greek letter ω specifies the carbon atom farthest from the carboxyl group, whatever the length of the hydrocarbon tail (Figure 9.2).

Fatty acids without a carbon-carbon double bond are classified as **saturated**, whereas those with at least one carbon-carbon double bond are classified as **unsaturated**. Unsaturated fatty acids with only one carbon-carbon double bond are called **monounsaturated**, and those with two or more are called **polyunsaturated**. The configuration of the double bonds in unsaturated fatty acids is generally cis. In IUPAC nomenclature, the positions of double bonds are indicated by the symbol Δ^n, where the superscript n indicates the lower-numbered carbon atom of each double-bonded pair (Table 9.1). The double bonds of most polyunsaturated fatty acids are separated by a methylene group and are therefore not conjugated.

A shorthand notation for identifying fatty acids uses two numbers separated by a colon; the first refers to the number of carbon atoms in the fatty acid, and the second refers to the number of carbon-carbon double bonds, with their positions indicated as superscripts following a Greek symbol, Δ. In this notation, palmitate is written as 16:0, oleate as 18:1 Δ^9, and arachidonate as 20:4 $\Delta^{5,8,11,14}$. Unsaturated fatty acids can also be described by the location of the last double bond in the chain. This double bond is usually found three, six, or nine carbon atoms from the end of the chain. Such fatty acids are called ω-3 (e.g., 18:3 $\Delta^{9,12,15}$), ω-6 (e.g., 18:2 $\Delta^{9,12}$), or ω-9 (e.g., 18:1 Δ^9).

The physical properties of saturated and unsaturated fatty acids differ considerably. Typically, saturated fatty acids are waxy solids at room temperature (22°C),

Chemistry for Biologists

whereas unsaturated fatty acids are liquids at this temperature. The length of the hydrocarbon chain of a fatty acid and its degree of unsaturation influence the melting point. Compare the melting points listed in Table 9.1 for the saturated fatty acids laurate (12:0), myristate (14:0), and palmitate (16:0). As the lengths of the hydrocarbon tails increase, the melting points of the saturated fatty acids also increase. The number of van der Waals interactions among neighboring hydrocarbon tails increases as the tails get longer, so more energy is required to disrupt the interactions.

Compare the structures of stearate (18:0), oleate (18:1), and linolenate (18:3) in Figures 9.3 and 9.4. The saturated hydrocarbon tail of stearate is flexible since rotation can occur around every carbon-carbon bond. In a crystal of stearic acid, the hydrocarbon chains are extended and pack together closely. The presence of *cis* double bonds in oleate and linolenate produces pronounced bends in the hydrocarbon chains since rotation around double bonds is hindered. These bends prevent close packing and extensive van der Waals interactions among the hydrocarbon chains. Consequently, *cis* unsaturated fatty acids have lower melting points than saturated fatty acids. As the degree of unsaturation increases, fatty acids become more fluid. Note that stearic acid (melting point 70°C) is a solid at body temperature, but oleic acid (melting point 13°C) and linolenic acid (melting point −17°C) are both liquids.

Free fatty acids occur only in trace amounts in living cells. Most fatty acids are esterified to glycerol or other backbone compounds to form more complex lipid molecules. In esters and other derivatives of carboxylic acids, the $RC{=}O$ moiety

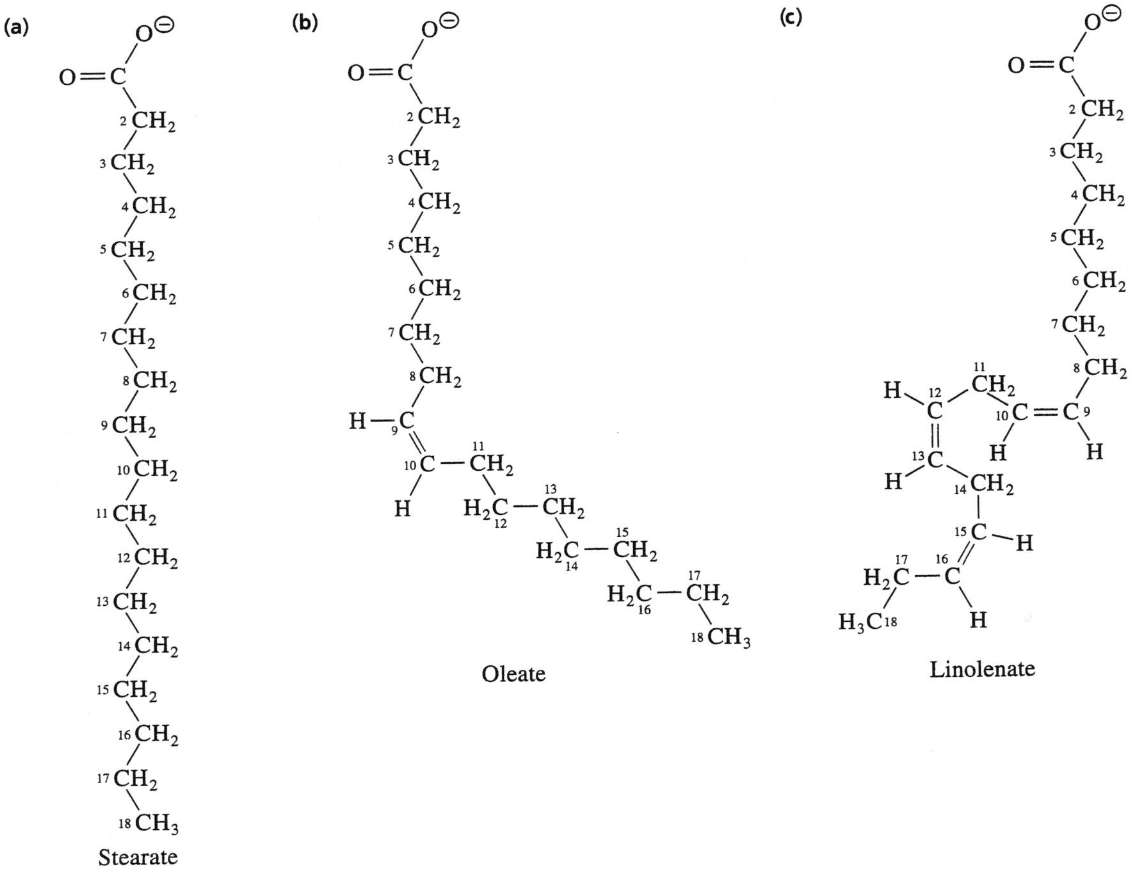

Figure 9.3 ▲
Structures of three C_{18} fatty acids. **(a)** Stearate (octadecanoate), a saturated fatty acid. **(b)** Oleate (*cis*-Δ^9-octadecenoate), a monounsaturated fatty acid. **(c)** Linolenate (all-*cis*-$\Delta^{9,12,15}$-octadecatrienoate), a polyunsaturated fatty acid. The *cis* double bonds produce kinks in the tails of the unsaturated fatty acids. Linolenate is a very flexible molecule, and can assume a variety of conformations.

Chemistry for Biologists

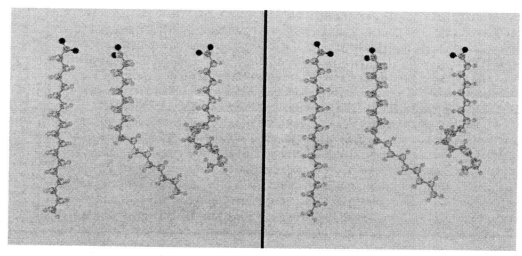

Figure 9.4 ▲
Stereo view of stearate (left), oleate (center), and linolenate (right). Color key: carbon, green; hydrogen, blue; oxygen, orange.

contributed by the acid is called the acyl group. In common nomenclature, complex lipids that contain specific fatty acyl groups are named after the parent fatty acid. For example, esters of the fatty acid laurate are called lauroyl esters, and esters of linoleate are called linoleoyl esters. (A lauryl group is the alcohol analog of the lauroyl acyl group.)

The relative abundance of particular fatty acids varies with the type of organism, type of organ (in multicellular organisms), and food source. The most abundant fatty acids in animals are usually oleate (18:1), palmitate (16:0), and stearate (18:0). Mammals require certain dietary polyunsaturated fatty acids that they cannot synthesize, such as linoleate (18:2), which is abundant in plant oils, and linolenate (18:3), which is found in plants and fish oils. Such fatty acids are called essential fatty acids. Mammals can synthesize other polyunsaturated fatty acids from an adequate supply of linoleate and linolenate.

Many fatty acids besides those listed in Table 9.1 are present in nature. For example, fatty acids containing cyclopropane rings have been found in the cell walls of certain bacteria, and branched-chain fatty acids occur on the feathers of ducks. Many of these fatty acids are rare and have highly specialized functions.

BOX 9.1   *Trans* Fatty Acids and Margarine

Although the configuration of most double bonds in unsaturated fatty acids is *cis*, some fatty acids in the human diet have the *trans* configuration. *Trans* fatty acids can come from animal sources such as dairy products and ruminant meats. Most edible *trans* fatty acids, though, are present as hydrogenated vegetable oils in some margarines or shortenings. Dietary *trans* monounsaturated fatty acids can increase plasma levels of cholesterol and triglycerides, and thus their ingestion may increase the risk of cardiovascular disease.

Plant oils such as corn oil and sunflower oil can be converted to "spreadable" semisolid substances known as margarines. Margarines can be produced by the partial or complete hydrogenation of double bonds in plant oils. The hydrogenation process itself not only saturates the carbon-carbon double bonds of fatty acid esters but can also change the configuration of the remaining double bonds from *cis* to *trans*. The physical properties of these *trans* fatty acids are similar to those of saturated fatty acids. Because *trans* fatty acids and saturated fatty acids are considered unhealthful, many margarines are now produced from plant oils without hydrogenation by adding other edible components such as skim milk powder.

9.3 Triacylglycerols

Fatty acids are important metabolic fuels. Because the carbon atoms of fatty acids are more reduced than those in proteins or carbohydrates, the oxidation of fatty acids yields more energy ($\sim$37 kJ g^{-1}) than the oxidation of proteins or carbohydrates ($\sim$16 kJ g^{-1} each). Fatty acids are generally stored as neutral lipids called **triacylglycerols**. As their name implies, triacylglycerols (historically called triglycerides) are composed of three fatty acyl residues esterified to glycerol, a three-carbon sugar alcohol (Figure 9.5). Triacylglycerols are very hydrophobic. Consequently, they (unlike carbohydrates) can be stored in cells in an anhydrous form; the molecules are not solvated by water, which would take up space and add mass, reducing the efficiency of energy storage.

Fats and oils are mixtures of triacylglycerols. They can be solids (fats) or liquids (oils), depending on their fatty acid compositions and on the temperature. Triacylglycerols containing only saturated long-chain fatty acyl groups tend to be solids at body temperature, and those containing unsaturated or short-chain fatty acyl groups tend to be liquids. A sample of naturally occurring triacylglycerols can contain as many as 20 to 30 molecular species that differ in their fatty acid constituents. Tripalmitin, found in animal fat, contains three residues of palmitic acid. Triolein, which contains three oleic acid residues, is the principal triacylglycerol in olive oil.

Most lipids in the average human diet are triacylglycerols. These lipids are broken down in the small intestine by the action of lipases. These enzymes are synthesized as zymogens in the pancreas and secreted into the small intestine, where they are activated. Pancreatic lipase catalyzes hydrolysis of the primary esters (at C-1 and C-3) of triacylglycerols, releasing fatty acids and generating monoacylglycerols. Because lipids are not water-soluble, lipid digestion occurs in the presence of strong detergents called bile salts (Section 9.6), which are amphipathic derivatives of cholesterol. Micelles of bile salts solubilize fatty acids and monoacylglycerols so that they can diffuse to and be absorbed by the cells of the intestinal wall. Lipids are transported through the body as complexes of lipid and protein known as lipoproteins.

In most cells, triacylglycerols coalesce as fat droplets. These droplets are sometimes seen near mitochondria in cells that rely on fatty acids for metabolic energy. In mammals, most fat is stored in adipose tissue, which is composed of specialized cells known as adipocytes. Each adipocyte contains a large fat droplet that accounts for nearly the entire volume of the cell (Figure 9.6). Although distributed throughout the bodies of mammals, most adipose tissue occurs just under the skin and in the abdominal cavity. Extensive subcutaneous fat serves both as a storage depot for energy and as thermal insulation and is especially pronounced in aquatic mammals.

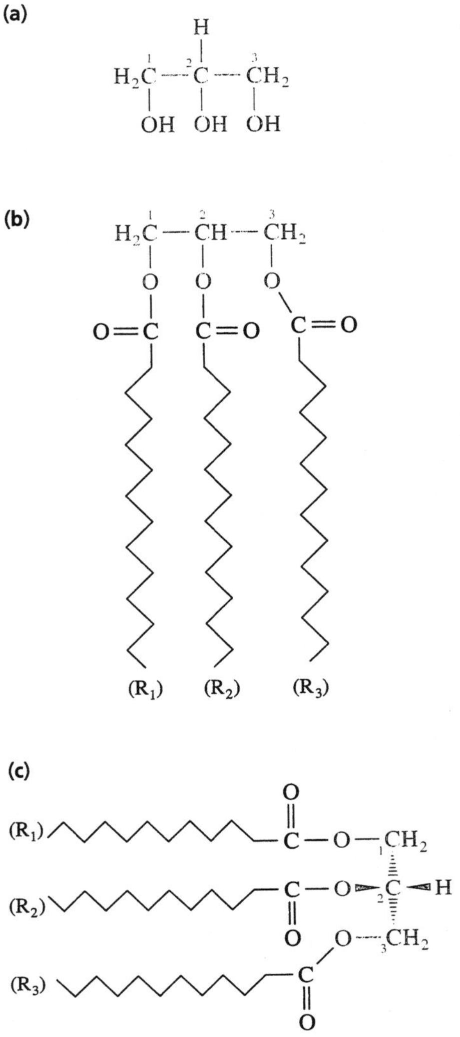

Figure 9.5 ▲
Structure of a triacylglycerol. Glycerol **(a)** is the backbone to which three fatty acyl residues are esterified **(b)**. Although glycerol is not chiral, C-2 of a triacylglycerol is chiral when the acyl groups bound to C-1 and C-3 (R_1 and R_3) differ. The general structure of a triacylglycerol is shown in **(c)**, oriented for comparison with the structure of L-glyceraldehyde (Figure 8.1). This orientation allows stereospecific numbering of glycerol derivatives with C-1 at the top and C-3 at the bottom.

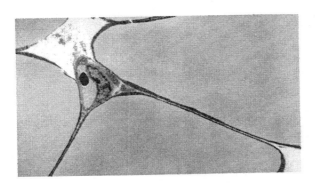

◀ Figure 9.6
Cross-section of adipocytes. A fat droplet occupies most of the volume of each adipocyte. A capillary is visible in the center left of the image.

The structures and functions of lipoproteins are discussed in Section 16.1B.

9.4 Glycerophospholipids

Although triacylglycerols are the most abundant lipids in mammals on the basis of weight, they are not found in biological membranes. The most abundant lipids in most membranes are **glycerophospholipids** (also called phosphoglycerides), which have a glycerol backbone. The simplest glycerophospholipids, phosphatidates, consist of two fatty acyl groups esterified to C-1 and C-2 of glycerol 3-phosphate (Figure 9.7). Phosphatidates are present in small amounts as intermediates in the biosynthesis or breakdown of more complex glycerophospholipids.

In most glycerophospholipids, the phosphate group is esterified to both glycerol and another compound bearing an —OH group. Table 9.2 lists some common types of glycerophospholipids. Note that glycerophospholipids are amphipathic molecules, with a polar head and long nonpolar tails. The structures of three types of glycerophospholipids—phosphatidylethanolamine, phosphatidylserine, and phosphatidylcholine—are shown in Figure 9.8.

TABLE 9.2   Some common types of glycerophospholipids

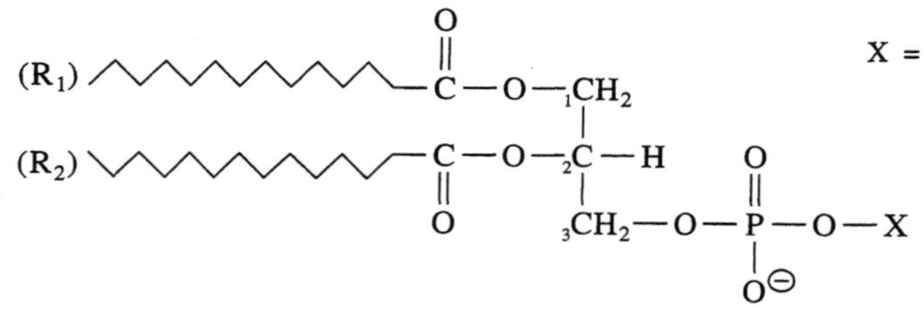

Precursor of X (HO—X)	Formula of —O—X	Name of resulting glycerophospholipid
Water	—O—H	Phosphatidate
Choline	—O—CH$_2$CH$_2$$\overset{\oplus}{N}$(CH$_3$)$_3$	Phosphatidylcholine
Ethanolamine	—O—CH$_2$CH$_2$$\overset{\oplus}{N}H_3$	Phosphatidylethanolamine
Serine	—O—CH$_2$—CH with $\overset{\oplus}{N}$H$_3$ and COO$^{\ominus}$	Phosphatidylserine
Glycerol	—O—CH$_2$CH—CH$_2$OH with OH	Phosphatidylglycerol
Phosphatidyl-glycerol	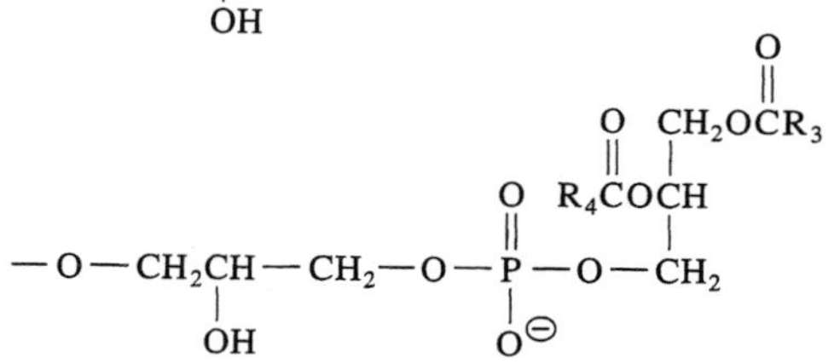 —O—CH$_2$CH—CH$_2$—O—P—O—CH$_2$ ...	Diphosphatidylglycerol (Cardiolipin)
myo-Inositol	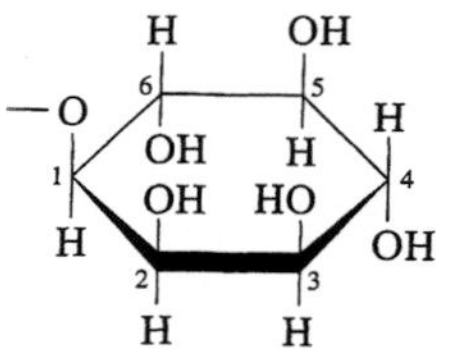 (inositol ring structure)	Phosphatidylinositol

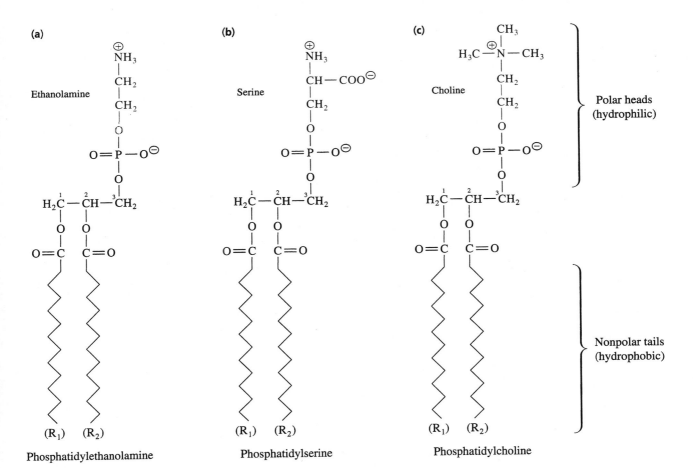

◀ Figure 9.7
(a) Glycerol 3-phosphate and **(b)** phosphatidate. A phosphatidate consists of glycerol 3-phosphate with two fatty acyl groups (R_1 and R_2) esterified to its C-1 and C-2 hydroxyl groups. The structures of glycerophospholipids can be drawn as derivatives of L-glycerol 3-phosphate, with the C-2 substituent on the left in a Fischer projection, as in Table 9.2; for simplicity, we usually show these compounds as stereochemically uncommitted structures.

Figure 9.8 ▲
Structures of **(a)** phosphatidylethanolamine, **(b)** phosphatidylserine, and **(c)** phosphatidylcholine. Functional groups derived from esterified alcohols are shown in blue. Since each of these lipids can contain many combinations of fatty acyl groups, the general name refers to a family of compounds, not to a single molecule.

Chemistry for Biologists

Figure 9.9 ▶
Action of four phospholipases.
Phospholipases A_1, A_2, C, and D can be used to dissect glycerophospholipid structure. Phospholipases catalyze the selective removal of fatty acids from C-1 or C-2 or convert glycerophospholipids to diacylglycerols or phosphatidates.

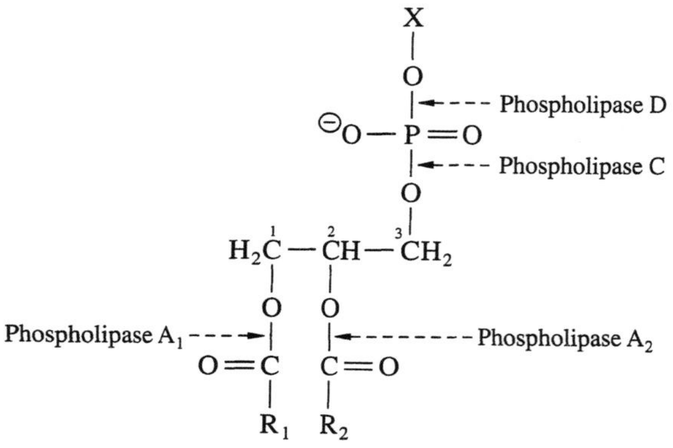

Each type of glycerophospholipid consists of a family of molecules with the same polar head group and different fatty acyl chains. For example, human red blood cell membranes contain at least 21 different species of phosphatidylcholine that differ from one another in the fatty acyl chains esterified at C-1 and C-2 of the glycerol backbone. In general, glycerophospholipids have saturated fatty acids esterified to C-1 and unsaturated fatty acids esterified to C-2. The major membrane glycerophospholipids in *Escherichia coli* are phosphatidyl-ethanolamine and phosphatidylglycerol.

A variety of phospholipases can be used to dissect glycerophospholipid structures and determine the identities of their individual fatty acids. The specific positions of fatty acids in glycerophospholipids can be determined by using phospholipase A_1 and phospholipase A_2, which specifically catalyze the hydrolysis of the ester bonds at C-1 and C-2, respectively (Figure 9.9). Phospholipase A_2 is the major phospholipase in pancreatic juice and is responsible for the digestion of membrane phospholipids in the diet. It is also present in snake, bee, and wasp venom. High concentrations of the products of the action of phospholipase A_2 can disrupt cell membranes. Thus, injection of snake venom into the blood can result in life-threatening lysis of the membranes of red blood cells. Phospholipase C catalyzes hydrolysis of the P—O bond between glycerol and phosphate to liberate diacylglycerol, and phospholipase D converts glycerophospholipids to phosphatidates.

The other major type of glycerophospholipids, **plasmalogens**, differ from phosphatidates in having the hydrocarbon substituent on the C-1 hydroxyl group of glycerol attached by a vinyl ether linkage rather than an ester linkage (Figure 9.10). Ethanolamine or choline is commonly esterified to the phosphate group of plasmalogens. Plasmalogens account for about 23% of the glycerophospholipids in the human central nervous system and are also found in the membranes of peripheral nerve and muscle tissue.

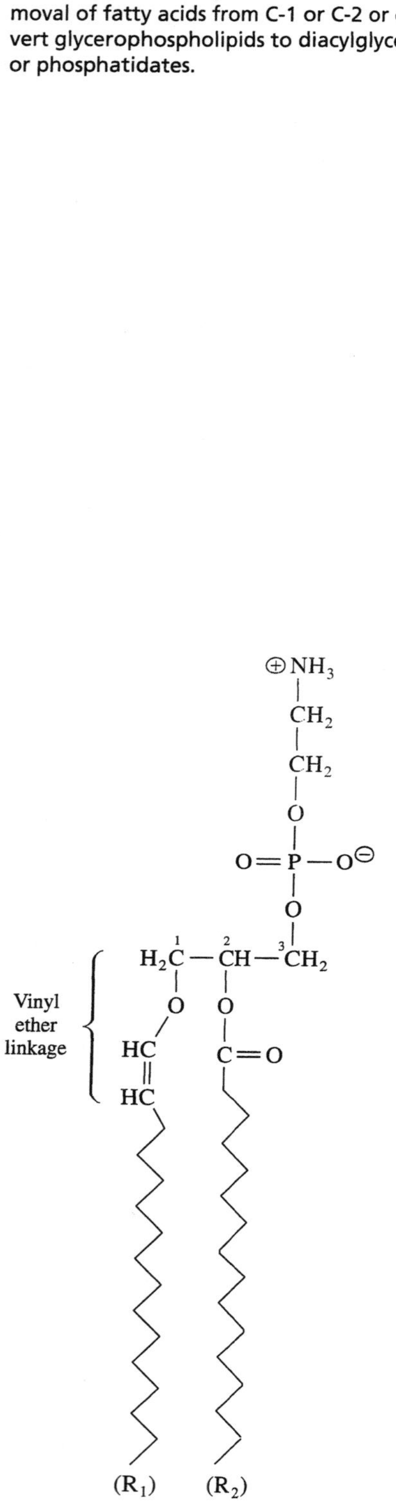

9.5 Sphingolipids

After glycerophospholipids, the most abundant lipids in plant and animal membranes are **sphingolipids**. In mammals, sphingolipids are particularly abundant in tissues of the central nervous system. Most bacteria do not have sphingolipids. The structural backbone of sphingolipids is sphingosine (*trans*-4-sphingenine), an unbranched C_{18} alcohol with a *trans* double bond between C-4 and C-5, an amino group at C-2, and hydroxyl groups at C-1 and C-3 (Figure 9.11a). **Ceramide** consists of a fatty acyl group linked to the C-2 amino group of sphingosine by an amide bond (Figure 9.11b). Ceramides are the metabolic precursors of all sphingolipids. The three major families of sphingolipids are the sphingomyelins, the cerebrosides, and the gangliosides. Of these, only sphingomyelins contain phosphate and are classi-

Figure 9.10 ▲
Structure of an ethanolamine plasmalogen. A hydrocarbon is linked to the C-1 hydroxyl group of glycerol to form a vinyl ether.

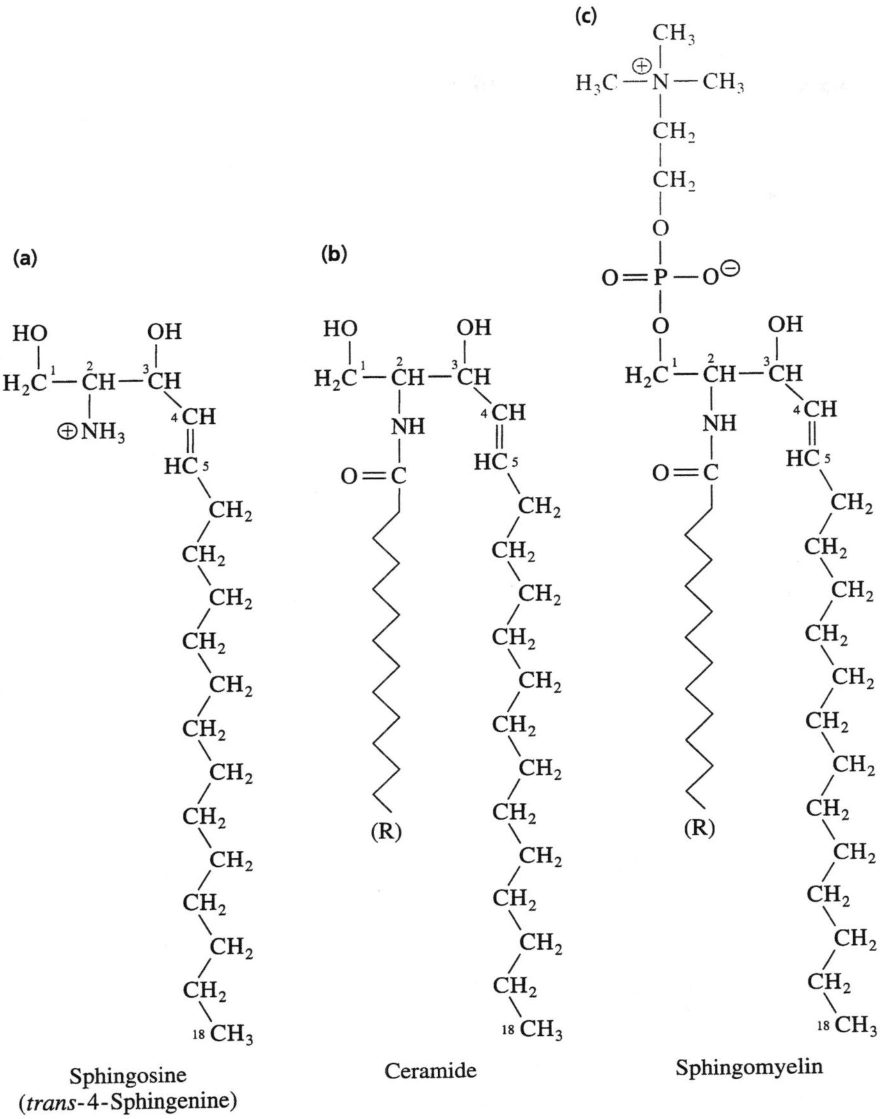

(c)

Structures of sphingosine, ceramide, and sphingomyelin. **(a)** Sphingosine, the backbone for sphingolipids, is a long-chain alcohol with an amino group at C-2. **(b)** Ceramides have a long-chain fatty acyl group attached to the amino group of sphingosine. **(c)** Sphingomyelins have a phosphate group (red) attached to the C-1 hydroxyl group of a ceramide and a choline group (blue) attached to the phosphate.

(a) Sphingosine (*trans*-4-Sphingenine)

(b) Ceramide

Sphingomyelin

β-D-Galactose

Ceramide

fied as phospholipids; cerebrosides and gangliosides contain carbohydrate residues and are classified as glycosphingolipids.

In **sphingomyelins**, phosphocholine is attached to the C-1 hydroxyl group of a ceramide (Figure 9.11c). Note the resemblance of sphingomyelin to phosphatidylcholine (Figure 9.8c)—both molecules are zwitterions containing choline, phosphate, and two long hydrophobic tails. Sphingomyelins are present in the plasma membranes of most mammalian cells and are a major component of the myelin sheaths that surround certain nerve cells.

Cerebrosides are glycosphingolipids that contain one monosaccharide residue attached by a β-glycosidic linkage to C-1 of a ceramide. Galactocerebrosides, also known as galactosylceramides, have a single β-D-galactosyl residue as a polar head group (Figure 9.12). Galactocerebrosides are abundant in nerve tissue and account for about 15% of the lipids of myelin sheaths. Many other mammalian tissues contain glucocerebrosides, ceramides with a β-D-glucosyl head group. In some glycosphingolipids, a linear chain of up to three more monosaccharide residues is attached to the galactosyl or glucosyl moiety of a cerebroside.

Gangliosides are more complex glycosphingolipids in which oligosaccharide chains containing *N*-acetylneuraminic acid (NeuNAc) are attached to a ceramide. NeuNAc (Figure 8.15), an acetylated derivative of the carbohydrate sialic acid, makes the head

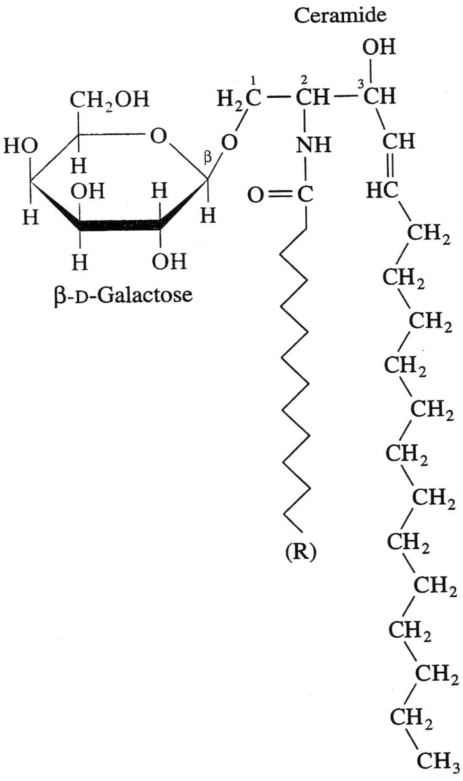

Figure 9.12 ▲
Structure of a galactocerebroside. β-D-Galactose (blue) is attached to the C-1 hydroxyl group of a ceramide (black).

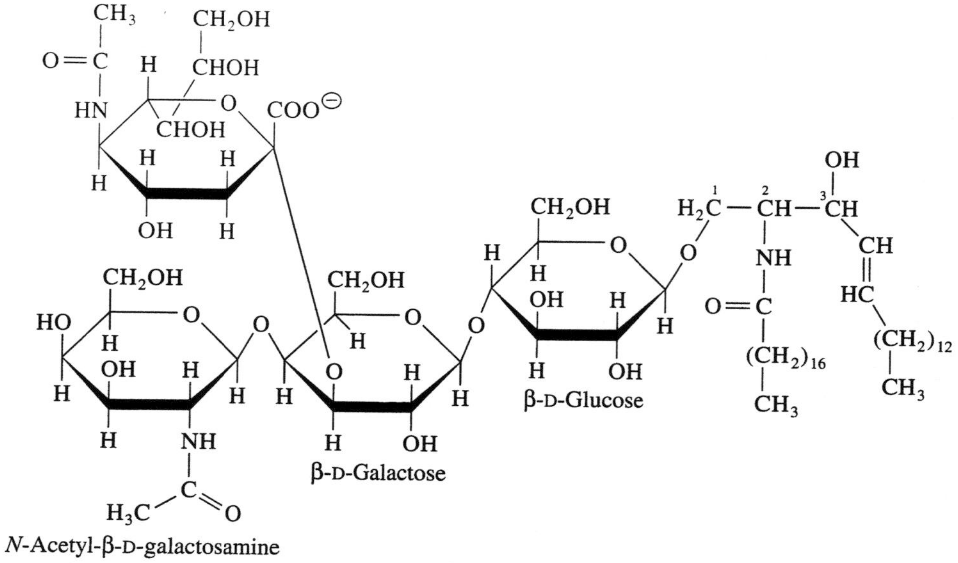

Figure 9.13 ▲
Ganglioside G$_{M2}$. The *N*-acetylneuraminic acid residue is shown in blue.

N-Acetyl-β-D-galactosamine

β-D-Glucose

β-D-Galactose

groups of gangliosides anionic. The structure of a representative ganglioside, G$_{M2}$, is shown in Figure 9.13. The M in G$_{M2}$ stands for monosialo (i.e., one NeuNAc residue); G$_{M2}$ was the second monosialo ganglioside characterized, thus the subscript 2.

More than 60 varieties of gangliosides have been characterized. Their structural diversity results from variations in the composition and sequence of sugar residues. In all gangliosides, the ceramide is linked through its C-1 to a β-glucosyl residue, which in turn is bound to a β-galactosyl residue.

Gangliosides are present on cell surfaces, with the two hydrocarbon chains of the ceramide moiety embedded in the plasma membrane and the oligosaccharides on the extracellular surface. For example, the ABO blood group antigens on the surface of human erythrocytes are the oligosaccharide chains of glycosphingolipids. Gangliosides and other glycosphingolipids provide cells with distinguishing surface markers that can serve in cellular recognition and cell-to-cell communication. The composition of membrane glycosphingolipids can change dramatically during the development of malignant tumors.

Genetically inherited defects in ganglioside metabolism are responsible for a number of debilitating and often lethal diseases, such as Tay-Sachs disease and generalized gangliosidosis. Certain rare genetic defects lead to deficiencies of enzymes responsible for the degradation of sphingolipids in the lysosomes of cells. In Tay-Sachs disease, there is a deficiency of a hydrolase that catalyzes removal of *N*-acetylgalactosamine from G$_{M2}$. Accumulation of G$_{M2}$ causes lysosomes to swell, leading to tissue enlargement. In the central nervous tissue, where there is little room for expansion, nerve cells die; this causes blindness, mental retardation, and death.

9.6 Steroids

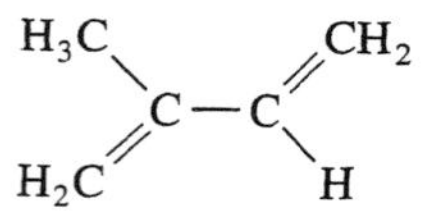

Steroids are a third class of lipids found in the membranes of eukaryotes. Steroids, along with lipid vitamins and terpenes, are classified as isoprenoids because their structures are related to the five-carbon molecule isoprene (Figure 9.14). Steroids contain four fused rings: three six-carbon rings designated A, B, and C and a five-carbon D ring. Substituents of the nearly planar ring system can point either down (the α configuration) or up (the β configuration). The structures of several steroids are shown in Figure 9.15.

Figure 9.14 ▲
Isoprene (2-methyl-1,3-butadiene), the basic structural unit of isoprenoids.

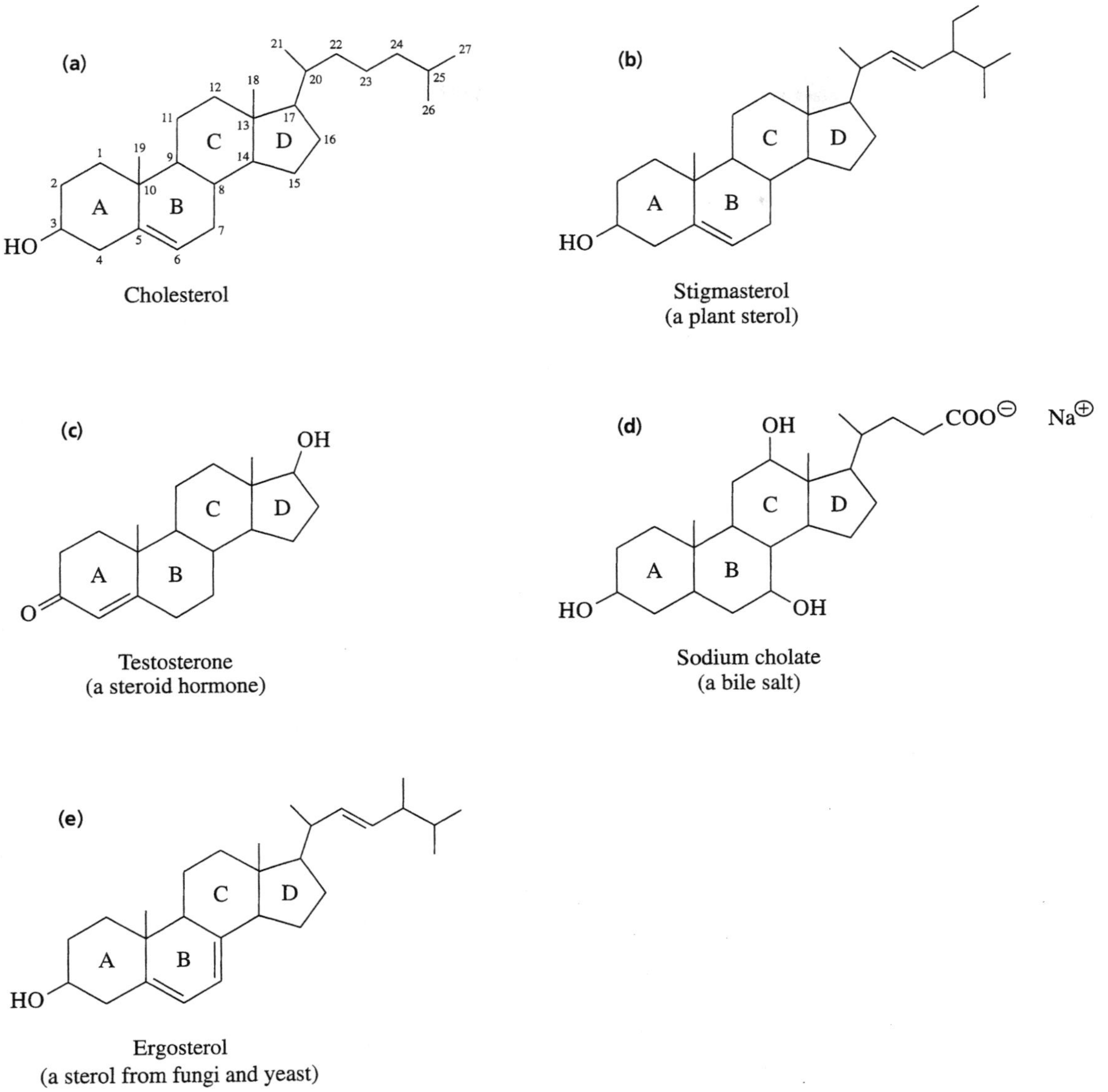

(a) Cholesterol

(b) Stigmasterol (a plant sterol)

(c) Testosterone (a steroid hormone)

(d) Sodium cholate (a bile salt)

(e) Ergosterol (a sterol from fungi and yeast)

Figure 9.15 ▲
Structures of several steroids. Steroids contain four fused rings (lettered A, B, C, and D).
(a) Cholesterol. **(b)** Stigmasterol, a common component of plant membranes.
(c) Testosterone, a steroid hormone involved in male development in animals.
(d) Sodium cholate, a bile salt, which aids in the digestion of lipids. **(e)** Ergosterol, a compound from fungi and yeast.

The steroid cholesterol is an important component of animal plasma membranes but is only rarely found in plants and never in prokaryotes, protists, or fungi. Cholesterol is actually a **sterol** because it has a hydroxyl group at C-3. Other steroids include the sterols of plants, fungi, and yeast (which also have a hydroxyl group at C-3); mammalian steroid hormones (such as estrogens, androgens, progestins, and adrenal corticosteroids); and bile salts. These steroids differ in the length of the side chain attached to C-17 and in the number and placement of methyl groups, double bonds, hydroxyl groups, and in some cases, keto groups.

Cholesterol often accumulates in lipid deposits (plaques) on the walls of blood vessels. These plaques have been implicated in cardiovascular disease, which can precipitate heart attacks or strokes. Many people limit their intake of animal fat because it contains cholesterol. Because plant oils usually do not contain cholesterol, many people prefer them to animal fats.

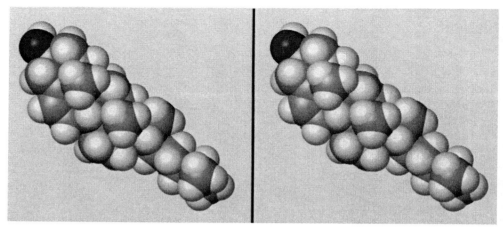

Figure 9.16 ▲
Stereo view of cholesterol. The polar hydroxyl group is on the left. Note that the fused ring system of cholesterol is nearly planar.

Figure 9.17 ▶
Cholesteryl ester.

Despite its implication in cardiovascular disease, cholesterol plays an essential role in mammalian biochemistry. Cholesterol, which is synthesized by mammalian cells, is not only a component of certain membranes but is also a precursor of steroid hormones and bile salts. The fused ring system of cholesterol, shown from the side in Figure 9.16, makes it less flexible than most other lipids. As a result, cholesterol modulates the fluidity of mammalian cell membranes, as we will see later in this chapter.

Since the hydroxyl group at C-3 is its only polar constituent, cholesterol is far more hydrophobic than glycerophospholipids and sphingolipids. In fact, free cholesterol's maximal concentration in water is only 10^{-8} M. Esterification of a fatty acid to the C-3 hydroxyl group forms a cholesteryl ester (Figure 9.17). Because the 3-acyl group of the ester is nonpolar, a cholesteryl ester is even more hydrophobic than cholesterol itself. Cholesterol is converted to cholesteryl esters for storage in cells or for transport through the bloodstream. Because they are essentially insoluble in water, cholesterol and its esters must be complexed with phospholipids and amphipathic proteins in lipoproteins for transport (Section 16.1B).

9.7 Other Biologically Important Lipids

Lipids that are not found in membranes, such as waxes, eicosanoids, and some isoprenoids, have many biological functions. **Waxes** are nonpolar esters of long-chain fatty acids and long-chain monohydroxylic alcohols. For example, myricyl palmitate, a major component of beeswax, is the ester of palmitate (16:0) and the 30-carbon myricyl alcohol (Figure 9.18). The hydrophobicity of myricyl palmitate makes beeswax very water-insoluble, and its high melting point (due to the long, saturated hydrocarbon chains) makes beeswax hard and solid at typical outdoor temperatures. Waxes are widely distributed in nature. They provide protective waterproof coatings on the leaves and fruits of certain plants and on animal skin, fur, feathers, and exoskeletons.

$$H_3C - (CH_2)_{14} - \overset{\overset{\displaystyle O}{\|}}{C} - O - (CH_2)_{29} - CH_3$$

Figure 9.18 ▲
Myricyl palmitate, a wax.

Chemistry for Biologists

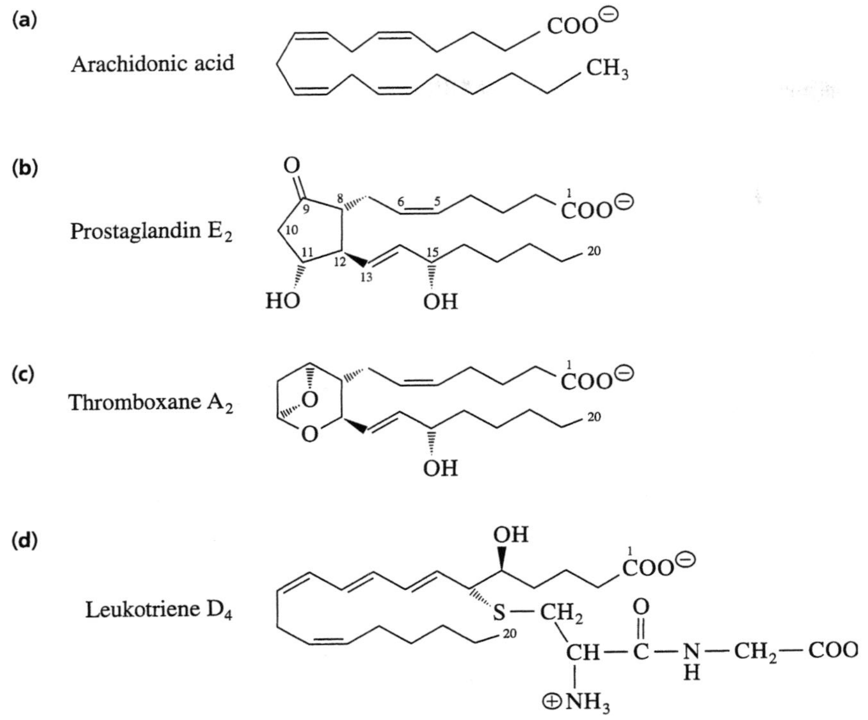

(a)

Arachidonic acid

(b)

Prostaglandin E₂

(c)

Thromboxane A₂

(d)

Leukotriene D₄

◄ **Figure 9.19**
Structures of arachidonic acid (a) and three eicosanoids derived from it. Arachidonate is a C_{20} polyunsaturated fatty acid with four *cis* double bonds.

Eicosanoids are oxygenated derivatives of C_{20} polyunsaturated fatty acids such as arachidonic acid; **prostaglandins** are eicosanoids that have a cyclopentane ring. Some examples of eicosanoids are shown in Figure 9.19. Eicosanoids participate in a variety of physiological processes and can also mediate many potentially pathological responses. For example, prostaglandin E_2 can cause constriction of blood vessels, and thromboxane A_2 is involved in the formation of blood clots, which in some cases can block the flow of blood to the heart or brain. Leukotriene D_4, a mediator of smooth-muscle contraction, also provokes the bronchial constriction seen in asthmatics. Aspirin (acetylsalicylic acid) alleviates pain, fever, swelling, and inflammation by inhibiting the synthesis of prostaglandins.

Lipid vitamins (A, D, E, and K) are isoprenoids that contain long hydrocarbon chains or fused rings (Section 7.12). The terpene limonene (Figure 9.20a) is a cyclic

Figure 9.20 ►
Some isoprenoids.

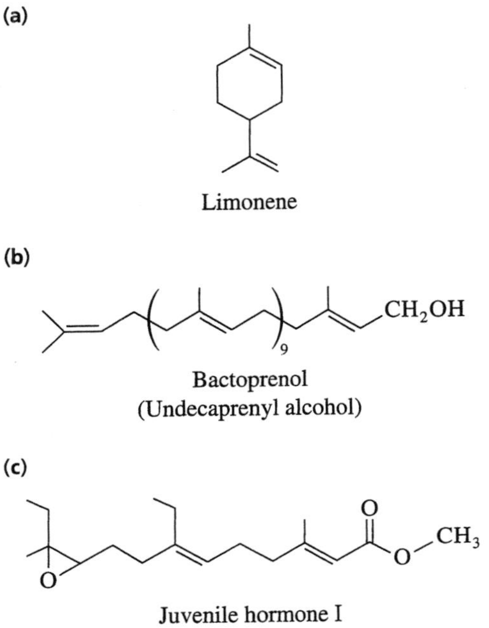

(a)

Limonene

(b)

Bactoprenol
(Undecaprenyl alcohol)

(c)

Juvenile hormone I

Chemistry for Biologists

BOX 9.2 Special Nonaqueous Techniques Must Be Used to Study Lipids

The study of lipids in the laboratory is rather unusual because it involves the use of organic solvents. Unlike the water-soluble or hydrophilic components of tissues or cells—such as carbohydrates and most proteins—lipids generally have very low solubility in water. In order to analyze the lipid components of organelles, cells, or tissues, the sample must be homogenized or dispersed in an organic solvent solution such as methanol in chloroform. The methanol precipitates proteins, whereas the chloroform effectively dissolves the lipids of membranes. The resulting lipid solution can be manipulated further to separate the major lipid classes and then to resolve the various components within each class. Plastic vessels must be avoided since many plastics can also dissolve in chloroform. Several new "lipids" have been "discovered" after placing chloroform extracts in plastic tubes. A schematic view of lipid purification is shown in the figure below and is described in the following paragraphs.

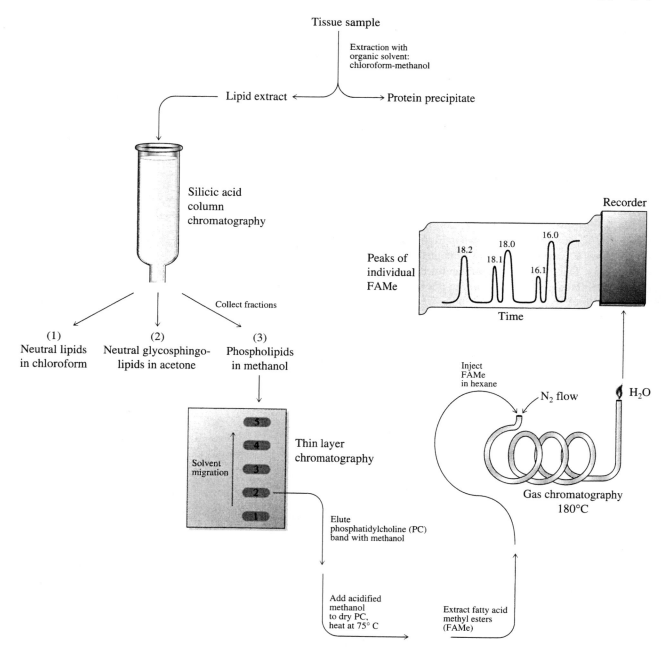

▲ Flowchart of lipid extraction and purification. Silicic acid column chromatography, thin-layer chromatography, and gas chromatography are used to separate and analyze lipid classes and component fatty acids.

Silicic acid, a chromatographic medium that resembles fine, white beach sand, is useful for lipid purification. For example, a lipid extract prepared from red blood cells can be layered on the top of a silicic acid column equilibrated with chloroform. By running chloroform through the column, neutral lipids such as cholesterol, triacylglycerols, and diacylglycerols can be eluted from the column, leaving the more polar lipids bound to the silicic acid. Changing the solvent to acetone allows the elution of neutral glycosphingolipids, and the application of methanol elutes the phospholipids.

Finer resolution of the compounds within each of these groups can be accomplished by thin-layer chromatography. A very thin layer (0.2 to 0.5 mm) of silicic acid is placed on a glass plate, and the lipid mixture (e.g., the phospholipid) is spotted on the thin layer near the bottom of the plate. The plate is then placed upright in a covered, shallow tank containing a small volume of a solution of chloroform, methanol, water, and acetic acid. The solvent slowly migrates up the plate, resolving the less polar lipid components (which move more quickly with the solvent) from the slower, more polar compounds. In this way, bands of phospholipid such as sphingomyelin, phosphatidylcholine, phosphatidylserine, phosphatidylinositol, phosphatidylethanolamine, and others are separated. The bands can be located by exposing the plate to iodine vapor or by spraying it with a fluorescent dye that permits visualization of the lipid bands under ultraviolet light. Each band can be scraped off the plate and the phospholipid eluted from the silicic acid with solvent. A convenient way to quantitate phospholipids is by acid hydrolysis and measurement of the released inorganic phosphate by a simple color assay.

Luckily for lipid chemists, many fats and their derivatives are volatile at high temperatures. Component fatty acids of phospholipids that have been separated by thin-layer chromatography can be analyzed by a technique known as gas chromatography. The phospholipids are treated with acidified methanol to produce fatty acid methyl esters; the mixture of fatty acid methyl esters is injected onto the top of a long, heated column containing a solid adsorptive medium. The methyl esters are carried by the flow of nitrogen gas through the column. The longer, more highly unsaturated fatty acids are separated from the faster-moving, shorter, more saturated chains. Since lipids burn at high temperatures, the methyl esters can be detected by a hydrogen flame positioned at the end of the column that burns each methyl ester as it emerges. This combustion is detected electronically and the signal inscribed by a recorder, permitting identification and quantitation of each peak.

The fatty acid profile in the figure indicates the diversity of molecular species within a phospholipid class. The individual species of phosphatidylcholine can also be resolved by treating the phospholipid with phospholipase C to produce the various diacylglycerol components. These diacylglycerols can be separated on the basis of chain length and degree of unsaturation of their fatty acids by high-pressure liquid chromatography (HPLC). In HPLC, the mixture of diacylglycerols is resolved by the flow of solvents under pressure through a column. It is common to see 20 to 30 different species in one phospholipid sample.

lipid chiefly responsible for the distinctive smell of lemons. Other isoprenoids are bactoprenol (undecaprenyl alcohol) (Figure 9.20b), which participates in the synthesis of cell walls in bacteria, and juvenile hormone I (Figure 9.20c), which regulates larval development in insects.

9.8 Biological Membranes Are Composed of Lipid Bilayers and Proteins

Biological membranes define the external boundaries of cells as well as separate compartments within cells. They are therefore essential components of all living cells. However, biological membranes are not merely passive barriers; they have a wide variety of complex functions. Some proteins contained in membranes serve as selective pumps that strictly control the transport of ions and small molecules into and out of the cell and also generate the proton concentration gradients essential for the production of ATP by oxidative phosphorylation. Receptors in membranes recognize extracellular signals and communicate them to the cell interior.

Many cells have membranes—both external and internal—with specialized structures. For example, many bacteria have double membranes: an outer membrane and an inner plasma membrane. The liquid in the periplasmic space between these two membranes contains proteins that carry specific solutes to transport proteins in the inner membrane. The solutes then pass through the inner membrane by an

ATP-dependent process. A mitochondrion's smooth outer membrane has proteins that form aqueous channels; its convoluted inner membrane is selectively permeable and has many membrane-bound enzymes. The nucleus also has a double membrane; nuclear contents interact with the cytosol by nuclear pores. The single membrane of the endoplasmic reticulum is highly convoluted. Its extensive network in eukaryotic cells is involved in the synthesis of transmembrane and secreted proteins and of lipids for many membranes.

A biological membrane consists of proteins embedded in or associated with a lipid bilayer. In this section, we explore the structure of biological membranes. In the remaining sections of this chapter, we discuss the properties and functions of biological membranes.

A. Lipid Bilayers

In Section 2.4, we saw that detergents in aqueous solutions can spontaneously form either monolayers or micelles. Like detergents, glycerophospholipids and glycosphingolipids, which are amphipathic, can form monolayers under some conditions. In cells, these lipids do not pack well into micelles but rather tend to form bilayers. **Lipid bilayers** are the structural basis for all biological membranes, including plasma membranes and the internal membranes of eukaryotic cells. The noncovalent interactions among lipid molecules in bilayers make membranes flexible and allow them to self-seal. Triacylglycerols, which are very hydrophobic rather than amphipathic, cannot form bilayers, and cholesterol, although slightly amphipathic, does not form bilayers by itself.

A lipid bilayer is typically about 5 to 6 nm thick and consists of two leaflets, or layers. In each leaflet, the polar head groups of amphipathic lipids are in contact with the aqueous medium, and the nonpolar hydrocarbon tails point toward the interior of the bilayer (Figure 9.21). The spontaneous formation of lipid bilayers is driven by the hydrophobic effect (Section 2.5D). When lipid molecules associate, the entropy of the solvent molecules increases.

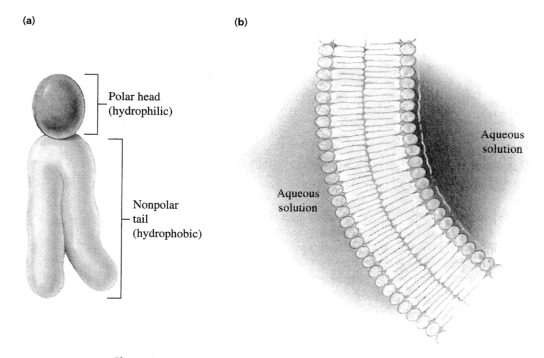

(a)

Polar head (hydrophilic)

Nonpolar tail (hydrophobic)

(b)

Aqueous solution

Aqueous solution

Figure 9.21 ▲
Membrane lipid and bilayer. **(a)** An amphipathic membrane lipid. **(b)** Cross-section of a lipid bilayer. The hydrophilic head groups (blue) of each leaflet face the aqueous medium, and the hydrophobic tails (yellow) pack together in the interior of the bilayer.

B. Fluid Mosaic Model of Biological Membranes

A typical biological membrane contains about 25% to 50% lipid and 50% to 75% protein by mass, with less than 10% carbohydrate as a component of glycolipids and glycoproteins. The lipids are a complex mixture of phospholipids, glycosphingolipids (in animals), and cholesterol (in some eukaryotes). Cholesterol and some other lipids that do not form bilayers by themselves (about 30% of the total) are stabilized in a bilayer arrangement by the other 70% of lipids in the membrane. The compositions of biological membranes vary considerably among species and even among different cell types in multicellular organisms. For example, the myelin membrane, which insulates nerve fibers, contains relatively little protein. In contrast, the inner mitochondrial membrane is rich in proteins, reflecting its high level of metabolic activity. The plasma membrane of red blood cells is also exceptionally rich in proteins.

In addition to having a characteristic lipid-to-protein ratio, each biological membrane has a characteristic lipid composition. Membranes in brain tissue, for example, have a relatively high content of phosphatidylserines, whereas membranes in heart and lung have high levels of phosphatidylglycerol and sphingomyelins, respectively. Phosphatidylethanolamines constitute nearly 70% of the inner membrane lipids of *E. coli* cells. The outer membranes of gram-negative bacteria contain lipopolysaccharides.

In addition to being distributed differentially throughout different tissues, phospholipids are also distributed asymmetrically between the inner and outer leaflets of a single biological membrane. For example, sphingomyelins and phosphatidylcholines each account for half of the phospholipid molecules in the outer leaflet of the plasma membranes of human erythrocytes, but together they represent less than one-fifth of the phospholipids in the inner leaflet of the same membrane.

A biological membrane is thicker than a lipid bilayer—typically 6 to 10 nm thick. The **fluid mosaic model** proposed in 1972 by S. Jonathan Singer and Garth L. Nicolson is still generally valid for describing the arrangement of lipid and protein within a membrane. According to the fluid mosaic model, the membrane is a dynamic structure in which both proteins and lipids can rapidly and randomly diffuse laterally or rotate within the bilayer. Membrane proteins are visualized as icebergs floating in a highly fluid lipid-bilayer sea (Figure 9.22). (Actually, some proteins are immobile, and some lipids have restricted movement.)

Figure 9.22 ▼
Structure of a typical eukaryotic plasma membrane. A lipid bilayer forms the basic matrix of biological membranes, and proteins (some of which are glycoproteins) are associated with it in various ways (Section 9.10). The oligosaccharides of glycoproteins and glycolipids face the extracellular space.

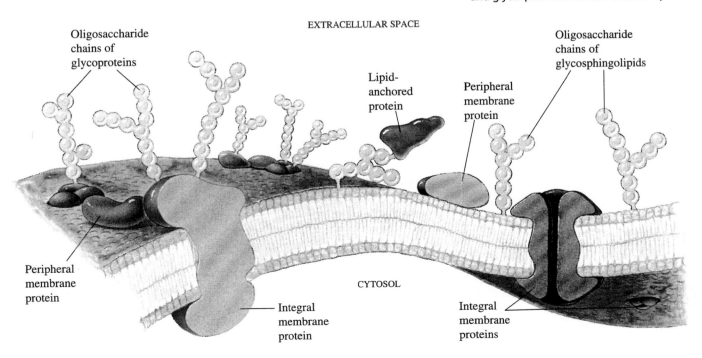

EXTRACELLULAR SPACE

Oligosaccharide chains of glycoproteins

Lipid-anchored protein

Peripheral membrane protein

Oligosaccharide chains of glycosphingolipids

Peripheral membrane protein

CYTOSOL

Integral membrane protein

Integral membrane proteins

Chemistry for Biologists

Figure 9.23 ▶
Diffusion of lipids within a bilayer.
(a) Lateral diffusion of lipids is relatively
rapid. **(b)** Transverse diffusion, or flip-flop, of
lipids is very slow.

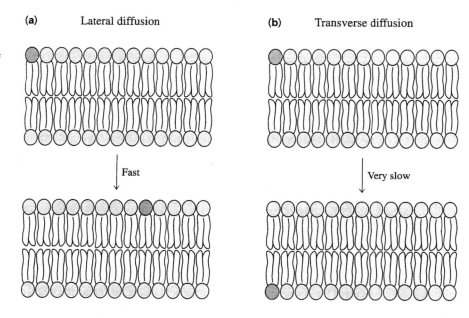

(a) Lateral diffusion

Fast

(b) Transverse diffusion

Very slow

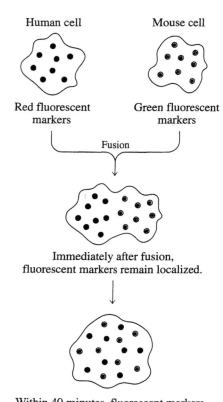

Human cell

Mouse cell

Red fluorescent markers

Green fluorescent markers

Fusion

Immediately after fusion, fluorescent markers remain localized.

Within 40 minutes, fluorescent markers appear to be randomly distributed over the entire surface.

Figure 9.24 ▲
Diffusion of membrane proteins. Human
cells whose membrane proteins had been
labeled with a red fluorescent marker were
fused with mouse cells whose membrane
proteins had been labeled with a green fluorescent marker. The initially localized markers became dispersed over the entire surface
of the fused cell within 40 minutes.

9.9 Lipid Bilayers and Membranes Are Dynamic Structures

The lipids in a bilayer are in constant motion, giving lipid bilayers many of the properties of fluids. Lipids undergo several types of molecular motion within bilayers.
Lateral diffusion, the movement of lipids within the plane of one leaflet, is very
rapid. For example, a phospholipid molecule can diffuse from one end of a bacterial cell to the other (a distance of about 2 μm) in about 1 second at 37°C. A lipid bilayer can therefore be regarded as a two-dimensional solution.

In contrast, **transverse diffusion** (or flip-flop), which is the passage of lipids
from one leaflet of the bilayer to the other, occurs very slowly. The polar head of a
phospholipid molecule is highly solvated and must shed its solvation sphere and
penetrate the hydrocarbon interior of the bilayer in order to move from one leaflet
to the other. The energy barrier associated with this movement is so high that transverse diffusion of phospholipids in a bilayer occurs at about one-billionth the rate
of lateral diffusion (Figure 9.23).

The very slow rate of transverse diffusion of membrane lipids allows the inner
and outer leaflets of biological membranes to have different lipid compositions.
Eukaryotic cells make their membrane lipids in an asymmetric arrangement in
the endoplasmic reticulum or the Golgi apparatus. They flow from these organelles—retaining the asymmetry—to other membranes. In mammals, lipid
asymmetry is generated and maintained by the activity of membrane-bound proteins that use the energy of ATP to move specific phospholipids from one leaflet
to the other. These proteins, called flippases or translocases, are present in many
cell types.

In 1970, L. D. Frye and Michael A. Edidin devised an elegant experiment to test
whether membrane proteins diffuse within the lipid bilayer. Frye and Edidin fused
mouse cells with human cells to form heterokaryons (hybrid cells). By using red
fluorescence-labeled antibodies that specifically bind to certain proteins in human
plasma membranes and green fluorescence-labeled antibodies that specifically bind
to certain proteins in mouse plasma membranes, they observed the changes in the distribution of membrane proteins over time by immunofluorescence microscopy. The
labeled proteins were intermixed within 40 minutes after cell fusion (Figure 9.24).
This experiment demonstrated that at least some membrane proteins diffuse freely
within biological membranes.

(a)

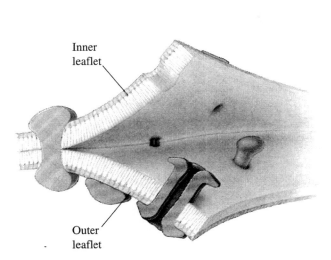

Inner leaflet

Outer leaflet

(b)

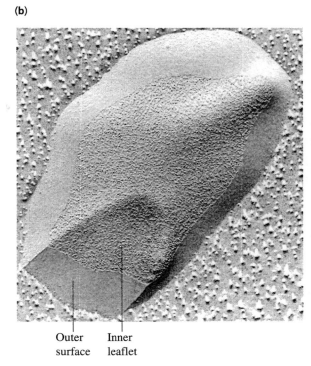

Outer   Inner
surface   leaflet

Figure 9.25 ▲
Freeze fracturing a biological membrane. **(a)** Splitting the lipid bilayer along the interface of the two leaflets. A platinum replica of the exposed internal surface is examined in an electron microscope. Membrane proteins appear as protrusions or cavities in the replica. **(b)** Electron micrograph of a freeze-fractured erythrocyte membrane. The bumps on the inner membrane surface show the locations of membrane proteins.

A few membrane proteins move laterally very rapidly. However, the majority of membrane proteins diffuse about 100 to 500 times more slowly than membrane lipids. The diffusion of some proteins is severely restricted by aggregation or by attachment to the cytoskeleton just beneath the membrane surface. Relatively immobile membrane proteins may act as fences or cages, restricting the movement of other proteins. The limited diffusion of membrane proteins produces protein patches, or domains, areas of membrane whose composition differs from that of the surrounding membrane.

The distribution of membrane proteins can be visualized by **freeze-fracture electron microscopy**. In this technique, a membrane sample is rapidly frozen to the temperature of liquid nitrogen and then fractured with a knife. The membrane splits between the leaflets of the lipid bilayer, where the intermolecular interactions are weakest (Figure 9.25a). Ice is evaporated in a vacuum, and the exposed internal surface of the membrane is then coated with a thin film of platinum to make a metal replica for examination in an electron microscope. The leaflets of membranes that are rich in membrane proteins contain pits and bumps indicating the presence of proteins. In contrast, the leaflets of bilayers that contain no proteins are smooth. Figure 9.25b shows the bumpy surface of the inner leaflet of a red blood cell membrane exposed by removal of the outer leaflet.

The fluid properties of bilayers depend on the flexibility of their fatty acyl chains. Saturated acyl chains are fully extended at low temperatures, forming a crystalline array with maximal van der Waals contact between the chains. When the lipid bilayer is heated, a phase transition analogous to the melting of a crystalline solid occurs. The acyl chains of lipids in the resulting liquid crystalline phase are relatively disordered and loosely packed. During the phase transition, the thickness of the bilayer decreases by about 15% as the hydrocarbon tails become less extended because of rotation around C—C bonds (Figure 9.26). Bilayers composed of a single

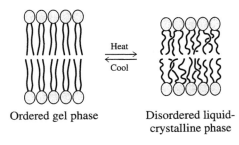

Heat

Cool

Ordered gel phase

Disordered liquid-crystalline phase

Figure 9.26 ▲
Phase transition of a lipid bilayer. In the ordered gel state, the hydrocarbon chains are extended. Above the phase-transition temperature, rotation around C—C bonds disorders the chains in the liquid crystalline phase.

type of lipid undergo phase transition at a distinct temperature called the phase-transition temperature. When the lipids contain unsaturated acyl chains, the hydrophobic core of the bilayer is fluid well below room temperature (23°C). Biological membranes, which contain a heterogeneous mixture of lipids, change gradually from the gel to the liquid crystalline phase, typically over a temperature range of 10° to 40°C. Phase transitions in biological membranes can be localized, so fluid- and gel-phase regions can coexist at certain temperatures.

The structure of a phospholipid has dramatic effects on its fluidity and phase-transition temperature. As we saw in Section 9.2, the hydrocarbon chain of a fatty acid with a *cis* double bond has a kink, which disrupts packing and increases fluidity. Incorporating an unsaturated fatty acyl group into a phospholipid lowers the phase-transition temperature. Changes in membrane fluidity affect the membrane transport and catalytic functions of membrane proteins, so many organisms maintain membrane fluidity under different conditions by adjusting the ratio of unsaturated to saturated fatty acyl groups in membrane lipids. For example, when bacteria are grown at low temperatures, the proportion of unsaturated fatty acyl groups in membranes increases. Goldfish adapt to a lower temperature of the water in which they swim. As the environmental temperature drops, there is a rise in unsaturated fatty acids in goldfish intestinal membranes and whole brain. The lower melting point and greater fluidity of unsaturated fatty acyl groups preserve membrane fluidity, allowing membrane processes to continue at colder temperatures.

In mammals that live in arctic conditions, in severe cold, triacylglycerols in the foot pads and extremities of limbs have much lower freezing points (more unsaturated fatty acyl groups) than those in the body core. Along their limbs, there is a gradient in the nature of the fat, with higher melting points seen closer to the trunk of the animal. This effect provides the necessary flexibility in foot pads and limbs. Possibly membrane phospholipids in these feet and limbs are also highly unsaturated to maintain their fluidity and function.

Cholesterol accounts for 20% to 25% of the mass of lipids in a typical mammalian plasma membrane and significantly affects membrane fluidity. By having two opposite effects, cholesterol broadens the phase-transition temperature range of a lipid bilayer (Figure 9.27). When the rigid cholesterol molecules intercalate between the hydrocarbon chains of the membrane lipids, the mobility of fatty acyl chains in the membrane is restricted and fluidity decreases at high temperatures. Cholesterol disrupts the ordered packing of the extended fatty acyl chains and thereby increases fluidity at low temperatures. Cholesterol in animal cell membranes thus helps maintain fairly constant fluidity despite fluctuations in temperature or degree of fatty acid saturation.

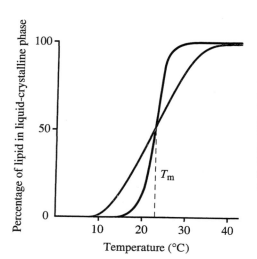

◀ **Figure 9.27**
Effect of bilayer composition on phase transition. A pure phospholipid bilayer (red) undergoes a sharp transition from the gel phase to the liquid crystalline phase at the phase-transition temperature (T_m). A bilayer containing 80% phospholipids and 20% cholesterol (blue) undergoes a phase transition over a broad temperature range.

Cholesterol also contibutes to the formation of protein-lipid rafts that occur in the external leaflets of cell membranes of some cells. At the Golgi apparatus, cholesterol-sphingolipid complexes bind specific proteins to form these rafts, which transport the proteins to various cell surfaces. This is one method by which newly synthesized proteins are sorted for proper distribution.

9.10 Three Classes of Membrane Proteins

Particular cellular and intracellular membranes are characterized by specialized membrane-bound proteins. These proteins are divided into three classes based on their mode of association with the lipid bilayer: integral membrane proteins, peripheral membrane proteins, and lipid-anchored membrane proteins (Figure 9.22).

Integral membrane proteins, also referred to as intrinsic proteins or transmembrane proteins, contain hydrophobic regions embedded in the hydrophobic core of the lipid bilayer. Integral membrane proteins usually span the bilayer completely, although at least one protein, cytochrome b_5, appears to be anchored in the membrane by a hydrophobic protein tail that may not traverse the entire bilayer. Some integral membrane proteins are anchored by only a single membrane-spanning segment; others possess several transmembrane segments connected by loops at the membrane surface. The membrane-spanning segment is often an α helix containing approximately 20 amino acid residues. Other transmembrane segments are β sheets.

Isolation of integral membrane proteins is often accomplished using a mild detergent, which solubilizes (Section 2.4) the protein by replacing most of the membrane lipids. To prevent their denaturation, once isolated, integral membrane proteins usually must be kept in the presence of the detergent.

One of the best-characterized integral membrane proteins is bacteriorhodopsin (Figure 9.28). This protein, found in the cytoplasmic membrane of the halophilic (salt-loving) bacterium *Halobacterium halobium*, helps harness light energy used in the phosphorylation of ADP to produce ATP. In bacteriorhodopsin, seven α-helical segments, each about 25 residues long, span the membrane. Nearly all the amino

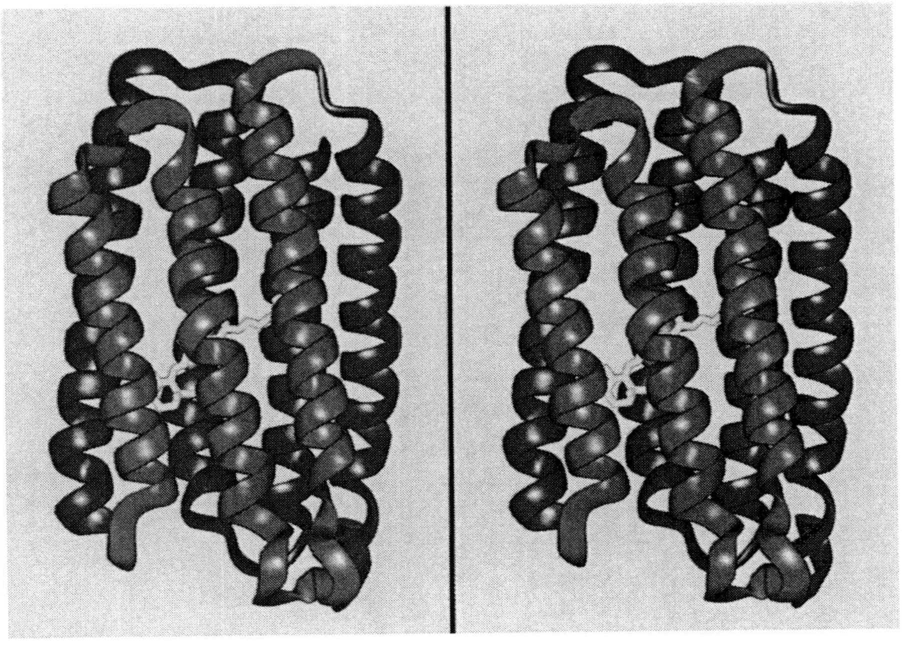

We consider the functions of some of these membrane proteins later in this chapter. We will also encounter membrane proteins in other chapters, including those on oxidative phosphorylation (Chapter 14), photosynthesis (Chapter 15), and protein synthesis (Chapter 22).

Figure 9.28 ▲
Stereo view of bacteriorhodopsin. Seven membrane-spanning α helices, connected by loops, form a bundle that spans the bilayer. The light-harvesting prosthetic group is shown in yellow.

acids in the transmembrane segments of bacteriorhodopsin are hydrophobic. Bacteriorhodopsin is one of several integral membrane proteins whose structure is known in detail. In the absence of data on three-dimensional structure, the presence of transmembrane helical regions in proteins can often be predicted by searching amino acid sequences for regions that are hydrophobic (i.e., that have high hydropathy values) (Section 3.2G).

Unlike integral membrane proteins, **peripheral membrane proteins** are associated with one face of the membrane through charge-charge interactions and hydrogen bonding with integral membrane proteins or with the polar head groups of membrane lipids. Because they are neither covalently attached to the lipid bilayer nor embedded within the lipid matrix, peripheral membrane proteins are more readily dissociated from membranes by procedures that do not require breaking covalent bonds or disrupting the membrane itself. A change in pH or ionic strength is often sufficient to remove these proteins from the membrane.

Lipid-anchored membrane proteins are tethered to a membrane through a covalent bond to a lipid anchor. In the simplest lipid-anchored membrane proteins, an amino acid side chain is linked by an amide or ester bond to a fatty acyl group, often from myristate or palmitate. The fatty acid is inserted into the cytoplasmic leaflet of the bilayer, anchoring the protein to the membrane (Figure 9.29a). Proteins of this type are found in viruses and eukaryotic cells.

Figure 9.29 ▶
Lipid-anchored membrane proteins attached to the plasma membrane. The three types of anchors can be found in the same membrane, but they do not form a complex as shown here. **(a)** A fatty acyl–anchored protein. **(b)** A prenyl-anchored membrane protein. Note that fatty acyl– and prenyl-anchored membrane proteins can also occur on the cytoplasmic (outer) leaflet of intracellular membranes. **(c)** Protein anchored by glycosylphosphatidylinositol. Shown here is the variant surface glycoprotein of the parasitic protozoan *Trypanosoma brucei*. The protein is covalently bound to a phosphoethanolamine residue, which in turn is bound to a glycan. The glycan (blue) includes a mannose residue, to which the phosphoethanolamine residue is attached, and a glucosamine residue, which is attached to the phosphoinositol group (red) of phosphatidylinositol. Abbreviations: GlcN, glucosamine; Ins, inositol; Man, mannose.

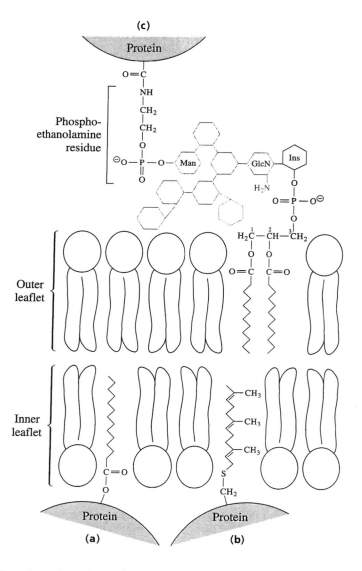

Other lipid-anchored membrane proteins are covalently linked to an iso-prenoid chain (either 15- or 20-carbon) through the sulfur atom of a cysteine residue at or near the C-terminus of the protein (Figure 9.29b). These **prenylated proteins** are found on the cytoplasmic face of both plasma membranes and intracellular membranes.

Many eukaryotic lipid-anchored proteins are linked to a molecule of glycosylphosphatidylinositol (Figure 9.29c). The membrane anchor is the 1,2-diacylglycerol portion of the glycosylphosphatidylinositol. A glycan of varied composition is attached to the inositol by a glucosamine residue, a mannose residue links the glycan to a phosphoethanolamine residue, and the C-terminal α-carboxyl group of the protein is linked to the ethanolamine by an amide bond. Over 100 different proteins are known to be associated with membranes by a glycosylphosphatidylinositol anchor. These proteins, which have a variety of functions, are present only in the outer leaflet of the plasma membrane. They are found in the cholesterol-sphingolipid rafts described in Section 9.9.

All three types of lipid anchors are covalently linked to amino acid residues posttranslationally, that is, after the protein has been synthesized. Like integral membrane proteins, most lipid-anchored proteins are permanently associated with the membrane, although the proteins themselves do not interact with the membrane. Once released by treatment with phospholipases, the proteins behave like soluble proteins.

> Some prenyl-decorated proteins will be encountered in the discussion of signal transduction (Section 9.12).

9.11 Membrane Transport

Plasma membranes physically separate a living cell from its environment. In addition, within eukaryotic cells, membranes surround various compartments, such as the nucleus and mitochondria. Membranes are selectively permeable barriers that restrict the free passage of most molecules. Nevertheless, water, oxygen, and other small molecules must be able to enter all cells and move freely between compartments inside eukaryotic cells. Larger molecules, such as proteins and nucleic acids, also have to be transported across membranes, including the membranes between compartments. Hydrophobic molecules and small uncharged molecules can freely diffuse through biological membranes, but the hydrophobic core of the bilayer presents an almost impenetrable barrier to most polar or charged species. Living cells move polar and ionic substances across membranes using transport proteins (sometimes called carriers, permeases, or translocators), and they transport macromolecules by endocytosis or exocytosis.

Nonpolar gases, such as O_2 and CO_2, and hydrophobic molecules, such as steroid hormones, lipid vitamins, and some drugs, enter and leave the cell by diffusing through the membrane, moving from the side with the higher concentration to the side with the lower concentration. The rate of movement depends on the difference in concentrations, or the concentration gradient, between the two sides. Diffusion down a concentration gradient (i.e., downhill diffusion) is a spontaneous process driven by an increase in entropy and therefore a decrease in free energy.

The traffic of polar molecules and ions across membranes is mediated by three types of integral membrane proteins: channels and pores, passive transporters, and active transporters. These transport systems differ in their kinetic properties and energy requirements. For example, the rate of solute movement through pores and channels may increase with increasing solute concentration, but the rate of movement through passive and active transporters may approach a maximum as the solute concentration increases (i.e., the transport protein becomes saturated). In addition, some types of transport require a source of energy. The characteristics of membrane transport are summarized in Table 9.3. In this section, we describe the different membrane transport systems, as well as endocytosis and exocytosis.

TABLE 9.3	Characteristics of different types of membrane transport			
	Protein carrier	**Saturable with substrate**	**Movement relative to concentration gradient**	**Energy input required**
Simple diffusion	No	No	Down	No
Channels and pores	Yes	No	Down	No
Passive transport	Yes	Yes	Down	No
Active transport				
Primary	Yes	Yes	Up	Yes (direct source)
Secondary	Yes	Yes	Up	Yes (ion gradient)

A. Pores and Channels

Pores and **channels** are transmembrane proteins with a central passage for ions and small molecules. (Usually, the term *pore* is used for bacteria, and *channel* for animals.) Solutes of the appropriate size, charge, and molecular structure can move rapidly through the passage in either direction by diffusing down a concentration gradient (Figure 9.30). This process requires no energy. In general, the rate of movement of solute through a pore or channel is not saturable at high concentrations. For some channels, the rate may approach the diffusion-controlled limit.

The outer membranes of some bacteria are rich in porins, a family of pore proteins that allow ions and many small molecules to gain access to specific transporters in the plasma membrane. Similar channels are found in the outer membranes of mitochondria. Porins are only weakly solute-selective; they act as sieves that are permanently open. In contrast, plasma membranes of animal cells contain many channel proteins that are highly specific for certain ions. Some of these channels are always open, and others open or close only in response to a specific signal.

For many years, biochemists thought that water moved through membranes by diffusion, despite the fact that tissues vary in their permeability to water. A few years ago, a membrane-bound protein called aquaporin-1 was isolated from human kidney tubules, from the region of the kidney responsible for the reabsorption of water. Aquaporin-1 is a pore that is selective for water whose passage is driven by osmotic pressure. More recent research has found that there are at least 10 mammalian

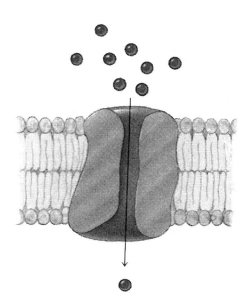

◀ **Figure 9.30**
Membrane transport through a pore or channel. A central passage allows molecules and ions of the appropriate size, charge, and geometry to traverse the membrane in either direction.

aquaporins and that they are involved in such functions as exit of excess water from the brain and generation of saliva and tears.

Membranes of nerve issues have gated (i.e., controlled) potassium channels that selectively allow rapid outward transport of potassium ions. These channels permit $K^{\oplus}$ ions to pass through the membrane at least 10 000 times faster than the smaller $Na^{\oplus}$ ions. Crystallographic studies have shown that the potassium channel has a wide mouth (like an inverted teepee) containing positively charged amino acids to attract cations and repel anions. Hydrated cations are directed electrostatically to an electrically neutral constriction of the pore called the selectivity filter. Potassium ions rapidly lose some of their water of hydration and pass through the selectivity filter. Sodium ions apparently retain more water of hydration and therefore transit the filter much more slowly. The remainder of the channel has a hydrophobic lining. Based on comparisons of amino acid sequences, the general structural properties of the potassium channel seem to also apply to other types of channels and pores.

B. Passive Transport

Passive and active transport proteins specifically bind solutes and transport them across the membrane. In passive transport, the solute moves down its concentration gradient, and in active transport, the solute moves against the gradient, a process that requires energy. The simplest membrane transporters—whether active or passive—carry out **uniport**; that is, they carry only a single type of solute across the membrane (Figure 9.31a). Many transporters carry out cotransport of two solutes, either in the same direction, **symport** (Figure 9.31b), or in opposite directions, **antiport** (Figure 9.31c).

Passive transport, also called facilitated diffusion, does not require an energy source. The transport protein accelerates the movement of solute down its concentration gradient, a process that would occur very slowly by diffusion alone. For a simple passive uniport system, the initial rate of inward transport, like the initial rate of an enzyme-catalyzed reaction, depends on the external concentration of substrate. The equation describing this dependence is analogous to the Michaelis-Menten equation for enzyme catalysis (Equation 5.14).

$$v_0 = \frac{V_{max}[S]_{out}}{K_{tr} + [S]_{out}}$$

where v_0 is the initial rate of inward transport of the substrate at an external concentration $[S]_{out}$, V_{max} is the maximum rate of transport of the substrate, and K_{tr} is a constant analogous to the Michaelis constant (K_m) (i.e., K_{tr} is the substrate concentration at which the transporter is half-saturated). The lower the value of K_{tr}, the higher the affinity of the transporter for the substrate. The rate of transport is saturable, approaching a maximum value at a high substrate concentration (Figure 9.32).

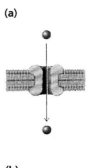

(a)

(b)

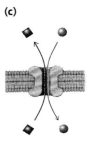

(c)

Figure 9.31 ▲
Types of passive and active transport. Although the transport proteins are depicted as having an open central pore, passive and active transporters actually undergo conformational changes when transporting their solutes (Figure 9.33). **(a)** Uniport. **(b)** Symport. **(c)** Antiport.

Figure 9.32 ▶
Kinetics of passive transport. The initial rate of transport increases with substrate concentration until a maximum is reached. K_{tr} is the concentration of substrate at which the rate of transport is half-maximal.

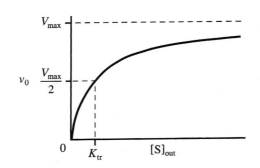

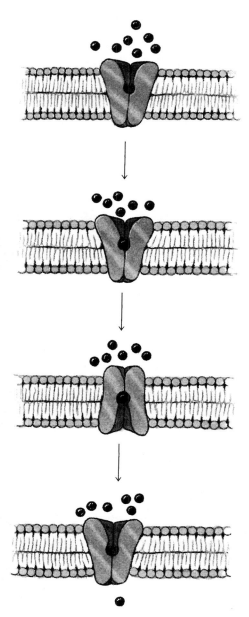

Figure 9.33 ▲
Passive and active transport protein function. The protein binds its specific substrate and then undergoes a conformational change allowing the molecule or ion to be released on the other side of the membrane. Cotransporters have specific binding sites for each transported species.

As substrate accumulates inside the cell, the rate of outward transport increases until it equals the rate of inward transport, and $[S]_{in}$ equals $[S]_{out}$. At this point, there is no net change in the concentration of substrate on either side of the membrane, although substrate continues to move across the membrane in both directions.

Passive and active transporters function somewhat like enzymes, but instead of catalyzing a chemical change in the substrate, they move it from one side of the membrane to the other. Models of transport protein operation suggest that a transporter undergoes a conformational change after it binds its substrate. This conformational change allows the substrate to be released on the other side of the membrane; the transporter then reverts to its original state (Figure 9.33). The conformational change in the transporter is often triggered by binding of the transported species, as in the induced fit of certain enzymes to their substrates (Section 6.9). In active transport, the conformational change can be driven by ATP or other sources of energy. Like enzymes, transport proteins can be susceptible to reversible and irreversible inhibition.

C. Active Transport

Active transport resembles passive transport in overall mechanism and kinetic properties. However, active transport requires energy to move a solute up its concentration gradient. In some cases, active transport of charged molecules or ions also results in a charge gradient across the membrane.

Active transporters use a variety of energy sources, most commonly ATP. Ion-transporting ATPases are found in all organisms. These active transporters, which include $Na^{\oplus}$-$K^{\oplus}$ ATPase and $Ca^{2\oplus}$ ATPase, create and maintain ion concentration gradients across the plasma membrane and across the membranes of internal organelles.

Primary active transport is powered by a direct source of energy such as ATP, light, or electron transport (Chapter 14). For example, bacteriorhodopsin (Figure 9.28) uses light energy to generate a transmembrane proton concentration gradient, which can be used for ATP formation. One primary active transport protein, P-glycoprotein, appears to play a major role in the resistance of tumor cells to multiple chemotherapeutic drugs. Multidrug resistance is a leading cause of failure in the clinical treatment of human cancers. P-Glycoprotein is an integral membrane glycoprotein (M_r 170 000) that is abundant in the plasma membrane of drug-resistant cells. Using ATP as an energy source, P-glycoprotein pumps a large variety of structurally unrelated nonpolar compounds, such as drugs, out of the cell up a concentration gradient. In this way, the cytosolic drug concentration is maintained at a level low enough to avoid cell death. The normal physiological function of P-glycoprotein appears to be removal of toxic hydrophobic compounds in the diet.

Secondary active transport is driven by an ion concentration gradient. The active uphill transport of one solute is coupled to the downhill transport of a second solute that was concentrated by primary active transport. For example, in *E. coli*, electron flow through a series of membrane-bound oxidation-reduction enzymes generates a higher extracellular concentration of protons. As protons flow back into the cell down their concentration gradient, lactose is also transported in, against its concentration gradient (Figure 9.34). The energy of the proton concentration gradient drives the secondary active transport of lactose. The symport of $H^{\oplus}$ and lactose is mediated by the transmembrane protein lactose permease.

In large multicellular animals, secondary active transport is often powered by a sodium ion gradient. Most cells maintain an intracellular potassium ion concentration of about 140 mM in the presence of an extracellular concentration of about 5 mM. The cytosolic concentration of sodium ions is maintained at about 5 to 15 mM in the presence of an extracellular concentration of about 145 mM. These ion concentration gradients are maintained by $Na^{\oplus}$-$K^{\oplus}$ ATPase, an ATP-driven antiport sys-

Figure 9.34 ▶
Secondary active transport in *Escherichia coli*. The oxidation of reduced substrates (S_{red}) generates a transmembrane proton concentration gradient. The energy released by protons moving down their concentration gradient drives the transport of lactose into the cell by lactose permease.

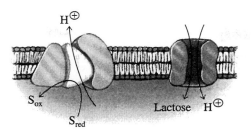

Extracellular space

Cytosol

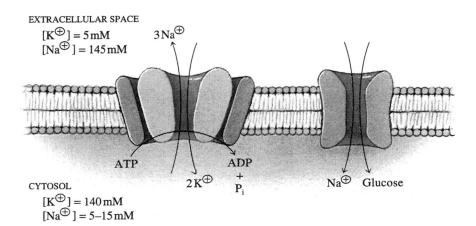

◀ **Figure 9.35**
Secondary active transport in animals. The $Na^{\oplus}$-$K^{\oplus}$ ATPase generates a sodium ion gradient that drives secondary active transport of glucose in intestinal cells.

tem that pumps two $K^{\oplus}$ into the cell and ejects three $Na^{\oplus}$ for every molecule of ATP hydrolyzed (Figure 9.35). Each $Na^{\oplus}$-$K^{\oplus}$ ATPase can catalyze the hydrolysis of about 100 molecules of ATP per minute, a significant portion (up to one-third) of the total energy consumption of a typical animal cell. The $Na^{\oplus}$ gradient that is generated by $Na^{\oplus}$-$K^{\oplus}$ ATPase is the major source of energy for secondary active transport of glucose in intestinal cells. One glucose molecule is imported with each sodium ion that enters the cell. The energy released by the downhill movement of $Na^{\oplus}$ powers the uphill transport of glucose.

D. Endocytosis and Exocytosis

The transport we have discussed so far occurs by the flow of molecules or ions across an intact membrane. Cells also need to import and export molecules too large to be transported via pores, channels, or transport proteins. Prokaryotes possess specialized multicomponent export systems in their plasma and outer membranes, which allow them to secrete certain proteins (often toxins or enzymes) into the extracellular medium. In eukaryotic cells, many—but not all—proteins (and certain other large substances) are moved into and out of the cell by **endocytosis** and **exocytosis**, respectively. In both cases, transport involves formation of a specialized type of lipid vesicle.

Endocytosis is the process by which macromolecules are engulfed by the plasma membrane and brought into the cell inside a lipid vesicle. Receptor-mediated endocytosis begins with the binding of macromolecules to specific receptor proteins in the plasma membrane of the cell. The membrane then invaginates, forming a vesicle that contains the bound molecules. As shown in Figure 9.36, the inside of such a membrane vesicle is equivalent to the outside of a cell; thus, substances inside the vesicle have not actually crossed the plasma membrane. Once inside the cell, the vesicle can fuse with an endosome (another type of vesicle) and then with a lysosome.

Chemistry for Biologists

BOX 9.3   The Hot Spice of Chili Peppers

Biochemists now know the mechanism by which spice from "hot" peppers exerts its action, causing a burning pain. The active factor in capsicum peppers is a lipophilic vanilloid compound called capsaicin.

Capsaicin

A nerve-cell protein receptor that responds to capsaicin has been identified and characterized. It is an ion channel, and its amino acid sequence suggests that it has six transmembrane domains. Activation of the receptor by capsaicin causes the channel to open so that calcium and sodium ions can flow into the nerve cell and send an impulse to the brain. The receptor is activated not only by vanilloid spices but also by rapid increases in temperature. In fact, the probable in vivo role of the receptor is detection of heat. Whereas the action of opioids suppresses pain, the action of vanilloids produces pain. Control of the capsaicin receptor might have value in the relief of chronic pain in conditions such as arthritis.

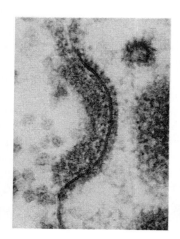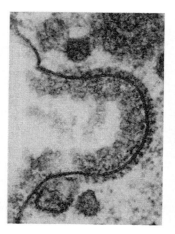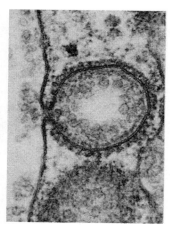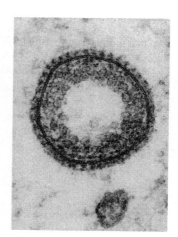

Figure 9.36 ▲
Electron micrographs of endocytosis. Endocytosis begins with the binding of macromolecules to the plasma membrane of the cell. The membrane then invaginates, forming a vesicle that contains the bound molecules. The inside of the vesicle is topologically equivalent to the outside of the cell.

Inside a lysosome, the endocytosed material and the receptor itself can be degraded. Alternatively, the ligand, the receptor, or both can be recycled from the endosome back to the plasma membrane.

Exocytosis is similar to endocytosis, except that the direction of transport is reversed. During exocytosis, materials destined for secretion from the cell are enclosed in vesicles by the Golgi apparatus (Section 1.8B). The vesicles then fuse with the plasma membrane, releasing the vesicle contents into the extracellular space. The zymogens of digestive enzymes are exported from pancreatic cells in this manner (Section 6.11A).

Chemistry for Biologists

9.12 Transduction of Extracellular Signals

The plasma membranes of all cells contain specific receptors that allow the cell to respond to external chemical stimuli that cannot cross the membrane. Plasma membranes contain lectins, carbohydrate-binding proteins that mediate the adhesion of one cell to another (e.g., a pathogenic bacterium to a host cell). In multicellular organisms, stimuli such as **hormones** (molecules that allow cells in one part of an organism to communicate with cells in another part of the same organism), **neurotransmitters** (substances that transmit nerve messages at synapses), and **growth factors** (proteins that regulate cell proliferation) are produced by specialized cells. These ligands can travel to other tissues where they bind to and produce specific responses in cells with the appropriate receptors on their surfaces. In this section, we see how the binding of water-soluble ligands to receptors elicits intracellular responses in mammals. The signal-transduction pathways discussed involve adenylyl cyclase, inositol phospholipids, and receptor tyrosine kinases.

A general mechanism for signal transduction is shown in Figure 9.37. After the ligand (also called the first messenger) binds to its specific receptor on the surface of the target cell, the signal is passed through a membrane protein **transducer** to a membrane-bound **effector enzyme**. The action of the effector enzyme generates an intracellular **second messenger**, which is usually a small molecule or ion. The diffusible second messenger carries the signal to its ultimate destination, which may be in the nucleus, an intracellular compartment, or the cytosol. Ligand binding to a cell-surface receptor almost invariably results in the activation of protein kinases. These enzymes catalyze the transfer of a phosphoryl group from ATP to various protein substrates, many of which help regulate metabolism, cell growth, and cell division. Some proteins are activated by phosphorylation, whereas others are inactivated. A vast diversity of ligands, receptors, and transducers exists, but very few second messengers and types of effector enzymes are known.

Receptor tyrosine kinases have a simpler mechanism for signal transduction. With these enzymes, the membrane receptor, transducer, and effector enzyme are combined in one enzyme. A receptor domain, on the extracellular side of the membrane, is connected to the cytosolic active site by a transmembrane segment. The active site catalyzes phosphorylation of its target proteins.

An important feature of signaling pathways is amplification. A single ligand-receptor complex can interact with a number of transducer molecules, each of which can activate several molecules of effector enzyme. Similarly, the production of many second messenger molecules can activate many kinase molecules, which catalyze the phosphorylation of many target proteins. This series of amplification events is called a **cascade**. The cascade mechanism means that small amounts of an extracellular

Kinases were introduced in Section 6.9.

◄ **Figure 9.37**
General mechanism of signal transduction across the plasma membrane of a cell.

The actions of the hormones insulin, glucagon, and epinephrine and the roles of transmembrane signaling pathways in the regulation of carbohydrate and lipid metabolism are described in Sections 11.5, 13.3, 13.7, 13.10, 16.1C, 16.4 (Box), and 16.7.

compound can affect large numbers of intracellular enzymes without crossing the plasma membrane or binding to each target protein.

Not all chemical stimuli follow the general mechanism of signal transduction shown in Figure 9.37. For example, because steroids are hydrophobic, they can diffuse across the plasma membrane into the cell, where they can bind to specific receptor proteins in the cytoplasm. The steroid-receptor complexes are then transferred to the nucleus. The complexes bind to specific regions of DNA called hormone-response elements and thereby enhance or suppress the expression of adjacent genes.

A. G Proteins Are Signal Transducers

Many hormone receptors in the plasma membrane rely on a family of guanine nucleotide-binding proteins—called **G proteins**—as transducers, the agents that transmit external stimuli to effector enzymes. G proteins have GTPase activity; that is, they slowly catalyze hydrolysis of bound guanosine 5'-triphosphate (GTP, the guanine analog of ATP) to guanosine 5'-diphosphate (GDP) (Figure 9.38). G proteins exist in two interconvertible conformations: an inactive GDP-bound form and an active GTP-bound form. The cyclic activation and deactivation of G proteins is shown in Figure 9.39. The G proteins involved in signaling by hormone receptors are peripheral membrane proteins on the inner surface of the plasma membrane, and each consists of an α, a β, and a γ subunit. The α and γ subunits are lipid-anchored membrane proteins (Section 9.10); the α subunit is a fatty-acyl anchored protein, and the γ subunit is a prenyl-anchored protein. The complex of $G_{\alpha\beta\gamma}$ and GDP is inactive. When a hormone-receptor complex diffusing laterally in the membrane encounters and binds $G_{\alpha\beta\gamma}$, it induces the G protein to change to an active conformation. Bound GDP is rapidly exchanged for GTP, promoting the dissociation of G_α-GTP from $G_{\beta\gamma}$. Activated G_α-GTP then interacts with the effector enzyme. The GTPase activity of the G protein acts as a built-in timer since G proteins slowly catalyze the hydrolysis of GTP to GDP. G proteins

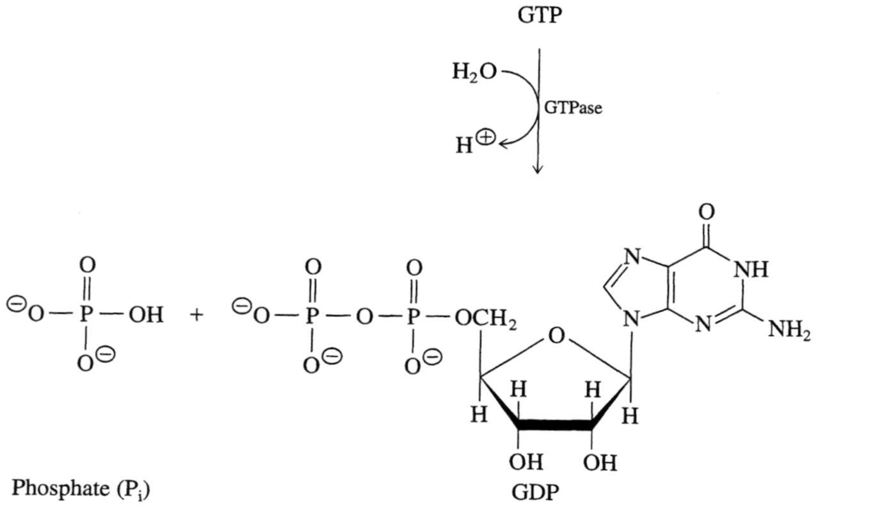

Figure 9.38 ▶
Hydrolysis of guanosine 5'-triphosphate (GTP) to guanosine 5'-diphosphate (GDP) and phosphate (P$_i$).

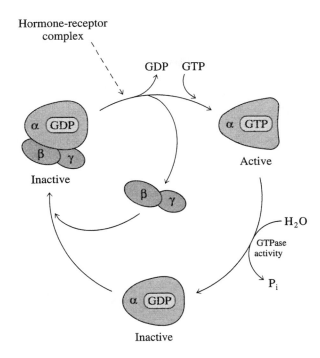

◀ **Figure 9.39**
G-protein cycle. G proteins undergo activation after binding to a receptor-ligand complex and are slowly inactivated by their own GTPase activity. Both G_α-GTP/GDP and $G_{\beta\gamma}$ are membrane-bound.

The response of *E. coli* to changes in glucose concentrations, modulated by cAMP, is described in Section 21.7B.

have evolved into good switches but very poor catalysts, typically having a k_{cat} of only about 3 min^{-1}. The hydrolysis of GTP to GDP deactivates the G protein and allows G_α-GDP to reassemble with $G_{\beta\gamma}$, halting the activity of the G protein on the effector enzyme.

G proteins are found in dozens of signaling pathways, including the adenylyl cyclase and the inositol-phospholipid pathways discussed below. An effector enzyme can respond to stimulatory G proteins (G_s) or inhibitory G proteins (G_i). The α subunits of different G proteins are distinct, providing varying specificity, but the β and γ subunits are similar and often interchangeable. Humans have two dozen α proteins, 5 β proteins, and 6 γ proteins.

B. The Adenylyl Cyclase Signaling Pathway

In eukaryotes, the cyclic nucleotides 3′,5′-cyclic adenosine monophosphate (cAMP) and its guanine analog 3′,5′-cyclic guanosine monophosphate (cGMP) are second messengers that help transmit information from extracellular hormones to intracellular enzymes. cAMP is produced from ATP by the action of adenylyl cyclase (Figure 9.40), and cGMP is formed from GTP in a similar reaction. Cyclic nucleotides are also involved in intracellular signaling in prokaryotes.

Many hormones that regulate intracellular metabolism exert their effects on target cells by activating the adenylyl cyclase signaling pathway. Binding of a hormone to a stimulatory receptor causes the conformation of the receptor to change, promoting interaction between the receptor and the G protein G_s. The receptor-ligand complex activates G_s, which in turn binds the effector enzyme adenylyl cyclase and activates it by allosterically inducing a conformational change at its active site.

Adenylyl cyclase is an integral membrane enzyme whose active site faces the cytosol. It catalyzes the formation of cAMP from ATP. cAMP then diffuses from the membrane surface through the cytosol and activates an enzyme known as protein kinase A. This kinase is made up of a dimeric regulatory subunit and two catalytic subunits and is inactive in its fully assembled state. When the cytosolic concentration of cAMP increases as a result of signal transduction through adenylyl cyclase, four molecules of cAMP bind to the regulatory subunit of the kinase,

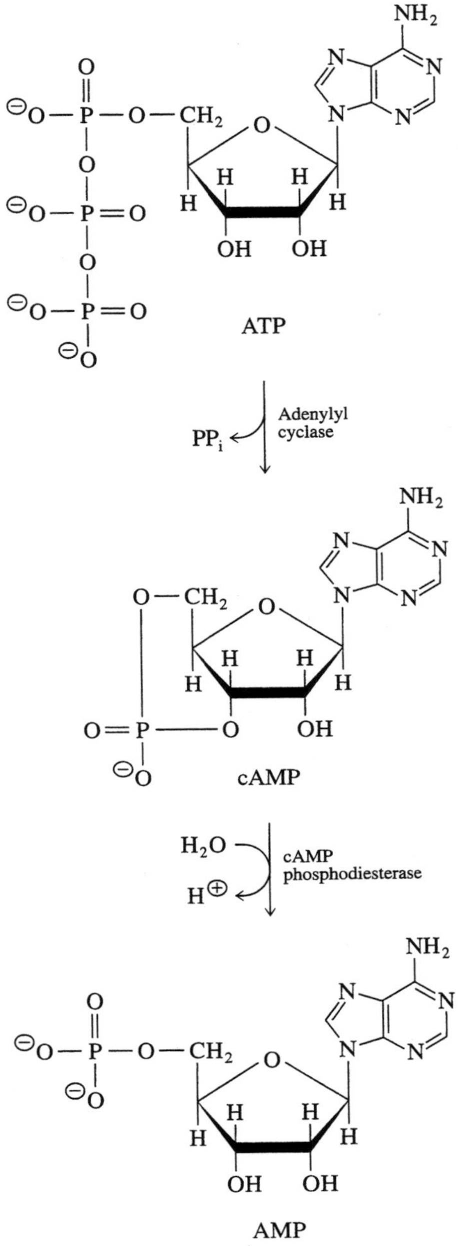

Figure 9.40 ▲
Production and inactivation of cAMP. ATP is converted to cAMP by the transmembrane enzyme adenylyl cyclase. The second messenger is subsequently converted to 5′-AMP by the action of a cytosolic cAMP phosphodiesterase.

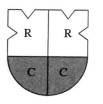

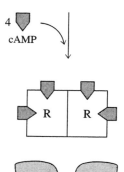

Inactive complex

Active catalytic subunits

◀ **Figure 9.41**
Activation of protein kinase A. The assembled complex is inactive. When four molecules of cAMP bind to the regulatory subunit (R) dimer, the catalytic subunits (C) are released.

releasing the two catalytic subunits, which are enzymatically active (Figure 9.41). Protein kinase A, a serine-threonine protein kinase, catalyzes phosphorylation of the hydroxyl groups of specific serine and threonine residues in target enzymes. Phosphorylation of amino acid side chains on the target enzymes is reversed by the action of protein phosphatases, which catalyze hydrolytic removal of the phosphoryl groups.

The ability to turn off a signal-transduction pathway is an essential element of all signaling processes. For example, the cAMP concentration in the cytosol increases only transiently. A soluble cAMP phosphodiesterase catalyzes the hydrolysis of cAMP to AMP (Figure 9.40), limiting the effects of the second messenger. At high concentrations, the methylated purines caffeine and theophylline (Figure 9.42) inhibit cAMP phosphodiesterase, thereby decreasing the rate of conversion of cAMP to AMP. These inhibitors prolong and intensify the effects of cAMP and hence the activating effects of the stimulatory hormones.

Hormones that bind to stimulatory receptors activate adenylyl cyclase and raise intracellular cAMP levels. Hormones that bind to inhibitory receptors inhibit adenylyl cyclase activity via receptor interaction with the transducer G_i. The ultimate response of a cell to a hormone depends on the type of receptors present and the type of G protein to which they are coupled. The main features of the adenylyl cyclase signaling pathway, including G proteins, are summarized in Figure 9.43.

Caffeine

Theophylline

◀ **Figure 9.42**
Caffeine and theophylline.

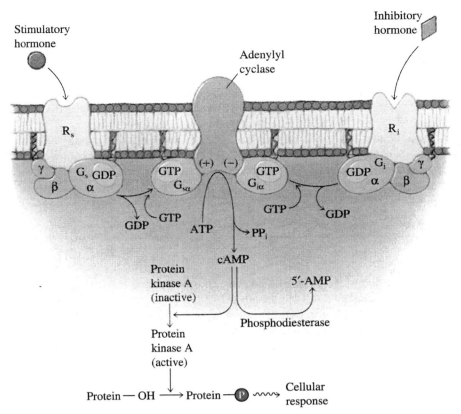

Figure 9.43 ▲
Summary of the adenylyl cyclase signaling pathway. Binding of a hormone to a stimulatory transmembrane receptor (R$_s$) leads to activation of the stimulatory G protein (G$_s$) on the inside of the membrane. Other hormones can bind to inhibitory receptors (R$_i$), which are coupled to adenylyl cyclase by the inhibitory G protein G$_i$. G$_s$ activates the integral membrane enzyme adenylyl cyclase, whereas G$_i$ inhibits it. cAMP activates protein kinase A, resulting in the phosphorylation of cellular proteins.

Some hormones stimulate the formation of cGMP (Figure 9.44), a second messenger similar to cAMP. cGMP is formed from GTP by the action of guanylyl cyclase and is hydrolyzed to 5′-GMP by the action of cGMP phosphodiesterase. cGMP is present at much lower concentrations than cAMP and consequently has not been as well studied. The second messengers cAMP and cGMP seem to mediate opposing intracellular signaling effects.

C. The Inositol-Phospholipid Signaling Pathway

Another major signal-transduction pathway, used by some hormones, growth factors, and other ligands, produces two different second messengers, both derived from a plasma membrane phospholipid, phosphatidylinositol 4,5-*bis*phosphate (PIP$_2$) (Figure 9.45). A minor component of plasma membranes, PIP$_2$ is located in the inner leaflet. It is synthesized from phosphatidylinositol by two successive phosphorylation steps catalyzed by kinases that require ATP.

Following binding of a ligand to a specific receptor, the signal is transduced through the G protein G$_q$. The active GTP-bound form of G$_q$ activates the effector enzyme phosphoinositide-specific phospholipase C, which is bound to the

3′,5′-Cyclic GMP
(cGMP)

Figure 9.44 ▲
3′,5′-Cyclic GMP.

Chemistry for Biologists

BOX 9.4   Bacterial Toxins and G Proteins

G proteins are the biological targets of cholera and pertussis (whooping cough) toxins, which are secreted by the disease-producing bacteria *Vibrio cholerae* and *Bordetella pertussis*, respectively. Both diseases involve overproduction of cAMP.

Cholera toxin binds to the surface of cells, and a subunit of it crosses the plasma membrane and enters the cytosol. This subunit catalyzes covalent modification of the α subunit of the G protein G_s, inactivating its GTPase activity. The adenylyl cyclase of these cells remains activated, and cAMP

levels stay high. In organisms infected with *V. cholerae*, cAMP stimulates certain transporters in the plasma membrane of the intestinal cells, leading to a massive secretion of ions and water into the gut. The dehydration resulting from diarrhea can be fatal unless fluids are replenished.

Pertussis toxin catalyzes covalent modification of G_i. In this case, the modified G protein is unable to replace GDP with GTP, and therefore adenylyl cyclase activity cannot be reduced via inhibitory receptors. The resulting increase in cAMP levels produces the symptoms of whooping cough.

cytoplasmic face of the plasma membrane. Phospholipase C catalyzes the hydrolysis of PIP$_2$ to inositol 1,4,5-*tris*phosphate (IP$_3$), a water-soluble molecule, and diacylglycerol (Figure 9.45). Both IP$_3$ and diacylglycerol are second messengers that transmit the original signal to the interior of the cell.

IP$_3$ diffuses through the cytosol and binds to a calcium channel in the membrane of the endoplasmic reticulum. IP$_3$ binding causes the calcium channel to open for a short time, releasing Ca^{2+} from the lumen of the endoplasmic reticulum into the cytosol. Calcium is also an intracellular messenger, activating calcium-dependent protein kinases that catalyze phosphorylation of various protein targets. The calcium signal is short-lived since Ca^{2+} is pumped back into the lumen of the endoplasmic reticulum when the channel closes.

Figure 9.45 ▶
Phosphatidylinositol 4,5-*bis*phosphate (PIP$_2$) produces two second messengers, inositol 1,4,5-*tris*phosphate (IP$_3$) and diacylglycerol. PIP$_2$ is synthesized by the addition of two phosphoryl groups (red) to phosphatidylinositol and hydrolyzed to IP$_3$ and diacylglycerol by the action of a phosphoinositide-specific phospholipase C.

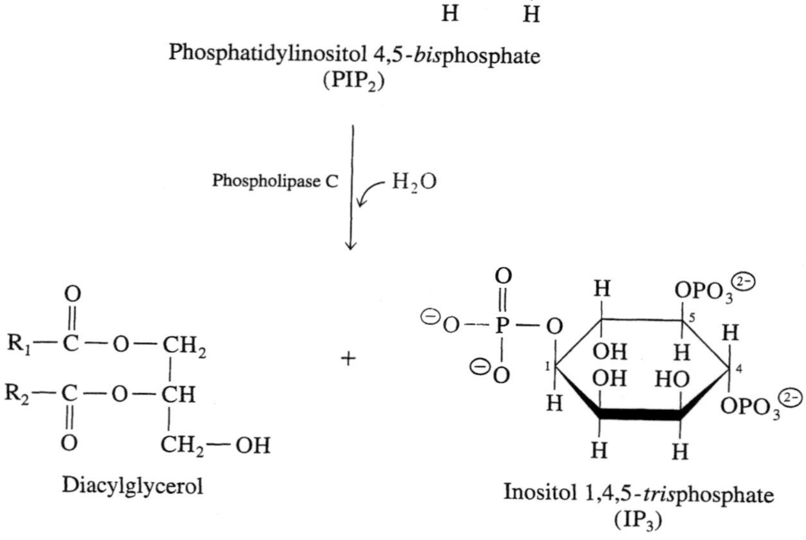

Phosphatidylinositol 4,5-*bis*phosphate
(PIP$_2$)

Phospholipase C $- H_2O$

Diacylglycerol

Inositol 1,4,5-*tris*phosphate
(IP$_3$)

The other product of PIP_2 hydrolysis, diacylglycerol, remains in the plasma membrane. Protein kinase C, which exists in equilibrium between a soluble cytosolic form and a peripheral membrane form, moves to the inner face of the plasma membrane, where it binds transiently and is activated by diacylglycerol and Ca^{2+}. A member of the serine-threonine kinase family, it catalyzes phosphorylation of many target proteins, altering their catalytic activity. Several protein kinase C isozymes exist, each with different catalytic properties and tissue distribution.

Signaling via the inositol-phospholipid pathway is turned off in several ways. First, when GTP is hydrolyzed, G_q returns to its inactive form and no longer stimulates phospholipase C. The activities of IP_3 and diacylglycerol are also transient. IP_3 is rapidly hydrolyzed to other inositol phosphates (which can also be second messengers) and inositol, and diacylglycerol is rapidly converted to phosphatidate. Both inositol and phosphatidate are recycled back to phosphatidylinositol. The main features of the inositol-phospholipid signaling pathway are summarized in Figure 9.46.

Phosphatidylinositol is not the only membrane lipid that gives rise to second messengers. Some extracellular signals lead to the activation of hydrolases that catalyze the conversion of membrane sphingolipids to sphingosine, sphingosine

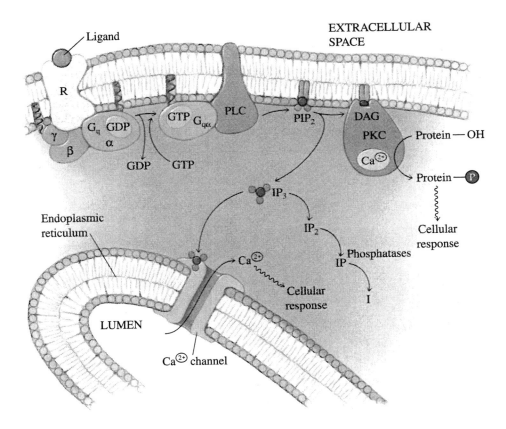

Figure 9.46 ▲
Inositol-phospholipid signaling pathway. Binding of a ligand to its transmembrane receptor (R) activates the G protein G_q. This in turn stimulates a specific membrane-bound phospholipase C (PLC), which catalyzes hydrolysis of the phospholipid PIP_2 in the inner leaflet of the plasma membrane. The resulting second messengers, IP_3 and diacylglycerol (DAG), are responsible for carrying the signal to the interior of the cell. IP_3 diffuses to the endoplasmic reticulum, where it binds to and opens a Ca^{2+} channel in the membrane, releasing stored Ca^{2+}. Diacylglycerol remains in the plasma membrane, where it—along with Ca^{2+}—activates the enzyme protein kinase C (PKC).

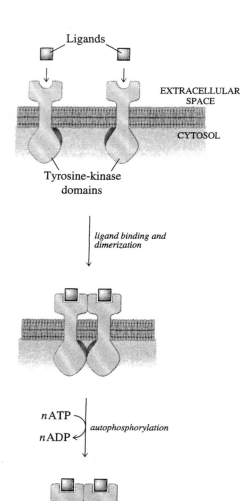

Ligands

EXTRACELLULAR
SPACE

CYTOSOL

Tyrosine-kinase
domains

*ligand binding and
dimerization*

nATP
autophosphorylation
nADP

Figure 9.47 ▲
Activation of receptor tyrosine kinases.
Activation occurs as a result of ligand-
induced receptor dimerization. Each kinase
domain catalyzes phosphorylation of its
partner. The phosphorylated dimer can
catalyze phosphorylation of various target
proteins.

1-phosphate, or ceramide. Sphingosine inhibits protein kinase C, and ceramide activates a protein kinase and a protein phosphatase. Sphingosine 1-phosphate can activate phospholipase D, which specifically catalyzes hydrolysis of phosphatidylcholine. The phosphatidate and the diacylglycerol formed by this hydrolysis appear to be second messengers. The full significance of the wide variety of second messengers generated from membrane lipids (each with its own specific fatty acyl groups) has not yet been determined.

D. Receptor Tyrosine Kinases

Many growth factors operate by a signaling pathway that includes a multifunctional transmembrane protein called a receptor tyrosine kinase. As shown in Figure 9.47, the receptor, transducer, and effector functions are all found in this protein. Binding of the ligand to an extracellular domain of the receptor activates tyrosine-kinase catalytic activity in the intracellular domain, by dimerization of the receptor. When two receptor molecules associate, each tyrosine-kinase domain catalyzes the phosphorylation of specific tyrosine residues of its partner, a process called autophosphorylation. The activated tyrosine kinase also catalyzes phosphorylation of certain cytosolic proteins, which sets off a cascade of events in the cell.

In the case of the insulin receptor, which is an $\alpha_2\beta_2$ tetramer to begin with (Figure 9.48), binding of insulin to the α subunit induces a conformational change that brings the tyrosine kinase domains of the β subunits together, activating them. Each tyrosine kinase domain in the tetramer catalyzes the phosphorylation of the other kinase domain. The activated tyrosine kinase also catalyzes the phosphorylation of tyrosine residues in other proteins that help regulate nutrient utilization.

Recent research has found that many of the signaling actions of insulin are mediated through PIP$_2$ (Section 9.12C and Figure 9.49). Rather than causing hydrolysis of PIP$_2$, insulin (via proteins called insulin-receptor substrates, IRSs) activates phosphatidylinositide 3-kinase, an enzyme that catalyzes the phosphorylation of PIP$_2$ to phosphatidylinositol 3,4,5-*tris*phosphate (PIP$_3$). PIP$_3$ is a second messenger

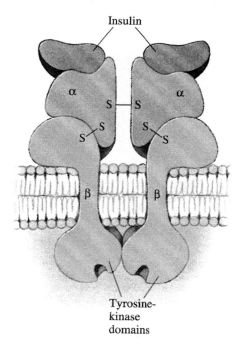

Insulin

α   α

S   S

S   S

β   β

Tyrosine-
kinase
domains

◀ **Figure 9.48**
Insulin receptor. Two extracellular α chains, each with an insulin-binding site, are linked to two transmembrane β chains, each with a cytosolic tyrosine kinase domain. Following insulin binding to the α chains, the tyrosine kinase domain of each β chain catalyzes autophosphorylation of tyrosine residues in the adjacent kinase domain. The tyrosine kinase domains also catalyze the phosphorylation of proteins called insulin-receptor substrates (IRSs).

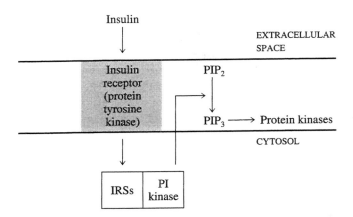

◀ **Figure 9.49**
Insulin-stimulated formation of phosphatidylinositol 3,4,5-*tris*phosphate (PIP_3). Binding of insulin to its receptor activates the protein tyrosine kinase activity of the receptor, leading to the phosphorylation of insulin-receptor substrates (IRSs). The phosphorylated IRSs interact with phosphatidylinositide 3-kinase (PI kinase) at the plasma membrane, where the enzyme catalyzes the phosphorylation of PIP_2 to PIP_3. PIP_3 acts as a second messenger, carrying the message from extracellular insulin to certain intracellular protein kinases.

that transiently activates a series of target proteins, including a specific phospho-inositide-dependent protein kinase. In this way, phosphatidylinositide 3-kinase is the molecular switch that regulates several serine-threonine protein kinase cascades.

Phosphoryl groups are removed from both the growth factor receptors and their protein targets by the action of protein tyrosine phosphatases. Although only a few of these enzymes have been studied, they appear to play an important role in regulating the tyrosine-kinase signaling pathway. One means of regulation appears to be the localized assembly and separation of enzyme complexes.

Summary

1. Lipids are a diverse group of water-insoluble organic compounds.

2. Fatty acids are monocarboxylic acids, usually with an even number of carbon atoms ranging from 12 to 20.

3. Fatty acids are generally stored as triacylglycerols (fats and oils), which are neutral and nonpolar.

4. Glycerophospholipids have a polar head group and nonpolar fatty acyl tails linked to a glycerol backbone.

5. Sphingolipids, which occur in plant and animal membranes, contain a sphingosine backbone. The major classes of sphingolipids are sphingomyelins, cerebrosides, and gangliosides.

6. Steroids are isoprenoids containing four fused rings.

7. Other biologically important lipids are waxes, eicosanoids, lipid vitamins, and terpenes.

8. The structural basis for all biological membranes is the lipid bilayer, which includes amphipathic lipids such as glycerophospholipids, sphingolipids, and sometimes cholesterol. Lipids can diffuse rapidly within a leaflet of the bilayer.

9. A biological membrane contains proteins embedded in or associated with a lipid bilayer. The proteins can diffuse laterally within the membrane.

10. Most integral membrane proteins span the hydrophobic interior of the bilayer, but peripheral membrane proteins are more loosely associated with the membrane surface. Lipid-anchored membrane proteins are covalently linked to lipids in the bilayer.

11. Some small or hydrophobic molecules can diffuse across the bilayer. Channels, pores, and passive and active transporters mediate the movement of ions and polar molecules across membranes. Macromolecules can be moved into and out of the cell by endocytosis and exocytosis, respectively.

12. Extracellular chemical stimuli transmit their signals to the cell interior by binding to receptors. A transducer passes the signal to an effector enzyme, which generates a second messenger. Signal-transduction pathways often include G proteins and protein kinases. The adenylyl cyclase signaling pathway leads to activation of the cAMP-dependent protein kinase A. The inositol-phospholipid signaling pathway generates two second messengers and leads to the activation of protein kinase C and an increase in the cytosolic Ca^{2+} concentration. In receptor tyrosine kinases, the kinase is part of the receptor protein.

Problems

1. Write the molecular formulas for the following fatty acids: (a) nervonic acid (*cis*-Δ^{15}-tetracosenoate; 24 carbons); (b) vaccenic acid (*cis*-Δ^{11}-octadecenoate); and (c) EPA (all *cis*-$\Delta^{5,8,11,14,17}$-eicosapentaenoate).

2. Write the molecular formulas for the following modified fatty acids:
   (a) 10-(Propoxy)decanoate, a synthetic fatty acid with antiparasitic activity used to treat African sleeping sickness, a disease caused by the protozoan *T. brucei* (the propoxy group is —O—$CH_2CH_2CH_3$)
   (b) Phytanic acid (3,7,11,15-tetramethylhexadecanoate), found in dairy products
   (c) Lactobacillic acid (11,12-methyleneoctadecanoate), found in various microorganisms

3. Increased consumption of ω-3 polyunsaturated fatty acids, relatively abundant in fish oils, may help reduce platelet aggregation and thrombosis (blood clotting). Increased consumption of ω-6 fatty acids, relatively abundant in corn and safflower oils, usually reduces plasma cholesterol levels. Classify the following fatty acids as ω-3, ω-6, or neither: (a) linolenate, (b) linoleate, (c) arachidonate, (d) oleate, (e) $\Delta^{8,11,14}$-eicosatrienoate.

4. Mammalian platelet activating factor (PAF), a messenger in signal transduction, is a glycerophospholipid with an ether linkage at C-1. PAF is a potent mediator of allergic responses, inflammation, and the toxic-shock syndrome. Draw the structure of PAF (1-alkyl-2-acetyl-phosphatidylcholine), where the 1-alkyl group is a C_{16} chain.

5. Many snake venoms contain phospholipase A_2, which catalyzes the degradation of glycerophospholipids into a fatty acid and a "lysolecithin." The amphipathic nature of lysolecithins allows them to act as detergents in disrupting the membrane structure of red blood cells, causing them to rupture. Draw the structures of phosphatidyl serine (PS) and the products (including a lysolecithin) that result from the reaction of PS with phospholipase A_2.

6. Draw the structures of the following membrane lipids: (a) 1-stearoyl-2-oleoyl-3-phosphatidylethanolamine, (b) palmitoylsphingomyelin, and (c) myristoyl-β-D-glucocerebroside.

7. (a) The steroid cortisol participates in the control of carbohydrate, protein, and lipid metabolism. Cortisol is derived from cholesterol and possesses the same four-membered fused ring system but with: (1) a C-3 keto group, (2) C-4-C-5 double bond (instead of the C-5-C-6 as in cholesterol), (3) a C-11 hydroxyl, and (4) a hydroxyl group and a —$C(O)CH_2OH$ group at C-17. Draw the structure of cortisol.
   (b) Ouabain is a member of the cardiac glycoside family found in plants and animals. This steroid inhibits Na⊕-K⊕ ATPase and ion transport and may be involved in hypertension and high blood pressure in humans.

Ouabain possesses a four-fused ring system similar to cholesterol, but has the following structural features: (1) no double bonds in the rings, (2) hydroxy groups on C-1, C-5, C-11 and C-14, (3) —CH_2OH on C-19, (4) 2-3 unsaturated 5-membered lactone ring on C-17 (attached to C-3 of lactone ring), and (5) 6-deoxymannose attached β-1 to the C-3 oxygen. Draw the structure of ouabain.

8. A mutant gene (*ras*) is found in as many as one third of all human cancers including lung, colon, and pancreas, and may be partly responsible for the altered metabolism in tumor cells. The *ras* protein coded for by the *ras* gene is involved in cell signaling pathways that regulate cell growth and division. Since the *ras* protein must be converted to a lipid-anchored membrane protein in order to have cell-signaling activity, the enzyme farnesyl transferase (FT) has been selected as a potential chemotherapy target for inhibition. Suggest why FT might be a reasonable target.

9. Glucose enters some cells by simple diffusion through channels or pores, but glucose enters red blood cells by passive transport. On the plot below, indicate which line represents diffusion through a channel or pore and which represents passive transport. Why do the rates of the two processes differ?

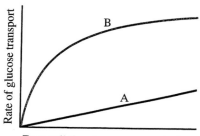

Extracellular glucose concentration

10. The pH gradient between the stomach (pH 0.8–1.0) and the gastric mucosal cells lining the stomach (pH 7.4) is maintained by an H⊕-K⊕ ATPase transport system that is similar to the ATP-driven Na⊕-K⊕ ATPase transport system (Figure 9.35). The H⊕-K⊕ ATPase antiport system uses the energy of ATP to pump H⊕ out of the mucosal cells (mc) into the stomach (st) in exchange for K⊕ ions. The K⊕ ions that are transported into the mucosal cells are then cotransported back into the stomach along with Cl⊖ ions. The net transport is the movement of HCl into the stomach.

$$K⊕_{(mc)} + Cl⊖_{(mc)} + H⊕_{(mc)} + K⊕_{(st)} + ATP \rightleftharpoons$$
$$K⊕_{(st)} + Cl⊖_{(st)} + H⊕_{(st)} + K⊕_{(mc)} + ADP + P_i$$

Draw a diagram of this H⊕-K⊕ ATPase system.

11. In the inositol signaling pathway, both IP_3 and diacylglycerol (DAG) are hormonal second messengers. If certain protein kinases in cells are activated by binding Ca^{2+}, how do IP_3 and DAG act in a complementary fashion to elicit cellular responses inside cells?

12. In some forms of diabetes, a mutation in the β subunit of the insulin receptor abolishes the enzymatic activity of that subunit. How does the mutation affect the cell's response to insulin? Can additional insulin (e.g., from injections) overcome the defect?

13. The ras protein (described in Problem 8) is a mutated G protein that lacks GTPase activity. How does the absence of this activity affect the adenylyl cyclase signaling pathway?

Selected Readings

General

Gurr, M. I., and Harwood, J. L. (1991). *Lipid Biochemistry: An Introduction*, 4th ed. (London: Chapman and Hall). A general reference for lipid structure and metabolism.

Vance, D. E., and Vance, J. E., eds. (1991). *Biochemistry of Lipids, Lipoproteins, and Membranes* (New York: Elsevier). Contains many reviews.

Membranes

Dowhan, W. (1997). Molecular basis for membrane phospholipid diversity: why are there so many lipids? *Annu. Rev. Biochem.* 66:199–232. Explains how genetic manipulation of phospholipids in bacteria indicates their biological roles.

Edidin, M. (1992). Patches, posts and fences: proteins and plasma membrane domains. *Trends Cell Biol.* 2:376–380. Discusses the organization of some membranes by protein-based domains.

Jacobson, K., Sheets, E. D., and Simson, R. (1995). Revisiting the fluid mosaic model of membranes. *Science* 268:1441–1442. Discusses the lateral diffusion of membrane proteins.

Simons, K., and Ikonen, E. (1997). Functional rafts in cell membranes. *Nature* 387:569–572.

Singer, S. J. (1992). The structure and function of membranes: a personal memoir. *J. Membr. Biol.* 129:3–12. Highlights the fluid mosaic model and discusses the relationship of recently discovered features to the model.

Zachowski, A. (1993). Phospholipids in animal eukaryotic membranes: transverse asymmetrical movement. *Biochem. J.* 294:1–14.

Membrane Proteins

Casey, P. J., and Seabra, M. C. (1996). Protein prenyltransferases. *J. Biol. Chem.* 271:5289–5292. Discusses the enzymes responsible for the prenylation of membrane proteins.

Fasman, G. D., and Gilbert, W. A. (1990). The prediction of transmembrane protein sequences and their conformations: an evaluation. *Trends Biochem. Sci.* 15:89–92. A concise assessment of the current methods used for prediction of membrane protein topography from the amino acid sequence.

McConville, M. J., and Ferguson, M. A. J. (1993). The structure, biosynthesis and function of glycosylated phosphatidylinositols in the parasitic protozoa and higher eukaryotes. *Biochem. J.* 294:305–324. Discusses the anchoring of membrane proteins by glycosylphosphatidylinositol moieties.

Membrane Transport

Agre, P., Bonhivers, M., and Borgnia, M. J. (1998). The aquaporins, blueprints for cellular plumbing systems. *J. Biol. Chem.* 273:14659–14662.

Borgnia, M., Nielsen, S., Engel, A., and Agre, P. (1999) Cellular and molecular biology of the aquaporin water channels. *Annu. Rev. Biochem.* 68:425–458.

Caterina, M. J., Schumacher, M. A., Tominaga, M., Rosen, T. A., Levine, J. D., and Julius, D. (1997). The capsaicin receptor: a heat-activated ion channel in the pain pathway. *Nature* 389:816–824.

Clapham, D. (1997). Some like it hot: spicing up ion channels. *Nature* 389:783–784. Discusses chilli peppers and the capsaicin receptor.

Doyle, D. A., Cabral, J. M., Pfuetzner, R. A., Kuo, A., Gulbis, J. M., Cohen, S. L., Chait, B. T., and McKinnon, R. (1998). The structure of the potassium channel: molecular basis of K^+ conduction and selectivity. *Science* 280:69–75.

Jahn, R., and Südhof, T.C. (1999). Membrane fusion and exocytosis. *Annu. Rev. Biochem.* 68: 863–911.

Loo, T. W., and Clarke, D. M. (1999) Molecular dissection of the human multidrug resistance P-glycoprotein. *Biochem. Cell Biol.* 77:11–23. A review of the structure and function of this protein.

Nikaido, H. (1994). Porins and specific diffusion channels in bacterial outer membranes. *J. Biol. Chem.* 269:3905–3908.

Pedersen, P. L., and Carafoli, E. (1987). Ion motiave-ATPases. I. Ubiquity, properties, and significance to cell function. *Trends Biochem. Sci.* 12:146–150. II. Energy coupling and work output. *Trends Biochem. Sci.* 12:186–189. Comprehensive reviews of the ion-translocating ATPases, including Ca^{2+} and Na^+-K^+ ATPases.

Signal Transduction

Berridge, M. J. (1985). The molecular basis of communication within the cell. *Sci. Am.* 253(10):142–152. An introduction to the adenylyl cyclase and inositol phospholipid signaling pathways.

Fantl, W. J., Johnson, D. E., and Williams, L. T. (1993). Signalling by receptor tyrosine kinases. *Annu. Rev. Biochem.* 62:453–481. A review of the biochemical mechanisms of signaling through tyrosine kinase growth-factor receptors.

Hamm, H. E. (1998). The many faces of G protein signaling. *J. Biol. Chem.* 273:669–672. A summary of recent structural and mechanistic studies of G proteins.

Hodgkin, M. N., Pettitt, T. R., Martin, A., Michell, R. H., Pemberton, A. J., and Wakelam, M. J. O. (1998). Diacylglycerols and phosphatidates: which molecular species are intracellular messengers? *Trends Biochem. Sci.* 23:200–205. An assessment of the second-messenger roles of phospholipase-generated lipids.

Hurley, J. H. (1999). Structure, mechanism, and regulation of mammalian adenylyl cyclase. *J. Biol. Chem.* 274:7599–7602.

Linder, M. E., and Gilman, A. G. (1992). G-Proteins. *Sci. Am.* 267(7):56–65. An introduction to G proteins.

Luberto, C., and Hannun, Y. A. (1999). Sphingolipid metabolism in the regulation of bioactive molecules. *Lipids* 34 (Suppl.):S5–S11. Describes the second-messenger roles of sphingosine, sphingosine 1-phosphate, and ceramide.

Prescott, S. M. (1999). A thematic series on kinases and phosphatases that regulate lipid signaling. *J. Biol. Chem.* 274:8345.

Shepherd, P. R., Withers, D. J., and Siddle, K. (1998). Phosphoinositide 3-kinase: the key switch mechanism in insulin signalling. *Biochem. J.* 333:471–490.

Colour Diagrams

(a)

$$\overset{\oplus}{H_3N} \blacktriangleright \underset{2}{\overset{1}{\underset{|}{C}}} \overset{COO^{\ominus}}{\underset{R}{\overset{|}{\underset{\alpha}{C}}}} \blacktriangleleft H$$

(b)

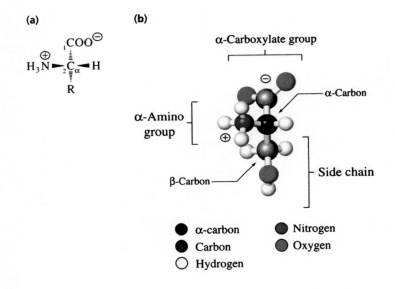

α-Carboxylate group

α-Carbon

α-Amino group

β-Carbon

Side chain

● α-carbon
● Carbon
○ Hydrogen
● Nitrogen
● Oxygen

◀ **Figure 3.1**
Two representations of an L-amino acid at neutral pH. **(a)** General structure. An amino acid has a carboxylate group (whose carbon atom is designated C-1), an amino group, a hydrogen atom, and a side chain (or R group), all attached to C-2 (the α-carbon). Solid wedges indicate bonds above the plane of the paper; dashed wedges indicate bonds below the plane of the paper. The blunt ends of wedges are nearer the viewer than the pointed ends. **(b)** Ball-and-stick model of serine (whose R group is —CH₂OH). Note the alternative numbering and lettering systems for the carbon atoms.

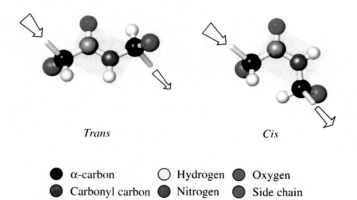

Trans   *Cis*

● α-carbon   ○ Hydrogen   ● Oxygen
◉ Carbonyl carbon   ● Nitrogen   ● Side chain

◀ **Figure 4.7**
Trans and *cis* conformations of a peptide group. Nearly all peptide groups in proteins are in the *trans* conformation, which minimizes steric interference between adjacent side chains. The arrows indicate the direction from the N– to the C-terminus.

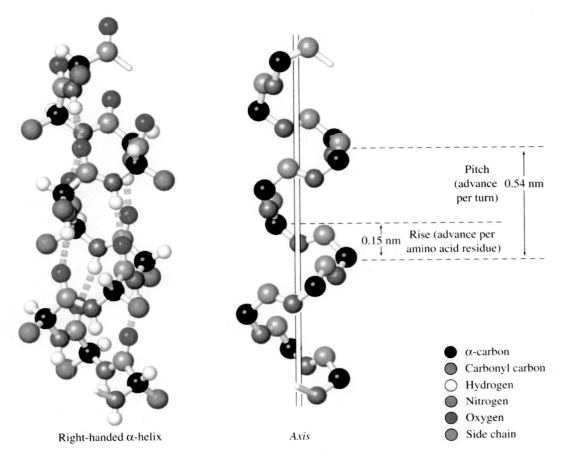

Right-handed α-helix

Axis

- ● α-carbon
- ● Carbonyl carbon
- ○ Hydrogen
- ● Nitrogen
- ● Oxygen
- ● Side chain

Pitch
(advance 0.54 nm
per turn)

0.15 nm Rise (advance per
amino acid residue)

Figure 4.10 ▲

α Helix. A region of α-helical secondary structure is shown with the N-terminus at the bottom and the C-terminus at the top of the figure. Each carbonyl oxygen forms a hydrogen bond with the amide hydrogen of the fourth residue further toward the C-terminus of the polypeptide chain. The hydrogen bonds are approximately parallel to the long axis of the helix. Note that all the carbonyl groups point toward the C-terminus. In an ideal α helix, equivalent positions recur every 0.54 nm (the pitch of the helix), each amino acid residue advances the helix by 0.15 nm along the long axis of the helix (the rise), and there are 3.6 amino acid residues per turn. The arrows at the ends of the helix indicate the direction from the N- to the C-terminus. In a right-handed helix, the backbone turns in a clockwise direction when viewed along the axis from its N-terminus. If you imagine that the right-handed helix is a spiral staircase, you will be turning to the right as you walk down the staircase.

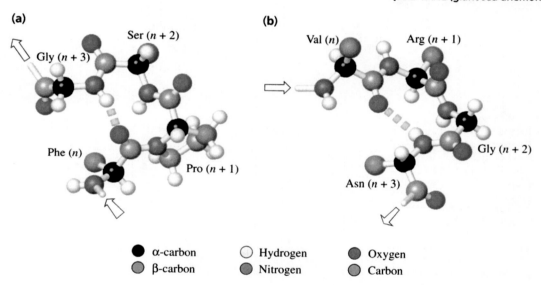

Figure 4.18
Reverse turns. **(a)** Type I β turn. The structure is stabilized by a hydrogen bond between the carbonyl oxygen of the first N-terminal residue (Phe) and the amide hydrogen of the fourth residue (Gly). Note the proline residue at position $n + 1$. **(b)** Type II β turn. This turn is also stabilized by a hydrogen bond between the carbonyl oxygen of the first N-terminal residue (Val) and the amide hydrogen of the fourth residue (Asn). Note the glycine residue at position $n + 2$. [PDB 1AHL (giant sea anemone neurotoxin)].

(a)

Gly ($n + 3$)

Ser ($n + 2$)

Phe (n)

Pro ($n + 1$)

(b)

Val (n)

Arg ($n + 1$)

Gly ($n + 2$)

Asn ($n + 3$)

- ● α-carbon
- ● β-carbon
- ○ Hydrogen
- ● Nitrogen
- ● Oxygen
- ● Carbon

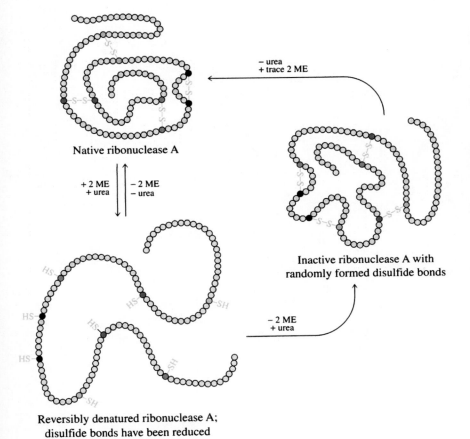

Native ribonuclease A

Reversibly denatured ribonuclease A;
disulfide bonds have been reduced

Inactive ribonuclease A with
randomly formed disulfide bonds

− urea
+ trace 2 ME

+ 2 ME
+ urea

− 2 ME
− urea

− 2 ME
+ urea

Figure 4.29
Denaturation and renaturation of ribonuclease A. Treatment of native ribonuclease A (top) with urea in the presence of 2-mercaptoethanol unfolds the protein and disrupts disulfide bonds to produce reduced, reversibly denatured ribonuclease A (bottom). When the denatured protein is returned to physiological conditions in the absence of 2-mercaptoethanol, it refolds into its native conformation and the correct disulfide bonds form. However, when 2-mercaptoethanol alone is removed, ribonuclease A reoxidizes in the presence of air, but the disulfide bonds form randomly, producing inactive protein (such as the form shown on the right). When urea is removed, a trace of 2-mercaptoethanol is added to the randomly reoxidized protein, and the solution is warmed gently, the disulfide bonds break and re-form correctly to produce native ribonuclease A.

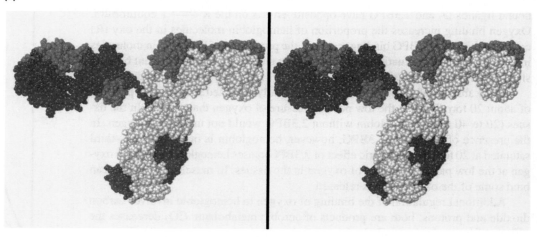

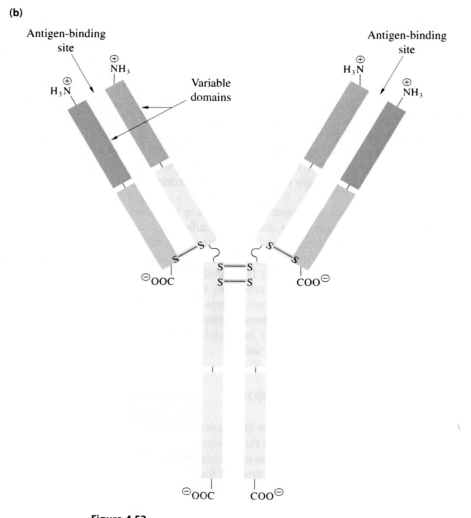

Antigen-binding site

Antigen-binding site

Variable domains

Figure 4.52
Human antibody structure. **(a)** Structure. **(b)** Diagram. Two heavy chains (blue) and two light chains (red) of antibodies of the immunoglobulin G class are joined by disulfide bonds (yellow). The variable domains of both the light and heavy chains (where antigen binds) are colored more darkly.

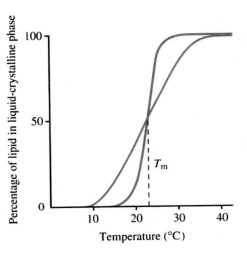

◀ **Figure 9.27**
Effect of bilayer composition on phase transition. A pure phospholipid bilayer (red) undergoes a sharp transition from the gel phase to the liquid crystalline phase at the phase-transition temperature (T_m). A bilayer containing 80% phospholipids and 20% cholesterol (blue) undergoes a phase transition over a broad temperature range.

Notes

Notes

Notes

Notes

Notes